DIGITAL STATE AT THE LEADING EDGE

The impact of information technology (IT) on government in the last five years has been profound. Using the governments of Canada and Ontario (both recognized as international leaders in the use of IT) as case studies, *Digital State at the Leading Edge* is the first attempt to take a comprehensive view of the influence of IT on the whole of government, including areas such as political campaigning, public consultation, service delivery, knowledge management, and procurement.

Using the concepts of channel choice, procurement market analysis, organizational integration, and digital leadership, this study explores the inter-relationships among various aspects of the application of IT to government and politics. The authors seek to understand how IT is transforming government and what the nature of that transformation is. In the process, they offer an explanation of Canada's relative success, and conclude with practical advice to politicians and public servants about how to manage IT in government more effectively. Based on original research undertaken over the last five years, the findings of this innovative study will be of particular interest to those studying or working in the fields of public administration, political science, and information technology.

SANDFORD BORINS is Professor of Public Management at the University of Toronto.

KENNETH KERNAGHAN is a professor in the Department of Political Science at Brock University.

DAVID BROWN is a senior associate at the Public Policy Forum in Ottawa, and a doctoral candidate in the Department of Political Science at Carleton University.

NICK BONTIS is an associate professor at the DeGroote School of Business at McMaster University.

PERRI 6 is a professor in the College of Business, Law and Social Sciences at Nottingham Trent University.

FRED THOMPSON is Grace and Elmer Goudy Professor of Public Management and Policy in the Atkinson Graduate School of Management at Willamette University.

**The Institute of Public Administration of Canada Series
in Public Management and Governance**

Editor: Donald Savoie

This series is sponsored by the Institute of Public Administration of Canada as part of its commitment to encourage research on issue in Canadian public administration, public sector management, and public policy. It also seeks to foster wider knowledge and understanding among practitioners, academics, and the general public.

For a list of book published in the series, see page 447.

Sandford Borins, Kenneth Kernaghan, David Brown,
Nick Bontis, Perri 6, Fred Thompson

Digital State at the
Leading Edge

IPAC
The Institute of
Public Administration of Canada

IAPC
L'Institut d'administration
publique du Canada

UNIVERSITY OF TORONTO PRESS
Toronto Buffalo London

© University of Toronto Press Incorporated 2007
Toronto Buffalo London
Printed in Canada

ISBN-13: 978-0-8020-9118-5 (cloth)
ISBN-10: 0-8020-9118-0 (cloth)

ISBN-13: 978-0-8020-9490-2 (paper)
ISBN-10: 0-8020-9490-2 (paper)

∞

Printed on acid-free paper

Library and Archives Canada Cataloguing in Publication

Digital state at the leading edge / Sandford Borins ... [et al.].

(Institute of Public Administration of Canada series in public management
    governance)

Includes bibliographical references and index.
ISBN-13: 978-0-8020-9118-5 (bound)
ISBN-13: 978-0-8020-9490-2 (pbk.)
ISBN-10: 0-8020-9118-0 (bound)
ISBN-10: 0-8020-9490-2 (pbk.)

1. Internet in public administration – Canada.   2. Information technology –
Government policy – Canada.   3. Internet in public administration.
4. Information technology – Government policy.   I. Borins, Sandford F.,
1949–   II. Series.

JL86.A8D44 2006   351.710285   C2006-904921-1

University of Toronto Press acknowledges the financial assistance to its
publishing program of the Canada Council for the Arts and the Ontario
Arts Council.

University of Toronto Press acknowledges the financial support for its
publishing activities of the Government of Canada through the Book
Publishing Industry Development Program (BPIDP).

To the memory of Joseph Galimberti,
Executive Director, Institute of Public Administration of Canada,
from 1975 to 2006

Contents

Acknowledgments

A research project involving six authors working together over four years is a major undertaking, and we owe a debt of gratitude to many institutions and individuals who have assisted us in bringing it to fruition.

The Social Sciences and Humanities Research Council of Canada, through its Initiative on the New Economy, provided generous research funding from 2002 to 2006. Gordana Krcevinac and Jean-François Fortin provided supportive liaison with SSHRC and its programs. The grants were helpfully managed by Judith Smith, business officer of the Department of Management, University of Toronto at Scarborough.

Empirical research enabled us to employ a legion of graduate and undergraduate students, and they have served us well in the following areas: scoping the project (Milica Uzelac), analysis of provincial party websites (Rachna Juneja, Danielle Katic, James Lo, Li Zhou), analysis of federal party websites and survey of parliamentarians' use of IT (Adam Angelone, James Lo), analysis of U.K. party websites (Heather Wilson), research on information technology in U.S. government (Maartje Booik, Donald Homuth, Sara Johnston), knowledge management case studies (Alexander Serenko), surveys of federal Government On-Line managers and their provincial counterparts (Milaine Alarie, Alana Cattapan, Jonathan Dignan, Gabe Eidelman, Crystal Hulley, Milena Isakovic, Patrick Kirby, Erick Lachapelle, Victoria Machado), and preparation of the manuscript (Venkat Kuppuswamy).

The CIO Branch of the Treasury Board Secretariat, Government of Canada provided David Brown with access to managers for both surveys and interviews. The Office of the Corporate Chief Information

Officer, Management Board Secretariat, Government of Ontario permitted Sandford Borins to observe its Information Technology Executive Leadership Council meetings from July 2003 to April 2005, and also provided access for interviews. In both cases, the views expressed in the book are entirely those of the authors and do not reflect those of the Treasury Board Secretariat of the Government of Canada, Management Board Secretariat of the Government of Ontario, or current or former governments of Canada or Ontario.

The publication process itself drew on the efforts of many people. Virgil Duff, executive editor at the University of Toronto Press, IPAC research director Patrice Dutil, and Donald Savoie, director of the IPAC book series, all supported the project. Two external reviewers provided much helpful advice. Parts of the manuscript were read by Greg Georgeff, Jim Hamilton, Rose Langhout, Brian Marson, Joan McCalla, Ross Peebles, and Charles Vincent. We received suggestions from a number of researchers in e-government and e-politics including Chris Bellamy, Stephen Coleman, Neil Nevitte, Charles Raab, and Stephen Ward. Draft chapters were copy-edited by Beth Herst and the entire manuscript was copy-edited by Ian MacKenzie. Barbara Schon compiled the index. Jowenne Herrera assisted with graphics.

DIGITAL STATE AT THE LEADING EDGE

Introduction

SANDFORD BORINS

The emergence of the Internet and e-mail as economic and cultural phenomena in the mid-nineties has challenged scholars to confront the transformations that information technology (IT) is effecting.[1] We are all digital now. But what exactly does this mean for key areas of social activity? For education? Business? Leisure? Governance?

The last question holds a particular urgency. It is through government that IT can and does shape the life of every citizen, however apparently far removed from the digital interface itself. And the study of IT in government has become, rightly, a rapidly growing scholarly field, with a corresponding proliferation of sub-fields: government websites; the use of IT in political campaigning and public consultation; IT procurement, organization, and management.[2] It is also an interdisciplinary field, in that it draws the attention of scholars in public administration, political science, economics, law, and information science. The subjects are diverse and the debates necessarily ongoing. What is missing, however, is a big picture. *Digital State at the Leading Edge* is an attempt to see the forest, to elucidate both methodology and materials for a comprehensive view of the impact, use, and management of IT in government.

Such a project can be undertaken at an entirely conceptual level, untethered from experience in any jurisdiction. It gains traction, however, if it is rooted empirically. This study uses holistic empirical research about the Government of Canada and the Government of the Province of Ontario as both a basis for, and a test of, conceptualization. Our rationale for choosing Canada and Ontario is that both are at the leading edge in the application of IT, and both are large enough, in population and in size and responsibilities of the public service, for their experiences to be applicable to large national or sub-national governments throughout the world. It is the signal achievement of the Government of Canada to have led in global rankings by the consulting firm Accenture of (national) e-government maturity for the last five years – a clear indicator of front-runner status (Accenture 2004, 2005). The Government of Ontario has received awards and recognition that include first prize in the Commonwealth Association for Public Administration and Management's (biennial) 1998 and 2002 international innovation awards for its IT-based innovations in service delivery, and third place ranking in the Bertelsmann Foundation's 2001 international study of e-government effectiveness (Human Resources and Stakeholder Education Branch 2004).

Our perspective, however, is comparative, encompassing chapters on the governments of the United States and United Kingdom too. In a field as non-traditional as this, a field that scrutinizes long-held verities, comparison of experiences, practices, and outcomes proves particularly valuable, especially when baseline commonalities clearly exist. To a great degree, Canada and the United States have common technology, both because the same technology providers are active in each and because their IT labour markets are closely related. Canada and the United Kingdom share a parliamentary system of government, so that the impact and management of technology is being mediated through similar institutions.

Our insistence on the integration of all aspects of public sector IT in our research also requires that this study be longitudinal, allowing us to trace the evolution of the impact and management of technology over a reasonable period of time. The period we have chosen ran from the beginning of this decade to the end of the year 2005. The start date of 2000 reduced the significance of two transitory events: Y2K and the dot-com boom. An end date of 31 December 2005 included the 2003 Ontario and 2004 federal elections, as well as the federal government's deadline for completion of its Government On-Line initiative. It also coincided with the Martin government's electoral defeat.

Beyond introducing the main theme of this research project, additional groundwork is laid here for subsequent chapters. In it we present data showing the extent to which the federal and Ontario governments have become digital workplaces, as well as outline functions now performed electronically. If we are *all* digital now, we argue that being digital has different implications in the public and private sectors, which stem from the intrinsic differences between public and private sector management, and we look at some of those defining differences here. Finally, we present brief outlines of subsequent chapters.

The Omnipresence of IT in Government

The most comprehensive look at the presence of IT in Canadian government is the Survey of Workplace Issues in Government, carried out in five Canadian jurisdictions, including the federal and Ontario governments, in 1998 and early 1999. The survey was completed by directors of work units of 5 to 100 employees. A telephone survey, followed by a mailed-out self-administered questionnaire, asked about issues including workplace practices, technological change, and labour–management relations. While we would have preferred a more recent replication for a topic as rapidly changing as IT, this survey at least serves as a baseline at the start of our study period (Lonti and Verma 2003).

Table I.1 presents results regarding access to technology for employees in the federal and Ontario governments (Lonti 2000, e-mail to the author 8 October 2004). When asked about employee access to technology, managers reported that almost all employees had networked personal computers and e-mail, and most had Internet access. Computer training was provided for employees in 94 per cent of the units in Ontario and 96 per cent in the federal government. The average employee in both governments spent slightly more than half of his or her time at work using a computer. On a scale where 1 indicates strong disagreement, 4 neutrality, and 7 complete agreement, managers in both jurisdictions agreed that the use of IT had increased the work capacity and effectiveness of their units. They were less certain, however, that the use of IT had changed the nature of the work performed by their units, or that all necessary supports were in place to allow employees to use technology to the fullest advantage.

These results paint a clear picture of IT well on its way to becoming omnipresent for government employees. Were the survey to be replicated today, virtually every employee would have a networked personal computer, e-mail and Internet access, and access to computer training.[3] It is also quite likely that the average employee would be spending even more of his or her working day using a computer.

The question that immediately comes to mind is what public servants are doing during the many hours they are sitting at their computers. More and more of their internal and external communications

6   Sandford Borins

Table 1.1
The presence of IT in the federal and Ontario governments, 1998–9

Employee access to technology, average for all branches
(3 = most employees, 4 = all employees)

Technology	Federal government	Ontario government
Networked PCs	3.82	3.66
E-mail	3.92	3.77
Internet	3.46	3.18
N	334	120

Branch provides or pays for computer training

	Federal government	Ontario government
Percentage (%)	96	94
N	334	115

Percentage of time spent using a computer by type of employee

Type of employee	Federal government (%)	N	Ontario government (%)	N
Managerial	45	320	43	110
Scientific	56	225	53	68
Technical	56	159	65	53
Clerical	66	320	68	105
Operational	61	96	45	35
Average	53		55	

Directors' perceptions of IT
(1 = disagree strongly, 4 = neutral, 7 = agree strongly)

	Federal government	Ontario government
Use of IT has increased potential work capacity of unit	5.8	5.8
Use of IT has increased effectiveness of unit	5.7	5.8
All necessary supports in place to use IT to fullest advantage	4.7	4.2
Use of IT has changed nature of work performed by unit	4.9	4.8
N	340	120

Source: Data from Z. Lonti e-mail 8 October 2004

are by e-mail, delivered to fixed workstations or wireless devices. More and more documents are being prepared and transmitted electronically. As a growing proportion of the workforce, in particular younger workers, have keyboarding skills, there has been a sharp decline in the number of clerical positions in the public service. More and more of government's communications and transactions with the outside world are being conducted over its websites, with the result that a substantial number of public servants build and maintain these sites, as well as oversee the transactions conducted through them. The government's administrative systems, whether internal, such as financial and human resource management, or external, such as a wide range of benefits programs, are being managed through increasingly complex software systems. Public servants or contractors are involved in building, maintaining, and using these systems. Finally, a large proportion of the government's intellectual capital is tied up in information systems. These include geographic information systems used by land use planners, police, or public health epidemiologists; case management systems used in social services; and economic modelling systems used in central banks and finance ministries.[4]

The increasingly digital character of the government has myriad structural implications for formal and informal communication patterns both within and outside, the sharing and storing of information, and the way departments and agencies are organized. As we trace these implications throughout the book, the question that necessarily arises is whether IT is transforming government. This question has far-reaching implications for politicians, public servants, and citizens. For politicians and public servants, the issue is how their work is changing, and for citizens it is how their relationships with government are changing. Politicians and public servants may encounter changes in the nature and roles of institutions that create winners and losers, while some citizens may be made better off, and others worse off, as a result of IT-driven transformation.

Public and Private Sector IT

The literature on public management has identified a number of key differences between managing in public and private sector contexts. Public sector management has been characterized as 'management in a fishbowl,' because anything that public sector managers do is potentially of interest to the media. Public sector managers are continually subject to a hostile takeover, in the sense that the parliamentary opposition's objective is to defeat the government in the next election by providing evidence of inappropriate public policies and inefficient public management. Public sector managers, unlike their private sector counterparts, cannot focus on a single bottom line, but must deal with a wide range of accountabilities, encompassing their departments, the government as a whole, as well as agencies responsible to Parliament such as the auditor general and commissioners for privacy and, in the federal government, official languages. Private sector managers can focus their strategy on the most lucrative market segments; equity requires that government provide service to all of society. Unlike business, government cannot fire the customer (Kernaghan and Siegel 1999, 7–11).

These contextual differences necessarily shape the management of IT in the public and private sectors. Consider the differences in the following areas: portals and websites, procurement, and human resource management. The development of government websites has been driven by the public sector's organizational complexity and service mandate. Portals such as http://www.gc.ca and http://www.gov.on.ca incorporate the three branches of government, and include the dozens of departments and agencies that populate the executive branch. Business portals are less complicated, simply because no business is as organizationally complex and all-encompassing as the senior levels of government. Business websites are focused on profit generation and will include not only information about or transactions with the company, but links to and advertising for other businesses as a means of generating revenue. Public sector websites are focused on information and service and virtually never incorporate advertising. Private sector sites can target a particular market segment, and as a consequence may be designed only for users with leading-edge hardware and software. Public sector sites must provide service to virtually all of society – an approach that necessitates maximum accessibility for people with older hardware and software and for people with disabilities. Private sector sites in Canada will choose to be bilingual if it is profitable; every aspect of the federal and Ontario websites must be bilingual, and there are also some provisions for other linguistic groups. Private sector sites may use cookies to find out about the customer; public sector privacy regulations are much more stringent, limiting the gathering of information about users.

In the area of procurement, the public sector also operates in a different context. Under the scrutiny of the media, auditors, and the Opposition, it must be able to show that its procedures themselves have been scrupulously fair to all potential bidders. As a consequence, we can expect procurement in the public sector to take longer and have higher transactions costs than in the private sector.

Skilled IT workers, scarce during the dot-com boom, continue to command a premium in the labour market. Private sector employers have responded with higher salaries and benefits, flexible working conditions, and compensation through stock options. Public sector human resource managers have sought flexibility to provide attractive employment packages that will allow them to compete for IT workers. While bonuses have sometimes been provided, they are not at all comparable to stock options. Often, the best the public sector can offer is competitive entry level (but not senior) salaries and the satisfaction of working on the most challenging problems. This may not be enough to provide the required workforce, and as a consequence the public sector may be required to use private sector consultants, often on long term-contracts, for much of its IT work.

This comparison of public and private sector IT management leads to the inescapable conclusion that the greater complexity of the public sector's mission (or missions) and its more onerous set of constraints make the management of public sector IT inherently more challenging. Successful management will require significant and continuous innovation. A key theme of this book will be to elaborate upon the federal and Ontario governments' responses to this enormous challenge.

Outline of the Book

Providing a comprehensive account of the management of IT in government was a project to engage more than one scholar. This research project was the work of a team that included Kenneth Kernaghan (Brock University), Nick Bontis (McMaster University), David Brown (Public Policy Forum, Ottawa), Fred Thompson (Willamette University), Perri 6 (Nottingham Trent University), and Sandford Borins (University of Toronto). The team was supported by the Social Sciences and Humanities Research Council of Canada's (SSHRC) Initiative on the New Economy, which provided research funding from 2002 to 2006. The team parcelled out the various aspects of the project, chapter by chapter, to its individual members.

Chapter 1, by Sandford Borins, provides a framework for the book, developing a conceptual model that distinguishes between traditional government and IT-enabled government. The model is driven by the following four key concepts:

- *Channel choice.* This concept captures the interaction between government, which establishes and manages channels (in-person, post, telephone, electronic) for service delivery and political participation, and users of public services, who choose among the channels available. User choice is affected by channel characteristics such as comparative speed and security, while government's setting of channel characteristics is driven by such factors as relative cost and political imperatives, for example, visibility to constituents.
- *IT-enabled integration.* This concept deals with the impact of IT on the internal workings of government. Information technology provides the potential to integrate service to the public, such as on government-wide web portals, and to improve internal efficiency through government-wide administrative applications. Integration poses a challenge to a system of government that is traditionally characterized by vertical departmental accountability to Parliament and political and bureaucratic departmentalism.
- *Procurement markets.* To deliver service electronically, government must buy hardware, software, and systems, and find the people to run them. Procurement markets represent the interface between government and suppliers of these goods and services. The characteristics of these markets influence government decisions about internal production versus outsourcing and the management of suppliers.
- *Digital leadership.* Technology will transform government only if government's leaders want it to. With the growing presence of IT in society at large, politicians and senior public servants are much more aware of technology than in the past, more sophisticated in their own use of technology, and more willing to exercise digital leadership.

Chapters 2 to 6 use these concepts to discuss the application of IT to service delivery and management within the bureaucracy (e-government). Chapter 2, by David Brown, discusses Government On-Line (GOL), the federal government's high-profile initiative in electronic service delivery centred on the Canada Site, from its inception in 2000 to its winding up in 2005. The chapter assesses the extent to which GOL has been transformative. The chapter draws on three surveys of managers involved in, or working in partnership with, GOL.

Chapter 3, by Sandford Borins, continues the discussion of managing IT within government in the provincial context. This chapter is based in part on Borins's attendance at biweekly meetings of Ontario's IT Executive Leadership Council (ITELC) from mid-2003 to mid-2005. The meetings discussed a wide range of topics, including service delivery, major projects, procurement, security, and new technologies. The chapter demonstrates how a change in political direction had substantial implications for the Ontario government's IT organization.

Chapter 4, by Kenneth Kernaghan, explores integrated service delivery at the front end – the interface with the user – as well as the back office. It discusses both difficulties posed, for example, concerns about privacy and data-sharing, and progress achieved, in integration.

Chapter 5, by Nick Bontis, continues the theme of integrated service delivery by examining integrated non-emergency telephone service (311) – an approach pioneered by the governments of several large cities in the United States. Some early Canadian initiatives are also discussed.

Chapter 6, also by Nick Bontis, deals with knowledge management (KM) in the federal and Ontario public services. Bontis links KM to the key themes of the book in several ways. It is an enabler for integrated service delivery. For expertise-based departments, the service model is one of providing information to their specialized clientele; hence, KM has a critical role. Digital leadership is also in evidence in KM, for example, in the activities of departmental KM champions. The chapter presents several Canadian case studies.

After these chapters on e-government, the focus of attention shifts to the use of IT in activities such as election campaigns and public consultation (e-democracy). Chapter 7, by Kenneth Kernaghan, deals with Internet campaigning, namely the ways that Canadian political parties have used their websites as a campaign tool. The chapter is based on close observation of party websites during 2003 Ontario election and 2004 federal election as well as interviews with webmasters thereafter. The seven other provincial elections held in 2003 and 2004 provide a comparative perspective. Though the January 2006 federal election took place after the chapter had been completed, Kernaghan continued his monitoring, and some of his initial observations are presented as a postscript.

Chapter 8, also by Kenneth Kernaghan, deals with the use of IT by politicians. It is based on surveys of Ontario MPPs and federal MPs in both 2003 and 2005, and hence takes a longitudinal perspective by including members of two federal parliaments (elected in 2000 and 2004) and two Ontario legislatures (elected in 1999 and 2003).

Chapter 9, by David Brown and Sandford Borins, examines federal and Ontario government e-consultation initiatives. Both governments have conducted e-consultations posted on departmental websites and have also experimented with e-consultation portals. Based on recent case studies, this chapter assesses the effectiveness and impact of these initiatives.

Chapter 10, also by Sandford Borins and David Brown, expands on the concept of digital leadership that was presented in chapter 1. As we see digital leadership occurring at both the political and public service levels, we have placed it after the discussions of e-government and e-democracy. The chapter puts a human face on IT by reporting the experience of individuals in the federal and Ontario governments involved in developing IT infrastructure (the theme of chapters 2 and 3), integrated service (chapter 4), knowledge management (chapter 6), and e-consultation (chapter 9), as well as enhancing the use of IT by politicians (chapter 8). The chapter discusses their accomplishments, frustrations, and challenges for the future.

The next two chapters provide perspectives on e-government and e-democracy in the United States and the United Kingdom. They take very different approaches to this task, however. Chapter 11, by Fred Thompson, focuses on whether IT in the public sector in the United States is decentralizing authority and undercutting hierarchy. It includes a case study contrasting the Republicans' decentralized and Democrats' centralized voter registration strategies in the 2004 presidential election and another examining the use of networked technology in the battlefield phase of the Iraq War.

Chapter 12, by Perri 6, discusses e-government and e-democracy in the United Kingdom. It deals with the full range of topics discussed in the Canadian context; for example, progress in e-government, changes in the structure of the central office for e-government, issues involved in data sharing in criminal justice and mental health, experience in online consultation, and Internet campaigning in the May 2005 U.K. election.

Chapter 13, which concludes the book, returns to the model of IT-enabled government presented in chapter 1 and examines how far the federal and Ontario governments have come to realizing the transformation outlined in the model. It then asks whether this transformation has left Canadians better off; for example, in better and more affordable public services and a more robust democracy. It outlines some expectations about the likely evolution of IT in government in the next half-decade, and draws lessons, especially for practitioners, from the experience of the federal and Ontario governments.

Notes

1   We will use *information technology (IT)*, the term commonly used in North America, rather than *information and communication technologies (ICTs)*, the term more commonly used in Europe. Given the convergence of information and communication technologies (for example, the provision of Internet service by telecom companies and, conversely, voice-over-Internet as an alternative to regular telephone service), *IT* and *ICTs* are essentially synonymous.
2   This proliferation of sub-fields is mirrored by a proliferation of terms with the prefix *e*, including *e-government* (the use of IT in the public service), *e-politics* (the use of IT by politicians), *e-consultation* (the use of IT in public consultation, whether managed by politicians or public servants), *e-democracy* (taken to include both e-politics and e-consultation), and finally *e-governance*, generally taken to mean all of the foregoing.
3   Mechling (1999, 183) suggested a possible milestone for 2010 of 95 per cent penetration of the Internet to all government workers. Thus, this milestone had already been achieved by the Ontario and federal governments in the same year Mechling suggested it.
4   This paragraph gives an accurate indication of the range of technologies to be discussed in this book. We are concerned with the social impact of technology, rather than the details of the technologies themselves. Not all technologies used by government are discussed; for example, we do not examine surveillance technologies such as iris scanning, vehicle tracking, or closed-circuit television monitoring.

1 Conceptual Framework

SANDFORD BORINS

This chapter begins by presenting a conceptual framework for understanding the potentially transformative impact of IT on government. The framework distinguishes between models of traditional and IT-enabled government and shows how they differ. The models are also illustrated diagrammatically. The chapter continues by setting out the components of the model of IT-enabled government more fully, anticipating the detailed evidence-based discussion of these components in subsequent chapters.

Consider, first, traditional government. There are three aspects to government's societal interface: voters, interest groups, and users of services. (Individuals can assume one or more of these roles at any given time, but the roles themselves are distinct.) Voters participate in election campaigns both by voting and by supporting their preferred party/candidate more actively; for example, by volunteering time or donating money. Individuals and interest groups attempt to influence public policy, both during and between election campaigns, and government may seek to consult them in developing policy. Government services are provided by the public service to individuals and businesses; the services themselves may be either information flows or transactions (that is, exchanges of money for goods or provision of entitlements based on authentication). The societal interface is enacted through a number of channels that, for simplicity, we have divided into two categories: in-person service channels, such as government office counters, and remote service channels, such as post, telephone, and fax. Voters, interest groups, and service users all choose the most convenient channel for their activity, and channel choices may vary significantly across the spectrum of roles. These channels are illustrated in figure 1.1.

Figure 1.1 Traditional Government

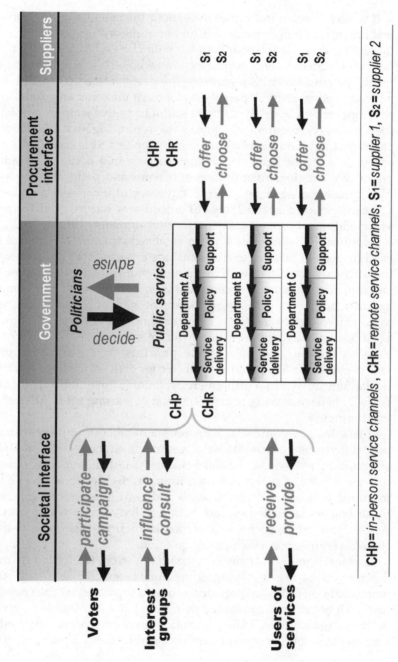

CHp= *in-person service channels* , CHR= *remote service channels*, S1= *supplier 1*, S2= *supplier 2*

It is useful to remind ourselves here of the essentially hierarchical and (internally) autonomous structure of traditional government, with its familiar division of labour between politicians who consult the public and then decide, and public servants who advise and then implement. The government is organized in departments, each of which has a service delivery unit, a policy development unit, and an administrative support unit. Each department's administrative support unit handles its own procurement, subject to central agency regulations, choosing from a number of competing suppliers. It is considered appropriate for procurement decisions to take into account considerations of the regional distribution of benefits and political patronage. New public management, with its advocacy of increasing autonomy for managers, and establishment of executive or service agencies, provided additional support for departmental autonomy (Borins 2002).

Coordination within this departmentalized structure is provided by central agencies, whose functions include ensuring that departmental initiatives are consistent with overall government priorities and other departments' missions, resource allocation to the overall government and to departments, enforcing government-wide policies in such areas as human resources and financial management, and the establishment of ad hoc units to support major government priorities. While central agencies impose government-wide priorities on departments, they take departments as a given, responsible for delivering policy in a particular functional area. Furthermore, traditional government has a tendency to behave as a 'loose confederation of warring tribes' (Blakeney and Borins 1998).

IT-enabled government demonstrates a number of important structural differences from traditional government. At the societal interface, electronic service becomes a third channel, and hence another option, for voters, interest groups, and service users. By electronic service we mean the Internet, with its websites and e-mail, as well as enhancements of older technologies, such as interactive voice response and call centres. How much societal interaction shifts from traditional to new channels is an important empirical question.

The most significant change that could flow from IT-enabled government, however, is a reshaping of the public service that consolidates many common functions previously located separately in each department. Three aspects, illustrated in figure 1.2, are integrated service delivery organizations, joined-up policy development and knowledge management, and integrated support organizations. These organiza-

Figure 1.2 IT enabled government

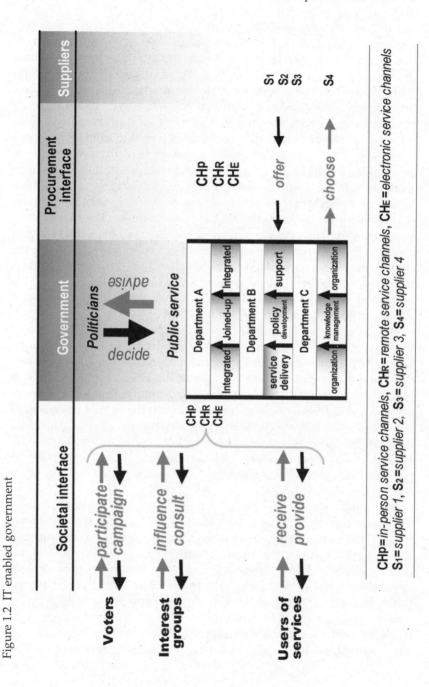

CHP=*in-person service channels*, **CHR**=*remote service channels*, **CHE**=*electronic service channels*
S1=*supplier 1*, **S2**=*supplier 2*, **S3**=*supplier 3*, **S4**=*supplier 4*

tional forms constitute a comprehensive level of coordination that goes beyond coordination by central agencies. We can identify multiple drivers for this phenomenon. On the societal interface, there are economies of scale and scope in websites, call centres, and front offices. Similarly, there are economies of scale in internal support functions, leading to the development of government-wide systems for financial management, human resource management, and procurement. Governments are anxious to realize the savings resulting from these economies, which can be regarded as the successor to earlier savings due to office automation. In the area of policy development and knowledge management, the ability to match and integrate databases can facilitate joined-up policy analysis and program delivery. Citizen preferences strongly support the latter; numerous surveys make clear that citizens want one-stop delivery of government services, and have little concern about which department or even level of government is delivering the service. Preferences for joined-up policy development are less clear; on the one hand, citizens are concerned about loss of privacy, but on the other, they want the enhanced service that would be its ultimate result (Crossing Boundaries National Council 2005b).

The reshaping of the public service is indicated by the direction of the heavy lines and arrows in the two figures. Current discussion among public administration scholars and practitioners describes traditional departments as vertical silos and the IT-enabled alternative as horizontal government, or horizontality. In our diagram, the axes are reversed, simply because our concern is with the face of government presented at both the societal and procurement interfaces. Traditional government presents as many faces as there are departments, while IT-enabled government presents far fewer, ideally a small number of integrated service delivery organizations and an integrated support organization.

This model also holds implications for the procurement interface. The electronic channel has been added to the traditional channels for contact between government and its suppliers. It has become increasingly popular with both because it reduces transaction costs. The use of the electronic channel (for example, online posting of procurement opportunities) also increases the number of potential suppliers for many products or services, which could be expected to reduce prices paid by government. As mentioned above, economies of scale in procurement will favour shifting responsibility from departmental procurement units to an integrated procurement organization. Ideally, citizens remain unaware of, and unconcerned with, procurement issues. It is at the societal interface that they are most likely to encounter government IT.

The Societal Interface

Politics and Consultation

Election campaigning, by definition, means voter contact; traditional methods include broadcast messages (advertising on television, radio, and in print) and individualized appeals (mailings and door-to-door visits). The electronic channel has added party websites as a form of broadcasting and e-mail as individualized appeal. During a campaign, voters may seek information about party platforms, politicians' strengths as representatives and leaders, and political reaction to campaign developments. Traditionally, voters informed themselves by reading newspapers, listening to television and radio commentary, and discussing politics with family and friends. The electronic channel adds visiting party websites and visiting external websites that provide advocacy and commentary (blogs). In addition to reaching voters, political parties are attempting to call on the efforts of their partisans; the electronic channel can be used for soliciting online donations or volunteers. Parties and politicians are also in frequent contact with members of the media, for example, in responding to stories during the campaign. Speed is of the essence in this context, and websites – in particular, the media room page – can be rapidly revised and e-mail used for instant contact with individual journalists. The role of the Internet and e-mail in political campaigns can be studied in a number of ways, such as sustained observation of party websites, which change virtually hourly, interviews with campaign strategists and with party webmasters who implement strategic decisions in the electronic media, and national election surveys that incorporate questions about voters' channel choices. We include all of these in our discussion of online campaigning in chapter 7.

Consultation with individuals and interest groups is another area where the electronic channel adds options, and these options may be bringing to the discussion new voices, particularly those of younger citizens more attuned to that channel. In addition to writing, phoning, or faxing their elected representatives, voters can send e-mails. Governments often launch consultation initiatives, which have traditionally included such channels as public hearings, written briefs, and polling. Electronic consultation adds to these options. Consultations can be posted on government websites and visitors encouraged to submit e-mails or complete online questionnaires.

One of the open questions in the early development of e-consultation is whether it will be hosted on the legislative or departmental components of government websites. Emerging practice in Canada appears to favour departmental websites, managed and maintained by the bureaucracy, and feeding it information to use in policy development. The legislative branch is not hosting e-consultation because politicians have chosen to limit their visibility online. The Ontario Legislature and federal House of Commons have restricted members' presence on their respective legislative websites to an official biography, and office and e-mail addresses. Unlike the U.S. Congress, neither body permits members to personalize their sites or to link to a personal site, for two reasons. First, personal sites are considered to be political advertising and thus inappropriate for an official government site. Second, strong party discipline prevents Canadian legislators from distinguishing themselves from the party, for instance, by developing their own policy positions.

Despite the dominance of departmentally hosted e-consultation, a few MPs and MLAs have created personalized websites and use them for blogging and e-consultation. The legislators who do so tend to be more enthusiastic about technology and more independent-minded about policy than their colleagues.

A second point of contention between politicians and public servants concerns the government's home page – a piece of prime real estate in cyberspace. Politicians want to use its limited space to highlight news about the first minister and new policy initiatives, while public servants want to highlight online services. The tension also extends to its look-and-feel, with politicians preferring their own party colours (Liberal red, Conservative blue) and public servants preferring something non-partisan. We have observed these tensions in both the federal and Ontario governments during our study.

Delivery of Public Services

Information technology has added the Internet and e-mail as new channels for service delivery and enhanced the telephone channel with interactive voice response (IVR) and call centres. Decisions about channel choice are made jointly by governments and users. Government decides which channels it will use to provide service and the characteristics of service on each channel; users compare characteristics of service channels (for example, time required, hours of availability, travel to point of service) to decide which they will use. This is not the standard interface of a competitive market, in which a multitude of suppliers provide service using a variety of channels, with the cost to the firm of providing service over a given channel figuring as a component of the total price paid by the customer. Because the government is often a monopoly provider of compulsory public services, it is expected to make a given service available on all channels. Governments may track the cost of providing service on different channels. Clearly, they would prefer to shift demand to the lowest-cost channel. In addition, the emerging evidence is, indeed, that the electronic channel (Internet and e-mail) is by far the least expensive, followed by IVR (Fountain with Osorio-Urzua 2001; Treasury Board Secretariat 2004). Nevertheless, public opinion – to which politicians and public servants are necessarily attuned – may prevent the government from using differential prices to shift demand.

Governments have other objectives besides cost minimization that are influencing decisions about service delivery. Points of service provide visibility for Canadian governments – a crucial consideration in a country of strong regional loyalties. Government offices are deemed an effective way for showing the flag, whether it be the federal red maple leaf, the Quebec fleur-de-lys, or the Ontario trillium (Gibbins 2000). The importance of regional and local job creation has made decentralization of government offices, particularly those providing service, an attractive option for regional and local economic development, in contrast to industrial projects requiring the subsidization of business. The job creation imperative also works against IT-based channels that substitute capital for labour.

By deciding on the characteristics of service, government can affect the distribution of use across channels. An equilibrium can thus be reached: government spends its budget for providing service, and service users distribute themselves across channels based on the service characteristics resulting from that budget. Over time, the equilibrium can change as government service budgets and their allocation across channels change, for example, because governments look to reductions in service delivery costs to free up resources. Similarly, changes in external factors affecting demand (for example, the availability and cost of broadband communications service) can affect users' channel choices.

Much of the literature on e-government has made two assumptions that we consider unwarranted. First, in comparative studies, governments have generally been evaluated on the basis of the *availability* of services over the electronic channel (Accenture 2004, United Nations 2004; West 2003). Second, following an e-business model, the literature has considered the dissemination of information over the Internet to represent a lower level of IT maturity than the provision of electronic transactions.

The availability of a service electronically is obviously a necessary condition for it to be used, but does not guarantee that it will be. The proof, we believe, is in the using, and in a pattern of shifting use from traditional channels to IT-enabled channels. Canadian governments have been at the forefront in measuring and explaining channel choice. In its 2005 annual report, to cite one example, the federal government's Government On-Line (2005) initiative provides the distribution of service across channels for forty-three federal information services and eighty-nine federal transaction services – all of which have been targeted for increased online use. For the information services, information was provided over the Internet 90 per cent of the time, by interactive telephone 8 per cent of the time (almost entirely weather information), and by each of telephone agent, in-person, and the mail 1 per cent of the time. Similarly, the federal government's website averages 1.2 million hits per month, twelve times as many as 1-800-O-Canada, its call centre, which receives 100,000 calls per month (Department of Finance Canada 2005a).

Transactional services are much more evenly split by channel, with 30 per cent of transactions completed on the Internet, 35 per cent by mail, 15 per cent by telephone agent, 12 per cent in person, and 8 per cent by interactive telephone (Government On-Line 2005). This overall variance is also reflected at the level of individual services: 90 per cent of applicants to the Public Service Commission submitted their resumés online, 43 per cent of personal income tax filings were online and 54 per cent by post, and 83 per cent of passport applications were filed in person and 17 per cent by post.

The Institute for Citizen-Centred Service, a research institute supported by the federal and provincial governments, has undertaken large surveys of individual and business users of public services (Institute for Citizen-Centred Service 2003, 2004) to explore drivers of satisfaction and patterns of channel choice. The most recent individual survey found that, in instances where only one channel was used, 11 per cent used the Internet or e-mail, and their satisfaction was higher than that achieved by any other channel. Individuals who made ten or more contacts with government were almost all using the Internet channel, reflecting the minimal effort required for an individual contact (Institute for Citizen-Centred Service 2003, 24, 31–4, 66). A surprising finding was the frequency that multiple channels are used to provide service: 71 per cent of business users and 50 per cent of individuals used more than one channel (Institute for Citizen-Centred Service 2003, 31; 2004, 42). These data bring out the complexity of channel choices by citizens and can assist governments in making their investments in service delivery infrastructure.

Now consider the second assumption commonly made in the literature, that transactions reflect a higher level of IT development or greater significance than the mere posting of information. In e-business – the source of this assumption – corporations provide relatively little information online. Information provided online generally includes only the overall nature of the business, investor relations, particularly if legally required, product features, and service. The aim of the site is to encourage and facilitate online purchasing. Information is supplied to further that end.

The informational content and objectives of government websites are vastly different. In contrast to corporations, much of what government does is done in public and is intended to form the public record.[1] Government has a special mandate to collect and publish information that citizens are compelled by law to provide (Alexander 2000). Government now runs an enormous online dissemination program, which includes

- Information on legislative and judicial processes that are intrinsically conducted in public (transcripts of debates and committee hearings, laws, judgments)
- Census and other statistical surveys and archival holdings
- Scientific information gathered by government such as environmental, meteorological, and geological monitoring
- Business and consumer information
- Information about government departments and programs such as departmental missions, activities, and budgets
- Performance and results information gathered by government such as league tables for schools and hospitals

Even if governments were not to provide any transactions online, their websites would be huge by virtue of the amount of information provided, and sufficiently sophisticated to support archiving, updating, and manipulation by users. Clearly, government initiatives in providing information online represent an enormous, and ongoing, challenge in knowledge management, the subject of chapter 6.

There is an important financial dimension to the informational aspect of government websites. Governments must make large initial investments to prepare databases for online publication and smaller ongoing investments for maintaining and updating the data. Once data are available online, governments can reap ongoing savings in reduced, or even eliminated, publication expenses, while the cost to the user is much reduced and availability is greatly enhanced. Easily accessed, regularly updated information is valuable, and thus raises the question of whether users should be charged prices that capture that value. The US government has followed a policy of making information available at only the cost of dissemination, which, on the Internet, is virtually free. Fallows (2005) argues that this policy stimulates the development of new firms and industries and helps individuals make better decisions. In contrast, Canadian governments have been more inclined to view their statistical agencies as revenue centres, and impose user charges for anything beyond basic data (Roberts 2006, 206).

Turning from informational to transactional services, the difference between business and government remains significant. Most online business transactions involve a relatively simple two-step process: payment by credit card for goods to be shipped subsequently. The public sector already provides online purchasing of publications, recreational licences, and permits. More complicated private sector transactions, with a higher security requirement, involve ongoing management of personal accounts, for example, electronic banking. Much of the role of government is more complex, involving the provision of expensive multi-year entitlements, such as social and health insurance. Government also produces documentary evidence of entitlements, such as passports and social insurance cards at the federal level, and birth certificates, driver's licences, and health (medical insurance) cards at the provincial level. These entitlements are extremely valuable in themselves – an Ontario health card entitles the holder to free (zero co-payment) treatment by any physician or hospital in Canada and reimbursement at Canadian rates for treatment outside Canada – and as proof of identity. Because Canada is an economically advanced country with an exceedingly diverse population, Canadian governments, for reasons of both security and cost, want to ensure that documentary evidence of entitlements is restricted to those who qualify. Here, too, if government wants to move to online creation of entitlement documents, it faces technical challenges and security concerns that the private sector rarely needs to confront (Bennett and Raab 2003, 139–59).

Reshaping the Public Service

While security concerns and technological limitations may currently constrain government initiatives to enhance transactional capability of the Internet, internal resistance may be slowing the transformational effects of IT within the public service – slowing, but not stopping. Traditional organization by department is, after all, entrenched by some very strong forces: ministerial accountability to the legislature on the basis of departmental budgets and personal political ambition. Ministers themselves, who are often political rivals, desire autonomy in their departmental affairs, and are often reluctant to share information and power with one another (Perri 6 2004a, 131–6; Kernaghan and Gunraj 2004). This departmentalism, however, is undercut by the potential for IT to provide crosscutting information that could improve government performance in service delivery, policy effectiveness, and internal efficiency, all of which would be desired by voters and the government as a whole – as opposed to its individual ministers.

In service delivery, Web portals organized on the basis of a variety of service-centred principles (issues, user groups, life events) have to deal with the 'back room' reality of department-based programs. This has necessitated the creation of virtual organizations that build and maintain portals, linking them to their constituent departments. Fountain (2001, 147–66) told the story of the U.S. Business Advisor, one of the first such portals ever launched. The initial enthusiasm of its founders, as well as support from Vice-President Gore's National Performance Review, gave way several years later to diminished commitment and an absence of resources to sustain the project. More recently, the U.S. government has become more successful in establishing and maintaining integrated portals and some (employment, student aid, product recalls, and government forms) are now being cited as examples of international best practice (United Nations 2004, 50). The Government On-Line initiative, discussed in chapter 2, involved the creation of a stable framework of three gateways and thirty-one portals for all Government of Canada services, and can be seen as an attempt to overcome the problems that undermined the U.S. Business Adviser.

Call centres go a step beyond the virtual organization of Web portals, employing workers who deal directly with the public. Yet they too have aspects of virtual organization, as constituent organizations provide information for operators to pass along and complete transactions that operators begin. And there must be a back office structure to ensure that the information is up to date and that the transactions are completed. This is discussed in the context of municipal 311 telephone service in chapter 5.

Beyond Web portals and call centres, some governments are in fact experimenting with integrated service delivery organizations. Bellamy and Taylor (1998, 77) and Mechling (1999, 176–7) provide rationales for such organizations to take advantage of economies of scale and scope in service delivery, reduce or eliminate wasteful 'hand-offs' of service recipients among government programs and departments, and provide more holistic and flexible service based on comprehensive individual or business records. The Institute for Citizen-Centred Service's finding that over half of transactions involve two or more channels and the Treasury Board Secretariat's finding of greatly reduced costs for the electronic channel strengthens the case for comprehensive management of service channels.

Two early examples of integrated service delivery organizations are Australia's Centrelink, which integrates the administration of cash benefits (Perri 6 2004b, 124), and Service New Brunswick, a Crown corporation that provides a variety of services on behalf of government departments. In February 2005, the federal government established Service Canada, its own integrated service delivery organization. Over a five-year period, it is expected to deliver $3 billion in operational savings. To achieve the savings, an investment of $500 million is required, half of which is in development of security systems for e-government transactions (Department of Finance Canada 2005a). Clearly, IT is integral to this initiative, as the government's plans reveal. Service Canada's evolution – for example, the menu of services it eventually provides and the accountability framework it assumes – will reveal much about the prospects of integrated public service-delivery organizations and the conditions that enable them to succeed.

A second aspect of IT-enabled integration is integrated support, or shared service, organizations. Their mandate includes implementation of government-wide software solutions, such as a common computer desktop or a common financial management system, and provision of a variety of support functions government-wide. Chapter 3 will discuss the Ontario government's initiatives in this area, beginning in the late nineties with the creation of the Shared Service Bureau. The February 2005 federal budget also took a major step in this direction by giving Public Works and Government Services Canada full authority for procurement and requiring departments to use standing offers negotiated by PWGSC (Department of Finance Canada 2005a). Here, too, there is much potential for evolution. What will be the balance of responsibility between a shared-service agency and departmental support units? How will the shared-service agency be structured, and what form of ministerial representation will it have (Kernaghan and Gunraj 2004)? Will it actually produce the intended savings?

If IT-based integration will lead to integrated service delivery organizations and integrated support organizations, then that leaves only the policy development function of departments as distinct. However, is there the potential for integration even here? Put differently, if departments can share limbs, can they also share minds? The change is not as revolutionary as it might appear. Traditional government has always displayed some degree of integrated policy development. One function of central agencies is to ensure that the impacts of any department's initiatives upon the missions of other departments are taken into account. Thus, central agencies generally have policy development units staffed by generalists who are capable of spotting cross-departmental impacts and ensuring that they are raised when policy proposals are considered by Cabinet committees or full Cabinet.

Policy integration in IT-enabled government, however, has a much deeper meaning. In addition to occasional cross-departmental policy impacts, there are some policy areas that are so closely linked as to have ongoing inter-relationships; an obvious example would be economic development and environmental sustainability. There are also thorny policy problems, such as homelessness or urban poverty, that have many dimensions, and, if any progress is to be made in alleviating them, they require integrated solutions involving many departments and programs. It is in developing these solutions that IT has an essential role to play, for they depend on the best applied social science research, which requires sophisticated analytical methodologies and comprehensive databases. Information technology provides the hardware and software to support integrative and holistic research.

By virtue of the wide-ranging economic and social data it collects, government has the capacity – to a greater degree than any other institution in society – to create comprehensive social and economic databases that would support integrated policy development. The question is whether public attitudes toward privacy will permit it to do so. A fundamental issue with new technologies, and IT in particular, is striking a balance between the technology's potential and what might be lost or threatened. In some instances, such as public health, the policy issue is of sufficient importance that legislative consent has been obtained. In other cases, a methodology such as geographic information systems (GIS) permits the construction of databases sufficiently detailed to support policy development, but without infringing on individual privacy. Occasionally, public attitudes have not been supportive, and the construction of integrative data sets has been halted. A recent example was the creation by Human Resources Development Canada of a comprehensive longitudinal database for virtually the entire Canadian population dealing with income, employment, taxation, and use of government programs such as employment insurance. While this database would have been extremely useful for policy research, public opposition to its perceived Orwellian potential as well as concerns expressed by the federal privacy commissioner led the department to dismantle it (Bennett and Raab 2003, 115; Good 2003, 119–22).[2]

While such battles over database integration will continue to be fought well into the future, a variety of integrated policy-development initiatives are under way in Canada and elsewhere. These include the Government of Canada's internal policy research secretariat and support for external policy research networks, both of which create capacity to deal with crosscutting policy problems, and several aspects of the U.K. government's joined-up government initiative, such as the establishment of new central policy units and crosscutting spending reviews (Perri 6 2004a, 122). Integrated policy development has also given rise to new patterns of program delivery, in particular neighbourhood or area-focused initiatives based on GIS data (Perri 6 2004a, 87–92; 2004b, 122). These integrated policy-development initiatives do not represent as extensive a restructuring as those occurring in service delivery and the provision of internal support. Yet it is clear that policy development is becoming more integrative in terms of a growing role for central policy units as well as a reshaping of the work of departmental policy units and their dealings with each other.

The Procurement Interface

There can be no doubt that the transformation in IT is affecting government procurement practices. Yet at the heart of the procurement interface lies a paradox. While the application of IT has made procurement, in general, much easier for government, the procurement of IT itself often remains a challenge. Posting government contract opportunities on websites, thus opening up the market globally (assuming the absence of domestic restrictions or preferences), electronic submission of documents, and posting results on websites to make future procurement more competitive all combine to improve the process and its outcomes. The remaining difficulties with IT procurement stem from the characteristics of some, though not all, IT markets.

Governments must purchase hardware, software, systems, and the services of IT professionals. Globerman and Vining's (1996) analysis of procurement provides valuable insight here. They identified three main environmental factors that affect procurement decisions: task complexity, contestability, and asset specificity. Task complexity describes the degree of difficulty in specifying and monitoring a transaction. Contestability refers to the number of firms currently or potentially available to bid for a contract. Asset specificity denotes the extent to which an asset makes a necessary contribution to the production of a particular good, but has a much lower value in alternative uses. Two polar cases in this framework are low complexity, high contestability, and low asset specificity, on the one hand, and high complexity, low contestability, and high asset specificity, on the other. The former is the more favourable. *Low complexity* implies that the government can readily specify and monitor the contract, *high contestability* means that there are many actual or potential bidders, and *low asset specificity* indicates that assets produced can be redeployed readily elsewhere. From the government's point of view, these parameters mean that inefficient or opportunistic contractors can quickly be replaced; from the contractor's point of view, opportunism on the part of the government is not a concern, because the product can be sold to someone else.

A mixture of high task complexity, low contestability, and high asset specificity presents the most difficult case for both government and contractor. The software and systems required for integrated service delivery, joined-up policy making, and integrated support cannot be purchased off the shelf, but must be tailor-made for the government acquiring them. Procurement consequently becomes a matter of contracting for, and managing, large and complex IT projects. Government will have difficulty specifying and monitoring outcomes, because the contractor's work is both technically complicated (for example, writing software involving millions of lines of code) and specialized. The degree of specialization results in few actual or potential bidders (low contestability). Moreover, those few bidders are necessarily wary of possible opportunism, since the assets they produce are not easily reconfigured and will be significantly less valuable to another client (high asset specificity).

If we think of Globerman and Vining's classification system as a spectrum, then in recent years some aspects of IT have moved towards the more favourable side. Basic computer hardware (desktops, laptops, and printers) has become increasingly standardized, with many competing producers, and a large market that includes businesses, consumers, and government (Carr 2004). The labour market for IT professionals was a seller's market during the dot-com boom of the last decade, and governments had difficulty staffing positions in that area. The problem was accentuated by the one-time demand created by the Y2K transition. The dot-com collapse, however, has cooled the market for IT professionals, and, as a consequence, governments now face less competition in hiring. In addition, the educational system is producing large numbers of graduates with basic or advanced technical skills in this area. Government is now in a stronger position when it hires junior IT professionals, such as website developers and help desk workers, as either permanent staff or temporary consultants. More difficult cases involve operating systems and office software, because of Microsoft's market dominance;[3] systems and networks, because of their inherent complexity, and senior IT professionals, because they continue to be in strong demand, and hence handsomely compensated (in particular with stock options) in the private sector.

The most challenging IT market is the procurement of large specialized systems. While this is usually contracted out, the relationship with contractors involves extensive negotiation and carries potential for conflict and ultimately unsuccessful outcomes (Globerman and Vining 1996). Yet the acquisition of these systems cannot be avoided: mainframe-based legacy systems using dying computer languages are increasingly coming to the end of their useful lives.

The literature on large IT projects, pioneered by the IT consulting firm the Standish Group (http://www.standishgroup.com), focuses almost exclusively on these challenges. While they are clearly substantial, it is important to retain perspective: the Standish Group, as a consulting firm, is dramatizing the problems for which it offers solutions. The Standish Group defines a successful project as one completed on time, within budget, and with full functionality. By this measure, performance has improved over the last decade: the group's initial 1995 study of 8400 public and private sector projects in the United States found that only 16 per cent were successful, 31 per cent were cancelled, and 53 per cent compromised (late, over budget, or delivered with less than full functionality). Its 2003 study found that 33 per cent were successful, 17 per cent cancelled, and 50 per cent compromised.

Let us look more closely at these measures. Are they appropriate as indices of success or failure? The essential problem is that they are defined in supplier terms, rather than in terms of the interaction between the project's value to end users and cost to produce. It is possible to have a project delivered on time, on budget, and with full functionality that fails because it does not gain user acceptance. Conversely, a project could be over budget, late, and delivered with less than full functionality but still accepted by users. A framework that more effectively takes into account both value to users and cost to producers is net present value.

If one accepts that the Standish Group's case has at least some validity, then the appropriate response is to find ways to improve project management. Dunleavy et al. (2004), in a cross-national survey of national government IT performance, give Canada and the United States high marks because they encourage open competition for contracts, resist market dominance by the largest IT suppliers, and retain substantial in-house capacity to monitor and, if necessary, manage large IT projects. They observe that the success rate of federal government IT projects in both Canada and the United States is comparable to the private sector – 'three quarters to four fifths of projects working within acceptable range of their intended major target aims' – a more realistic standard than that of the Standish Group. In contrast, they criticize the United Kingdom for precisely the opposite policy choices, and claim that these choices are responsible for an abnormally high rate of project failures.

Other practitioner groups have developed guidelines for the management of large IT projects (Organization for Economic Co-operation and Development 2001; Parliamentary Office of Science and Technology 2003), and these have included such recommendations as having a project champion at the senior management level, dividing projects into self-contained modules, undertaking gateway reviews of projects, including in contracts with private sector partners incentives and penalties, maintaining close communication between the project team and private sector suppliers and between the project team and end users, and establishing clear lines of responsibility and accountability for project management.

Digital Leadership

To this point, our analysis and models have focused on impersonal factors such as costs, user preferences, and organizational structure. While these factors are important, they ignore the shaping role that individuals play in the development of public sector IT. We now address this human factor under the rubric of digital leadership.

Historically, the late eighties and early nineties were a very fertile period for the application of IT in the public sector. The spread of numerous new technologies – GIS, smart cards, electronic kiosks, e-mail, and the Internet, among them – spurred public servants to imagine applications. The public servants who were doing the imagining were those who were familiar with the technologies, and they tended to be front-line workers or middle managers, rather than agency heads or politicians. Borins (1998) studied a sample of 217 of the best innovations in the Ford Foundation–Kennedy School of Government state and local government innovation awards between 1990 and 1994. He found that 70 per cent of the innovations involving IT were initiated by middle managers or front-line workers – a far higher percentage than in any other policy or management area. The typical IT innovator was described as

> a person close to and knowledgeable about a particular technology and its use ... The IT innovator has a long-term vision of how the technology will grow to serve new purposes and markets and leadership skills that can be used to communicate this vision to others less familiar with the technology, who control the resources needed to make the vision a reality. (Borins 1998, 141)

Innovators were experimenting beneath agency heads' and politicians' radar but, when they came up with something workable, secured the necessary resources. While politicians were rarely involved in decision making about these innovations, they were eager to be photographed beside the successful innovation. A notable example was

Schoolnet, an early website developed in Industry Canada to support elementary and secondary school teachers. It originated on the front lines, with the idea put forward by an undergraduate student on a work term. It was eventually funded and often used for photo ops by federal politicians, including then prime minister Jean Chrétien (Alexander 2000; Borins 2001).

By the mid-nineties, the landscape had altered. Public consciousness of IT dramatically increased. Additionally, the public sector itself experienced highly visible failures and successes in the management of its large technology projects. This new IT environment has given rise to three arenas for digital leadership: the political, the senior bureaucratic, and the front-line. Information technology has emerged from being an element of general administrative support to a specialty in its own right, with an organization headed by a chief information officer (CIO), a process discussed with respect to the federal government in chapter 2 and Ontario government in chapter 10. If IT creates the conditions for integrated service delivery organizations, joined-up knowledge management and policy development, and integrated support organizations, then governmental and departmental CIOs will be deeply involved in establishing them. Similarly, if governments are to exert control over their large IT projects, CIOs and the IT organization will play a major role.

Front-line digital leadership will play a less autonomous role than fifteen years ago, but it will not be absent. Government will continue to recruit recent graduates with advanced technical skills, and they will work on projects like Web development and software applications. Some of their work may be too advanced for public sector acceptance, for example, because it introduces leading-edge technologies that are not yet widely available. Front-line digital leaders will, nevertheless, advance the baseline of government IT sophistication, enabling it to respond to the expectations of younger citizens.

The political context for digital leadership has changed dramatically. Politicians have become the hinge in the model of IT-enabled government, in the sense that they are involved in online campaigning and consultation, on one arm, and in overseeing the public service's use of technology, on the other arm. Some politicians, particularly younger ones, are personally comfortable with IT. In addition, they and their campaign organizations and parties will have used the technology to be elected, and it is reasonable to expect they will continue using the technology when in office. For example, they may want the government website to have the same look and feel as the party website they used during the election campaign.

Politicians are also becoming aware of the potential benefits and costs in the management of IT. Establishing integrated service organizations, support organizations, and joined-up policy development will entail large and expensive IT projects. If managed well, the projects can deliver savings and improve service. If delivered poorly, the projects will produce cost overruns and embarrassing headlines. In effect, in IT-enabled government the riskiness of the procurement and project-management interface has increased. Considerations of regional benefits and political patronage, previously important in procurement, in the context of IT-enabled government increase risk by giving work to firms with a higher probability of failure. Similarly, there are a host of security issues involving public sector IT, such as the security of public sector systems and data from hackers and viruses. Here, too, lies much potential embarrassment. While poor IT management may not defeat a government, it certainly won't help it be re-elected.

IT has become so pervasive in government that it is a major factor in a number of Cabinet portfolios. These include:

- Treasury or Management Board, which oversees the government's overall use of technology, and is particularly responsible for managing its risks
- Public Works or government services portfolios, which oversee procurement and common services
- Service delivery organizations, especially if they are assigned a growing number of responsibilities formerly held by functional area ministries
- Industry portfolios that deal with the IT industry as a constituency

While in theory ministers are generalists capable of handling any portfolio, in practice the complexity of policy and management issues means that premiers and prime ministers tend to assign portfolios to ministers who have some expertise. We can thus expect ministers with strong technology backgrounds to be chosen for these portfolios. We can also expect some portfolios, such as Public Works, that were previously driven by considerations of regional benefits and patronage, to shift their attention to risk minimization through effective management. We will take up the issue of digital leadership in more detail in chapter 10.

Conclusion

This chapter developed a conceptual model to compare traditional and IT-enabled government and ask whether the latter represents transformative change. Our focus was the major differences between the two worlds. First, new channels – the Internet, e-mail, and Web-supported IVR and call centres – have been added at all the interfaces between government and society: political campaigning, policy consultation, public services, and procurement. Second, technology provides the potential for greater inter-agency (and intergovernmental) integration in all aspects of public sector organization: service delivery, procurement and support, and policy development. If the electronic channel becomes increasingly popular at the interfaces, government will look very different to those who deal with it. If increased internal integration comes about, the nature of political and bureaucratic work will change. If IT can bring about major cost savings in government, important questions will arise about how to allocate them. Together, there is the potential for a transformation of the public sector. The chapter then outlined a set of concepts – channel choice, organizational integration, procurement markets, and digital leadership – that can be used to understand the developmental dynamics of IT-enabled government both at its interfaces and internally. This chapter has thus laid out a program for observing and explaining the development of IT-enabled government. Subsequent chapters apply this program to both the federal and Ontario governments by discussing in detail developments over the last five years.

Notes

1 Access to information (in federal government parlance) or freedom of information (in Ontario parlance) requests can require government to make available to the requester vast libraries of data and documents held in electronic form. For a discussion of the issues involved in requests involving electronic records, see Roberts (2006, 199–227).

2 The set of technological, legal, and policy issues regarding privacy is more complex than can be treated in depth in this book. They include surveillance (Lyon 2001, 2003), commercial practice regarding consumers, and government regulation of the private sector through privacy law (Bennett and Raab 2003). Our concern in this book is somewhat more limited: to

service delivery and policy development. The former could benefit from data integration, but such integration is prohibited unless individual permission is given, for example, the federal government's permanent voters list, which operates on the basis of taxpayers agreeing on their income tax returns to release their address information to Elections Canada. Data integration for policy development does not necessarily depend on individual consent, but rather on broad public support for initiatives in which individual cases are stripped of personal descriptors.

3 An apparently inexpensive alternative to Microsoft and other commercial software developers is open-source software and, as discussed in chapter 3, governments have become increasingly interested in it.

2 The Government of Canada: Government On-Line and Citizen-Centred Service

DAVID BROWN

Technology has a long history in the federal government, as a subject of public policy and as a feature of public administration. In the past decade, the information highway, networked computing, and the World Wide Web have combined to blur traditional policy and jurisdictional boundaries and to take the government into new modes of administration and service delivery. Technology, globalization, and related management concepts have interacted with a society and economy defined by knowledge and characterized by new relationships, skills, and forms of wealth creation.

The foundations of this new environment emerged in the mid-1990s, with the work of the Information Highway Advisory Council and the establishment of a Government of Canada presence on the Internet. From a public administration perspective, the period between 1999 and 2006 was shaped by an active program of reform – Government On-Line (GOL) – that sought to profoundly change the way the government deals with the public and related internal administrative practices and culture. Although by no means all-encompassing, GOL was sufficiently successful that for five years, from 2001 through 2005,[1] Canada was ranked first by the Accenture consulting firm in its annual international survey of e-government service delivery. Their assessment gave particular weight to efforts to make government services available to the public in an integrated way, using information technology to permit government to share the perspective of the citizen using those services (Accenture 2005).

Government On-Line formally ended on 31 March 2006. Its 1999–2006 time frame is the focus of this chapter. We begin with a brief discussion of IT in Canadian public policy, in order to provide the context for the discussion of IT in federal public administration that is the chapter's primary concern. The second section looks at the federal government's measures to harness IT in administration and service delivery in the period before and during GOL, as well as initiatives taken by the Martin government after December 2003 to move beyond GOL.

One of the most innovative aspects of GOL was its promotion of citizen-centred World Wide Web–based service-delivery portals that were placed on the government's primary Internet portal, the Canada Site, as a means of reshaping the service relationship between the government and the public. These citizen-centred websites, known in the federal government as Clusters, and the three Gateways into which they were organized, raised issues about governance and management practice and also led the federal government into new relationships with other Canadian jurisdictions and the private sector. The third section of the chapter discusses this new paradigm, drawing on surveys of federal, provincial, and municipal officials. The chapter's fourth section discusses four themes that emerge from the surveys and from the history of GOL.

Information Technology in Canadian Public Policy and Governance

Information technology has had a major effect on all dimensions of public policy and governance: government's roles and relationships with the economy and society, with its citizens and with the international environment, as well as the operations of state institutions and their internal relationships (Brown 2005). Canada's geography has led governments since World War II to encourage technology-based industry, in particular in the telecommunications sector, through its own research and programs to support Canadian industry. A Department of Communications was created in 1969, with responsibilities that included developing and promoting new technologies. The 'hardware' side of Communications was merged into a new Department of Industry in 1993, which also assumed responsibility for science and technology policy, while the cultural industries 'software' side became part of the Department of Canadian Heritage.

The foundation for the Government of Canada's policy framework for the knowledge economy was laid through the work of the Information Highway Advisory Council (IHAC), an external blue-ribbon committee that was appointed in 1994 and reported in late 1995. The government's response to the IHAC report (Industry Canada 1996) set out a four-part action plan:

1. Build the information highway by creating a competitive, consumer-driven policy environment conducive to innovation.
2. Grow Canadian online content to strengthen national culture.
3. Ensure that all Canadians have the opportunity to participate in the information highway.
4. Attain better levels of government services in an affordable manner and make government serve as a catalyst for information-highway development across Canada.

Subsequent federal economic policy stressed the development of a national infrastructure required for the information highway, including broadband telecommunications capacity and policies to promote enterprise creation and skills development in the knowledge economy. As a result of the IHAC report, a major objective of social policy in the knowledge economy became fostering public access to technology and technology-enabled public and private services and mitigating the effects of the digital divide. Industry Canada's Connecting Canadians program in the mid-1990s promoted the extension of Internet facilities to remote and Aboriginal communities, schools, and libraries. Perhaps the most spectacular example was SchoolNet, in which Industry Canada realized the ambitious goal of linking all schools in Canada to the Internet by the end of the decade. This achievement was paralleled by major efforts by Industry Canada to promote use of the Internet by business and by Heritage Canada, the National Library, and related agencies to promote cultural industries and digitization of national cultural assets.

Information technology also contributed to major changes in the relationship between the Canadian state and the international environment, introducing new international institutions and changing the roles of existing ones, while also transforming the nature of international economic activity, capital flows, and national security. The state remains the cornerstone of the international system, but its mode of operating internationally has been dramatically affected by the World Wide Web, including bringing it closer to the citizens of other countries. Similarly, there have been important changes in how government interacts with the Canadian public and in how it administers itself. The balance of this chapter takes a closer look at some of the most signifi-

cant impacts on federal government administration, notably the provision of technology-enabled services to the public, which has been
central to its success in the annual Accenture surveys.

Information Technology and Federal Public Administration

The evolution of e-government in the Government of Canada can be
traced through three periods of development, each building on earlier
efforts: the lead-up to the launch of Government On-Line (GOL) in 1999;
the life cycle of GOL from 1999 to 2006; and the move to the generation
beyond GOL. Government On-Line is used as the reference point, both
because it matches the time frame of this book and because its emphasis
on citizen-centred service delivery is important; however, it by no
means captured all of the IT-related activities and initiatives undertaken
during this period. It is also important to recall that GOL was an initiative launched by the Chrétien government. The government of his Liberal successor Paul Martin, in office from December 2003 to February
2006, chose to see GOL through to its conclusion, taking a number of
steps to broaden and deepen the changes introduced by GOL, and to
integrate them into the wider operations of government.[2]

Laying the Foundation: Pre-1999

Government On-Line grew out of a long tradition of administrative
reform in the federal government. The foundation of much of this
reform was the Royal Commission on Government Organization (the
Glassco Commission), which reported in the early 1960s. In support of
the axiom that the government should 'let the managers manage,'
Glassco established a framework for management of the government
as a whole based on three organizational types:

- Central agencies, which support collective (Cabinet) ministerial
  decision making, provide management policy direction to the public
  service, allocate budgets, and lead government-wide administrative
  reform
- Common service agencies, which provide centralized services to
  government in areas where this is deemed appropriate, in support of
  government policy objectives (as opposed to leaving departments to
  develop their own services or go outside government to obtain
  them)

- Line departments, which provide programs and services to the public

This taxonomy has informed all subsequent reform efforts and debates. Four other enduring reform themes since Glassco are also important, individually and cumulatively. Continuing efforts to reform financial administration have sought to ensure that managers have the financial authorities they need, while observing public service standards of stewardship and ethics. There have also been several waves of reforms to the management of the public service as a body and of human resources as a key instrument of knowledge-based government. A third reform strand has been institutional bilingualism, which since 1969 has given the Canadian public the right to ask for services from the federal government in either English or French. Finally, measures since the early 1980s to increase public access to government information, while safeguarding government-held personal information, have highlighted the importance of information as a critical resource of public administration.

In the late 1980s and early 1990s, the information highway's convergence of telecommunications and computing technologies began to infiltrate public administration. This transformation would eventually lead to networked computers providing desktop access to the World Wide Web as a universal operating assumption across the federal government. Reflecting these trends, Progressive Conservative Prime Minister Kim Campbell made extensive changes to the machinery of government in 1993, including reconstituting the Department of Industry with a major role in promoting the use of information technology in the larger economy and appointing the first government CIO (at first a chief informatics officer, later chief information officer), located in the central agency responsible for management and budget, the Treasury Board Secretariat. The CIO's significant early accomplishment was the development of a *Blueprint for Renewing Government Services Using Information Technology* (Treasury Board Secretariat 1994), which was published in 1994.

Prime Minister Jean Chrétien's Liberal government, which entered office later in 1993, introduced the principle that government did not have to implement public programs itself in order to achieve public policy objectives. This position was intended to help the federal government address a serious deficit, but it was also compatible with the spirit of public-private partnerships, an increasingly common feature of administrative projects with a major technology dimension. One of the Chrétien government's early measures was the appointment of the Information Highway Advisory Council in 1994. In 1995, the government launched the Canada Site (http://www.canada.gc.ca) as its portal on the World Wide Web. Although the Canada Site became an important part of the government's technological toolkit, the government in the late 1990s was most concerned with managing the risks involved in major IT projects and with ensuring that its computing infrastructure would not be vulnerable to the Y2K 'millennium bug.'

Government On-Line: 1999–2006

In 1999, the Cabinet committee on government communications approved the establishment of a federal online presence, combining a citizen-centred service strategy with electronic service-delivery programs. Three complementary service programs were created: Service Canada, based on in-person service centres and a national telephone service centre (1-800-O-CANADA); the Service Improvement Initiative (SII), seeking to establish a government-wide service-delivery standard based on client satisfaction surveys; and GOL, which was 'all about using IT to provide the best possible service to Canadians and to spur economic growth in the global marketplace' (Government On-Line 2003). All three programs were administered by Treasury Board Secretariat (TBS), GOL by the Chief Information Officer Branch, and the SII and Service Canada by a separate Service and Innovations Sector, whose mandate extended to the full range of service channels (in-person, telephone, mail, etc.). In 2002 the SII was transferred to the TBS GOL office and Service Canada to a line department, Human Resources Development Canada, in view of its operational nature.

These initiatives were foreshadowed in the 1997 Speech from the Throne announcing the government's priorities to Parliament by an undertaking that information and knowledge infrastructure would be accessible to all Canadians by the year 2000, 'thereby making Canada the most connected nation in the world' (Canada, Governor General 1997). In the 1999 Speech from the Throne, this was expanded to a commitment that by 2004, Canadians would be 'able to access all government information and services online at the time and place of their choosing' (Canada, Governor General 1999).

Originally, GOL applied to the twenty-eight (eventually thirty-four) major government departments and agencies in three 'tiers.' Tier 1 constituted a commitment to make information about government and government services available online by 31 December 2000. In Tier 2, key 'transactional' services were to be made available online by the end of the 2004–5 fiscal year. An important underpinning of Tier 2 was the development of a capacity for secure online transmission of personal information and financial transactions. Tier 3 was to proceed at the same time as Tiers 1 and 2 and called for collaborative delivery of services to common client groups, working with other levels of government.

In 2000, the Treasury Board – the Cabinet committee responsible for management – approved the *Cluster Blueprint* (Mantagaris 2003) as a basis for relaunching the Canada Site on 1 January 2001. Building on extensive client consultation and public opinion research, including biennial *Citizens First* surveys of public preferences in government service provision, the services on the Canada Site were reorganized into three Gateways: for individual citizens and residents (the Canadians Gateway),[3] for the business community (Canadian Business Gateway),[4] and for international clients (Non-Canadians Gateway).[5] Within each Gateway, several portals (Clusters) restructured information found on departmental and program websites to provide more effective access to government information and services by subject (for example, health), by audience (for example, seniors), and by life event or activity (for example, travel abroad). An inventory was taken of all government services to the public, and 135 (by the end of GOL, 130) priority services were identified to be included in the single windows provided by some thirty Clusters. At the same time, the deadline for having these services available online was extended to the end of the 2005–6 fiscal year: 31 March 2006. This became the target date for completion of GOL as a government-wide reform program.

Complementing the Gateways and Clusters were measures to strengthen the government's information management policies and to establish a public key infrastructure-based 'Secure Channel' for online transmission between government and the public of personal, financial, and other sensitive information. A project office was established in the Treasury Board Secretariat's CIO branch to spearhead GOL. It was responsible for providing overall leadership to GOL, using $880 million in supplementary funding through to 2005–6 to leverage departmental spending on GOL projects, encourage redesign of service-oriented Internet sites, and finance development of the Secure Channel.[6]

The GOL initiative and the Gateways and Clusters had an extensive governance structure, led and supported by the Treasury Board Secretariat CIO and the GOL office. Overseeing the process was the Treasury Board Secretariat Advisory Committee Information Management Subcommittee (TIMS), a committee of deputy ministers appointed by the Cabinet secretary. Three other groupings reported to TIMS: the Service and Information Management Board (a committee of senior program managers and departmental CIOs that backed up TIMS in providing inter-ministerial direction and coordination for GOL); the council of departmental CIOs (which served as a network for that community); and a committee of the GOL champions (senior managers that each department was required to designate in order to lead the GOL internally) that linked to GOL implementation. These structures provided an umbrella for a host of interdepartmental committees and working groups at all levels to deal with everything from technical to policy and content issues. The Gateways and Clusters developed their own structures, with each Cluster setting up a dedicated project office and numerous working groups to develop common standards and working tools for Web page design, measurement of client satisfaction, and other steps to increase a consistent and interoperable approach among the Clusters. Outside support and advice was provided by a blue-ribbon Government On-Line Advisory Committee, which issued three annual public reports to the president of Treasury Board commenting on GOL progress (Canada, Government On-Line Advisory Panel 2002a, 2002b, 2003).

From the outset, a notable feature of GOL was the extent of interjurisdictional collaboration. Informal networking led, in the mid-1990s, to the creation of the Public Sector CIO Council (PSCIOC), eventually made up of all fourteen federal, provincial, and territorial chief information officers plus two municipal representatives. During the same period, the Canadian Centre for Management Development, the federal government's executive training agency, sponsored the Citizen-Centred Service Network (CCSN), an action-research initiative that included national and regional working sessions and resulted in the Citizens First surveys and studies promoting best practices in service delivery, including the development of a common measurement tool. After the CCSN completed its work, a more permanent forum for intergovernmental collaboration emerged, evolving into the Public Sector Service Delivery Council (PSSDC). In 2001, the PSSDC established the Institute for Citizen-Centred Service (the ICCS),[7] supported by the participating governments and 'incubated' by the Institute of

Public Administration of Canada (IPAC), the national network for public administration academics and practitioners. In 2002 the PSCIOC and PSSDC began working more closely together, with the ICCS acting as a research secretariat supporting the joint activities of the two councils. Beginning in 1997, *IT World Canada*, a publisher of information technology trade journals, working with the PSCIOC and later the PSSDC and IPAC, sponsored annual Lac Carling conferences that brought senior IT and service officials from all levels of government together with senior private sector IT executives.[8]

By mid-2005, GOL was well on the way to meeting its original objectives. Departments reported to the GOL office at the end of 2004 that they had achieved over 55 per cent of the targeted service levels for the 2005–6 completion of GOL (with strongest results in the Canadian Business Gateway), and that the remaining services were mostly on course to meeting their goals. Sixty-eight per cent of client activity was being conducted over the Internet, as compared to the other service channels (such as mail, phone, and in person),[9] and half of the services involved other jurisdictions or private sector partners (Government On-Line 2005). There were also risks. Managers of the Gateways and Clusters spent the final year of GOL developing sustainability strategies to ensure their continued existence when GOL funding terminated at the end of March 2006, and the GOL office prepared to close down at the same time. While no formal initiative was announced to replace GOL, the emphasis in its final year was on embedding its accomplishments across government under the broad theme of service transformation.[10] Nevertheless, the government was able to announce in its final GOL report that the 130 most frequently used government services all met their 31 March 2006 GOL targets (Government On-Line 2006, 73–80).

The Martin Government: 2003–2006

The Martin government made clear that it was comfortable with technology and wished to use it extensively. The appointment of a former provincial public servant and known technology aficionado, Reg Alcock, as Treasury Board minister signalled this priority to both the public service and the private sector. In addition to creating a department of Human Resources and Skills Development, with a mandate to meet skills needs in the knowledge economy, the government took two other significant organizational steps on coming into office in December 2003: it transferred the GOL office to Public Works and Government Services Canada (PWGSC – the federal government's main common service agency) and created an Information Technology Services Branch (ITSB) within PWGSC to administer IT services and infrastructure in support of government administration. The GOL transfer represented a judgment that GOL was well on its way to completion and had essentially become an operational function. The establishment of ITSB was a clear signal of intent to consolidate the IT common services functions in government and thus to realize the potential synergies and economies of scale in government administration. These measures left the Treasury Board Secretariat CIO branch more freedom to concentrate on its strategic central agency policy and budget roles.

The February 2005 budget, which included funding projections beyond fiscal year 2005–6, signalled other important changes (Department of Finance Canada 2005b). Service Canada became a stand-alone government agency, with its own deputy minister, providing single-window services to individual Canadians and residents on behalf of a range of departments. The new organization, which was formally launched in September 2005, built on a combination of the Canadians Gateway's Web-based services and the in-person 'over-the-counter' services provided in offices across the country, notably the network of employment offices (Service Canada 2005). While not announced in the budget, parallel steps were taken to establish a new unit called Canada Business, situated within Industry Canada and combining the Clusters located in the Canadian Business Gateway with the Canada Business Service Centres, which provide over-the-counter, Internet, and other services to business jointly on behalf of federal, provincial, and municipal governments.

The second major announcement in the 2005 budget was the planned creation of a single organization to provide services to government across the range of administrative functions. It would build on the infrastructure provided by PWGSC's IT Services Branch but would be a separate organization providing multi-channel services in areas such as financial and human resources as well as IT management. Underpinning these initiatives was additional financing for implementing the Secure Channel, which was to be built through a private sector consortium under government contract.

The Martin government avoided launching a formal reform initiative with a high-profile 'brand' label, such as GOL or the earlier Public Service 2000, but in practice it set out to introduce major changes to federal government administration. Taken together, these changes fit a private sector 'three rooms' model, in which services to public clients are consolidated in a single 'front room' (for example, Service Canada and Canada Business), and services to clients within government are provided by a consolidated 'back room' (such as the IT Services Branch of PWGSC and the emerging shared corporate and administrative services organization, building on PWGSC's traditional common services role). The program responsibility centres constitute the 'middle room,' retaining their policy development, program design, and monitoring roles but with reduced program delivery functions, especially where service to the public is involved. Underpinning this division of labour is an integrated technology infrastructure and data management capability. Some of the issues raised by these ambitious moves, in particular the implications for traditional accountability models, are discussed in the final section of this chapter. But first, the next section looks at the experience with the Gateways and Clusters – the most innovative aspect of GOL.

Gateways and Clusters: Perspectives on Public Service Reform

The three Gateways and thirty-odd Clusters (the number fluctuated over time) were introduced when GOL was relaunched on 1 January 2001. The Clusters, in particular, represented an effort to turn government service provision inside out, using the single-window potential of World Wide Web portals to organize services according to the needs and interests of defined segments of the population. Although conceived through planning led by Treasury Board, and carrying ministerial endorsement, the Gateways and Clusters were, for much of the GOL period, developed and implemented outside the established public service hierarchy. Each Cluster had a full-time management unit and was housed in a 'host' department; however, the Clusters were oriented to reflect the citizen's view of government – from the outside looking in – focusing on demand for services, placing organizational and jurisdictional lines in the background. This crosscutting service orientation was also reflected in the horizontal, team-based nature of Cluster governance, creating a policy community whose strategic direction, energy, and problem-solving were provided largely by networks of working groups and committees operating in a collaborative and at times even evangelical atmosphere; in this environment, Clusters staff were providing a new kind of leadership for the public service. These structures began to be brought into the mainstream as the 2005–6 GOL deadline approached, and a longer-term question will be whether the process itself had a lasting imprint on public service organizational culture.

Given their novelty and intrinsic interest, the Public Policy Forum, as part of this research project, conducted three surveys to gauge the views of public servants who were involved with Gateways and Clusters and with their counterparts in other jurisdictions. Surveys conducted in 2003 and 2005 focused on headquarters-based federal public servants. In both surveys, the core participants were individuals at all hierarchical levels who had worked on the Gateways and Clusters initiative, supplemented by other groups with an interest in the approach, including in 2005 the universe of federal assistant deputy ministers. In 2004, a modified version of the survey, using the more generic term *citizen-centred, Web-based service delivery*, was sent to all provincial and territorial deputy ministers, a cross-section of municipal chief administrative officers, and the managers of federal government field offices across Canada. Altogether, 1153 survey instruments were distributed in the three surveys, and 247 responses were received. The survey methodology and complete results of the three surveys are available on our website at http://www.digitalstate.ca/supp/ch2.html (Brown et al. 2006; Brown, Eidelman, and Isakovic 2004; Kirby and Brown 2005). The following discussion is based on the surveys and follow-up interviews and workshops.

Gateways and Clusters Are a Successful Model To Build Upon

In a short space of time, Gateways and Clusters, and their citizen-centred counterparts in the provinces, made their mark. The majority of federal respondents to the three surveys rated Gateways and Clusters 'generally' or 'highly' successful, while fewer than 5 per cent of survey participants in all three years assessed these initiatives as 'not successful' (Q 28).[11] Although the provinces, territories, and municipalities do not have precise counterparts to Gateways and Clusters, they have all developed portal-based approaches to electronic service delivery on the World Wide Web, incorporating methodologies to structure services in line with citizen needs and interests rather than according to the structure of government machinery and programs. Respondents to the 2004 and 2005 surveys were asked to assess which level of government had most successfully implemented citizen-centred Web-based

Table 2.1

Responses to survey question*: In your experience, which three types of services will be most successfully implemented by the Clusters by March 2006 (formal conclusion of the Government On-Line initiative)?

Type of service	2005 (%)	2004 (%)	2003 (%)
Information about government services and information sources	92.6	86.7	92.1
Forms	35.2	42.2	20.3
Publications and documents online	66.7	69.5	70.3
Links to sites	63.0	38.3	78.1
Accessible databases	9.3	10.9	7.8
Submission of completed forms	9.3	15.6	1.6
Financial transactions	3.7	8.6	3.1
Handling of personal and commercially sensitive information	1.9	0.0	0.0
Comments on policy documents	1.9	2.3	0.0
Use of online voting tools	0.0	0.0	0.0
Moderated policy discussion	0.0	1.6	0.0
Unable to assess	7.4	6.3	7.8
Other (please specify)	1.9	2.3	4.7

*Q 6 in 2006.

Note: Results do not add up to 100%, because some participants selected more than three responses. In the 2004 survey, questions were referenced to citizen-centred websites.

Source: Brown et al. 2006.

service delivery. Both surveys ranked the federal government first, although in 2005 federal headquarters officials ranked provincial sites a close second (Q 29).

Government On-Line – and indeed all Web-based service strategies – have distinguished between information and transactional services, with a general expectation that progress on the former will lead the latter. When asked to select the three most successfully implemented types of services, all three surveys rated information on government services most highly, followed by provision of documents online (see table 2.1). Links to sites and access to government forms were also frequently mentioned.

These highly ranked services all fall into the category of information services and correspond to the Tier 1 services in the original GOL formulation. Transactional services (the fifth through the eighth services listed in table 2.1) received a much lower rating – the highest being accessible databases and submission of forms – while services relating to the policy process (the ninth through the eleventh listed in table 2.1) were barely mentioned. The last result undoubtedly reflects the fact that policy services were not included in GOL.

All government services are also designed to embody crosscutting public policy objectives. All three survey groups were asked to assess how well these goals had been met by their own citizen-centred government websites (Q 16). Federal respondents gave highest marks to English-French bilingualism, reflecting well-established federal official languages policies. Meeting requirements to provide common identification as government sites and standard presentation and navigational formats (branding/common look and feel) received the next-highest ratings, followed by privacy and accessibility among federal respondents and security requirements among those from other jurisdictions. Two areas had clearly negative ratings: all three surveys gave lowest marks to 'management of information' and then 'user support.'

In the integrative nature of the Clusters, an important issue was their relationship with other areas of government work, including other jurisdictions dealing with the same segments of the population. The three surveys asked respondents to assess a number of these connections (Q 17). Points of strength for the Clusters included their integration into the larger GOL initiative, the working relationship among Clusters, and to a lesser extent their integration with other channels of service delivery. Work remained to be done, however, in other types of relationships that were looked at, notably working relationships with regional offices (which provide most of the over-the-counter service to the public), alignment with established departmental programs, and integration with services provided by other jurisdictions. Integration with the services provided by other jurisdictions was rated somewhat lower in the 2005 survey (which involved only federal officials) than in the 2004 survey, which had substantial provincial and municipal participation.

Clusters Are an Important Part of the Future of Public Administration

Officials from all three levels of government were clear that the Cluster/citizen-centred model should be built upon in the future, in internal management and in service delivery. Thus there was strong agreement with the proposition that Clusters/citizen-centred websites are an example of horizontal collaboration that will lead the future

Table 2.2

Responses to survey question*: In your opinion, which will be the preferred *electronic* service channel in the longer term (2008 and beyond)?

	2005 (%)	2004 (%)	2003 (%)
Citizen-centred websites (Gateways and Clusters)	67.3	56.6	51.6
Departmental/ministry websites	5.8	12.3	7.8
Program-oriented websites	3.8	12.3	**
Unable to assess	5.8	13.1	12.5
Other (please specify)	17.3	5.7	28.1

*Q 20 in 2006. **Question not posed.
Source: Brown et al. 2006.

evolution of the public service (Q 27). Notwithstanding challenges and uncertainties – in particular, the financial difficulties anticipated at the termination of special GOL funding at the end of the fiscal year 2005–6 – the surveys indicated strong support for Clusters as a central part of public service delivery in the future. In the context of electronic service delivery alone, Clusters and citizen-centred websites were cited as the preferred channel by a strong margin, compared with departmental or program-oriented websites (table 2.2). The 'other' responses almost entirely supported Clusters in combination with one of the other types of Web-based sites.

This preference carries over into the 'multi-channel' service environment, combining electronic service 'channels' such as Clusters with in-person, mail, and telephone services. Just over half of the 2005 respondents considered Clusters well positioned to play a central role in the then recently announced Service Canada and Canada Business (52 per cent positive, 38 per cent negative – Q 21), which provide services through all channels. Perhaps most important was the view held by 62 per cent of the 2005 respondents that the citizen-centred structure of the Clusters should provide the starting point for organizing Service Canada and Canada Business, as opposed to 34 per cent who considered that the Clusters should be structured to align with the organization of Service Canada and Canada Business: the 'architecture' of the Clusters should shape the service front room (table 2.3).

Returning to the types of online services that are linked to the Cluster concept, survey participants were asked to identify their three priorities for future development, using the same list as in table 2.1 (table 2.4). Not surprisingly, the most frequently cited priorities were in

Table 2.3
Responses to survey question*: Which statement best reflects your views?

	2005 (%)
The citizen-centred structure of the Clusters should provide the starting point for organizing Service Canada and Canada Business	62
The Clusters should be restructured to align with the organization of Service Canada and Canada Business	34
There is no requirement for the Gateways and Clusters and Service Canada / Canada Business to take account of each other	4

*Q 22 in 2005.
Source: Brown et al. 2006.

Table 2.4
Responses to survey question*: Beyond March 2006, which three additional types of services should be given priority?

	2005 (%)	2004 (%)	2003 (%)
Information about government services and information sources	9.3	12.5	12.5
Forms	27.8	17.2	14.1
Publications and documents online	16.7	10.2	6.2
Links to sites	5.6	10.2	4.7
Accessible databases	46.3	44.5	35.9
Submission of completed forms	59.3	52.3	57.8
Financial transactions	38.9	44.5	57.8
Handling of personal and commercially sensitive information	42.6	22.7	42.2
Comments on policy documents	16.7	18.0	15.6
Use of online voting tools	7.4	18.8	14.1
Moderated policy discussion	5.6	16.4	17.1
Unable to assess	1.9	5.5	1.6
Other (please specify)	11.1	0.8	10.9

*Q 7 in 2005.
Note: Results do not add up to 100%, because some participants selected more than three responses.
Source: Brown et al. 2006.

transactional services, with submission of forms most frequently mentioned, and strong support for accessible databases, handling of sensitive information, and financial transactions – the elements of Tier 2. The scorecard prepared by the GOL office in 2004 identified the more complex transactions as the area requiring the most work (Public Works and Government Services Canada 2004). The surveys gave some support to areas not included in the original GOL framework, notably including comments on policy, but also the development of tools such as online voting and interactive policy discussion.

A central issue is the nature of Clusters: are they simply a sophisticated set of electronic 'links' through a single window to other government websites – a kind of electronic staging point – or should they be able to create content in their own right, independent of material carried on the sites of established program responsibility centres? Opinion was divided (Q 14), with a strong minority unable to decide. When the responses were broken down in 2005 by respondent responsibilities in relation to Clusters, the lowest support for an independent content role came from those with direct responsibilities for developing and maintaining Clusters, while those who collaborated with Clusters (or who had no role in relation to Clusters) more strongly supported a content role.

Cluster Sustainability Presents a Major Challenge

Towards the end of GOL, there was considerable uncertainty about whether efforts to ensure the sustainability of Clusters had been successful (Q 17). In the first instance, sustainability was seen as a financial issue, but also as one of program integration. Another critical component was leadership. In the 2005 survey, 44.2 per cent of the respondents stated they did not believe the Clusters would have adequate funding to achieve their full medium-term potential, that is, to 2008 (Q 25), while the state of the relationship between Clusters and government financial planning was also given a low rating (Q 17). Conversely, when asked to identify the best way to maximize the financial resources of the Gateways and Clusters (table 2.5), strongest support was for further integration with established departmental programs and budgets, followed closely by partnership or other joint financing arrangements with other government institutions, which would include other jurisdictions. There was very little support for commercial or user financing of the Clusters and citizen-centred websites, as a general matter, and only slightly more for cost recovery.

Three other areas of management were cited as requiring attention in order to ensure the longer-term viability of the Clusters: information management, privacy, and security. Given the nature of the Clusters, information and database management are critical issues, and this was consistently rated as the least satisfactory aspect of the Clusters (see,

Table 2.5
Response to survey question*: In order to maximize their financial resources, the Gateways and Clusters might make use of any or all of the following. Which approach do you consider to have the most potential?

	2005 (%)	2004 (%)	2003 (%)
Cost recovery	2.0	12.4	12.5
Partnership or other joint financing arrangements with other government institutions	37.3	31.4	46.9
Partnership or other joint financing arrangements with the private sector	7.8	5.0	12.5
Advertising and promotion	0.0	5.8	12.5
Further integration with established departmental programs and budgets	45.1	38.0	65.6
User fees	5.9	4.1	**
Other (please specify)	2.0	3.3	4.7

*Q 26 in 2005. **Question not posed.
Note: Columns may not add up to 100%, because of rounding.
Source: Brown et al. 2006.

for example, Q 16). This challenge is compounded by the fact that much of the information collected, especially through the Canadians Gateway, is personal information that requires protection in accordance with the Privacy Act and related Treasury Board policy. The first two surveys agreed with the proposition that there was a tension between the information-sharing goals of Clusters and the requirements of privacy policy, but by 2005 the response pattern had reversed, with 50 per cent disagreeing and fewer than 40 per cent agreeing (Q 15). Interviews suggested there may have been some progress in resolving the perceived tension. Although a relatively good assessment was given to meeting security policy aims (Q 16), the link with the Secure Channel was rated as one of the weakest Cluster relationships (Q 17). Interviews suggested this was because development of the Secure Channel began well before the Clusters were launched and efforts to integrate the two came relatively late in GOL.

The question remains: what will be the 'drivers' for future development of citizen-centred websites? (table 2.6) When asked to rate factors that might affect the future directions of Clusters, the single most important element was user demand – echoing the citizen-oriented philosophy of the Clusters. Intriguingly, technological improvements were ranked towards the bottom among the suggested possible fac-

Table 2.6
Responses to survey question*: How would you rate the factors listed as 'drivers' for future development of citizen-centred websites?

	Very important/ important (%)	Somewhat important/ not so important (%)	Unable to assess (%)
Citizen-centred website policy and governance	80.8	11.5	7.7
Data and information management	82.7	11.5	5.8
Finances	78.4	13.7	7.8
Globalization	30.0	60.0	10.0
Government priorities and direction	86.5	9.6	3.8
Official languages considerations	53.8	38.5	7.7
Public sector leadership	80.7	13.4	5.8
Technological improvements	71.1	25.0	3.8
User capability	78.4	17.7	3.9
User demand	92.3	3.8	3.8

*Q 24 in 2005.
Note: Rows may not add up to 100%, because of rounding.
Source: Brown et al. 2006.

tors, as were official languages considerations, probably reflecting their high rating in performance to date (Q 16). Globalization was rated lowest as a future driver, suggesting that multi-jurisdictional linkages have not yet extended beyond Canada's borders.

Leadership Takes New Forms

Leadership and accountability are central to management of Gateways and Clusters, as they are to any area of administration. Horizontal mechanisms such as interdepartmental committees and central agencies have played a major role in all aspects of GOL. The two Ottawa-oriented surveys (2003 and 2005) both indicated that two committees were the most influential in the development and implementation of Clusters. The interdepartmental committee of deputy ministers TIMS met monthly during most of the GOL period and oversaw planning and allocation of GOL discretionary funding. The Gateway Directors committee – the managers of the three Gateways and the Canada Site, chaired by the director of the Gateways and Clusters unit in the central GOL office – met weekly and provided hands-on direction and problem solving for the lower-level structures. Although three hierarchical levels below TIMS, this committee was made up of the highest level of

Table 2.7
Response to survey question*: In your experience, clusters are, in practice, fully accountable for their work.

	2005 (%)	2004 (%)	2003 (%)
Strongly agree	15.1	1.6	17.5
Agree	45.3	39.3	49.2
Disagree	20.8	18.0	23.8
Strongly disagree	1.9	2.5	3.2
Unable to assess	17.0	38.5	6.3

*Q 11 in 2005.
Note: Columns may not add up to 100%, because of rounding.
Source: Brown et al. 2006.

Table 2.8
Response to survey question*: In your experience, top management (DMs, ADMs,
central agencies) are, in practice, fully accountable for clusters.

	2005 (%)	2004 (%)	2003 (%)
Strongly agree	5.5	8.0	1.6
Agree	31.5	40.8	32.3
Disagree	29.6	28.0	51.6
Strongly disagree	18.5	5.6	3.2
Unable to assess	14.8	17.6	11.3

*Q 12 in 2005.
Note: Columns may not add up to 100%, because of rounding.
Source: Brown et al. 2006.

management devoted full-time to Gateways and Clusters and, as interviews indicated, enjoyed good access to decision making 'up the line'
to TIMS as well as interacting intensively with the Cluster organizations, which generally operated as a team.

A more enigmatic result was provided by the juxtaposition of two
sets of survey responses on accountability. When asked whether Clusters (or citizen-centred sites in provinces, territories, and municipalities) were accountable for their work, the greatest number of responses
in all three surveys agreed (table 2.7). But when asked to react to the
statement that top management (including deputy ministers and central agencies) are in practice fully accountable for Clusters, half of the
two Ottawa-oriented respondent groups disagreed (table 2.8). A factor
may have been the working-level team leadership model adopted by
the Clusters, wherein the Cluster-related groups acted within Treasury

Board policy frameworks but with a high level of discretion to innovate and largely outside established departmental hierarchies, taking their direction from an influential interdepartmental committee of deputy ministers. A strength in the development and early implementation stages of the Clusters, this autonomy risked translating into a lack of institutional ownership in the later stages.

Conclusions about Gateways and Clusters

While conscious of the risks and deficiencies, senior public service managers in all levels of government clearly supported Gateways and Clusters and their citizen-centred counterparts in the provinces as the centrepiece of electronic service delivery and of the emerging 'multi-channel' service environment reflected in organizations such as Service Canada. In order to be successful in the longer term, however, a number of challenges emerged by the end of GOL that will be important in determining whether the Gateways and Clusters leave a lasting legacy. The most basic was to bring the Cluster methodology and innovative culture into the organizational mainstream and to integrate Clusters into the government's program and financial planning. There were also significant information management issues to be addressed, as well as issues in the related areas of privacy and security, notwithstanding the considerable attention they had already received in the context of GOL. The more open-ended question, however, hinted at in the links vs. content debate, is whether the 'virtual' model provided by the Clusters will be a catalyst for future organizational development in the public sector. As the citizen-centred Web-based service concept puts down roots, this point will bear watching.

Issues for Canadian Public Administration

The massive infusion of information technology into all aspects of government has affected everything from the nature and use of public policy instruments to the internal skills and processes of public administration. These dynamics translate into a number of issues for Canadian public administration. Four warrant comment in light of the particular experience of the Government of Canada, although it is likely that variations on these themes occur in all governments. The most profound challenge is the implications of the citizen-centred service model for public services, as sensitivity to citizen interests and needs is increasingly part of public expectations of government. A second set of issues is the growing importance of information as a public resource. A third set of consequences is the new skills and relationships that are brought into the mix and the internal and external pressures they create. Finally, and cumulatively, there are implications for governance and accountability, within the public service itself and in its relationship to the larger political process.

The Growth of Citizen-Centred Government and Service

A central feature of GOL, reinforced by the Service Improvement Initiative, was online provision of government services to the public and the use of information technology to restructure ('transform') those services. This approach, which owes much to e-commerce models, implied taking the structure and delivery of services through several evolutionary stages. In the early phase of GOL, Treasury Board Secretariat identified four stages, moving from online presence through service availability, to mature electronic service delivery, and finally service transformation, characterized by seamless interconnectedness among all channels to deliver services independent of the channel access point.

The Gateways and Clusters took this approach a step further by building on the possibilities provided by the World Wide Web to create single windows to organize all of the information and services of interest to particular segments of the population – looking at government from the perspective of the citizen, regardless of where the service comes from. For example, the Seniors Cluster (http://www.seniors. gc.ca) provides links to sites in several departments dealing with personal finances and pensions, health and wellness, and travel and leisure, among a variety of topics of interest to seniors.

The single window in turn builds on the concept of self-service. Arguably one of the most significant developments in twentieth century management thinking, this was the source of much of the expected financial savings through the use of IT-supported management techniques such as process re-engineering and continuous improvement, both of which are integral to a single window approach. Self-service empowers citizens by giving them greater access to and control over what government knows about them and what it does for them. At the same time, it represents a significant 'downloading' of government clerical functions on to citizen 'users,' predicated on an assumption that citizens have the technological capacity and skills to play the new roles that they have been given.

Citizen-centred service has a number of important implications. Within government departments, it creates a coordination issue among program units that provide services to the department's client groups, especially when multi-channel features are introduced. The coordination challenge is compounded when the front room / middle room model is introduced – as with the reconstituted Service Canada and its counterparts in the provinces – and organizational responsibility for service delivery is separated from policy and program responsibility. Policy, public communications, and information technology functional communities also become involved, and Cluster management units were found in any of these areas within a given department. The situation becomes more complex when, as is generally the case, a Cluster of services designed in the image of the citizen brings together activities from more than one department or agency, and more complex still when the other jurisdictions that serve the same populations are also involved. In the first instance, a citizen-oriented single window raises basic issues of identity and information management – in whose 'space' is the service being provided? Whose budget is involved and therefore which minister, or even which legislature, has authority? Who controls the related information and therefore which privacy regime applies? In the longer run, it raises questions about whether programs and organizations should be redesigned to bring them in closer alignment with the citizen's interests and requirements – that is, whether and how far the front room should extend back into the middle room.

The surveys found that the citizen-centred model is clearly the preferred basis for the future development of electronic service delivery and as the framework for structuring the work of the federal government's integrated service front room, Service Canada. This view suggests that the model will be increasingly central to the future evolution of the public service. At the same time, it is unlikely that citizen-centred service will ever become the only framework for the government's relationship with the public or for designing its programs. Where government departments have regulatory or 'active' programmatic roles designed to shape citizen behaviour, they are likely to maintain a capacity to deal directly with the public, while more 'passive' services and ones that are designed to facilitate citizen behaviour will be more conducive to a citizen-centred approach. It may also be that the citizen-oriented approach will work best with transactional services as opposed to information services, where the service requirement may simply be a good search engine.

The Challenge of Information as a Public Resource

Information is the essence of e-government, being its greatest asset and providing its biggest headaches. It pervades GOL. A central part of GOL was the updating of the Management of Government Information Policy, the instrument by which Treasury Board ministers provide a common framework for information management procedure and practice across the public service. The policy gives administrative direction for the life cycle management of government information, as well as for facilitating information storage, access, and transmission in a networked environment. When the GOL office was transferred to Public Works and Government Services Canada (PWGSC) in December 2003, the unit providing leadership to the 'communities of practice' defined by Treasury Board information and technology policies initially went with it but was then returned to the Treasury Board CIO branch, reflecting the strategic importance of communities of practice. Information management was a central element of the agenda of all the major GOL-related interdepartmental committees, and the national librarian and archivist was designated the champion for information management on TIMS.

And yet, it was not clear by the end of the GOL process that the government had a much better handle on information management than at the beginning. The three surveys and related interviews consistently cited this issue as the area of greatest concern. This concern had several dimensions arising from the diversity of policies linked to information management. The most far-reaching was the management of personal information and related privacy policy issues. By networking personal information and consolidating it in databases, its analytical value is considerably enhanced but so too are the opportunities – and temptations – for secondary uses. This feature runs directly against the basic privacy policy principle that information should be used only for the purpose for which it was collected unless the consent of the information subject has been explicitly collected or can reasonably be assumed (itself a thorny policy issue). The growing technical feasibility of pooling personal information, together with pressures such as the desire to harness government information holdings for use in the post-9/11 war on terrorism, creates pressure to make the fullest possible use of the government's investment in collecting and preserving such information. At the same time, the underlying reality is that the personal information holdings of government are based on information that is generally provided voluntarily and whose accuracy depends on voluntary ·compliance, much like the tax system. In addition, also like in the tax system, there exists an implied contract between the citizen and the state that personal information will be safeguarded, or else the prized quality of that information risks degradation through incomplete and inaccurate information provision from the source (the citizen).

Other areas of information management add to the dilemma. The access to information (ATI) regime, which is closely related to the privacy regime, puts considerable administrative pressure on government information management in view of its basic requirement that requested records be located, reviewed, and produced within thirty days. This pressure has been compounded by the weakness of electronic record keeping, especially of e-mails, and uneven integration between electronic and paper records management. A further dimension is created by the political sensitivity of many of the ATI requests, reflecting the objectives of more open government that originally led to ATI legislation. In practice, both ATI and privacy policy intersect with government security policy, which at root is a subset of information policy. Information technology – in particular IT infrastructure – creates its own security requirements, but the basic tension is between the need to protect government from harmful effects of the disclosure of sensitive information and the principles of openness created by ATI. These tensions are compounded when linked to the tenets of government communications, starting with the premise that government has a duty to inform the citizenry so they can exercise their rights and responsibilities, not least as voters and taxpayers.

Notwithstanding these linkages and the central importance of information and knowledge management to the knowledge economy and society, and therefore to the digital state, the management of information and related technologies in the federal government has been less integrated and cohesive – operating in a less mature policy and institutional environment – than the management of the other major assets of public administration, financial and human resources, and the physical assets of the state. The Treasury Board policy centres of expertise in information, communications, and security policy were combined from the mid-1980s to the mid-1990s; however, they were dispersed among parts of the Treasury Board Secretariat (TBS) by the time GOL was launched. The CIO branch did not see itself as defined by these policies and their implementation in the way that the TBS human resources and comptrollership branches are shaped by their respective policy and statutory responsibilities. While that decision was later partially reversed, the statutory policy and program framework of information and technology management remained less comprehensive and integrated than was the case for financial and human resources management. This situation was characterized by the fact there is no comprehensive legislative framework for information management comparable to the Financial Administration Act or the Public Service Employment Act.

The underlying issue is that networked information creates relationships among activities and organizations of government that were not anticipated in the classic public administration models. In the case of the Government of Canada, this in turn opens up larger issues about the central agency role of the Treasury Board in directing the government as a whole in management practice.

New Skills and Relationships

A third set of challenges for public administration is the relationships created by the IT environment and the skills required to manage them. Earlier sections of this chapter discuss the relationships that information technology creates or accentuates between government and the economy and society in the various areas of public policy. The different working relationships created within government organizations were also noted. The federal government's experience with GOL and Gateways and Clusters suggests that two other sets of relationships – with other jurisdictions and with the private sector – assume a much more central place.

From a mandate and accountability perspective, the more important set of issues arises from changes in the federal government's relationship with other jurisdictions, in particular the provinces and territories, but also municipalities. The client-service and citizen-centred service models cut across constitutional jurisdiction as well as boundaries within governments and government departments. The logic of the Internet has allowed governments to extend their activities into areas that might be regarded as the preserve of other levels of government (for example, the federal government's promotion of SchoolNet). It has also led to widespread and growing efforts by governments to collaborate in delivering services to common segments of the public – most visibly through common citizen-centred service windows on the World Wide Web – and to cooperate in related policy and even infrastructure development. The role played by the Public Sector CIO Council and the Public Sector Service Delivery Council was discussed earlier in this chapter, and interviews confirmed that similar interjurisdictional collaboration is happening within policy sectors.

Perhaps the most changed relationship for the federal government, however, has been the one it has with the private sector. The effects of IT on public policy have already been noted, including the prominence of the view expressed by the IHAC, among others, that government should be a model actor on the information highway. As the largest institutional buyer of technology in the country, Government of Canada purchasing of IT goods and services – an estimated $3.1 billion out of total spending on IT of $4.95 billion in 2003/04[12] – has a major impact on the Canadian IT industry, an effect that is compounded when provincial and municipal purchasing is included. This is, therefore, one of the few areas where government administrative practices are important for national industrial policy as well as for public administration.

The other side of the coin is the government's dependence on the private sector for the up-to-date technology that it uses, as well as many of the technology applications and technology skills and most of the technology-enabled management models. The private sector integrates IT-related services for government and provides the entire range of such services, from data centres to hardware, software, and staff working in government offices. Three of the six CIOs appointed since 1993 were recruited from the private sector, and contract IT workers can be found at every level of public service work. The resulting requirement for collaborative working relationships with contractual partners creates a set of dynamics that are very different from those of the classic public service model, requiring government officials and private sector vendors each to develop an appreciation for the other's interests and incentives. Procurement, contract management, change management, and risk management all become additional components of the standard managerial toolkit. While the federal government has been its own technology manager, several provinces and some international jurisdictions have contracted out most, if not all, of their technology functions, and all jurisdictions deal with the same universe of national and multinational suppliers of IT goods and services.

Governance and Accountability in the Digital Environment

A fourth set of issues is the implications of IT for the internal governance and leadership of the public service. The most important issue is accountability. The horizontal and group nature of activities such as Gateways and Clusters makes it more difficult to apply the vertical accountability of the traditional Westminster model. At the same time, clear ministerial support and accountability is required if there is to be much hope of parliamentary and public support for the extensive changes underway, in particular ones such as self-service that require new skills and behaviours by the public. Compounding the complexity is the technical, often risky, nature of many IT-related decisions, contrasted with the lay understanding that most senior decision-makers have of the subject matter.

The issues that IT poses for public service governance create a need for a leadership model that can encompass significant components of horizontal action, collaborative approaches, and leadership from innovative line staff. Citizen-centred service also creates a new kind of relationship between line staff and the public; this in turn can create tensions with traditional assumptions about accountability as staff can come to feel more validated by their contact with the public than by their contacts with their ministers, through the vertical model of ministerial accountability to Parliament. Program ministers are asked to represent activities for which they are not totally responsible while having to share accountability and political credit for their programs with implementing departments. Similarly, the collective accountability model of government is placed under pressure by IT. After nearly a generation of decentralizing measures to increase empowerment of and delegation to individual managers, the networked environment and the three rooms shift the focus back to the total picture – the 'enterprise' – with a corresponding weakening of local autonomy and a renewed emphasis on a 'whole of government' role for the central agencies and common service agencies. Enterprise management was one of the themes running through the changes made by the Martin government.

Perhaps the best illustration of this evolution is the central and common service arrangements for managing information and technology. The first CIO, appointed in 1993, was a former comptroller general who had an engineering background. The new CIO office brought together the Treasury Board policy unit for the management of information technology and units responsible for a number of centrally led efforts to develop public service-wide technology applications, notably shared IT services to support financial and human resources management. Only a year and half later were the remaining Treasury Board Secretariat information, security, and communications policy centres – the traditional basis for Treasury Board involvement in management issues – included in the CIO's mandate. At the same time that the CIO organization was established, two common service agencies – the government telecommunications agency and the government computing services – were merged in the new Department of Public Works and Government Services to form the Government Telecommunications and Informatics Services (GTIS). For two years in the mid-1990s, the CIO function was combined with that of comptroller general. When a full-time CIO was appointed again in 1997, the position was filled from the private sector, as it was again in 1998. The fifth federal government CIO, appointed in 2000, came from the public service, having previously been responsible for implementing the IHAC recommendations on e-commerce in Industry Canada. When she left in 2004, the position was filled on an acting basis for a year by the head of the GOL office and then, again on an acting basis, in 2005 by the CIO branch official responsible for promoting the development of shared services in support of government management.

During much of this period, the CIO's role within the public service was to lead the information and technology functional communities of practice and the major government-wide reform and infrastructure initiatives: GOL and the Secure Channel. The CIO was also responsible for administering supplementary GOL funding, but had a more limited role in management policy development and in the budgetary process. Unlike a private sector CIO, or its Ontario counterpart, the federal government CIOs at no point had direct authority over the information and technology functions in departments and agencies, or over the government's IT-related spending envelope.

The Martin government introduced changes to give a more strategic role to the CIO and to establish a better balance between central agency and common service agency functions. The changes included transferring what were regarded as operational roles from the CIO's office to PWGSC, reconstituting GTIS to become the Information Technology Services Branch of PWGSC, while establishing a parallel Government Information Services Branch within PWGSC. The situation evolved further with the creation of Service Canada as a separate agency and the foreshadowing of a new shared services agency, both operating within policy and governance frameworks established by the Treasury Board. At the same time, it left the CIO position vacant, and a new associate secretary – a former CIO – was appointed in the Treasury Board Secretariat with an overview of initiatives in the IT and services area — a change that could be seen as a downgrading of the CIO position.

The Harper government maintained much of the course set by its predecessors, but with potentially important changes. Service Canada remained the focal point for services to Canadians but was incorporated back into a reconstituted Department of Human Resources and Social Development. The Canada Site was also redesigned, with a less prominent position for the three Gateways. The chief executive officer of the IT Services Branch of Public Works and Government Services Canada was reassigned to be the CIO at the Treasury Board Secretariat. And, at least in the first six months, no successor was announced to Government On-Line.

Conclusions

The Government of Canada has been remarkably successful in absorbing information technology into its internal operations and into public policies and programs. In doing so, it has built on earlier public service reform and responses to technological forerunners of the Internet and the World Wide Web. This has not always been an easy process. Major IT projects have not always fared very well, the most notorious case being the firearms registry, which in addition to being based on controversial policy assumptions has had problems with everything from technology and data quality to cost over-runs and incomplete cost accounting to Parliament (Canada, Office of the Auditor General 2003, 2006). Over a ten-year period there has been considerable organizational churn at the centre of government and in departments, and in the nature of a large, complex organization, there has been a continuing tension between the government-wide view and the perspective and needs of departmental managers, with a significant shift towards the former in recent years after a long period of promoting the latter.

Two aspects of the federal government's approach have been particularly important. In public policy, the government has consistently seen itself as needing to act as a model user of the information highway, setting an example for other major institutions and employers, and conscious of its potential influence on developments in other parts of the public sector and other sectors of the economy. On the public administration side, as recognized by Accenture, the government has continued to emphasize service to the public and of meeting public needs and interests in shaping its internal adoption of information technologies. In the case of GOL, this step involved regularly reworking established approaches and using service and financial benchmarks to keep the process under continuous review. This development probably led to de-emphasizing elements that will necessarily be part of the long-term picture, notably a government-wide approach to knowledge management and use of client-centred approaches in the design and provision of services to government departments and employees. At the same time, much of the needed infrastructure and methodologies are in place to move in these directions.

The changes introduced by the Martin government represented an effort to generalize earlier reforms and to realize economies of scale. Its approach was largely maintained by the Harper government when it came into office in the dying days of GOL, with changes that may or may not signal a longer-term change of direction. There are a number of risks involved, not least those created by the political uncertainty of minority government. Nor is it clear how easy it will be to realize significant savings in IT spending, given the relentless pace of technological change. At the same time, there has been very little partisan controversy over either GOL or the moves since December 2003, at least in part because many of them parallel the direction taken by a number of provinces, allowing for differences that necessarily arise from the considerably greater scale of operations of the federal government. The biggest unknown is whether sufficient political support and direction will be available to ensure that the latest round of reform and renewal, represented by GOL, will be sustained.

Notes

1 In its May 2006 report, Accenture did not rank governments (Accenture 2006).

2 The Conservative government led by Steven Harper came into office in February 2006, less than two months before the end of GOL, and issued a final GOL report in March 2006 that provides a good overview of the GOL process and results. See http://www.gol-ged.gc.ca/rpt2006/rpt/rpt00_e.asp.

3 Later renamed Service Canada: http://servicecanada.gc.ca/.
4 Later renamed Canada Business: http://canadabusiness.gc.ca/gol/cbec/
   site.nsf.
5 Later renamed Canada International: http://canadainternational.gc.ca/.
6 Of this amount, $475 million was spent on the Secure Channel, $95 million
   on Gateways and Clusters, $26.5 to support online service delivery, and
   $47.5 million on developing policies and standards (Public Works and Gov-
   ernment Services Canada 2006, 68).
7 See http://www.iccs-isac.org/. The ICCS has continued to sponsor Citizens
   First surveys and in 2004 conducted a Business First survey.
8 For information on the 2005 Lac Carling meeting, see http://www.
   itworldcanada.com/Pages/ContentPage.aspx?name=laccarling2005.
9 This statistic does not distinguish between information and transactional
   services – the categories into which GOL services were divided for planning and monitoring. It is likely that it is weighted by information services,
   which were the area where GOL had progressed most quickly.
10 This approach was reflected in the reconstitution of TIMS to become the
    Treasury Board Service Transformation Advisory Committee (STAC),
    chaired by the secretary of TBS.
11 References cited with a question number (for example, Q 28) relate to the
    question number in the 2005 survey. The 2005 survey results, as well as
    those for the 2004 and 2003 surveys, are found in Brown et al. 2006, at
    http://www.digitalstate/supp/ch2.html.
12 See Treasury Board Secretariat CIO branch report on Government of Can-
    ada IT spending from 1999/2000 to 2003/4, issued in June 2005: http://
    www.tbs-sct.gc.ca/cio-dpi/pres/2005/spending-depense/page01_e.asp.
    The remainder of IT spending was on government staff costs, the one area
    of continuing growth in an otherwise stable spending profile. Spending on
    IT represents about 10 per cent of the core federal government budget, after
    removing transfer payments and interest payments on the national debt.

3 What Keeps a CIO Awake at Night? Evidence from the Ontario Government

SANDFORD BORINS

The IT Executive Leadership Committee (ITELC) is the senior forum for IT policy and management in the Ontario Public Service, bringing together the Ontario government's top IT managers to discuss virtually all important IT issues and initiatives. It is also an excellent perspective from which to survey the increasingly complex terrain of public sector IT management. Charting ITELC's reflections and decisions over an eventful twenty-month period that saw both a change in government and the launch of a major government-wide cost-cutting initiative, this chapter identifies issues and imperatives whose significance go well beyond the experience of a single jurisdiction. The aim is to offer a more detailed view of IT management in government than has been provided in the literature to date. By doing so, this chapter also tells a larger story whose moral is becoming increasingly germane: this is what a government's chief information officer who is managing a billion dollar IT operation must worry about. The worries discussed in this chapter emanate from many sources: political initiatives, major IT projects, relationships with suppliers, technological change, and security issues. The CIO's final worry discussed in this chapter is a result of all the others: his own job security.

Research Methodology

From September 2003 to April 2005, ITELC held thirty-eight biweekly meetings. I was accorded status as an observer and attended thirty-one of them. This proved to be a particularly opportune observation period, beginning just after the 2003 provincial election call and continuing through the first eighteen months of the McGuinty government's mandate. I also had access to the minutes and PowerPoint decks presented at the meetings. My only restriction was that I would not quote individuals. My observation of ITELC meetings was supplemented by formal and informal interviews with public servants in the Ontario Public Service's IT area.

This anthropological approach enabled me both to observe Ontario's public sector IT culture in action and to study its top-level representatives without the defence mechanisms of self-censorship and professional discretion that interviews generally activate. Additionally, the relatively long observation period allowed me to familiarize myself with the complex and constantly changing IT landscape and to identify 'hot button' issues that might well have gone unmentioned in a more formal interview setting. While this chapter is based on 'fieldwork,' it has been supplemented by research conducted for a panel on the future role of government, commissioned by the previous government. The papers I prepared dealt extensively with the management of large IT projects, focusing on several undertaken in the 1990s (Borins 2003a, 2003b). They were based on reviews of documents, such as legislative debates and reports by the provincial auditor, as well as interviews with public servants and consultants involved in the projects.

ITELC and Ontario's IT Organization

In 1998, Ontario adopted a highly centralized approach to managing IT through the Office of the Corporate Chief Information Officer (CCIO).[1] The CCIO heads an office of several hundred people that until July 2005 was located within the secretariat to the Management Board of Cabinet.[2] Units within the CCIO's office oversee most aspects of e-government, including electronic service delivery on the government's Web portal, strategic planning, technology forecasting and planning, human resources management for IT professionals, and infrastructure and common services. For IT purposes, government ministries are organized into eight Clusters, with CIOs and support staff for each. This structure eliminates the need for a CIO and staff within each ministry. It is further intended to promote collaboration in IT development among ministries whose programs have common themes and whose clients share similar interests and needs. Cluster CIOs report to the CCIO and the deputy ministers of the ministries within their Cluster.

The term *IT organization* refers to the Office of the Corporate CIO and the Cluster CIOs and their staff. It is a measure of the centralized control this structure enables, that approximately half of the Ontario government's total IT spending is controlled directly by its IT organization, rather than individual ministries. In contrast, many jurisdictions have an IT unit in every department or ministry, and the corporate CIO is an advisory position located in a central agency, but with a very small budget and staff complement, and no authority over departmental IT spending.

Ontario's corporate chief information officer at the time the research was done, Greg Georgeff, was the chair of ITELC, and he used ITELC both as an advisory body and as a forum for discussion, decision, and communication within the IT organization. The members of ITELC include the eight Cluster CIOs as well as the senior members of Georgeff's office who reported directly to him: the corporate chief strategist, the chief technology officer, the head of corporate security, the corporate chief for service delivery, and the director for human resources and stakeholder education. The assistant deputy minister for supply chain management and one ministry's chief administration officer also attend, the latter to provide a link with his counterparts across the government.

The IT Executive Leadership Committee meets every second week for three hours. Each meeting has four or five presentations, and they deal with a wide range of topics including the IT organization's budget, management of common infrastructure, procurement policy, major projects, human resource management, technology forecasting, and system security. Presentations are for either decision or discussion, with notes taken and minutes of decisions recorded by a junior staff member in the corporate CIO's office. Presentations are introduced by the appropriate member of ITELC, but are almost always made by middle managers who are subject matter experts and who are considered to be of 'high potential.' The rationale is to expose these individuals to ITELC discussion and decision making, and to enable senior managers to assess their presentation skills.

At the 38 ITELC meetings from September 2003 to April 2005, 160 presentations were given: 135 (84 per cent) were made by the corporate CIO and his staff, 20 (13 per cent) by Cluster CIOs and their staff, and 5 (3 per cent) by outsiders to the IT organization. This division of responsibility demonstrates that most of the time, the corporate CIO and his staff are presenting new management developments originating either internally or at the political level. They are seeking reaction at the Cluster CIO, or line ministry, level. Cluster CIO presentations were mainly 'show and tell' to explain a major project or a new practice.

Politics Matter: ITELC and the McGuinty Government

The provincial election of October 2003 changed the political environ-ment for the Ontario Public Service (OPS) and its IT organization. The point seems self-evident: changes of administration will do that. Yet the advent of the McGuinty Liberals, and its effect upon the OPS's IT structure in particular, point to a phenomenon worth exploring in some detail. Generally, the literature on public sector IT still distin-guishes only between politicians who support technology and those indifferent to it. The experience of ITELC makes it clear that such a dis-tinction is no longer adequate to address the complexity of the subject.

The McGuinty government arrived in office with an image of sophistication in its own use of IT and enthusiasm about the applica-tion of IT. As a party, the Liberals had fielded a much more effective Internet campaign than their Conservative rivals had. (This is dis-cussed in chapter 7.) In addition, the newly-elected premier, who has long used the Internet for research, early on displayed his digital cre-dentials. When shown the Cabinet room after his election, his first question was where PowerPoints were presented. Informed that his predecessor's government used only paper, he asked to have Power-Point available for the first Cabinet meeting. This was more than a per-sonal predilection. The Liberal government took office enthusiastic about using the government website to highlight priorities and to host policy consultation. They also mandated the creation of an information system within Cabinet Office to track the progress of election cam-paign promises. McGuinty himself frequently visits the premier's home page and the Web pages associated with key government priori-ties, and makes suggestions to the webmasters for improving them.

Yet this embrace of technology was not without significant, publicly aired, reservations. While the Liberals were in opposition, the provin-cial auditor reported critically on two of the Conservative govern-ment's major IT projects: the Integrated Justice Project, and the Ministry of Community and Social Services Business Transformation Project (both discussed below). These projects were also discussed in the Legislature's Public Accounts Committee, where the Liberals attacked the Conservative government for mismanagement. One aspect that the Liberals criticized vociferously was the Conservatives' use of high-priced IT consultants. The Liberal platform claimed that the Conservatives 'wasted $662 million on private consultants last year alone.' The Liberals also opposed the Conservatives' practice of confidentiality regarding contracts and promised 'to require that all future contracts signed by the government be subject to public scrutiny' (Ontario Liberal Party 2003). Thus, the McGuinty government took office committed to major changes in IT practice. This chapter will discuss how this commitment was implemented. More generally, it demonstrates that politicians may support some and be critical of other aspects of IT, and shows some possible differentiating factors.

Money Matters: Deficits and IT Restructuring

Once the new government was in office, its fiscal situation would become an important contextual factor for its decisions about IT. The Conservatives entered the election campaign claiming a balanced budget. Outside analysts disputed this calculation, arguing there was really a deficit in the order of $5 billion (approximately 6 per cent of total spending of $80 billion). Immediately after the election, McGuinty asked the recently retired provincial auditor to examine the government's books. The auditor sided with the outsiders. Thus, the McGuinty government took office having made ambitious promises predicated on the books being no more than $2 billion in the red. These would be much harder to deliver in the face of a $5 billion deficit. Couple a tight fiscal environment with a perception that public sector IT projects were wasteful, unsuccessful, and relied too heavily on high-priced private consultants, and the stage was set for the new government to take a critical attitude towards the IT organization.

The politician who would be most directly involved with the IT organization was the chair of the Management Board of Cabinet, Gerry Phillips. Phillips is an experienced politician and minister. He was first elected in 1987, had served as a minister in the Peterson government (1987–90), and had been finance critic when the Liberals formed the official opposition. Phillips was not particularly experienced in the IT area or an avid Internet user, and asked his parliamentary assistant, MPP Wayne Arthurs, to focus on the political oversight of the IT organization.

The IT Organization Responds to the New Political Environment

This section discusses three areas where the new government challenged the IT organization to do things differently: its use of consultants, its overall budget, and its management of large projects. I outline each challenge and the IT organization's response, and then summarize by explaining the IT organization's view of the government in the middle of its mandate, and speculate about how the relationship between politicians and public servants might evolve during the remainder of the mandate.

High-Priced Consultants

The first issue on which the new government wanted action was reduced spending on consultants. The reliance on consultants in Ontario, as in other jurisdictions, developed in the late 1990s, when IT professionals were at a premium, and hiring them as consultants was a way to compete with the private sector. Even after Y2K and the dot-com bust, the use of IT consultants persisted and, indeed, the IT area accounted for approximately 80 per cent of the government's total spending on consultants. The Ontario Public Service Employees Union was a source of pressure to change this policy, arguing that in many Ontario government workplaces, consultants were sitting side-by-side with permanent staff and being paid substantially more to do the same work. While the union's position received little sympathy from the Conservative government, the new government was much more supportive.

The issue of consultants was discussed in ITELC on 17 October and 14 November 2003 and finalized on 9 January 2004. Members of ITELC expressed several concerns about the new government's policy directions. They did not want binding numerical targets for the percentages of positions that would shift from consultants to full-time public servants, but preferred to have a set of principles to guide them. Many of the consultants had been in place for quite some time, and ITELC members were concerned that if they were forced out, there would be a loss of organizational memory. Members of ITELC were also asking if they would be able to retain the savings in their budgets. In the discussions, it became clear that Management Board was looking for a rapid and major reduction – approximately 25 per cent – in government expenditure on IT consulting and, given, the size of the deficit, it was not willing to let ministries keep the savings.

The Office of the Corporate Chief Strategist developed, and Management Board approved, a framework for ministries to convert positions from consultants to full-time staff, beginning with an analysis of their spending pattern on consultants, a subsequent analysis of opportunities to convert these positions, and by 2005–6 targets for reductions in the use of consultants (Procurement Policy and IT Procurement Branch 2004c). The Procurement Policy Branch also developed a framework to bring down the price of consulting services under vendor-of-record[3] arrangements. This involved reducing the highest per diems from approximately $2500 to $1500, and shifting from open-ended per diem contracts to contracts with fixed price deliverables and a prescribed end point. It was expected that this would lead some of the large, expensive, international consulting firms to stop bidding, but that the pool of smaller, Canadian-based firms would be sufficient to pick up the slack (Procurement Policy and IT Procurement Branch 2004b). One indication that the new policies had an immediate impact was that IT spending on professional services fell from $256 million in fiscal 2002–3 to $193 million in fiscal 2003–4, while spending on salaries, wages, and benefits rose from $211 to $253 million (Information and Information Technology Controllership Branch 2004a). In the three previous fiscal years, spending on consultants had been decreasing slightly and on full-time staff had been increasing slightly, but the 2003–4 results marked a clear policy-induced shift.

The IT Budget

In the first few months of its mandate, the McGuinty government, contemplating its options for tackling the deficit, was not yet giving the bureaucracy precise marching orders. Members of ITELC held two apparently contradictory attitudes towards the IT budget: the first, that Ontario runs an efficient and low-cost IT operation, and the second, that there is still room for additional cost savings. The first idea was repeated frequently in the IT organization's performance reports. While total IT spending had grown rapidly towards the end of the previous decade, in particular in response to Y2K, it had levelled off by 2001–2 and declined thereafter. Specifically, IT spending was $835 million in 1999–2000, peaked at $953 million in 2001–2, but declined to $926 million in 2003–4. Ontario compared its IT spending to that of the other provinces and showed that, on both per capita and percentage of government spending bases, it was spending less than any other province except Newfoundland and Labrador. If we accept that there are some economies of scale to IT spending in government, the best reference group would be the other large provinces. In 2003–4, Ontario was spending $71 per capita on IT, while Quebec, British Columbia, and Alberta averaged $104. Similarly, Ontario allocated 1.25 per cent of total government spending to IT – while the other three provinces averaged 1.5 per cent (Information and Information Technology Controllership Branch 2004a).

The view that there was room for additional savings was expressed at an ITELC retreat held a few days after the McGuinty government took office. It was observed that savings could be delivered by consolidating investments such as servers, increasing the use of common infrastructure, and having the OPS provide IT services for agencies, boards, and commissions that were now operating independently and, as a result, failing to take advantage of opportunities of scale (Information Technology Executive Leadership Council 2003).

One of the McGuinty government's major steps in dealing with the deficit was to commission eight reviews of aspects of internal management. This is similar to the approach taken in the expenditure review in the Martin government's 2005 budget, which produced $11 billion in savings, of which $10 billion were in internal efficiencies and only $1 billion in program cuts. This preference reflects the preference of Liberal governments to respond to fiscal constraint by improving efficiency rather than cutting programs.

The IT review was conducted by Ron Vrancart, a former Ontario deputy minister, and delivered in February 2004. Vrancart advocated an e-Ontario strategy, which involved intensifying the use of IT in the broader public sector, as well as among consumers and business, so as to improve competitiveness, attract investment, and create high value jobs. Vrancart's vision was in close accord with that of the leadership of the IT organization. Vrancart did not, however, address the government's immediate fiscal problems. The IT Executive Leadership Council was initially asked by the Management Board to identify quick wins in reducing costs. At a special meeting held on 9 March, a number of proposals were discussed including developing a common structure for portals on the Ontario website, consolidating public sector servers both in Toronto and in other locations, decommissioning legacy software systems and mandating use of new government-wide systems, and making greater use of open-source software (Office of the Corporate CIO 2004).

By the spring, Cabinet had decided that, to reduce the deficit, the public service would be required to produce $750 million in base budget cuts during the government's mandate. A committee chaired by Cabinet Secretary Tony Dean was charged with identifying the cuts. When Georgeff was called to meet the committee, they asked their standard.

question: what could the IT organization do to help? He offered approximately $50 million in savings; the committee asked for more, $100 million, or approximately 10 per cent of Ontario's IT spending. Georgeff did not push back, and $100 million was the agreed total. Georgeff believed that the savings could be achieved through the efficiencies discussed at ITELC. He also believed that, while the existing base would be cut by $100 million, over time IT spending would increase because the IT organization would be asked to undertake new projects to improve service delivery and/or achieve efficiencies in other areas. Management Board recognized this point but felt that it was nonetheless necessary to maintain downward pressure on the unit cost of technology.

A cut of $100 million certainly captured the attention of the IT organization. An internal task force was established to determine how to implement it. The task force worked from August 2004 until March 2005, and reported at most ITELC meetings. Some of the sources of savings identified were

- Ongoing conversion of consultant positions to permanent public servants
- Consolidating IT infrastructure, for example, servers, throughout the OPS
- Shutting down redundant services and applications, reducing the number of websites and portals, developing and sharing new common applications, such as a common e-mail system and a common computer desktop for the entire OPS
- Making greater use of open-source software
- Moving from leasing to owning computer equipment (discussed below)
- Extending consolidated infrastructure, services, and applications to Ontario government agencies, boards, and commissions, and then the broader public sector
- Seeking opportunities for service collaboration with the federal government (Office of the Corporate Chief Strategist 2005)

The cost-saving program was outlined in detail to 200 senior IT managers throughout the OPS at a leadership forum held on 20 April 2005 at Queen's Park with the theme Mission Possible. One Cluster CIO urged the managers to get on board, to avoid getting in the way and hoping the measures fail. In wrapping up the session, Georgeff urged his staff to live up to their moral obligation as public servants to deliver service as efficiently as possible. Georgeff quoted Management Board Chair Phillips as acknowledging that he had tortured his IT team by continually demanding detail about where the cuts would be made. Georgeff challenged his team to get the maximum value out of public spending on IT. After finishing that job, he intended to help the broader public service deliver similar savings.

Major Projects

Perhaps the most uncomfortable topic at ITELC was the management of large IT projects. At the ITELC retreat held just after the McGuinty government took office, one member stated that the failure of such projects had made the IT organization into the 'whipping boy' of the OPS. In addition, this perception was to prove something more than paranoia. Chapter 1 advanced the hypothesis that large IT projects present the most difficult procurement context for government, and Ontario's recent experience is certainly consistent with that view. The issue is worth examining in some detail, since large IT projects are the most likely to produce highly visible results – whether successful or otherwise. The potential for political crises, and resulting intervention, is high. This section will begin with three projects whose sometimes troubled histories undoubtedly shaped the McGuinty government's relations with the IT organization, creating a challenge ITELC struggled to meet.

THREE TROUBLED PROJECTS
The Integrated Justice Project (IJP) involved three provincial ministries responsible for the police, the courts, the Crown attorneys, and the correction system.[4] Computer systems in the project included dispatch and records management for the police; case management for Crown attorneys; case management, scheduling, electronic document filing, and digital audio recording for the courts; and an offender tracking and information system for corrections (Borins 2003a).

In September 1997, the government contracted with a consortium led by SHL Systemhouse (now part of the U.S.-based multinational EDS) to deliver the project. At the outset, total project costs were estimated at $180 million and benefits at $326 million. The computer systems were to be completed by August 2002. By March 2001, estimated costs had risen to $359 million, benefits had been reduced to $238 million, and not all systems were expected to be completed by the deadline. According to a report by the provincial auditor, the project management's plan to introduce new systems and procedures in the court system was resisted by court staff and the judiciary; securing their cooperation required extensive consultation and increased implementation costs. The project was reviewed for the government by Ray Hession, a former deputy minister of Supply and Services Canada and an expert in managing IT projects. He concluded that the requirements for the case management system for the courts were too complex for software developers and consultants to implement (Borins 2003a).

After the deadline for completing work on the project passed and not all systems had successfully been delivered, the Eves government and the consortium began litigation. The claims were settled out of court in October 2004, and the McGuinty government agreed to pay the consortium $63 million for a licence to use the custom software developed under the project. This settlement was not announced by either party, but was reported several months later by a journalist who obtained it through a freedom of information request (Makin 2005).

The Business Transformation Project (BTP) was an initiative undertaken by the Harris government to update obsolete mainframe-based computer systems used for social assistance programs by the Ministry of Community and Social Services. The project intended to develop tools such as a computerized system for reviewing program eligibility, a system for screening persons applying for social assistance through call centres prior to scheduling in-person office visits, an automated telephone system for program recipients, and automated case management hosted on the ministry's website. In January 1997, the government chose Andersen Consulting (now Accenture) to deliver the project within five years for a maximum fee of $180 million. The project had some delays getting started. A key decision made by the assistant deputy minister in charge of the project was to bring in Ray Hession as full-time project manager. Ultimately, the deadline of January 2002 was met. The total cost of the project, incurred by both Andersen and the government, was approximately $400 million, somewhat higher than envisaged. Benefits, including time savings for staff and clients and reduced fraud, were measured at $587 million by 2002, and the government claimed the project would continue to deliver $200 million in benefits annually. The project won a number of awards, both internal to the OPS and internationally (Borins 2003a).

The provincial auditor reported on BTP in 1998 and 2000 and, in both cases, refused to recognize any of the benefits claimed by the gov-

ernment, arguing that the government did not have to resort to consultants and that determining benefits by means of a statistical analysis
of claims did not provide absolute certainty. The Harris government
vigorously disputed these arguments.[5]

Regardless of the validity of the auditor's claims about benefits for
BTP, his reports did constitute a powerful critique of the procurement
approach used for both IJP and BTP. They operated under a procedure
introduced by the Harris government known as common purpose procurement. Rather than let a detailed contract, the government first
chose the most capable partner. The government and the partner then
designed the project jointly. Project definition included both the work
to be done and a methodology for measuring benefits to be achieved.
A contract was then signed along the following lines: the government
and its partner both contributed resources (known as the cost pool)
and, once benefits had been achieved, shared the benefits in proportion
to the resources they had contributed to the cost pool; if the benefit
pool ultimately was not larger than the cost pool, both lost money. The
objective of this approach was to create a common interest on the part
of both the government and its partner in making the project succeed
(Borins 2003a).

The Integrated Justice Project and BTP demonstrated, however, that
the government's attempt to shift upfront financial exposure to its partners created a financial hot potato. In both cases, the private sector partners were management consulting firms accustomed to being paid as
they do the work and, therefore, did not carry much working capital.
The partners responded to this unaccustomed uncertainty of return in
several ways: trying to claim as large a share of the cost pool as possible,
in particular by incorporating high overhead charges into per diem fees,
because overhead did not represent their actual cash outflows; attempting to renegotiate the agreement so as to be compensated as soon as benefits started to accrue; and attempting to keep some services outside the
common procurement framework and thus payable when rendered.
From the partner's point of view, there were also risks involved in dealing with government, such as the risk that government staff would be
unable to perform their tasks on schedule (as happened with both IJP
and BTP) or that political decisions would force expensive changes in
mid-project. Building in a profit margin at the outset and maximizing
cash flow are ways the private sector tries to protect itself from risk. The
private sector's under-capitalization and risk aversion thus led it to
attempt to shift risk back to the public sector (Borins 2003a).

The provincial auditor's criticisms of common purpose procurement were readily embraced by the opposition Liberals. At hearings of the Legislature's Public Accounts committee regarding BTP, they asked numerous questions about the contract with Andersen Consulting (Ontario, Public Accounts Committee 1998, 1999a, 1999b). Three Liberal MPPs at the forefront were committee chair John Gerretsen, Sandra Pupatello, and Joseph Cordiano, all of whom were appointed to the McGuinty cabinet. This experience led to the Liberals targeting wasteful spending on consultants in the 2003 election campaign.

The Business Transformation Project re-emerged as a source of controversy in the Liberals' first year in office. When the new government decided to increase social assistance and disability benefits by 3 per cent, it was discovered that this increase would require changing the software and would take some time. Management Board chair Phillips and then minister of community and social services Pupatello put the cost of this change at $20 million and the delay at almost a year (Brennan and Benzie 2004). In the view of both Accenture and IT experts in government, most of the $20 million was attributable to previously scheduled upgrades in software and hardware, and programming the rate change alone would cost only $1.5 million and require just a month (Alden Cuddihey interview 14 November 2005; Greg Georgeff interview 10 November 2005; Ticoll 2004).

The third troubled project was a three-year procurement contract the Ministry of Consumer and Business Services signed in September 2001 with a consortium consisting of Bell Canada, Bearing Point Consulting, and the computer software firm CGI. By the end of March 2003, twenty-four high-volume routine transactions (for example, licence plate renewals) were to be available through the Internet, from call centres, or at 300 public access e-terminals (Borins 2003b). The last were to replace the successful but now outdated electronic kiosks (see note 4). Bearing Point would be responsible for project management and specifications, and CGI would be responsible for software development and implementation. Bell Canada would bear the risk, as it would compensate Bearing Point and CGI on a progress basis, and then earn a return on its investment through transaction fees when the infrastructure was in place. Georgeff described the contract as a strategic change initiative that would drive the creation of reusable infrastructure to provide more electronic services in the future (Office of the Corporate CIO 2002, 11).

Unfortunately, the Bell Canada consortium failed to deliver. Representatives of both sides spoke off the record about what went wrong. The IT organization felt that the contractors did not understand what was wanted, bid low, and hence did not have the necessary capability. The contractors felt that the IT organization's proposed specifications were driven by the objective of reusability, and were more demanding than necessary to provide the transactions originally envisaged. By fall 2003, both sides informally agreed to stop work on the project. By then Bell had paid Bearing Point and CGI close to $100 million and the government had spent approximately $10 million. At the time of writing, both sides had not reached a formal agreement to terminate the contract. One key outstanding issue is whether a performance bond of $15 million Bell paid to the government should be returned to Bell or retained by the government as compensation.

DISCUSSIONS AT ITELC

The monitoring of large projects was discussed four times during the period I observed ITELC, and the discussions clearly reflect the experience of the troubled cases. In October 2003, the Controllership Branch in the Office of the Corporate Chief Strategist asked for ITELC's approval to develop a 'dashboard' to show the condition of major projects. The Controllership Branch proposal intended to track twenty-two large projects costing over $10 million. A red-yellow-green scoring system would be employed. A rating of red would indicate a project with an expected cost overrun of 30 per cent or a more, a delay over schedule of 30 per cent or more, or deliverables not accepted by clients: it would trigger an executive project review meeting among the accountable project executive, the Cluster CIO, and the corporate CIO leading to corrective action (Information and Information Technology Controllership Branch 2003). The IT Executive Leadership Council members were concerned about the very idea of a dashboard with formal categories. Cluster CIOs did not want formal reports going to the Management Board and felt they were being put into the difficult position of being accountable but not responsible for projects in their Clusters. The meeting decided that the Controllership Branch would consult with individual ITELC members to reframe the proposal.

The Controllership Branch returned to ITELC with a new proposal in March 2004. It would require the Cluster CIOs to update the corporate CIO on major projects in their regular one-on-one meetings and would have ITELC schedule periodic in camera meetings to share information and lessons learned on major projects (Information and Information Technology Controllership Branch 2004c).

The Controllership Branch presented its first quarterly report to ITELC on major IT projects on 18 November 2004 (Information and Information Technology Controllership Branch 2004b). The page that provoked the most discussion was a table summarizing the status of the major projects on the basis of four categories: on track, manageable variances, serious variances, and other (which could refer to those that were the subject of legal disputes). To ITELC members, this looked like the objectionable red-yellow-green template of the previous year. The group expressed a clear preference that assessments would be used for helping projects at risk, rather than for performance reviews of individuals. Finally, there was a concern about sharing this material more widely within the OPS, as well as about finding its way into the media. The next quarterly report on major projects was presented at ITELC on 3 March 2005. In this case, distribution was restricted to ITELC members. It contained information on more of the projects, and most were rated as being on track or showing only minor variances. There were still concerns about distribution, and the conclusion was not to distribute the report beyond ITELC.

THE EXTERNAL REVIEW

At the same time that ITELC was wrestling with the issue of managing large projects, the Liberal government was also focusing on it. The difficulty of implementing an increase in social assistance rates, which surfaced in July 2004, forcefully reminded the Liberals that they had inherited the problems for which they had criticized the Conservatives while in Opposition. In August 2004, the Management Board decided to commission a special external task force on the management of large-scale IT projects. The task force was chaired by Denis Desautels, a former auditor general of Canada, and had three other members: David Johnston, president of the University of Waterloo; Carol Stephenson, dean of the Ivey School of Business at the University of Western Ontario; and Howard Dickson, assistant deputy minister for Information Management in the Department of National Defence. The review was to analyze relevant experience in the OPS and elsewhere to recommend improvements in planning, governance, management, procurement, and accountability. The conclusions the task force reached were based on interviews with senior public servants in the IT and project management areas as well as industry representatives, a consultant study of several large Ontario projects including IJP and BTP, and research about practices in other governments.

The report was presented by minister Phillips and task force chair Desautels at a press conference on 28 July 2005 (Government of Ontario 2005). The first recommendation was that the government establish a deputy minister for overseeing major projects. The task force envisioned this as a new position, while Phillips saw this responsibility as being assigned to an existing deputy minister. Secondly, the task force recommended that the Management Board of Cabinet strictly limit the number and size of major projects, and establish a maximum duration of two years for any project. This position was certainly consistent with the McGuinty government's thinking and, in his remarks at the press conference, Phillips made it clear that he saw these constraints on projects as contributing to the government's cut of $100 million in IT spending.

The task force supported the dashboard-style reporting that the OCCIO had developed and recommended frequent, full, and open reporting to the Management Board – a recommendation that was immediately endorsed by the minister, effectively bringing to an end eighteen months of opposition by ITELC members. On the other hand, the report had some recommendations ITELC members could view more favourably, such as the one that their primary role should be sponsoring and specifying business application projects rather than day-to-day infrastructure management, and another that total compensation be reviewed for IT executives, especially those with project management responsibilities. The task force also recommended that project leadership should be exercised by the public service and not delegated to external service providers, and that implicitly terminated the Conservatives' common purpose procurement policy. All these recommendations were ultimately accepted by the government (Ministry of Government Services 2005). The government resolved the one area of ambiguity – the deputy ministerial appointment for project management – by giving that responsibility to the deputy minister of the new Ministry of Government Services, which is introduced in the section on organizational integration below.

Conclusion

By the middle of its mandate, the McGuinty government had clearly asserted its control over, and redirection of, the IT organization. Reducing reliance on consultants and cutting IT spending were relatively easy to implement, in that the Management Board gave the orders and persisted in ensuring that the organization responded. Dealing with major projects was more complicated, because it required substantial problem identification and diagnosis before new orders could be given. By establishing an external task force, the government made clear that it would not accept the IT organization's efforts alone, but wanted to bring to the problem a variety of other views.[6]

My observation of the IT organization showed that this three-part assertion of political control led to disillusionment within. Its staff felt that they had conducted themselves as professional public servants; after having stated their concerns about the government's plans, they went about loyally implementing the government's decisions. In the public servants' eyes, the McGuinty government is enamoured of IT's publicly visible front end, such as using eye-catching websites that trumpet government priorities or engaging in public consultation (see chapter 9). Politicians and staffers are also enthusiastic about personal technology, such as PowerPoint and the BlackBerry. On the other hand, the government appears, to the IT organization, to know and care much less about IT's less visible, but equally important, back end, such as servers and systems. The IT organization is also much more sanguine than the government about incurring the risks inherent in major projects, because it believes it has a clearer vision of the projects' benefits of enhanced service and reduced cost.

While the relationship between the IT organization and the politicians may have been at a low point in mid-2005, it could improve during the remainder of the mandate. Because the IT organization has been made a 'whipping boy' for large project failures, if the external task force's remedies will lead to better performance, albeit in fewer projects, the IT organization can only benefit. The task force made clear that the OPS's large projects involved business transformation using IT, thus extending responsibility for them beyond the IT organization. The recommendation that Cluster CIOs shift their attention from infrastructure to projects could end the syndrome of accountability without responsibility for projects. The IT organization is also being presented with two new challenges: achieving efficiencies in IT infrastructure in government agencies and the broader public sector, and, as will be discussed in the next section, working with its major clients in service delivery and organizational support in a larger and more closely integrated organization. Finally, the recommendation for a review of total compensation for IT executives could lead to compensation increases that buy support.

Organizational Integration: The Role of IT

As was discussed in chapter 1, IT can support the creation of integrated external service delivery and internal support service organizations. Embracing this potential, the Ontario Government embarked upon a major restructuring of both IT and service delivery, announced as part of a Cabinet shuffle at the end of June 2005. While this was after my observation period, some of its antecedents were apparent at earlier ITELC discussions.

In service delivery, two overlapping initiatives were unfolding for several years. In the context of the cancellation of the Bell Canada contract, the Ministry of Consumer and Business Services took the lead in establishing ServiceOntario, an in-house integrated service delivery organization. The Web-based face of ServiceOntario went live on the Government of Ontario website, which the IT organization manages, in fall 2004. The website is already integrated to the extent that it currently presents a variety of services by theme (for example, life events, user groups, and popular topics) rather than by ministry. ServiceOntario's vision goes substantially beyond that, to take over routine transactions on any channel. It would thus assume responsibility for government information centres, electronic kiosks, and call centres (Mary Tate interview 21 July 2004). The success of ServiceOntario's efforts depends on the IT organization to support the databases and applications that enable the different channels to provide seamless and integrated service and to deliver cost savings.

The IT organization's contribution to integrated service is the federation of portals it is developing. The basic idea is to revamp the service elements of the gov.on.ca website as a federation of portals. The central IT organization will set standards and develop tools (content management, search tools, payment capability, and authentication) that will enable either individual ministries or multi-ministry groups to develop thematic portals. By April 2005, the IT organization had completed most of its development work and was establishing service and pricing models for use of the tools by prospective portal developers. Two demonstration portals now live on the site are children's and seniors' information portals. Given the inherent overlapping between the ServiceOntario and federation of portals initiatives, placing the

Ministry of Consumer and Business Services and the IT organization under a common minister and deputy minister can be seen as a way of ensuring that both initiatives are moving in the same direction.

The second context for integration, the establishment of an integrated support organization, involves consolidating internal functions such as financial and human resource management that are not visible to the public. The political and bureaucratic payoff of integrated support is the achievement of economies of scale that can produce savings to redeploy elsewhere. The Ontario government has been in the forefront of this movement with the establishment of the Shared Services Bureau in 1998. Its initiatives include establishing an employee Intranet portal containing applications such as corporate learning and travel; moving to a common financial system; and consolidating support offices (Technology in Government 2005). Because the procurement function involves policy for and purchasing of the full range of products and services used by government, the Procurement Policy and IT Procurement Branch was merged with the Shared Services Bureau to create Ontario Shared Services (Bouey 2004).

The creation of Ontario Shared Services and the overlapping work of the Ministry of Consumer and Business Services and the IT organization set the stage for a much larger merger involving the creation of the Ministry of Government Services. The new Ministry of Government Services combines the Ministry of Consumer and Business Services, elements of the former Management Board Secretariat including the IT organization, Ontario Shared Services, and the human resources organization (previously a part of Cabinet Office). The merger puts the IT organization under the same roof as Consumer and Business Services, its major client in the area of service delivery. It creates the potential for greater integration of service delivery because ServiceOntario has a multi-channel mandate that the IT organization, confined to the electronic channel, lacked. It also puts integrated service delivery and integrated support under the same organizational roof. The change separates the management of IT from the minister who chairs the Management Board, but it is expected that the Management Board will still call upon the Office of the Corporate CIO for advice on IT issues and for the monitoring of large IT projects.

The minister of Government Services and a continuing member of the Management Board is Gerry Phillips. While he previously tended to view IT from a cost-cutting perspective, his new portfolio puts him in a position where he might become more receptive to its transformative aspect as well. At the press conference announcing the external task force report, he made it clear that he saw his new ministry as responsible for the transformation of government. How the IT organization functions when housed within this new ministry should be of interest to other IT organizations because of the far-reaching and ambitious nature of the merger.

Procurement Issues

The discussion of large projects dealt with Ontario's difficulties in the most challenging procurement context. It was argued in chapter 1 that basic computer hardware (desktops, laptops, printers, servers) was increasingly becoming commoditized, and was therefore less challenging. This section will show that even if the hardware is commoditized, there are management challenges when an organization must acquire millions of dollars' worth. It was also argued in chapter 1 that the context for procurement of standard office software and operating systems was influenced by Microsoft's dominant position; this section will report on the IT organization's negotiations with Microsoft, as well as its consideration of open-source software as an alternative. The section also shows that IT procurement does not exist in a vacuum; a variety of management policies and capacities elsewhere in the government influence procurement policies and decisions. These issues will certainly arise in other governments that face comparable procurement decisions regarding hardware and software.

Commodity Hardware: To Lease or to Buy?

The OPS's procurement policy for hardware has been one of three-year leases, with the exception of two-year terms for notebook computers. Leasing requires contracting with a private sector firm that acquires the equipment from manufacturers and leases it to the OPS. One of the major lessors was GE Capital, which in mid-2003 had a total portfolio of equipment leased to the OPS valued at $84 million. On 15 July 2003, representatives of the firm met with the Procurement Policy Branch and delivered a surprising ultimatum: the accounts payable of Ontario government ministries had risen to approximately $11 million, with some ministries' accounts more than 150 days in arrears; in addition, machines valued at $3 million had not been returned at the end of their leases. As a consequence, GE would lease no additional equipment to the OPS until the accounts payable problem was resolved. GE Capital itself was under pressure from the computer manufacturers, whom it couldn't pay because the OPS, a major client, was not making timely payments. This ultimatum, as intended, got the immediate attention of the Procurement Policy Branch. They put pressure on ministries to pay their bills and return equipment that had reached the end of its lease cycle. By October, accounts payable were down to $4 million and both the Procurement Policy Branch and GE Capital agreed to a lifting of the leasing freeze (Procurement Policy and IT Procurement Branch 2003b). This episode illustrates a simple but essential truth: a policy of leasing millions of dollars in equipment does not absolve a government of management responsibility.

In reaction to the problems with GE Capital, and because the vendor-of-record agreement for equipment leases would expire in April 2005, the Office of the Chief Corporate Strategist took a comprehensive look at the question of leasing or buying. It recommended moving to an optional strategy of buying some assets, to be managed centrally by the IT Clusters. In the past, the rationale in favour of leasing had been that it forced regular replacement of machinery, facilitated standardization, smoothed spending patterns, and provided a disposal strategy for used equipment. On the other hand, leasing was leading to disputes over returned equipment, instances where users forgot to return equipment after leases expired and thus continued to make payments, and administrative costs for the government in the management of leases. There were also environmental concerns about how lessors were disposing of used computers.

Buying had several advantages. It could save money because the government's cost of capital is lower than the vendor's. In addition, the useful life of computers is getting longer, and government would likely keep computers longer under a policy of buying. The OPS could use old equipment internally (for example, as terminals in a 'thin client' system where all the data and processing power would reside on a network), make it available to non-profits such as the federal government's Computers for Schools program, or dispose of it in a more environmentally responsible way than a private sector lessor would. The success of buying would depend on several factors: good asset management to track, service, replace, and dispose of equipment; replacement terms for each class of equipment based on industry best practice; and a policy of capitalizing equipment, so that acquisition expense would be spread over the life of the equipment. Current Ministry of Finance policy, however, treats equipment as an operating expense in the year of purchase, which is one of the factors that led to a leasing strategy in the first place (Office of the Corporate Chief Strategist 2004a, 2004b).

When the proposal was discussed at ITELC on 19 March 2004, the group was unwilling to endorse a dramatic shift in policy direction. Instead, it asked for detailed cost-benefit analysis of the alternatives, as well as consultation with all Clusters. The proposal was revisited by ITELC two months later. While the financial analysis showed that buying was less expensive if the equipment was kept one or two years longer than was the case for leasing, the consultations strongly favoured leasing. Some ministries felt they would not be able to manage the uneven expenditure flows that would result from buying under the Ministry of Finance's current policy. In addition, the OPS's financial management system will not have the capacity to support capital asset management for a few years. Finally, it was felt that the OPS does not yet have in place effective asset management policies. As a consequence, the decision was to continue the current policy of leasing, while the IT organization would work with the Ministry of Finance to change its accounting treatment of IT equipment and develop better asset management capacity. Once this change was complete, the leasing versus buying decision would be revisited on a case-by-case basis for each class of equipment (Office of the Corporate Chief Strategist 2004b).

The question of leasing or buying arose again at ITELC's 10 February 2005 meeting. As part of the review of spending on IT, there was interest at the political level in buying out leases at the end of the leasing period in April 2005. This was estimated to save an immediate $7 million compared with continuing the leases. The plan was criticized at ITELC for a number of reasons, primarily that it would be a de facto change from leasing to buying without adequate review, that the short-term savings would be eroded by longer-term increases in maintenance and disposal cost, and that the necessary asset management capacity was still not in place. Members agreed to this change only as a last resort.

At the end of the observation period, the IT organization's position on leasing or buying hardware was still conflicted. Cost-savings from buying had been identified and, in the context of the budget review, those savings assumed greater importance. On the other hand, the capacity to move to buying was not in place, and putting that capacity in place depended on the Ministry of Finance's policies about cost accounting and Ontario Shared Services' schedule for developing the necessary financial management systems. The IT Executive Leadership Council demonstrated an understandable tendency to embrace the status quo regarding leasing at a time when so much change was happening in so many other areas.

The Microsoft Agreement

As the OPS's licence agreement with Microsoft was due to expire on 30 September 2004, the Procurement Policy Branch approached ITELC on 11 June 2004 seeking authorization to negotiate a new one. In entering the negotiations, it was clear that Microsoft earns a substantial margin on software leases to large organizations, so the government's strategy would be to offer a large volume and seek a substantial discount. The Management Board might raise concerns about making a single source agreement with a near-monopolist, but the answer would be that Microsoft operating systems and office software are a necessity, at least in the short term.

The Procurement Policy Branch obtained Management Board authorization to negotiate the new agreement during the summer, and on 2 December it returned to ITELC with the details of the negotiation. The previous three-year fixed-term master agreement with the OPS was replaced with a perpetual agreement either party could terminate with sixty days' notice. The advantage of the latter was that any government or broader public sector agency could initiate its own three-year agreement, rather than being constrained to the remainder of a three-year master agreement. Ministries or Clusters with more than 100 desktops purchasing licences for standardized software (for example, Office) would receive a 55 per cent discount from the list price. Ministries would receive discounts of 35 per cent on more specialized software, with no volume requirement. The Microsoft agreement would be mandatory for the OPS, and the Procurement Policy Branch would attempt to enrol as many ministries as possible at the outset for the standardized software agreement, thus receiving one blanket authorization from the Management Board. Ministries' payments to Microsoft would be spread out evenly over three years, and would thus eliminate peaks and valleys for this budget item. It was expected that the agreement would save $42 million over the next three years, compared to the cost of having no agreement. Finally, the terms of the agreement were open to organizations in the broader public sector that wanted to participate (Procurement Policy and IT Procurement Branch 2004a).

The agreement was approved enthusiastically by ITELC, which felt that a deal with Microsoft was a necessity and that this was a good deal. Six months later, the U.K. government signed a similar deal with Microsoft, and pointed to £84 million in savings it would receive as a result – illustrating the global nature of both Microsoft's strategy and governmental responses (PublicTechnology.Net 2005).

Open-Source Software

The main competitor to the Microsoft monopoly is non-proprietary open-source software products. At the same time that the Procurement Policy Branch was negotiating the agreement with Microsoft, the Offices of the Corporate Chief Strategist and Chief Technology Officer were examining how the OPS could use open-source software (OSS). On 21 October 2004, ITELC approved the development of a policy framework for OSS. Pending the development of such a framework, restrictions were placed on its use because the Management Board Secretariat legal branch warned that some OSS might have proprietary software embedded within it. Therefore, the OPS was confined to using OSS that it had obtained through an existing vendor-of-record agreement and prohibited from downloading new OSS from the Internet, except for testing.

Open-source software was again discussed at ITELC on 3 and 31 March 2005. Interest in OSS had quickened, as it was seen as having the potential to contribute savings to the mandated budget cut. The Office of the Chief Technology Officer had developed criteria for evaluating OSS and was ready to begin trials of specific products. The first products to be evaluated were the Linux operating system and Open Office, an alternative to Microsoft's Office suite (Corporate Architecture and Standards Branch 2005).

By way of international comparison, the Norwegian government has moved further towards open-source, and is requiring all public sector bodies to have in place a plan by the end of 2006 for using open-source codes and standards (Tatle 2005).

Reusable Software

One implication of the IT organization's drive to create common reusable software components for the federation of portals was in terms of procurement. If the initial components were developed within the OPS, there was no problem with reuse because they were already the property of the entire OPS and not any one part of it. The much more likely scenario was that the components had been acquired from a vendor. A vendor might object to reuse for two reasons: first, if the software is to be reused, the potential additional value should be recognized in the purchase price; second, if the software is to be reused in different contexts, that could increase risk and hence the vendor's liability, which would also affect the purchase price. Transferring software created for one context to other contexts is implicit sole-sourcing, as opposed to holding an open competition for software to be used in those contexts. ITELC discussed this problem on 30 September 2004 and recognized both that future requests for proposals would explicitly mention reuse and that a mechanism should be established to examine whether proprietary products being considered for reuse are the most cost-effective and appropriate, or whether those applications should be subject to competition.

Labour Relations, Emerging Technology, and Security: Other Problems That Keep CIOs Awake at Night

This section presents a number of other managerial and technical problems ITELC wrestled with, and that managers in other jurisdictions can also expect to face.

Electronic Service on Strike?

Ultimately, IT is not automatic, and to be operational, needs a host of people to keep websites current, oversee or complete transactions, and keep the system running. During a strike by the Ontario Public Service Employees Union in 2002, electronic service delivery was disrupted because the government took down some websites where unionized staff would not complete transactions that had been initiated electronically. When negotiations with that union were ongoing in 2005, because of the need to maintain secrecy, on several occasions ITELC members met in closed sessions, without outsiders present and without notes taken, to plan strike strategy. Presumably, discussions revolved around maintenance of service and system integrity during a strike.

Emerging Technologies

The IT Executive Leadership Council's discussions of emerging technologies displayed a paradox: when a technology had rapidly attained popularity, ITELC was scrambling to react to it, but when a technology was not on the immediate horizon, ITELC was not particularly interested in formulating a policy for it.

The emerging technology that attracted the most attention was the BlackBerry. By early 2005, 3500 of the 60,000 members of the OPS were using BlackBerrys, paid for out of their own departmental budgets. My own observation suggests that senior public servants and political staff were the most frequent users. Indeed, as a temporary visitor to the OPS, I was surprised often to receive near immediate responses via Black-Berry to e-mails sent to deputy ministers or political staff. 'CrackBerry' addiction appears to be occurring in the OPS, as in other large organizations. Premier McGuinty's executive assistant sent a memo to all ministerial office, premier's office, and Cabinet office staff asking them not to bring their BlackBerrys into meetings with the premier (Sobers 2004).

The IT organization was scrambling to respond to the implications of the rapid growth in popularity of the BlackBerry. It established a users' group to share lessons learned and common experiences. The Office of the Corporate Chief Technology Officer undertook a more comprehensive study looking at the history and likely evolution of multifunctional wireless devices and chronicled those currently available (Office of the Corporate Chief Technology Officer 2004a). Security precautions for the BlackBerry were also discussed, including deactivation of devices that were lost or stolen or had experienced five consecutive unsuccessful login attempts (Corporate Security Branch 2005). From a procurement point of view, the next step would be to establish a list of acceptable handheld devices, and then develop a vendor-of-record agreement for all the devices on that list. It was recognized that there would be no support at the political level for an approach that gave Research in Motion a monopoly, even though it is an Ontario-based firm.

In addition to working on new technologies that have arrived, the Office of the Chief Technology Officer does anticipatory work, studying information technologies likely to become available in the next five years. The studies are organized around themes such as pervasive computing – the use of wireless connectivity and mobile devices – and deep computing, which involves visualization, data mining, and pattern recognition (Office of the Corporate Chief Technology Officer 2004b). The reaction to these presentations at ITELC was that they were too technical, too future-oriented, and insufficiently connected to the real world. Members of ITELC wanted outcome-oriented case studies that would look at particular technologies and focus on the state of development, lessons learned, and potential impact on the way the OPS conducts its business.

Security

Early in the observation period, the IT organization received a wake-up call about the security of the computer system. The Blaster Worm, which was released on 11 August 2003, quickly spread to OPS computers, and on 19 August, Nachi, a variant of Blaster, overwhelmed the government's system. On 14 August, a massive power outage sent the OPS home, and, to conserve energy while service on Ontario's power grid was being restored, Premier Eves ordered all non-essential Ontario public servants to stay off work during the week of 18 August. As a consequence, the computer system was under minimal use that week, making it easier for personnel in the IT organization designated as essential to clean infected machines and install patches (Corporate Security Branch 2003). The Blaster Worm represents one of the most successful attacks on computer systems throughout the world in recent years. The OPS computer system now experiences, and repels, 1.6 million hack attempts every month, or one every 1.6 seconds. The attacks come through government websites, e-mail and attachments, and simply by being connected to the Internet (Information and Information Technology Controllership Branch 2004a).

The impact of Blaster led the IT organization to reconsider its approach to security. Its problems were compounded by operating computers at widely dispersed locations; having limited ability to deploy patches electronically; having some computers running outdated operating systems for which patches are no longer provided; and having computer systems of agencies, boards, and commissions, which have lower security standards, connected to the OPS system. A special committee was established in fall 2003 to develop a patch management strategy, the Corporate Security Branch was given a mandate to acquire hardware and software for delivering patches electronically, and patch management training was initiated for technical support staff (Corporate Security Branch 2003). Some of the responses that were quickly developed included defining levels and threat severity, and hence speed of response; putting forward an RFP for vendors of patch management software; and requiring all computers to be left 'powered on' during non-office hours to implement electronic patching (Corporate Security Branch 2004a).

In addition to its involvement in patch management, the IT organization is active in repelling security threats before they can infect the system. This responsibility involves working with police agencies and vendors, constantly monitoring of the system, and scanning e-mail for viruses (Corporate Security Branch 2004b).[7] Another aspect of the security issue is that many public servants want to be able to work from home. This preference becomes problematic if they want to use computers they own, rather than OPS-owned laptops; hence, the IT organization is faced with a choice of two costly options: providing security for employee-owned equipment, or buying more laptops.

A final aspect of security concerns employee behaviour, such as use of the OPS system for file sharing for music downloading, or visiting websites for personal reasons. The IT organization filters Web page visits and reported that in March 2004, for example, public servants visited approximately 600 million Web pages. Permitted visits included portal and search engines (28 per cent), news (22 per cent), sales (8 per cent), sports (7 per cent), travel (5 per cent), investing (3 per cent), gaming and gambling (3 per cent), match-making (2 per cent), and chat (2 per cent). Access was denied for visits to 570,000 pages, or 0.1 per cent of the total. The pages most frequently denied were webmail (70 per cent) and sex (2 per cent). The OPS posts terms of use when employees log on to their computers – an approach rarely experienced in a university environment – and the terms of use, followed rigorously, would exclude many of the permitted visits listed above. Monitoring of individual users requires senior executive approval from the IT organization as well as the ministry involved, but has on occasion occurred, and has led to individuals being fired for violating the Work Place Harassment and Discrimination Policy as it applies to technology use (Corporate Security Branch 2004b).

Terminating the Corporate CIO

The creation of the Ministry of Government Services meant that corporate CIO Greg Georgeff was reporting to a new deputy minister, Michelle di Emanuele. She had begun her career in the OPS, rose to the rank of assistant deputy minister in the Ministry of Health and Long-term Care, and then left the public sector for a senior executive position at the Canadian Imperial Bank of Commerce. She returned to the OPS in April 2004 as deputy minister for human resource management in Cabinet Office. When her appointment was made, observers noted that both di Emanuele and Georgeff have forceful personalities and questioned whether the two would work well together.

The IT organization held its annual conference on 19–21 September 2005. On Friday, 23 September, Greg Georgeff was preparing for the Canadian CIO Council meetings in Halifax the following Monday. He was told to cancel his trip to Halifax and to meet Ms. Emanuele on Monday morning. At that meeting, he was given a letter terminating without cause his employment in the OPS. According to Georgeff, it would have been difficult to prove cause, given that all his evaluations had been good. (Indeed, Cabinet Secretary Tony Dean introduced Georgeff's keynote speech at the annual conference and praised his leadership.) The reason given for the termination was insufficient support from the deputy minister community. Georgeff was terminated that day, taken to his office to retrieve his immediate personal effects, required to return his security pass, and escorted to the lobby – the nearest public space.

The new corporate CIO, Ron McKerlie, began work on 11 October. McKerlie had been vice-president of e-business with Rogers Communications and had previously worked in that area at the Bank of Montreal. The speed of this replacement, as well as the absence of an open competition, makes clear that a search had been launched before Georgeff was terminated. The significance of this termination and replacement will be discussed at greater length in chapter 10, which deals with digital leadership. At this point, suffice it to say that just as this chapter has demonstrated that the IT organization was not exempt from the politicians' imperatives, its leader was not immune from the internal politics of the senior bureaucracy.

Conclusion

This chapter has provided a detailed look at the ongoing management of IT in a major government and has therefore touched upon a wide range of issues. Though it focused on only one government, there are quite a few general lessons that flow from the Ontario government's experience.

The traditional dichotomy between policy and administration assumes that politicians are responsible for policy and public servants for administration. The maxim that war is too important to be left to generals now appears relevant to the management of IT: it has become too important – to politicians – to be left to CIOs and their staff. This point has become true for five reasons.

First, the face of government has become electronic: for example, policy statements and press releases appear on the government website, and it is to the website that citizens increasingly turn for information and transactions.

Second, the application of IT has the potential to deliver significant savings in both administrative overhead and program spending. These savings serve different, but equally important, purposes along the political spectrum: the left sees them as a way of funding new programs, while the right sees them as a means of accommodating tax cuts. If forced to cut overall spending, the left prefers reducing overhead to cutting programs (for example, seeking efficiencies in IT infrastructure), while the right is more likely to cut programs, especially in low priority areas (for example, the Harris government's use of IT to cut both overhead and program spending on social assistance).

Third, IT carries major risks to politicians. While they may like the fanfare accompanying the launch of a major project, the planned economies can evaporate, leaving embarrassing cost-overruns later. Other risks, such as computer systems being attacked by hackers or protected information being disclosed inadvertently, accompany day-to-day operations.[8] Ultimately, politicians must account for failures and problems.

Fourth, management of government has become a topic of political debate, as illustrated in the area of federal government grants and contributions by Good (2003). The risks of IT are high enough that it is likely that some problems will occur during any government's mandate. The problems will be seized upon by the media and public auditors as evidence of mismanagement, and the political opposition will use them to support the claim that the government should be defeated because of its management failures. If there is any systemic component to the problems, a newly elected government will want to do things in a way that is different from its vanquished predecessor – a dynamic demonstrated in Ontario.

Fifth, managing IT always raises issues about where to draw the border between public and private sectors, and the nature of the relationship across that border. Here too the left and right sides of the political spectrum see things differently. The right, operating under the perception that public managers are incapable and inefficient, prefers private sector partnerships and the use of consultants, while the left, suspicious that private sector contractors are expensive and rapacious, prefers to shift the management of IT to permanent public servants – another dichotomy demonstrated in Ontario.

All of these reasons build a case for any government wanting to manage IT in a hands-on, forceful, and effective manner. If so, the government is likely to be presented with what the television series *Yes Prime Minister* referred to as the clash between the 'political will and the administrative won't.' While this phrase overstates recent Ontario experience, the evidence did show that the bureaucracy acted as a constraint on political initiatives for a number of reasons. Public servants are cautious about change, as evidenced by the many rounds of discussions about introducing reporting on major projects and moving from leasing to buying. They prefer having discretion to being bound by numerical rules or targets, as indicated by their reaction to targets for full-time employees. They prefer to operate under the cover of confidentiality, as evidenced by the concern about the circulation of traffic-light ratings of major projects. They prefer predictable and smooth budget lines. Thus, as long as the Ministry of Finance's rules treat computers and software as current expenditure, they prefer leasing to buying and endorse Microsoft's spreading of licensing costs evenly over three years. These preferences are quite consistent with standard theories of bureaucracy (such as Allison and Zelikow 1999) and are likely to be applicable to IT organizations in other governments as well.

Because all hardware and most software are produced outside government, a second major constraint on political will is the procurement process. Large projects necessarily involve detailed contracts that the bureaucracy writes and enforces. In this process, the IT organization negotiates with Microsoft, the near-monopoly supplier of standard office software. Ontario, and likely other governments as well, would like to build its IT structures of common components that are readily reusable. Procurement policies based on the objective of encouraging competition, as is the case in Ontario and likely in other jurisdictions, erect a barrier to reuse, because reuse is implicit sole-source acquisition. All these procurement issues will have a bearing on political initiatives in IT.

To conclude, the distinction made in the literature between politicians who do and do not support IT is not nearly nuanced enough. The Ontario Liberal government and its premier were certainly knowledgeable about and supported IT, but their policies have been affected by their political ideology, their reaction while in Opposition to the policies of their predecessors (in effect, a form of path-dependence), and the fiscal, bureaucratic, and procurement constraints they must work with. The chapter also shows the relevance of Fountain's (2001) point about the importance of the context within which technology is embedded. By exploring the reaction of a new government to the policies of a predecessor that embraced a different ideology, we see that how technology is implemented depends on, and is shaped by, political choices.

Notes

1 The creation of Ontario's centralized IT organization is discussed in chapter 10 in reference to Scott Campbell, its architect.

2 A reorganization occurred in July 2005, after the end of the period I studied ITELC, and involved relocating the Office of the Corporate CIO to the new Ministry of Government Services. It is discussed in the section of this chapter on organizational integration.

3 A vendor-of-record (VOR) arrangement is a fixed contractual procurement arrangement with multiple vendors for the ongoing acquisition of commonly purchased goods or services within a defined term. Vendors agree to common terms and conditions, including pricing, and buyers do not need to repeat a full open competitive process to get access to volume pricing. A corporate VOR is established by the Management Board of Cabinet and applicable to all ministries. It has the virtue of reducing procurement cost and delay for individual ministries (Procurement Policy and IT Procurement Branch 2003a).

4 Though this section deals with troubled IT projects, there were some earlier ones – predating the establishment of the IT organization – that were more successful. For example, in the early 1990s, the NDP government entered into a partnership with IBM, which developed, provided, and continues to maintain a system of electronic kiosks. IBM is compensated by a fee of $1 per transaction on the approximately 1 million transactions performed at the kiosks (Borins 2003b).

5 I side with the government and consider the auditor's claims to be specious. The possibility that the program could have been delivered in a dif-

ferent, and even less expensive, way does not negate the benefits from the way the government chose to deliver the program. A statistical study of claims by its very nature cannot produce absolute certainty; measures of statistical significance are used to determine whether one can be confident there were benefits, and in this case, a sufficient degree of confidence was achieved (Borins 2003a).

6 Corporate CIO Greg Georgeff was not averse to establishing an external task force. He recognized its political necessity after ministers resumed their criticism of the Business Transformation Project. He also felt it would respond to his own organization's reluctance to embrace enhanced project monitoring. He recommended the task force membership to the politicians (Greg Georgeff interview 10 November 2005).

7 My experience working in both a university environment and in the OPS as scholar-in-residence in 2003–4 is that the OPS is much more effective at blocking viruses and spam.

8 In December 2004, Ontario experienced a technological invasion of privacy when 27,000 people received child-care supplement cheques with other individuals' names and social insurance numbers attached to the stubs (Ferguson 2004). While the software error that caused the problem did not occur in the IT organization, Management Board Chair Phillips, in dealing with the problem, made clear that he expected the IT organization to find a solution.

4 Beyond Bubble Gum and Goodwill: Integrating Service Delivery

KENNETH KERNAGHAN

Canadians want integrated, citizen-centred service delivery. The Citizens First research reports (Erin Research Inc. 1998, 2001, 2003; Phase 5 Consulting Group Inc. 2005) have shown that Canadians want the delivery of government services to be organized from the perspective of citizens, not governments, and they want these services delivered seamlessly across jurisdictions and across delivery channels. Over the past decade, integrated service delivery (ISD) has been driven by citizens' desire to find and access the services they need and to have these services brought together so that they can be accessed as conveniently as possible (Bent, Kernaghan, and Marson 1999, 2). More recently, ISD has been increasingly driven by governments' need for lower service-delivery costs. The fall 2004 IPAC survey of deputy ministers and municipal chief administrative officers found that 'governments are looking for innovative ways to deliver services for lower cost. This means a harder look at delivery via the electronic service channel, as well as the development of service delivery partnerships to reduce the cost of delivery' (Marson and Ross 2005, 8).

Canada's governments have responded to the demand for ISD with vigorous efforts to improve service to citizens, to put 'citizens first.' The federal government has been formally recognized as a world leader in the provision of ISD, and governments across Canada, especially the Ontario government, have received national and international awards for innovative approaches to service delivery. The aim of the federal Government On-Line (GOL) initiative (1999 to 2006) has been 'to use information and communication technology to provide Canadians with enhanced access to improved citizen-centred, integrated services, anytime, anywhere and in the official language of their choice' (2003). Provincial, territorial, and municipal governments have taken similar initiatives.

For each year between 2001 and 2005, Canada ranked first in the Accenture global survey of the breadth and maturity of e-government. The 2005 report noted, however, that e-government is only part of overall service delivery and challenged Canada to accelerate its 'implementation of the next wave of *seamless, multi-jurisdictional* service offerings' (Accenture 2005, 61; emphasis added). Helen McDonald, Canada's acting chief information officer, acknowledged at this time that dramatic improvements in services to Canadians could be achieved only by rethinking the way that services are designed and delivered (Accenture 2005). This would require, among other advances in e-government, the successful implementation of ISD.

There are, however, formidable challenges to achieving and sustaining ISD. This chapter examines how government services are being integrated across channels, within and between departments, across departments, across orders of government, and between governmental and non-governmental service providers.[1] The chapter begins by explaining the meaning of ISD and the critical importance of IT to achieving it. The second section sets out an idealized model of ISD, and the third describes the evolution of ISD arrangements since the early 1990s. The fourth section examines the variety and complexity of ISD arrangements. Section 5 discusses the major challenges to achieving ISD, and section 6 examines governments' responses to these challenges. Sections 7 and 8 focus respectively on challenges and responses in the sphere of integrated *channel* delivery (ICD). The final section describes efforts to formalize ISD mechanisms and to promote their long-term sustainability. While examples of ISD and ICD are drawn from all levels of Canadian government and from the private sector, the primary focus is on initiatives in the federal and Ontario governments.

What Is Integrated Service Delivery?

Integrated service delivery is the result of bringing together related government services so that citizens can access them in a single seamless experience based on their wants and needs. A seamless service delivery system is *'fluid, agile, integrated, transparent, connected,'* providing 'a smooth, virtually effortless experience for those who interact with it' (Linden 1994, 4; emphasis in original).

Information technology is intrinsic to ISD. It is the primary enabler in the delivery of seamless service for Canadians. More specifically, it is the Internet that forms the backbone of a multi-channel delivery system. The telephone and walk-in channels are supported by the information available through the Internet and by the capacity of public organizations to collect, create, process, and share that information (Kernaghan and Gunraj 2004, 529–31). At a minimum, employees operating the telephone and walk-in channels would have access to the organization's website and would, over time, become skilful in navigating the website to find the answers to callers' or visitors' frequently asked questions. The system could also be built with access to service-oriented databases and to software for tracking organizational transactions. A good example of what can be done is New York City's 311 telephone dial system described in the next chapter.

Integrated service delivery aims to ensure single-window service (one-stop access), largely through 'the three Cs' of coordination, collaboration, and clustering. *Coordination* refers to the sharing of *work* for mutual benefit with a view to avoiding duplication, eliminating gaps, and reducing fragmentation. *Collaboration* involves the sharing of *power* for the same purposes (Rounce and Beaudry 2002, 13). *Clustering* is the result of bringing together related government services delivered by one or more service providers so that citizens can access the services in one place. A helpful distinction can be made between service clustering as 'services that are grouped together,' and ISD as 'services that fit together' (d'Auray 2002). Integrated service delivery is clustering plus coordination and collaboration.

Like coordination and collaboration, both ISD and clustering are closely linked to the concept of partnering defined here as the process of bringing together individuals and organizations to share power, work, support, information, benefits, and risks for the achievement of joint goals and/or mutual benefits. The successful pursuit of ISD requires effective partnering (also described more broadly as collaborative arrangements) between and among departments, governments, and sectors. Discussion of ISD is an integral part of the current movement, in Canada and elsewhere, towards *horizontal* government. Many of the challenges to ISD are the same as those to horizontal policy making and management in general.

Finally, the concept of ISD is closely related to that of *citizen relationship management* (CzRM), a concept that developed in the private sector as *customer* relationship management. In essence, CzRM is a strategy that puts service to the citizen at the centre of a comprehensive, concerted, and committed effort to integrate services, not only across departments, governments, and sectors but also across service channels. The next chapter provides a detailed examination of the implementation of CzRM through the integration of call centre services.

Envisioning ISD

As a basis for identifying and overcoming challenges to successful ISD, it is helpful to visualize a highly integrated system of government service delivery. An idealized model of ISD would include the following features:

1. A single-entry portal for each delivery channel provides access to the entire network of services of all orders of government. There is no wrong door.
2. Each portal is clearly and consistently organized from the citizens' perspective.
3. Service delivery is seamless, regardless of which government has responsibility for the service and of how many services, providers, and channels are involved.
4. Service delivery is highly integrated at both the front and back ends of the system.
5. Citizens can receive customized (personalized) service tailored to their particular wants and needs.
6. The privacy and security of the system are assured.
7. Citizens can receive through each delivery channel the level of service they require.
8. Citizens can receive through each delivery channel the level of service they require regardless of their social, demographic, geographical, or technological circumstances.
9. Citizens can readily understand which level of government is responsible for the service being provided.

Evolution of ISD

First Steps

Before the turn of this century, governments in Canada had already responded to citizen demand by embarking on several ISD initiatives. The 1998 Citizens First national survey (Erin Research Inc. 1998) (3000 respondents) found that Canadians wanted improved service through single-window operations. In particular, they wanted services involving multiple contacts with government(s) to be integrated so that one-stop service would be available, regardless of which government departments and which orders of government were involved. The survey also showed that Canadians wanted to be able to choose among the various service delivery *channels* so that, depending on their personal circumstances, they could, for example, receive information or complete a transaction either at a walk-in centre or via the Internet.

A 1999 study (Bent, Kernaghan, and Marson) examined ISD progress by describing and classifying eighteen cases of single-window service delivery across Canada. The study set out a matrix that summarized ISD developments to that date. The matrix classified single-window initiatives by their purpose and by their structure. The first purpose was to improve access to government information and referral services through single-window gateways that took the form of call centres, Internet sites, and general information offices. The second purpose was to improve convenience through one-stop shops where citizens could access in one physical or electronic location both related and unrelated government services (for example, Service New Brunswick, Atlantic Canada On-Line). The third purpose of single-window initiatives was to provide seamless service in a particular service area or for a particular client group by integrating related services within or between governments (such as the Aboriginal Single Window Initiative in Winnipeg, the Vancouver Neighbourhood Integrated Service Teams). Single-window initiatives were also classified according to their structure (for example, owner-delivered, shared delivery through integration, delegated delivery, corporate service utility). While the matrix reflected the reality of the time by not including examples of service utilities, we shall see that the service utility model has since become very popular. We return to this topic later in this chapter.

The matrix also showed that several of the first single-window initiatives had their origins in the early 1990s, but the earliest single-window initiative in Canada seems to have been the Government Agents offices in British Columbia, which date back to the mid-1800s. Not only have most of these pre-2000 initiatives survived, but several of them prospered to the point of winning prestigious national and international awards.

The study also identified several challenges arising from the efforts of departments and jurisdictions to collaborate horizontally and vertically to provide ISD. The obstacles they encountered included turf tension, technological incompatibilities, unrealistic expectations, and partnership problems, as well as accountability and visibility concerns. Since such challenges have proven to be a common feature of ISD initiatives, they are examined in detail later in this chapter.

Governments' response to citizens' demand for ISD has been driven to a large extent by the collaboration of public service champions of ISD drawn from all levels of Canadian government. Foremost among these collaborative efforts has been the work of the Citizen Centred Service Network (CCSN) established in July 1997 and composed, by the spring of 1998, of 220 senior managers and academics from across Canada. The CCSN worked with the Canadian Centre for Management Development (CCMD) (now the Canada School of Public Service) on several of CCMD's groundbreaking research studies on citizen-centred service,[2] including the 1998 Citizens First survey. Prominent among the early – and enduring – champions of the CCSN's work were Ralph Heintzman and Brian Marson from CCMD and Art Daniels from the then Ontario Ministry of Consumer and Commercial Relations. All three were instrumental in the 1998 conversion of the CCSN into the Senior Service Delivery Officers Council (SSDOC), which in 2001 was renamed the Public Sector Service Delivery Council (PSSDC). The CCSN won the IPAC Gold Award for Innovative Management in 1999 and the Silver CAPAM International Innovation Award in 2000. In 2001, the PSSDC created the Institute for Citizen-Centred Service (ICCS) (http://www.iccs-isac.org) to 'promote high levels of citizen satisfaction with public sector service delivery ... by undertaking research to identify citizens' service expectations, and by then assisting the public sector in applying innovative solutions' (Vincent and Prychodko 2002, 19). The ICCS was incorporated in 2005 as a not-for-profit organization.

The Public Sector Chief Information Officers Council (PSCIOC), composed of the chief information officers of the federal, provincial, and territorial governments, began in 2001 to meet informally with the PSSDC through the annual Lac Carling conference on electronic government. The council's mission is to enhance service delivery to Canadians through inter-jurisdictional collaboration and leadership in the management of information and technology. In 2002, the two councils established a more formal relationship and provided joint support to the ICCS. The individual and collaborative work of the two councils, now buttressed by the ICCS, has been – and continues to be – central to thinking and action in the sphere of ISD.

Another actor in the ISD community is the Crossing Boundaries National Council. Crossing Boundaries operated from 1997 to 2003 as a research and consultation initiative dealing with the impact of IT on government and democracy. In January 2004, this initiative was transformed into a non-profit national forum called the Crossing Boundaries National Council, composed largely of senior public servants and elected representatives from all levels of Canadian government. Integrated service delivery is one of many National Council projects designed to help Canadian governments 'make a successful transition from the Industrial to the Information Age' (Crossing Boundaries National Council 2005a).

ISD in the New Century

In the early 2000s, governments continued to focus on providing a one-stop portal for each of the major delivery channels: Internet, telephone, and walk-in centres (Kernaghan and Berardi 2001). Use of such terms as *single-window delivery, one-stop access,* and *clustering* were increasingly complemented by use of the term *ISD*. The scope of the challenge of providing ISD through each channel – the first criterion in the idealized model of ISD – can be illustrated by reference to the newest developed channel, the Internet. Movement toward ISD through the Internet channel is a multi-stage process that begins with a simple Web presence for a government department and moves through the stages of one-stop access / single department, one-stop access / single government, and one-stop access / multiple service providers, to the final stage of integration. While many governments around the world had not moved beyond the second stage by 2000, governments in Canada had taken many initiatives at the third-stage level and were looking ahead to further integration, not only of services but of delivery channels as well.

The 2000 Citizens First survey (Erin Research Inc. 2001) (6000 respondents) confirmed the findings of the 1998 survey on citizen demand for ISD. In addition, the 2000 survey identified five primary drivers of citizens' perception of quality service: timeliness, knowledge and competence of staff, going the extra mile (originally defined as courtesy), fair treatment, and outcome. Moreover, the survey showed that the importance of these determinants varied by service delivery channel. For instance, the drivers of courtesy and fairness were ranked highly for walk-in services but not for telephone services.

Clients Speak (2001), a large survey of both business people and citizens who had used a single-window service, found that over 80 per cent of them used either walk-in or telephone as their initial channel for accessing the service. Only 10 per cent used the Internet as their first channel. The survey also found that almost three-quarters of the business and citizen respondents supported 'seamless' or one-stop service delivery. The federal government's GOL advisory panel (Canada, Government On-Line 2002b, 4) reinforced these findings by noting that 'people want to access public sector services that are comprehensive and seamless and [they] have little patience for inter-jurisdictional constraints ... People expect the same level of integrated response regardless of the channel they choose.' This emphasis on channel 'choice' was increasingly supplemented during this period by the call for channel 'integration': the linking, coordination, and rationalization of the main service channels in the pursuit of citizen-centred service.

The Citizens First (2003) survey (9000 respondents) found that service quality has a significant effect on citizens' confidence in government. Other notable findings were that in seeking services, citizens use two or more delivery channels half of the time; that the telephone is the most frequently used delivery channel but is rated low in satisfaction; that when multiple contacts are required to deliver a service or when service delivery is difficult, the Internet channel can provide greater satisfaction than the other channels; and that citizens' unrealistically high expectations regarding e-mail response time were softening.

Taking Care of Business (TCOB) (Phase 5 Consulting Group 2005), a survey based on a representative sample of almost 6000 businesses across Canada, found that governments could improve business perception of government services by improving service quality. The findings indicated that a 10 per cent increase in service quality could enhance the perceived value of government service, in such terms as satisfaction and value for tax dollars, by as much as 7 per cent. In addition, the survey showed that businesses want to receive seamless service across departments and governments. Moreover, since 73 per cent of business service transactions with government involve the use of more than one delivery channel, businesses want easy access through and across all of the main channels.

Varieties of ISD

The range of actors involved in ISD includes departmental administra-

Figure 4.1 Single-dimensional to multi-dimensional integrated service delivery[18]

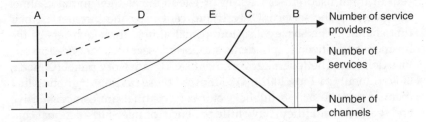

A – uni-dimensional: single departmental unit providing single service through a single delivery channel

B – multi-dimensional: several service providers providing several services through several channels

C – inter-departmental: a large number of departments providing a variety of services through several channels

D – inter-jurisdictional: two governments providing a single service through a single channel

E – cross-sectoral: several departments, governments, business organizations, and NGOs delivering services through a single channel

tive units, departments as a whole, governments, business organizations, and third sector organizations. These are the main actors in the four categories of ISD examined in this chapter: intra-departmental, inter-departmental, inter-jurisdictional, and inter-sectoral ISD. While ISD arrangements can be classified according to a considerable number of factors, the focus here is on three major criteria:

1. The number of providers involved in the service delivery
2. The number of services being provided
3. The number of delivery channels being used

As shown in figure 4.1, these criteria can be depicted on separate continua running from a single-dimensional to a multi-dimensional arrangement. For any specific ISD arrangement, an ISD *profile* depicts that arrangement's particular mix of the three criteria. A wide variety of ISD arrangements can be depicted along these continua. At the uni-dimensional end is a single departmental unit providing a single service through a single delivery channel (profile A). At the multi-dimensional end is an arrangement involving several service providers from different governments and from the business and third sectors providing several services through several channels (profile B). It cannot be assumed that the closer an arrangement's profile is to the multi-dimensional end of the continua, the greater the challenge to integration. An *inter-departmental* arrangement involving a large number of departments and a variety of services delivered over several channels (profile C) may be more challenging than an *inter-jurisdictional* arrangement involving only two governments, a single service, and a single channel (profile D). Even a cross-sectoral arrangement involving several departments, governments, business organizations, and NGOs may be relatively uncomplicated if it operates on only the Internet channel, and especially if it does not require a stringent partnership agreement (profile E). A good illustration of this last arrangement is the Canadian Consumer Information Gateway (http://consumerinformation.ca), which is a considerably less complicated arrangement than, for example, the Canada Business Service Centres network (http://www.cbsc.org). The former is an electronic partnership of more than 400 federal departments and agencies, provincial and territorial ministries, and non-governmental entities involving cooperation and coordination but not collaboration among the partners. The latter is a multi-channel, inter-jurisdictional, collaborative arrangement involving forty-three federal departments and provincial and territorial governments with thirteen centres across the country. Figure 4.1 indicates the challenges posed for the designers and operators of ISD arrangements.

In terms of sheer size and complexity, by far the most challenging ISD initiative is Service Canada, which was discussed in chapter 2. The federal government has described Service Canada as 'one of the biggest single reforms ever in federal operations' (Department of Finance Canada 2005a, 13). It is a multi-channel one-stop service initiative that aims to provide services on behalf of fourteen federal departments and agencies and, over the next few years, to partner with other levels of government and other sectors to promote seamless citizen-centred service. By mid-2006, Service Canada had 22,000 employees serving Canadians through all of the main service channels for the stated purpose of transforming service to Canadians.

Challenges to ISD

For analytical purposes, ISD challenges are divided here into four categories: political/legal, structural, operational/managerial, and cultural. An examination of integrated *service* delivery is followed by a discussion of integrated *channel* delivery.

Political/Legal Challenges

Mollifying ministers. Political resistance to ISD can be a 'showstopper' in the sense that public servants cannot pursue ISD in the absence of legislative and regulatory approval from ministers and legislators. Moreover, the individual responsibility of ministers for the conduct of their departments encourages them to focus on the vertical dimension of government. The political motivation of ministers to avoid risk and blame underpins the traditional 'silo' design of departments that stands as a barrier to the horizontal linkages required for ISD. Moreover, ministers become increasingly wary as collaborative arrangements move from the inter-departmental realm to the inter-jurisdictional and inter-sectoral ones.

Valuing visibility. Both individual ministers and the governing party as a whole strive to ensure visibility or 'profile' in the sense of credit for their financial and other contributions to improved service delivery. Collaboration with other departments and especially with other governments can blur the relative contributions of those involved. An example of public servants' sensitivity to this important political consideration can be seen in the commitment of the then federal Department of Human Resources Development to develop a partnership strategy for multi-channel service delivery that will 'get the most value and federal presence from our partnerships' (1999, 12). Governments sometimes receive little public recognition for their substantial investment in ISD arrangements.

Legal challenges. As noted, legislative and regulatory barriers can be showstoppers because they require political consent for their removal or modification. However, some legal impediments to ISD are more obvious than others. It is clear, for example, that privacy acts restrict the sharing of some kinds of data between government and business partners. Less obvious is a situation like that involving Canada Revenue Agency (CRA) employees who have legal immunity when giving tax advice – an immunity that does not extend to ISD partners such as a Canada Business Service Centre whose employees may act on the CRA's behalf.

Structural Challenges

Reducing departmentalism. The main structural challenge is the departmental model of organization. This constraint is closely related to the ministerial concern about accountability that perpetuates the departmental approach to organizational design. This silo system runs strongly counter to the current movement towards horizontal government and, in particular, to the collaborative arrangements required for successful ISD. The current reality is that 'governance structures favour departmental projects, not interdepartmental partnerships' (Velenosi 2002, slide 26).

The decisions of public servants, like those of their ministers, are greatly constrained by accountability considerations. The challenge for public servants is to maintain an appropriate measure of vertical accountability while supporting horizontal initiatives for which the lines of accountability are much less clear. In general, the difficulty and the risk increase as collaborative efforts go beyond inter-departmental arrangements to inter-jurisdictional and inter-sectoral ones.

Even *within* departments, structural barriers can significantly impede accountability for ISD. There is, for example, a longstanding need in most federal departments to enhance accountability by more closely aligning the strategic objectives set at the 'grass tops' level with the activities of those at the grass roots level who deliver the services, notably in the regions. Without rigorous monitoring of the connection between strategic objectives and regional activities, asymmetrical service delivery can result. The extent of ISD, and thus the quality of service, can vary substantially from one part of the country to another, from one region to another, and even from one office to another within a region.

Minimizing interdepartmental tensions. The requirements of ministerial and public service accountability pose significant structural impediments to coordination and collaboration across departmental, governmental, and sectoral boundaries. The barriers to inter-departmental ISD, however, are usually less challenging than those across governments and sectors. While collaboration between departments often requires the use of influence rather than control, there are powerful incentives for inter-departmental collaboration. The collective responsibilities of ministers to the government as a whole and the duty of senior departmental officials to support these responsibilities provide impetus for inter-departmental collaboration. In Ontario, the Deputy Minister's Committee on Ontario Public Service Transformation, established in late 2002, drives cross-ministry ISD initiatives and decides on the allocation of costs among the ministries.

Minimizing inter-jurisdictional tensions. The tensions and complexities that characterize the pursuit of coordination and collaboration in Canadian federalism are reflected in efforts to promote ISD across governments. The political competition for visibility noted above inhibits the creation of structures such as joint planning committees that would facilitate effective ISD. Consider the challenge of joining up federal social and economic departments with their provincial counterparts and with municipal and non-governmental actors to deal with socio-economic issues in a large city like that of Toronto. The difficulty of formalizing an overall plan that coordinates funding and targets spending results in a fragmented delivery system. The many ad hoc arrangements worked out at the grass roots level are not as well integrated as they otherwise would be, and in many projects either a federal or provincial partner is missing (for example, where there is joint planning between a non-governmental organization and the federal government alone).

In less contentious and narrower program areas, intergovernmental ISD initiatives are easier to establish and operate. For example, Seniors Canada On-Line involves several federal departments and several provincial governments in providing ISD through the Internet channel. Similarly, the Canadian Consumer Information Gateway within the federal Department of Industry joins up a very large number of provincial and non-governmental partners to provide information to consumers via the Internet.

A noteworthy mechanism for promoting inter-jurisdictional collaboration is the 2004 memorandum of agreement between the federal and Ontario governments (Canada-Ontario 2004). The focus is on new collaborative approaches for achieving such objectives as improved quality and seamlessness of services, enhanced efficiency and service through the co-location of offices, and the alignment of complementary programs from each jurisdiction. If successful, this mechanism could be adopted by other provinces and thereby facilitate inter-jurisdictional service arrangements, including ISD, that would otherwise be difficult to achieve. Moreover, Service Canada and its several provincial counterparts, including ServiceOntario, have been established to provide seamless integrated services. The development of these federal and provincial entities provides the basis for future bilateral efforts to advance the ISD agenda.

Even carefully crafted inter-jurisdictional ISD arrangements can be confounded by unpredictable changes in one or more of the partners, especially at the political level. The election of a new government or the appointment of a new minister in a current government can be accompanied by reduced funding or even by a government's withdrawal from the partnership. A further complication arises from the fact that, to secure the participation of certain provincial governments in ISD arrangements, the federal and the wealthier provincial governments may have to contribute more than their fair share of the funding. At the public service level, the success of inter-jurisdictional ISD arrangements often depends on the continuing commitment of 'champions.' When a champion moves on, the arrangements can falter or fail.

Finding funding. The challenge here is to overcome the reluctance or inability of governments to fund projects on a horizontal basis. Integrated service delivery projects are often multi-year initiatives that require substantial up-front investment and take considerable time to harvest savings. Moreover, the savings may accrue to the government as a whole rather than to the department making the investment. Changing a department's or a government's budgetary system to permit dedicated funding of horizontal projects can be extremely difficult. 'Research shows that the public does not distinguish between branches, divisions, departments, ministries or levels of government. Yet, our silo approach to conducting business, strongly reinforced by policy and legislative requirements, continues to impede the flexibility and innovation required to finance integrated service delivery initiatives' (Public Sector Service Delivery Council 2003a, 84).

Operational and Managerial Challenges

Ensuring inter-operability. This issue is usually discussed in the context of technological barriers to electronic service delivery resulting from the incompatibility of technologies across departments and particularly across governments. However, inter-operability can be conceptualized as a broader issue that presents several problems for ISD that do not lend themselves easily to technological solutions. Formidable managerial and operational difficulties can arise from differences between partners in respect of laws, policies, rules, regulations, and standards. Multiple accountabilities have to be sorted out, financial rules have to harmonized, and different human resource policies, including salary levels, have to be accepted or accommodated. These considerations have very practical implications for efficient and effective ISD. Federal language policies have frequently impeded or prevented ISD arrangements between the federal government on the one hand and the provinces and the third sector on the other. In the area of human resource management, unions can complicate efforts to improve service by using part-time workers, and morale can be reduced if different pay rates are given to staff doing the same work but coming from different governments.

Satisfying staff. Inter-operability issues are especially challenging in the sphere of human resource management. A study of human resource challenges facing public organizations involved in inter-jurisdictional ISD (Public Sector Service Delivery Council 2003b) found that most of the challenges affect inter-departmental and inter-sectoral ISD initiatives as well. Among the key challenges were *employee fairness* (for example, overcoming differences in pay rates between federal and provincial employees), *communication* (the need to be open and clear at the outset), *employee involvement* (which must be early and continuous), *attempts to build a common culture* (to promote shared commitment to integration), and *attention to detail* (to identify and resolve differences in the human resource frameworks of both employers).

Disincentives for staff to pursue ISD exist *within* the partner organizations as well between them. The organizations' pay, reward, and recognition systems may provide little or no incentive to pursue ISD arrangements in the first place, much less to maintain them. Employees will focus their efforts on tasks for which they are formally accountable. With particular reference to e-government initiatives, Jane Fountain argues that the incentives are actually the obverse of those for e-commerce: 'Whereas dramatic efficiency gains and cost savings in the economy are rewarded through profits, promotions, stock price increases, and market share, similar gains in government are rewarded with budget cuts, staff reductions, loss of resources, and consolidation of programs' (Fountain 2001, 13).

Getting the representation right. A significant challenge to both inter-departmental and inter-jurisdictional ISD is inappropriate or inadequate representation in decision making. For example, those in charge of one of the main delivery channels may not be represented in deliberations on integration. Even when all relevant parties are represented, some of them may not have final decision-making authority on such important issues as harmonizing policies, rules, and standards across departments or governments. Furthermore, representatives from different departments or governments can meet and agree to do certain things but then fail to live up to their commitments. This failure is less likely to happen within a single department where people are evaluated on the basis of how well they do what they agree to do.

Ensuring privacy and security. Proponents of ISD are acutely aware of the critical importance of dealing effectively with privacy and security challenges. While these challenges are difficult to manage within individual departments, they are even more daunting when information is being shared across departments and especially across jurisdictions. The nature of the privacy challenge can be illustrated by reference to ServiceOntario's proposed privacy policy (Ontario, Ministry of Consumer and Business Services 2005, slide 7), which aims to 'support seamless, multi-channel, cross-jurisdictional service delivery' by building trust with partners and customers. Success can be achieved by

- Demonstrating to the government, overseeing bodies, the public, and partners that ServiceOntario has built privacy safeguards into the integrated service delivery program through a clear process
- Ensuring compliance with privacy legislation and standards, and identifying where there may be gaps
- Clearly demonstrating compliance
- Guiding the design, construction, and implementation of ServiceOntario initiatives to ensure that privacy requirements are met at all stages of the program life cycle

Only brief reference can be made here to privacy and security issues because a discussion of their implications for ISD must be set within the broad context of privacy and security challenges for government generally. The scope of the issues involved ranges from policy questions about the permissible extent of data mining and sharing to technical questions about mechanisms for authentication.

The issue of authentication has become increasingly significant as governments have moved from simply providing information to permitting service transactions involving the transmission and use of personal information. It is now much more important for governments to be assured that clients seeking access to information and services are who they say they are. The PSCIOC and the PSSDC recognized the significance of this issue for ISD by establishing a joint working group to propose identification, authentication, and authorization standards to facilitate citizen-centred and seamless electronic service delivery across jurisdictions. The group's recommendations for a framework policy and guidelines were released in a consultation draft (PSCIOC/PSSDC 2004). Implementation of these recommendations is intended to complement the broader legislative and regulatory requirements already existing in each jurisdiction.

Cultural Challenges

A strong organizational culture can be conducive to *intra*-departmental ISD, but it can be a major challenge to the blending of organizational cultures required by many ISD arrangements that extend across departments, governments, and sectors. Long experience working in silos under strict accountability requirements creates a culture of tunnel vision rather than the peripheral vision needed for horizontal government. The staying power of the silo mentality can be seen in the fact that many ISD arrangements retain a strong element of the silo approach, which often takes the form of simply making existing services available online rather than exploiting ISD to its fullest to consolidate services and reduce costs.

Tunnel vision is often accompanied by turf tension as individuals and organizations strive to protect established mandates and processes, and even their jobs, in part by restricting the sharing of information. These barriers can be exacerbated by the absence of incentives and a culture of innovation supporting creative efforts to pursue ISD. There is

> an ingrained and rewarded cultural resistance to change. There are fears about whether sharing turf, information, power and control really means 'the beginning of the end of my job.' These concerns can manifest themselves as a desire to be seen to embrace change and integration while still maintaining the status quo. In other words, integrated service delivery is the right thing for other people to do. (Public Sector Service Delivery Council 2003a, 20)

Since values are the essence of organizational culture, it is essential to cultivate shared commitment to those values – citizen-centred service, trust, teamwork, leadership, and accountability – most likely to support ISD initiatives. Culture change can take a long time, however, and should not be viewed as the kind of short-term solution that structural change often is.

Responses to ISD Challenges

Integrated service delivery should not be sought for its own sake. There are obstacles to ISD, especially across governments, that may prove intractable – even over time. For example, a municipal government may not want to join with other levels of government in an online integration of the sale of business licences for fear of losing revenue. A high level of integration may be the ideal solution for common services being offered by a single department through a single channel, but a much lower level of integration may be the most desirable solution for services offered by several departments or governments through several channels.

An important measure of ISD maturity is the extent to which service delivery is integrated not just at the front counter or on the computer screen or telephone line but also in the back-office systems that support the front-office service delivery. Accenture has noted that substantial cost savings 'are only realized when there is a true integration between the Web front-end and the back office systems. Achieving the end-to-end integration requires changes to administrative structures, development of new skills and re-design of processes' (2002, 12). Use of the Internet channel can reduce the extent of the restructuring that is required. Lucienne Robillard, a former federal cabinet minister, has cited Seniors Canada On-Line as an ISD initiative that in effect has created a new department without a change in structure.

> Most citizens don't know or care if this department exists. What they do care about are the information and transactions and relationships that this virtual 'seniors' department is providing. They don't care that a host of public servants from all three levels of government have signed [memoranda of understanding], have extensive accountability procedures and information management approaches to make this work ... The Internet is, in effect, allowing us to restructure government, without restructuring government. (Robillard, 2003)

The ways in which governments are striving to meet the challenges to ISD are described below. There follows a separate examination of challenges to cross-channel integration and efforts to overcome them.

ISD Governance Models

Proponents of ISD call for exploration of 'another dimension between the silos' through the development of new models of ISD. By the late 1990s the most common single-window service delivery structures were in the categories of *owner-delivered* (for example, Revenue Canada Business Number), *owner-delivered in a co-located environment* (for example, Aboriginal Single Window Initiative), and *shared delivery through integration*. This last model can be very effective in providing seamless service across governments and between governments and non-governmental partners as well. In 2003, the Canada/Manitoba Business Service Centre had thirty-six federal, twelve provincial, and eight non-governmental partners. Among the measures taken to meet such problems as partner competition and managing staff from different governments, the centre has focused on getting the up-front agreement right, blending different cultures into one, and sharing costs and pooling resources.

In the early 2000s, to promote seamless service by overcoming ISD challenges, there has been increased use of delegated service delivery through a *service utility*. A service utility is 'an organization that delivers services on behalf of other government organizations but delivers no services (or very few) of its own' (Bent, Kernaghan, and Marson 1999, 2–5). Variations on the service utility theme include *corporate* and *NGO* models.

A corporate service utility provides single-window delivery of a range of services from one government. It can be created as a public corporation with a board of directors reporting to a departmental minister – as in the case of Service New Brunswick or Australia's celebrated Centrelink (which took the form of a statutory authority). Under this organizational form, ministers' accountability concerns about risk and blame lessen because ministers are required to answer only for the overall policy direction of the utility, not for the day-to-day operations. Like other public corporations, the service utility enjoys greater autonomy and flexibility in management in general and in innovative ISD initiatives in particular. The potential benefits of the corporate service utility model include greater coordination, collaboration, and integration resulting from reduced 'departmentalism'; clearer lines of accountability; less reliance on the use of influence to get things done; a diminution in such inter-operability problems as different policies, standards, rules, and salary levels; and a reduction in turf tension.

Similar benefits could accrue from an *inter-jurisdictional* corporate service utility that would pursue seamless service in various policy fields (such as health, business development) on behalf of more than one level of government. The tensions and differences among governments, together with legal impediments to joint federal-provincial corporations, make this option less viable. There are, however, some instances in which federal or provincial public agencies have been created and then have evolved into de facto intergovernmental platforms by appointing members to their board from the partner jurisdictions. The Canadian Tourism Commission is a federal agency with an intergovernmental and inter-sectoral board.

An increasingly popular alternative to the corporate inter-jurisdictional model is the use of *a non-governmental organization* (NGO) to promote ISD across governments and sectors while avoiding or reducing inter-jurisdictional tensions. This model is exemplified by the award-winning Victoria Connects,[3] an independent, not-for-profit entity with partners from all orders of government and the private sector that delivers services to small business through all three major delivery channels. Victoria Connects began as a separate entity involving a three-way partnership of the federal, provincial, and local governments. The Canadian Institute for Health Information is a not-for-profit organization, financed in large part through bilateral funding agreements with federal and provincial ministries of health, and with a board of directors representing the various health sectors and regions of Canada.

Learning points for integrated service delivery can be drawn from private sector experience. In the case of Interac Association, the reward of mutual benefits convinced bitter competitors to collaborate through a service utility arrangement. Interac is an unincorporated, non-profit organization of 120 members, virtually all of which are financial institutions, that is governed by a board of directors. The member organizations share the cost of running the Shared Cash Dispensing service (through ABMs) and the Interac Direct Payment service. These services are connected to a single network that covers all of Canada. The founding banks overcame destructive competition by seconding employees to this new entity that was expected to develop a culture that was distinct from that of each of the banks. Interac became a 'facilitating structure,' and the employees were viewed as trusted facilitators who provided a safe bridge between the member organizations.

Integrated service delivery is also being pursued through structural arrangements other than the service utility model. A relatively new model is the *ISD department* that takes the form of a department or agency dedicated to improved service delivery with a division responsible for promoting ISD, in part through coordinated channel management. For example, Ontario created an Integrated Service Delivery Division within the Ministry of Consumer and Business Services (MCBS) to work with other ministries to promote seamless service through a multi-channel delivery system. The division subsequently became ServiceOntario. Service Nova Scotia and Municipal Relations is a department providing a range of services through the three major delivery channels; all three channels are managed within the Service Delivery Division. British Columbia has brought together all of the government's service delivery organizations into Service BC, which is a division within the Ministry of Labour and Citizens' Services. This division includes several corporate service-delivery channels: in-person (Government Agents), telephone (Inquiry BC), and online (Enterprise Portal and BC OnLine).

Each of these models has the potential to facilitate effective ISD. No single model best meets all of the diverse challenges of integrating service delivery within departments and across departments, governments, and sectors. As noted, among the attractions of the service utility model are its non-departmental status or non-governmental status and its consequent flexibility in avoiding or dealing with interoperability and territorial issues.

The creation of inter-jurisdictional service utilities can help avoid the political competition for visibility by providing a 'neutral' platform for service delivery that is neither federal nor provincial. A common solution to the need for visibility is joint branding. In the more complex electronic world that is emerging, the solution may lie in ensuring that there is no wrong door through which citizens may enter, but when they pass through doorways from one government's or department's area to another, each door is clearly branded. A good example here is the Nova Scotia Business Registry, where you can come in through any door but as you move around it is clear which government or department you are dealing with.

Perfecting Partnerships

Most ISD initiatives involve partnering within and between departments, between governments, and between governments and the business and third sectors. By 2005, the 130 most commonly used federal services had an 'on-line presence with various degrees of functionality' (Government On-Line 2005, 2). Ninety-one per cent of these services involved one or more of three types of partnership for service integration: across programs within a department, across federal departments, or across jurisdictions or sectors. The use of IT was intrinsic to achieving this integration.

Several of the barriers discussed earlier in this chapter can be lowered or removed through effective partnering. The political competition for visibility, the structural obstacle of departmentalism, the operational/managerial concerns about representation and resources, and the cultural barrier of turf protection can all be lessened by the careful creation and cultivation of partnerships. Partnerships do, however, complicate the issue of accountability because the partners have dual accountabilities: vertical accountability to their government or organization, and horizontal accountability to their partners. The accountability dimension of ISD, like that of ISD arrangements in general, becomes more difficult as the arrangements move from the interdepartmental scene to the inter-jurisdictional and inter-sectoral ones.

Establishing the Governance Framework

Getting the 'pre-nuptial' agreement right is extremely important to getting the partnership arrangement right, which is, in turn, central to the success of ISD. This is especially the case with inter-jurisdictional and inter-sectoral arrangements. Many of the impediments to ISD can be avoided or minimized by paying scrupulous attention to the crafting of the initial agreement, often described as a memorandum of understanding (MOU). Since the devil really is in the details, it is essential to set out the governance and management arrangements as fully as possible. At the same time, it is necessary to ensure sufficient flexibility to adapt to unforeseen problems.

A clear, comprehensive, and transparent agreement at the start helps to avoid conflicts or resolve them more easily when they do arise. This is the time to deal with such political issues as ensuring adequate visibility for all of the partners, especially in inter-jurisdictional arrangements. The negotiations leading to the creation of the Canada/ Manitoba Business Service Centre (C/MBSC), which were moving very smoothly, 'ground to a halt when it came time to involve communications folks and agree on logos, colours, positioning' (Coughlin 2003, slide 7). Public organizations do not 'go into a partnership to lose their visibility' (Coughlin 2003, slide 9). This is also the time to seek an appropriate balance between the vertical and horizontal accountabilities of the partners by spelling out their accountabilities to one another. 'If governance and accountability are not established or remain unclear from the outset of the partnership, organisational politics and redundancies have the potential to flourish, performance can suffer and "turf wars" can surface. These problems often emerge as a result of interrelated accountabilities' (Public Sector Service Delivery Council 2003a, 13).

While the political and structural issues of visibility and accountability are major governance concerns, the success of ISD arrangements depends in very large part on operational and managerial considerations. As explained earlier, formidable inter-operability problems can arise from differences among the partners in such areas as business processes, administrative rules, and financial and human resource policies, with consequent detrimental effects on morale and, therefore, on service. It is advisable at the outset to think through and harmonize as many of these differences as possible. Working out differences at this point also constitutes a first major step in the important process of blending organizational cultures. Experience with the creation of Ontario's Integrated Service Delivery Division taught that 'a common culture is even more difficult to establish the more different the partners are (such as private/public, large ministry/small ministry, province/municipality). Just how difficult depends on the strength of the common interest' (Public Sector Service Delivery Council 2003a, 83). The governance agreement should also provide for such matters as its own revision and for dispute resolution.

Negotiating the founding agreement provides an opportunity to ensure that the governance arrangements make adequate provision for representation of the partners and that these representatives have decision-making authority appropriate to the task of integrating service delivery. At this stage, careful attention must also be paid to the sources and allocation of funding, since the funds contributed by the partners become the budget of the integrated organization. Thus, the founding agreement should contain a funding agreement.

Dedicated Funding

The lack of dedicated and long-term funding is a major impediment to ISD between departments and especially between governments and sectors. Allocating monies from a central fund for worthy ISD projects and then letting these projects wither on the vine for lack of funds sends a clear message. Even the commitment of well-recognized 'champions' of ISD will wane in the face of inadequate or uncertain funding.

The funding challenge is directly related to the departmental model of organizational design. Program budgets are allocated by department, and departments compete with one another for funds to support their major policy objectives rather than collaborative initiatives across departments or governments. An Ontario senior public servant explains that 'our silo approach to conducting business, strongly reinforced by policy and legislative requirements, continues to impede the flexibility and innovation required to finance integrated service delivery initiatives' (Public Sector Service Delivery Council 2003a, 84).

Public servants focus on those responsibilities for which they have relatively secure and continuing (multi-year) funding and for which they will be held accountable. Moreover, despite considerable enthusiasm for 'horizontal' funding, there is concern that allocating a pool of money for ISD initiatives in a particular program area can skew priorities as departments follow the money into program areas that would otherwise receive less attention. The Ontario provincial auditor, after noting the federal government's dedicated funding for its world-leading online strategy, recommended that Ontario's Management Board Secretariat ensure that the funding provided for electronic service delivery (ESD) be 'directed at the most strategic initiatives from a government-wide perspective' (2002, 150).

There are solutions to the funding challenge short of major reform of the budgetary system. Governments can decide what ISD initiatives should be pursued on a government-wide basis, what departments should be involved, and how much funding each should receive. The Ontario Deputy Ministers Committee on OPS Transformation operates along these lines. A related option is for departments to join together in coordinated proposals to ministers that would be handled in a similar fashion.

Leadership and Marketing

Chapter 10 of this book celebrates the contributions of political and public service leaders to electronic government. In addition, reference has already been made to the role of public service leaders – or *champi-*

ons – of ISD. In a study of twenty cases of ISD in the federal and provincial spheres of government, public service leadership emerged as the single most frequently cited critical success factor. In the words of an Ontario senior public servant, 'Leadership needs to be provided by champions who are passionate about and committed to the project at all levels of the organisation. Champions at the senior level are required who are willing to make the ISD partnership a priority at the working level' (Public Sector Service Delivery Council 2003a, 12).

While ISD success depends to a large extent on champions at the middle and senior levels of departments, it also depends significantly on ministerial and central agency leadership. 'Keeping ISD on the agenda has proven challenging for some jurisdictions. One of the reasons for this challenge is the lack of ISD/citizen-centred champions to promote and encourage cross-ministry partnerships and initiatives. In particular, a lack of senior ISD leaders (political and bureaucratic) has limited some ISD initiatives' (Public Sector Service Delivery Council 2003a, 10). Central agencies can foster ISD by working against 'siloism' both within and across governments. They can, for example, create ISD organizations and then hand them off to departments – as in the case of the Canada Business Service Centres initiative led by the federal Treasury Board and then transferred to Industry Canada.

Public servants need to take the lead in educating ministers and backbenchers on the implications of ISD, especially through the Internet channel. At the same time, both politicians and public servants must be sensitive to the proprieties of their respective roles. While public servants increasingly favour the Internet channel, many politicians continue to prefer the traditional walk-in channel. Ministers like to see the physical presence of government, in the form of public servants, in their communities and constituencies. Moreover, politicians in general are accustomed to serving their constituents by referring them to the bricks-and-mortar manifestation of government.

Compared to the challenges of effective ISD between departments, governments, and sectors, the challenges *within* departments are easier to overcome, especially if there is strong support from senior officials who have authority to make things happen. Indeed, ISD initiatives within departments involve in large part the exercise of authority and control, whereas initiatives involving more than one department, government, or sector usually involve or require the exercise of *influence*. Reliance on influence, persuasion, and negotiation is characteristic of horizontal government in general. In the absence of command and compliance, some senior officials will still strive to overcome all obstacles to ISD, whereas others will – and can – simply refuse to collaborate.

Beyond the issue of political and public service leadership is the general need for public servants to market ISD to a broad range of political actors. Vigorous marketing efforts are needed to promote understanding and recognition of ISD initiatives and achievements not only within government to politicians and public servants, but also outside government to the media and the general public. The integration of services can, for example, be accompanied by their relocation. Citizens need to know about the existence of new or modified services and how to access them. 'Unfortunately, finding the funding for marketing or branding initiatives prohibits many jurisdictions from promoting their new ISD initiatives' (Public Sector Service Delivery Council 2003a, 11).

Advocates and practitioners of ISD find its benefits so evident that they sometimes forget that horizontal management is a new emphasis in government, that the benefits of ISD are not well enough known, that there are insufficient incentives for public servants to pursue ISD, and that many important actors remain to be convinced of its advantages. Initiatives in ISD need to receive adequate funding for a long enough time to produce some 'good news stories' that will elicit both citizen satisfaction and political support. While cultural change can take a long time, there has been significant progress in making devotion to meeting citizens' needs a strong part of the public service culture. The Citizens First research has been helpful in overcoming the natural resistance to horizontal initiatives because managers can see that ISD is what citizens want and need.

Challenges to Integrated Channel Delivery

Given the importance of multi-channel service delivery, the next two sections examine some of the challenges and responses associated with integrated channel delivery (ICD). Integrated channel delivery is the result of joining up the major service delivery channels (primarily the Internet, telephone, and service counters) to provide seamless service to citizens. It involves more than providing service delivery through multiple channels; it requires surmounting barriers to the rationalization and convergence of the channels in the pursuit of such benefits as better service and cost efficiency. *Citizens First 3* shows that Canadians use an average of two channels to receive the service they want; half of them use a single channel and half use two or more channels (2003, 31).

The *TCOB* study (Phase 5 Consulting Group 2005, 35) showed that businesses use more than one channel 71 per cent of the time. Thus, providing seamless transitions from one service channel to another is a central aspect of ICD.

The more channels that are being integrated and the more they are being integrated across departmental, governmental, and sectoral boundaries, the more difficult integration becomes. All of the categories of challenges discussed in the previous section have an impact, in varying degrees, on ICD.

A major *political* challenge is the argument that citizens should receive through each delivery channel the level of service they require, regardless of their social, demographic, geographical, or technological circumstances. Politicians have a strong interest in ensuring equitable service to citizens. This point can be illustrated by the April 2005 announcement that the Canada Revenue Agency (CRA) would replace over-the-counter service at all of its tax service offices with 'service by appointment' to be used only by taxpayers with special needs or complex issues. Most tax services would now be provided through the telephone and Internet channels. Many politicians criticized this money-saving measure as an unjustifiable reduction of service, especially for such groups as seniors, low-income families, and new Canadians. The CRA's service and efficiency rationales for its decision received little publicity.

This example highlights the limits to ICD arising from political considerations, including the need to ensure appropriate service levels for disadvantaged persons. There is strong political pressure to ensure equitable service on each channel in the sense of special arrangements for such groups as blind persons. There is also strong pressure for equitable service in providing the same level of service on each channel so that, for example, poorly educated or low-income Canadians are not obliged to access certain services solely through the Internet. At the same time, as explained below, there is increasing emphasis on persuading citizens to 'migrate' to the self-serve channels.

An important *structural* challenge to ICD is the fact that service channels, even within a single department, are often organized as silos that sometimes compete with one another and are accountable to different masters. A simple example is a situation where the introduction of telephone interactive voice response (IVR) frees up capacity at a mail centre, and this spare capacity is then used by the mail centre to unduly improve the mail centre's capacity rather than to support increased use of the telephone channel. When call centres and the Internet channel come together, the two organizations operating the channels have to be integrated. Incompatible databases may also have to be joined up.

The various service channels emerged at different times, and only recently has attention been focused on linking and rationalizing them. There are practical limits to the extent to which this can be done. Each channel provides a different mix of information and transactions, in large part because certain services (for example, consultations involving the presentation of records) are best provided at walk-in centres. However, the capacity of the Internet to handle transactions is gradually improving. In addition, the overall capacity of the Internet channel to provide seamless service across departmental, governmental, and sectoral boundaries exceeds that of the other channels.

Among the *operational and managerial* challenges to ICD, the issue of resources is especially notable. The service delivery policy of the former Department of Human Resources Development (HRDC) articulated the reality of ICD when it noted that 'we cannot possibly provide all services and activities through all channels – for simple reasons of cost. The challenge is to set priorities and declare preferred modes of service based on choices that will be attractive to the broadest range of citizens as well as affordable' (1999, 10). Data compiled by the Treasury Board Secretariat (2004) show the Internet at $0.84, telephone agents and IVR at $2.99, regular mail at $18.86, and in-person service at $38.24 per transaction. The pressure for a channel shift towards the less expensive self-help channels of telephone IVR and the Internet requires the coordination and rationalization of the service channels so that citizens have reasonably equitable access to whatever services they need. *Citizens First 3* found that citizens' satisfaction with a service was higher if they obtained the service through their preferred channel (2003, 39).

There are inter-operability constraints as well. Each channel operates in a way that is different from the others, and it is difficult to create a common look and feel across channels. Walk-in centres are the most distinctive channel and the toughest to manage, in part because their practices are longer-established and in part because of the relatively greater human resource challenges involved in providing in-person service to the public. Pixels are easier to manage than people are.

The dominant *cultural* challenges to ICD, like those to ISD in general, are turf tension and tunnel vision. Some managers of the older channels (such as walk-in centres) resent and resist the growth of the telephone and Internet channels and the consequent need to reallocate resources as citizens migrate to these newer channels. While there is widespread acceptance of a multi-channel approach to service delivery, there is need for a change in organizational culture towards horizontal thought and action that will facilitate effective channel integration.

Responses to ICD Challenges

Governments' responses to ICD challenges have been very similar to those for the ISD challenges already discussed. Restructuring is an especially important means of overcoming channel silos and channel cultures, both of which impede ICD within departments as well as between departments and across governments and sectors. Managing all delivery channels through a single structure helps to minimize channel silos and competitions and, over time, to foster channel ratio-nalization and convergence. Examples have already been provided of departmental service utilities in provincial governments that include divisions with the specific responsibility for channel management, including ICD. Other service delivery models also permit effective ICD. Service New Brunswick – a corporate utility – has achieved sub-stantial cross-channel integration. The Canada/Manitoba Business Service Centre, which is an example of the shared delivery through integration model, provides multi-channel service across govern-ments. In the sphere of local government, the Regional Municipality of Halton, ON, has developed an effective multi-channel delivery system. In addition, the next chapter provides several municipal examples of the operationalization of CzRM by integrating call centres through the use of the 311 telephone dialing system. A potentially significant advantage of the greater operational autonomy enjoyed by service util-ities is that they can more easily encourage channel migration by tak-ing account of cross-channel cost differences.

Given the growing importance of ICD, formal up-front agreements setting out the governance arrangements for ISD should make careful provision for the management and integration of the service channels. Special attention should be paid to the many problems of inter-opera-bility that will arise from efforts to integrate channel delivery. In gen-eral, it is desirable to achieve ICD *within* each organization before seeking it across departmental, governmental, and sectoral boundaries.

Pressure for enhanced citizen-centred service delivery has arisen in part from perceived service improvements in the private sector, especially by financial institutions. Despite the major differences between government and business organizations, some useful learning points for ICD can be drawn from the experience of the Bank of Montreal, which is notable for the governance arrangements and the restructuring and re-engineering measures it used to integrate its service channels. Especially significant were the measures to overcome problems of interoperability, broadly defined here as including issues not only of technology but also of business and communication processes and human resource policies.

Governments' responses to the channel equity issue explained above can be illustrated by reference to the Canada Business Service Centre network. The network received a 2004 United Nations Public Service Award, in large part because of its effective response to the demand for both components of channel equity – equitable service on each channel and channel choice. The network's strategies include 'teletypewriter telephony service for the hearing-impaired; Braille; audio and enlarged print format on request; wheelchair friendly locations; and graphic-free view capability on Web sites' as well as 'special outreach activities directed to audiences that may be unaware of, or uncomfortable accessing, government services, e.g., new Canadian and Aboriginal entrepreneurs' (http://unpan1.un.org/intradoc/groups/public/documents/un/unpan015778.pdf). In addition, the network provides several channel choices, described as 'service delivery modes': telephone (telecentres), the Web, e-mail, in person, and Talk To Us – a new feature for personal service on the Web that connects the user immediately by voice to a business information officer who searches the Internet with the user for the information required.

The pressure on governments to reduce costs by moving citizens to the Internet channel involves difficult political, policy, and program decisions. The following are a sample of the questions to be answered:

- What priority should be placed on Internet service delivery?
- Can we aim for a common time frame for migration of particular clients? What should take-up targets be? Should some services be offered only electronically?
- What communications strategies are needed to influence channel choice or encourage migration in order to achieve take-up targets?
- Should there be common service standards – hours of operation, response times, etc.? (McDonald 2003)

Providing the same level of service on each channel at reasonable cost to government can pose an especially difficult challenge. For example, use of IT enables citizens to receive documents immediately over the Internet. Does this mean that those who do not have Internet access should receive the documents by courier? Should the user-pay principle be applied to those choosing to use the more expensive channels to encourage them to migrate to the Internet?

Research cited by the Chief Information Officer Branch of the federal Treasury Board Secretariat suggests that Canadians are concerned that the use of IT will result in 'less personal service; fewer informed service agents; a reduced government presence in smaller communities; and an over-reliance on self-service, which in the case of e-services ... could reduce service to those without computer access or to people with disabilities' (2004, section 5.0). The federal government is sensitive to these concerns, but it is notable that the 2005 annual report of Government On-Line promised an aggressive marketing campaign to promote the benefits of online services: 'The challenge we face now is to ensure that all audiences view the Internet as the channel of choice' (2005).

These considerations highlight the need to manage service channels to balance the public service values of efficiency, effectiveness, and service with those of fairness and equity. They also highlight the importance of marketing as a solution in that governments will have to decide how far to go – and how soon – in limiting channel choice for certain services and persuading citizens to switch channel preferences, especially to the self-serve channels of the Internet and IVR telephony. The challenge is to stream services into the self-serve channels by making them as irresistible as possible (for example, CRA's NETFILE) without short-changing any segments of the population. Users of NETFILE receive financial compensation for using this lower cost channel in that they obtain their tax refund more quickly. When the Ontario government imposed a $.50 per claim processing fee on doctors submitting OHIP claims by mail, they switched immediately to electronic submission.

ISD: The Way Forward

The 2005 Accenture Report singled out several noteworthy Canadian ISD initiatives, including Seniors Info (http://www.seniorsinfo.ca) and BizPaL (http://www.bizpal.ca). These two initiatives provide illustrations of the current state of ISD and a basis for looking to future developments.

Seniors Info was launched on 31 October 2003. It is an integrated Web-based service that provides information and services for seniors, their families and caregivers, and service providers. Seniors Info was conceived by the Ontario Seniors Secretariat and was developed in partnership with other organizations in the Ontario government, federal departments, the City of Brockville (Ontario), and local seniors and community organizations. The information on the Seniors Info website is tailored to Brockville and surrounding areas, and the site is available from the websites of the participating organizations as well as from other sites designed to serve seniors. The long-run objective is to bring together local and community information from as many municipalities across Canada as possible.

Seniors Info is sponsored by the Canadian Seniors' Partnership (CSP), which was created in November 2001. The CSP has also sponsored Seniors Canada On-line, which provides links to information for seniors on federal, provincial, and territorial websites. The CSP aims to foster an integrated approach to inter-jurisdictional, multi-channel service delivery for seniors. The Governing Council of the CSP is co-chaired by the Ontario Seniors Secretariat and the federal Department of Veterans Affairs, with members and participants drawn mainly from federal, provincial, and territorial governments. In recognition of the need to coordinate its efforts with other initiatives devoted to seniors, the CSP intends to connect seniors' portals across the country. The information available online will serve as the backbone for services provided through the telephone and walk-in channels.

BizPaL is also an integrated Web-based service. It enables business clients to create a customized list of the licences and permits they need from all levels of government. The pilot for this project was launched in 2005 by the federal government (Industry Canada) together with a small number of provincial, territorial, and municipal governments. The intention is to make BizPaL available to all governments across the country. While BizPaL will be accessible through a single portal, it will also be available through each government's website. There will be 'no wrong door.'

The project responds to the aggravation that business people face in meeting the licence/permit requirements of a variety of departments at different levels of government. It is expected to save time and money for business clients, who will ascertain all of their requirements at one time and one place, and for governments, avoiding duplication of effort. The Business Transformation Enablement Program (BTEP), a standardized process for business/service mapping, will identify each jurisdiction's licence/permit requirements in various business sectors. This information will offer opportunities to reduce duplication within governments and between them.

The eventual governance arrangements for BizPaL will likely take the form of a not-for-profit organization, with a board of directors representing the participating governments. As BizPaL evolves, the composition of the board is also likely to change. One can envisage that in its initial stages BizPaL will bundle and customize information on licences/permits to meet the basic needs of business clients. This structure could be followed by a move to online transactions and eventually to the harmonization of standards, regulations, and policies on licences/permits where there is conflict among jurisdictions. Finally, integration of services could proceed to the point where one jurisdiction could take on all or much of the licence/permit work of the others. A much larger and longer-run ISD challenge, with complex governance implications, arises from the recognition that BizPaL is only one of many horizontal initiatives for improving service to business. There are likely to be substantial benefits to designing umbrella service-delivery organizations to coordinate the work of these initiatives across departments, governments, and sectors. These umbrella organizations could be developed not only for the business sphere but also for such areas as social and health policy.

As ISD initiatives like Seniors Info and BizPaL mature, they move closer to the idealized ISD model set out earlier in this chapter. Many ISD arrangements, however, have a long way to go in terms of integration at the back end of the system and, thereby, a long way to go to meet the Accenture challenge that Canada implement the next wave of seamless, multi-jurisdictional service offerings. Most inter-jurisdictional programs serving common clients are not even interoperable, much less integrated, in the back office, with the result that clients cannot simply provide information once, that can then be re-used.

The maturity models[4] shown in figure 4.2 indicate the direction of ISD evolution. The 1980s were characterized largely by the development of intra-departmental approaches to ISD (for example, telephone call centres); the 1990s emphasized inter-departmental approaches (such as Service New Brunswick); and these two approaches have been complemented in the first half of the 2000s by an emphasis on inter-jurisdictional ISD (for example, the Seniors Partnership). Movement towards inter-sectoral ISD has been slower than that of the other ISD

Figure 4.2 Integrated service delivery (ISD) maturity models: An evolution matrix

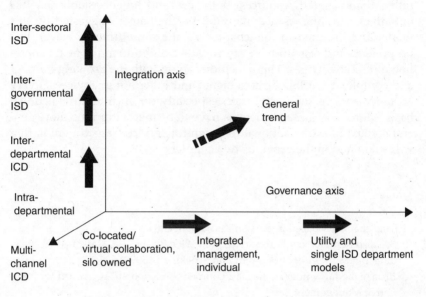

categories but may pick up its pace after inter-jurisdictional challenges have been met more effectively. Progress in inter-sectoral arrangements can be seen in the experience of cities like Toronto and Vancouver with 211 calls for information about social, health and government services. In Toronto, the 211 system involves a partnership among the city, Community Information Toronto, the United Way of Greater Toronto, Human Resources Development Canada, and the Ontario Ministry of Training, Colleges, and Universities.

The horizontal axis of figure 4.2 shows the evolution of the governance arrangements for ISD that were discussed in the section on responses to ISD challenges. Figure 4.2 also indicates the trend in the integration of channels from no integration, through multi-channel integration, to full CzRM involving seamless integration across delivery channels as well as across departments, governments, and sectors.

To highlight the difficulty of developing and sustaining ISD arrangements, Canada's ISD community often refers to the 'bubble gum and goodwill' model of ISD. The argument is that many ISD initiatives have been stuck together in a jerry-rigged fashion for the sake of collaboration; they have been stretched around barriers (and sometimes around rules); and their survival depends largely on benevolence rather than assured resources. Both new and longer-established ISD initiatives continue to face many of the challenges suggested by this model and outlined in this chapter. At the same time, however, ISD proponents and practitioners are already caught up in the next generation of ISD challenges. These include coping with the growing number and complexity of ISD arrangements and integrating service delivery arrangements in the back office, especially on an inter-jurisdictional basis. Moreover, these challenges have to be met within the more general context of organizational redesign for service transformation that was examined in the previous two chapters.

Notes

1 This chapter is based in part on Kernaghan 2005.
2 See also Bent, Kernaghan, and Marson 1999; Blythe and Marson 1999; Dinsdale and Marson 1999; Schmidt and Strickland 1999.
3 Bronze medal winner in the 2001 competition for the IPAC Award for Innovative Management.
4 Designed by Brian Marson of the Treasury Board of Canada Secretariat and used with permission.

5 Citizen Relationship Management in Canadian Cities: Starting to Dial 311

NICK BONTIS

Citizen relationship management (CzRM) is a business strategy designed to deliver a broad range of government services to citizens, and to facilitate dialogue with citizens. The objectives of CzRM are to optimize service quality, timeliness, and citizen satisfaction, and to increase the level of engagement of citizens in all aspects of the democratic process. Citizen Relationship Management will respect the public policy imperatives of universality of access and the rights of individuals to privacy. To realize CzRM, governments must implement processes and technologies that support coordinated citizen interactions throughout all channels (Diamond and Cooper 2003).

In response to global, economic, social, and technological changes in contemporary markets, many organizations embarked on the implementation of customer relationship management (CRM). Customer relationship management is a customer-centric business philosophy and culture that relies on the use of information technologies, effective marketing models, organizational integration, and business processes alignment (Kalakota and Robinson 2000). Through CRM, companies may offer high-quality personalized services at lower prices. Businesses utilize all available information about their current and prospective customers to redirect their needs in advance and present timely solutions.

Most importantly, wide employment of CRM has facilitated substantial changes in customer behaviour. Customers now believe they are empowered. They also want to be involved in the process, assume information availability, and expect fast, inexpensive, and personalized high-quality service (Lewis and Bridger 2000). They anticipate all these benefits not only from businesses but also from government institutions, and they demand that elected officials offer more account-able, responsive, and cost-effective approaches. As a result, govern-ments of all levels are expected to provide better services while reducing the burden on taxpayers.

In order to keep abreast of industry, the public sector has also embarked on the implementation of customer relationship manage-ment solutions (Pan, Tan, and Lim 2006). Citizen relationship manage-ment has become particularly important strategically because it can deliver e-government solutions efficiently, make governments more customer-oriented, cut costs, build trust, and enable the implementa-tion of knowledge-management practices and self-services. In a gov-ernment setting, customer relationship management' is often referred to as 'citizen relationship management,' 'constituent relationship management,' or CzRM – terms that better reflect the nature of this approach. Currently, periodicals and academic literature use these definitions interchangeably to describe CzRM projects in the public domain.

Despite a number of indisputable similarities between private and public organizations, at least four major differences further prove the need for CzRM solutions in governments (Pan et al. 2006). The first is the dynamic nature and diversity of public sector customers. The sec-ond distinction is the lack of alternatives for citizens forced to use pub-lic agencies in their geographical area, regardless of their service quality. The third is governments' need to interact with occasional users who apply for services very infrequently and large numbers of people who may complain about the same problem within several days or months. The fourth distinction is that citizens often cannot adequately describe the nature of their request (Sibley 2003). In con-trast to profit-oriented organizations, governments cannot identify favourable and unfavourable categories of customers to offer different levels of service. Governments should treat all citizens equally. Dis-abled or disadvantaged citizens may require additional attention. The public sector should attempt to employ CzRM to maximize the value of every customer interaction at minimum cost.

Three-one-one call centres are a realization of citizen relationship management that has already demonstrated benefits for all stakehold-ers. They represent a unified non-emergency centre with a single 311 phone number that area residents use to contact the government, regardless of the nature of their inquiries. It is part of the overall e-gov-ernment services initiative with the goal of simplifying people's interactions with municipal agencies. Three-one-one consolidated call centres exemplify the differences between public and private CRM: they focus on enhancing citizen experiences with the government while considering cost reduction as a secondary, yet important, effect. Currently, citizens of many U.S. and two Canadian cities may access their local authorities by dialling a single number.

311 Historical Background

We need a new national community policing number that's just as simple and easy to remember as 911, so that if you have a tip for the police, if you see a suspicious activity, if a car alarm is going off, you will still be able to call a community policing number. (Bill Clinton 1996)

The first 311 system originated in 1996, in Baltimore, Maryland, in response to the overload of their 911 operators with non-emergency questions (Schultz 2003). The goal was to improve the level of government service at lower costs. Inspired by mayoral vision, direction, and dedication, various departments merged their resources to develop a uniform solution for everyone. A decision was made to concentrate on call centres rather than the Internet, to ensure service accessibility for lower-income citizens. The following year, the U.S. Federal Communications Commission assigned 311 as the national three-digit number for non-emergency access to local public agencies.

In 1999, Baltimore was ranked first among large U.S. cities in per capita murder, crime, and drug-related hospital emergency visits (DeWitt 2003). By 2001, the government's investment in the new technology and citizen-service approach had paid off. Baltimore had become the leader in reducing these shocking statistics. The crime rate fell, the unemployment rate decreased, property values began to rise, and major construction projects started in the downtown area. Citizens received better services, the government's revenues increased, and costs for overtime and operational improvements fell. The project's start-up and yearly support costs were US$2.5 million and US$4.6 million respectively (Myron 2004). The financial return, however, dramatically exceeded expenses. In the first year, Baltimore saved over US$13 million, and after three years of successful operation, the aggregate savings were over US$100 million.

Inspired by the experience of Baltimore, several other cities including Chicago, Dallas, and Chattanooga embarked on the implementation of similar 311 programs. According to *Dispatch Monthly Magazine*, in March 2005, there were at least twenty-five 311-enabled U.S. cities, and six other municipalities were embarking on a 311 CzRM solution (Dispatch 2005). Among a variety of successful 311 initiatives, New York City's experience is perhaps the most illuminating, given both the scale of the project and the magnitude of the resources involved.

311 in New York City

The city of New York has one of the largest and most complex governments in the United States. It employs over 300,000 people and has a budget of $40 billion. The municipality provides over 900 different services to its 8 million residents through over fifty public agencies. It has a large and diverse immigrant community: almost 3 million New York City residents are foreign-born, and 46 per cent of the population speaks a language other than English at home (New York City 2000).

Every interaction with the government represented a substantial challenge for New Yorkers. The contact information of the municipality included 4000 entries on fourteen pages of the city phone book. Forty call centres were in operation. People were uncertain what number to call, and isolated departments often referred citizens to inappropriate agencies.

Mayor Michael Bloomberg's vision for the city focused on the development of an open government, the creation of a citizen-centred culture among the city's employees, and the improvement of the quality and accessibility of services provided by the city's widely dispersed departments. In January 2002, the mayor announced a plan to create a 311 Citizen Service Centre that would provide a centralized, all-purpose information centre for all non-emergency government services.

Accenture, a world leader in CRM solutions, became the partner of New York City in this ambitious endeavour. Accenture was also chosen because it already had a comprehensive understanding of the city's infrastructure gained through working with New York City on previous projects. To meet tight deadlines, four teams of experts were formed consisting of employees of both Accenture and the city's Department of Information Technology and Telecommunication. The teams cooperated to implement the four key phases of the project. First, a searchable knowledge repository of all available services was built. For this, the basic structure of information was established and data were transferred to the new CzRM system. The result was a comprehensive knowledge base of over 6000 aspects of the city's government, allowing call service representatives to locate answers to questions quickly. Second, a new call centre, hosting 450 service representatives, was constructed, and the necessary telecommunications infrastructure was put in place. This centre was designed to handle up to 10 million citizen requests per year. Third, a host of operational processes was designed, based on contact software applications by Siebel Systems and content-management tools by Interwoven. The software provided a uniform view of the city's operations, regardless of the point of access. For example, a New Yorker might submit a request by calling a 311 operator. Later, he or she might check the status of this order online on the city's website at http://www.nyc.gov and receive updated information on its current status. Fourth, the city's 122 police precincts were networked and connected with the 311 system, allowing citizen service representatives to route incoming emergency and non-emergency calls to a specific precinct that could quickly provide the most relevant answer.

In October 2002, only ten months after the initiation of the project, the Department of Housing Preservation and Development was connected to the 311 hotline. In February 2003, the New York Police Department joined the service, and in March 2003, the entire 311 Citizen Service Center began to operate. Now, to access the Service Center, citizens dial 311 in New York City and (212) NEW YORK from outside. The services are delivered by human operators in 170 languages, around the clock. As of December 2004, the centre receives 22,000 calls per day on average, and the average response takes twenty-six seconds.

The system was successfully tested in extreme situations. For example, in one day, the centre processed 111,000 calls when most people inquired about flu vaccine availability and the new STAR tax rebate program. In August 2003, when a power outage occurred in many parts of the United States and Canada, the centre processed 150,000 calls in two days.

As of February 2005, seventeen out of forty of the city's call centres were consolidated. The centre employs 200 full-time and fifty part-time call takers. All citizen representatives receive training in an extensive four-week program that focuses on customer service, technology, and available information. The centre hires continuously; as of February 2005, the New York City website advertised fourteen open positions in the 311 Citizen Service Center.

Overall, the implementation of the 311 Center provides fast, high-quality service for New York City residents, reduces the workload of 911 operators who have to deal with non-emergency situations less frequently, saves resources from the consolidation of different agencies, and offers an example of how the government may be more accountable to taxpayers (Accenture Digital Forum 2005a, 2005b).

New York City's experience with 311 illustrates several key lessons. First, to ensure project success, 311 initiatives should be supported by the key decision makers, for example, the mayor. Second, a credible and experienced partner should be found who can not only implement the system but can also offer long-term support. Preference may be given to companies already familiar with city infrastructure and with established business connections with the municipality. Third, expert teams should include city representatives from various departments, including information technology and telecommunications experts. Fourth, city services should be connected to the 311 line in several phases, allowing early identification of emerging problems before other departments go live. If the initial implementation is successful, it also generates a certain degree of confidence and trust. Fifth, the training of citizen service representatives should be organized in advance through either local facilities or other 311-enabled municipalities.

Today, many American cities of all sizes are considering 311 call centres supported by CzRM technologies. Three-one-one projects are being implemented at the municipal level because most federal or provincial agencies already operate call centres. As a pioneer in this field, Baltimore constantly shares its expertise. Since 1996, representatives from more than two hundred cities from all over the world have travelled to Baltimore to learn about the value and realization of its 311 project. In recent years, Canadian officials visited Baltimore, Chicago, and other U.S. cities to consider adapting 311 technology-based CzRM systems in Canada (Oldenburg 2003). Tillsonburg, ON, Halton, ON, and Halifax, NS, are among the earliest adopters of consolidated call centres in Canada (see our website http://www.digitalstate.ca/supp/ch5.html for a review of the Tillsonburg case).

CRM in Critical Situations: The City of Halifax

On 29 September 2003, Hurricane Juan made landfall in Nova Scotia, the most powerful and damaging hurricane to strike this region for the past hundred years. Juan claimed the lives of eight people, caused power outages, destroyed houses, and damaged the city's infrastructure. Then, in February 2004, Halifax received over 80 cm of snow in one day, breaking the previous fifty-year-old record. A state of emergency was declared in both cases. With its new CzRM software, the local government was able to control these crises efficiently, successfully managing its relationship with citizens throughout (Hansen 2004).

One year before the first disaster, Halifax Regional Municipality implemented a customer service module developed by Hansen Information Technologies of Mississauga, Ontario. This system represented an integrated call centre including the municipality's Public Works, Transportation, Parks, Finance, Transit, Solid Waste, Community Projects, and Pesticide departments. Over two hundred staff members received training on system use. During both catastrophes, Halifax's citizens fully realized the value of the new CzRM, making over 45,000 service requests. During Hurricane Juan alone, the normal call activity of the centre increased by 353 per cent. By using CzRM, the staff was able to log the requests on the system efficiently, forward them to the appropriate division, and trace order completion. Most requests were addressed within a few days (J. Brown 2000).

While the value and benefits for both taxpayers and authorities of the examples above are indisputable, there is some room for improvement. Although substantial attempts have been made to integrate services in a single call centre, not all municipalities have managed to centralize their incoming requests. In addition, the lack of back-end integration of information systems can exacerbate the delay. For example, in the case of the City of Halifax, people still have to call different numbers to reach different departments, since their disparate back-end systems are not yet integrated. The 311 call number is another form of operationalization of CzRM in the public domain. What 411 did for information and 911 for emergency service, 311 is doing for public service. To enable the implementation of 311, in November 2004, the Canadian Radio-television and Telecommunications Commission (CRTC) approved the assignment of the 311 code for access to non-emergency municipal government services (Canadian Radio-television and Telecommunications Commission 2004). Less than a year after that, two Canadian cities began to offer 311 services to the public.

Calgary and Ville de Gatineau Initiate 311 Services in Canada

On 18 May 2005, Calgary, AB, became the first Canadian municipality to offer a 311 phone service to the public. One month later, Ville de

Gatineau, QC, also went live with a similar service. Residents of both cities may access a variety of municipal services by dialing 311 within city limits. In Gatineau, citizen service representatives are available around the clock, making it more convenient for residents to contact the authorities. Ville de Gatineau receives from four hundred to five hundred calls per day, with most inquiries related to general information. At the first stage of project implementation, the city attempted to understand the needs of the people and to learn how to respond better to their requests. Marc Phaneuf, Ville de Gatineau 311 spokesperson, indicated that many calls pertain to tax issues, and citizens may now receive answers to their specific questions immediately without call transferring to the taxation department. Several other Canadian municipalities are currently working on the implementation of 311 call centres (Eaton 2005).

Benefits of 311

The development of customer relationship management systems has brought substantial benefits to corporations and customers because businesses were able to offer better service at lower costs. The implementation of CRMt platforms, especially 311 consolidated call centres, allows governments to leverage their expertise by providing a better return on taxpayers' money.

Currently, in most North American cities, every interaction with local government represents an ordeal for an ordinary citizen. The first problem is what number to call, given that in large municipalities the blue pages may list thousands of phone numbers, while the individual may not even know which department to contact. In the best case, the call would be transferred internally. Often, the citizen is merely given another, perhaps correct, number to call. The second dilemma is how to formulate the request. The municipality of Toronto receives over 5 million citizen calls every year, and it is often an ordeal for residents to locate a service representative who may answer a particular question, because of the lack of a centralized system (*Toronto Star* 2005). The third problem is consistency of information. Many people are not surprised when they receive a different answer to the same question from another service representative, or when information in a brochure contradicts that found online (Meckbach 2001). The fourth issue is the existence of an audit trail of customer inquiries. In the absence of an integrated intake and order tracking system, a call taker records the order details on a paper slip, which is later delivered to the manager of a related service department. At that point, it is the sole responsibility of the manager to trace order completion, and the citizen is unable to receive an update on service progress. If the work has not been done within a certain period of time, he or she would have to call the authorities again and place another request.

Implementation of a centralized citizen service approach may address the issues described above. Three-one-one systems may thus provide significant benefits for individuals and governments. The key benefits for citizens include convenience, empowerment, service quality, and more efficient 911 emergency response. The major incentives for governments include increased productivity, lower costs, transparency, accountability, and improved constituent relations.

Convenience is the major benefit for citizens, who now have to remember only one phone number to interact with their local government, regardless of the nature of the problem, whether a utility bill payment, a barking dog, or a pothole. Citizens are able to make service requests through the Internet, telephone, mail, fax, or in person, and to receive a consistent response through either the same or a different channel.

Calling the 311 number may also *empower* people (Gonzales, Henke, and Hart 2005). Citizens have an opportunity to discuss important non-emergency issues with the authorities, for example, problems related to neighbourhoods and crime patterns. If someone reports a non-emergency security issue over a non-emergency line, a call taker has more time to capture all related information, enter it into the system, and inform the appropriate department.

Quality of service should also improve with the implementation of 311. Mazerolle et al. conducted a survey to gauge Baltimore citizens' attitudes toward and satisfaction with the 311 system (2003). Overall, most people viewed the new citizen service approach favourably. For example, 79 per cent of respondents said they believed that 311 improved city service, 90 per cent mentioned that the call taker was helpful, and 91 per cent were satisfied with the way the inquiry was handled.

Improved efficiency of 911 emergency services should also be mentioned. Usually, 911 operators spend a considerable amount of time handling non-emergency calls that do not require immediate action, for example, gambling, suspicious persons, property damage, or parking. By choosing between 311 and 911, citizens make a decision on the urgency of assistance they need. Analysis of call patterns in Baltimore shows a 25 per cent reduction in 911 calls for non-emergency service (Mazerolle et al. 2003). At the same time, the data reveal an increase in 311 non-emergency calls for some categories of crime, such as loud noise complaints, because more people felt comfortable contacting the authorities through the 311 number.

Increased productivity is an important justification for governments implementing 311 systems (Newcombe 2001). By accepting all incoming requests through a single point of contact, all complaints pertaining to a similar issue can be forwarded to the same department. Such uniformity helps avoid inconsistency and saves resources, preventing multiple services from attempting to address the same issue. An extreme example of such duplication occurred when a number of citizens contacted the city of Lynchburg, VA, to report unsafe activities in a derelict house. Different city departments began to act independently, submitting various complaints to the court. The judge, however, dismissed the case because of the redundant violations filed by the city.

Experience demonstrates that the new service approach also *saves government resources*. First, as a result of self-service opportunities, citizens can check the status of their requests online rather than calling a service representative. The availability of consistent, reliable information on the website also frees the time of call takers. Second, a new citizen service approach increases collaboration among multiple departments and reduces work duplication. Third, by having a centralized database of all citizen–government transactions, the authorities may analyze historical records to identify the most frequent inquiries, locate problems with request completions, or develop lists of best practices for call takers. This type of data mining transforms the CzRM system into a real-time performance-management system. For example, the New York Police Department analyzed the nature and origin of non-emergency complaints over a long period of time, allowing it to identify locations with higher rates of quality of life offences and to reallocate police resources accordingly.

A consolidated call centre also improves the image of the authorities by *increasing transparency and accountability*. Since all records are always accessible, government officials may produce statistical reports to assess the service-request activity and the quality of response. Usually, most 311-enabled governments make this information available to the public to justify the investment of the taxpayers' dollars in a new system. Such an approach builds citizens' trust in the government and improves constituent relations. The benefits of a consolidated call centre are numerous and unarguable. There are several challenges, however, that authorities should be aware of before embarking on 311 projects.

311 Challenges and Solutions

Because governments are non-profit, their objectives tend to be either very general or ambiguous, so it is difficult to measure return on investment in order to justify innovations. Public sectors at all levels are highly fragmented, hierarchical, and bureaucratic, often hindering new initiatives and impeding the realization of projects. In 311 CzRM projects, two key challenges need to be carefully addressed to ensure a smooth transition to the new citizen service approach. The first relates to citizens or 311 customers and includes people's perception of privacy and possible confusion between 311 and 911 services. The second challenge involves governments as service providers and embraces the difficulty of measuring return on CzRM investment, the facilitation of wireless 311 access, system adoption issues, and the increased responsibility of the authorities. These challenges are not insurmountable, however, and there are a number of suggestions that governments may consider when embarking on CzRM.

Challenges for Citizens

Privacy concerns can impede the full realization of public sector CzRM initiatives, raising fears of government intrusion. When an individual calls 311 and requests a service, all his or her personal information is entered into the system. In a few years, the government will form a single comprehensive database that will include personal information on most local residents. If proper privacy and information protection mechanisms are missing, individuals will be concerned about the misuse of this information. Indeed, access to that database will eventually become a dream of most telemarketers. In addition, government privacy policies may also obstruct the implementation of various CRM functions.

Three-one-one systems do not, in fact, represent new threats to the privacy of citizens. Citizen relationship management does not facilitate the collection of new private information; it merely consolidates what was previously dispersed among isolated public bodies. The issue, therefore, boils down to public perceptions of privacy. To address the privacy concerns of their citizens, governments at all levels should establish clear privacy and information use policies. They must also educate their constituencies by demonstrating proper information usage. For example, the New York City 311 Citizen Service Center offers a detailed description of their privacy protection principles. Moreover, a 311 privacy compliance officer is available for questions and comments from the public.

Possible *caller confusion* needs to be addressed at the early stage of 311 system implementation. Some individuals, especially seniors and people with limited proficiency in English, may mistake 311 for 911, and vice versa, thus seriously undermining the ability of the 911 service to discharge its duties and may put at risk those who require urgent assistance. ·

Caller confusion is a time-limited issue that will be resolved as people use the 311 system more frequently. In the initial phases of service implementation, however, it is unarguable that some individuals may dial 311 instead of 911. Three steps should be taken to respond to this dilemma. The first is to educate the public and create citizen awareness of key differences between types of 311 and 911 calls. When the CRTC approved the assignment of the 311 number in Canada, it indicated that 'the Commission considers it necessary and in the public interest for the Municipalities to promote awareness of their 311 services, especially for the purpose of minimizing confusion between emergency and non-emergency services ... The Commission expects the Municipalities to fulfill their commitment to undertake comprehensive and effective public awareness campaigns' (Canadian Radio-television Commission 2004, item 100). All parties involved in the implementation of 311 solutions are legally and morally bound to educate citizens regarding their use. The second step is to create the infrastructure that allows quick call-routing between emergency and non-emergency call centres. In this case, if someone who needs urgent assistance from medical, fire, or police personnel mistakenly dials 311, he or she may be immediately transferred to the emergency call taker. The third, but not the least, issue that needs to be addressed is the inclusion of emergency-call response procedures as part of service representative training. Emergency call response is a vital component of a New York City four-week orientation program for all service representatives. Another alternative is to provide 311 staffed by former 911 call-centre operators.

Challenges for Governments

The *measurement of return on CzRM* investment is a substantial challenge. In contrast to the private sector, public institutions cannot measure the success of their projects by growing revenues, sales, market share, and profitability (Diamond and Cooper 2003). The implementation of a system is likely to have an indirect impact on government revenues that may be difficult to identify (Ferris 2004). Conventional industry principles do not apply directly to any government projects, including citizen-relationship management. Therefore, other approaches should be employed to report on the value and success of CzRM solutions. One such approach is to concentrate on other benefits that can be measured and reported to the public, such as costs savings, improved quality of service, and convenience.

It may be difficult to facilitate both regular telephone and *wireless 311 access*, since mobile services are offered by a variety of independent providers. The provision of wireless 311 access is solely a matter of coordination between the authorities and private wireless operators, because no major technological or infrastructure changes are required. To enable mobile service accessibility, legislation should be passed and cooperation between the Canadian Wireless Telecommunications Association (CWTA) and providers should be achieved. There are signs that this will be possible. Currently, CWTA permits wireless carriers to charge subscribers regular airtime rates for access to 311 services (Canadian Wireless Telecommunications Association 2002). In response to the Canadian Radio-television and Telecommunications Commission's approval of the 311 number, Telus, one of Canada's leading wireless providers, stated that it is prepared to enable access to non-emergency municipal government services by Canadians in its wireless networks (Telus 2004, item 5).

The city of Toronto plays catch-up. In many cases, municipal governments are facing a nexus of confounding technology challenges that all seem to surface at the same time. This is mainly an issue for Canada's largest city, Toronto. It struggled through an imposed amalgamation and still faces the daunting task of trying to integrate its disparate systems. At the same time as reviewing the business case for 311, the city must also consider integrating a host of other services all requiring call centres.

'The City of Toronto is undergoing a re-engineering of its business processes in anticipation of 311,' reported Colleen Bell, manager of corporate client services. 'We will do that whether 311 is approved or not, because we need to do some significant service improvement,' she explained. If approved, the 311 service would be divided into three areas: general inquiry, service transactions, and customer advocacy. The major challenge in setting these streams up relates to areas requiring harmonization of information from each of the municipalities that are now part of the city of Toronto since amalgamation. Funding for pilot projects in the works and emergency services, public health, and revenue services departments has been identified. Toronto residents will be able to use the 311 call centre by mid-2007 (Mononey 2005). 'Because of the size of the city we have more than 40 service areas,' said Bell. 'We realize we won't be able to process every single call in its entirety through 311; we may have to do call transfers. What we are going to set up in terms of a model is a main 311 team and specialized 311 teams that reside within the departments, so if you need specialized expertise, you get transferred' (Sibley 2004).

According to Michael Jordan, associate partner with Accenture's government operating practice in Toronto, the city of Toronto is aware that it is not nearly as advanced technologically as other Ontario municipalities, such as the city of Mississauga, largely as a result of the immense task of amalgamation. 'I think if you talk to people in [Toronto Mayor David] Miller's office they're aware of challenges the city faces,' he said. 'They look at neighbouring municipalities and I think they appreciate they've got a ways [sic] to go to catch up' (Sibley 2004).

Governments also face a *technological and system adoption* dilemma. This issue is not unique to 311 systems; most organizations adopting new technologies experience challenges related to changes in a supporting infrastructure and user behaviour. Technological challenges relate to legacy systems, network infrastructure, and information processing procedures. Often, there is no integrated, coordinated multi-agency service request system (Automated Business Systems and Services 2003). In some cases, legacy applications need to be replaced with the modern alternatives. In others, interfaces should be developed to bridge dissimilar, independent systems operated by different departments. Usually, the technology provider working together with the local IT department can handle this issue. The major challenge, however, is the acceptance of entirely new information technologies.

The issue of technology adoption has traditionally attracted the attention of both management information system researchers and practitioners (Legris, Ingham, and Collerette 2003). On average, the success rate of technology implementation in budgets and timelines is below 30 per cent. Often, it is the end-users who impede the adoption of the system, as a result of either a lack of involvement in the process from the very beginning or the absence of proper training. This principle holds true in CzRM projects. Failure to address end-user needs may result in unexpected delays or an increased attrition rate. Even if all user issues are accounted for, some people may leave during the transition stage because they fail to accept a new application. High-quality technology, such as turnkey 311 packages, does not represent a single solution. Instead, technology implementation requires careful, long-term strategic planning and end-user involvement at earlier stages.

The *increased responsibility* of 311 service providers is perhaps the most significant challenge. Usually, the implementation of a new system, a novel citizen service approach, and potential benefits are widely promoted by the authorities. The public, in turn, forms high expectations of the future quality of services. According to the marketing literature, prior expectations of service features, reliability, and quality strongly influence the degree of actual customer satisfaction with this service (Anderson and Fornell 2000). Disappointment of customer expectations results in low satisfaction, frequent complaints, and unwillingness to continue using the service. Assume, for example, a situation in which a citizen requests a service by calling 311. She receives a confirmation number. After that, she keeps checking the municipality website, only to see that no action has been taken. In this case, the citizen's dissatisfaction will be greater than that of a person experiencing the same problem with a pre–311 service approach. In the minds of taxpayers, the authorities are now more empowered and more able to keep their promises. Simply capturing information from people and storing it in the database is no longer a solution. If the municipality is not committed to addressing issues revealed by CzRM data collection, there is no point in implementing a new solution. Instead, the authorities should make the best use of available resources and technologies to respond effectively to people's needs.

True realization of CzRM requires a long-term commitment by the public sector. To address the challenges discussed above, governments need to listen to the concerns of their constituencies and educate their citizens. They should also consider multiple dimensions of return on investment in both financial and non-monetary value. Governments should work closely with wireless-communication regulating bodies and adapt some of the best practices of the private sector in end-user technology adoption. The experiences of those who have succeeded at CzRM and the case studies found in academic literature may offer valuable insights. Most importantly, government-wide transforma-tions of most business processes are required, with a focus on the qual-ity of service, citizen satisfaction, and transparency.

311 Implementation

There are several additional issues that officials who consider the implementation of a centralized 311 call centre should be aware of. These are start-up and operating costs, as well as call traffic manage-ment under regular and extreme conditions (Austin City Council 2004). Table 5.1 presents a summary of start-up costs, yearly expenses, and centre operations statistics for nine U.S. cities that implemented 311 successfully.

According to this table, the start-up costs of a 311 call centre are below three U.S. dollars per citizen. Every person who resides in the 311 juris-diction calls the centre once per year on average. During emergencies, however, daily call traffic may increase up to 400 per cent, as demon-strated by the examples of Halifax and New York. Depending on the city size and the number of municipal services connected to 311, a call centre may employ from seven to more than two hundred call takers. Each call taker processes 100 calls per day on average, with a range from 60 to 170. The number of city departments connected to 311 depends on the city size. Larger municipalities tend to combine more services.

A white paper by Motorola, a leader in delivering 311 solutions, presents six key principles for successful public-sector call-centre implementation, based on its experience (Motorola 2002). First, key stakeholders should be identified and a consensus on requirements obtained. The major 311 stakeholders are residents, municipal employ-ees, and elected officials. The involvement of all stakeholders is critical because it allows the needs of all parties involved to be identified at early stages of service development. For example, after announcement of a 311 implementation, a number of citizens may express their con-cerns or provide valuable suggestions on the project. Since the intro-duction of a new system requires city employees to upgrade their computing skills or change system usage, their consensus is crucial to ensure project success. Second, to ensure consistency among de-partments and the facilitation of inter-departmental communication, project ownership and management should be assigned to a single

Table 5.1
311 Call centre comparative analysis 2004

City	Start-up costs ($ mil)	Operations costs per yr ($ mil)	No. of incoming calls per day	No. of incoming calls per yr (mil)	No. of city departments connected to 311	No. of call takers	City population (mil)	Start-up costs per citizen ($)	No. of daily incoming calls per call taker	No. of yearly incoming calls per citizen
Austin	1	0.55	1,000	n/a	61	6.5	0.7	1.57	153	0.53
Baltimore	3	4.6	2,740	1.0	300	45	0.7	3.79	60	1.52
Chattanooga	n/a	n/a	490	0.2	12	7	0.3	n/a	70	1.20
Chicago	5	n/a	10,410	3.8	500	61	2.9	1.72	170	1.31
Dallas	5	n/a	3,836	1.4	600	n/a	1.1	4.46	n/a	1.25
Houston	3	4.0	5,753	2.1	300	50	2.0	1.25	115	1.05
Los Angeles	21	n/a	19,726	7.2	1,500	180	3.8	5.53	109	1.89
New York	25	n/a	22,300	8.1	n/a	220	8.0	3.13	101	1.02
San Antonio	n/a	1.3	3,288	1.2	169	26	1.2	n/a	126	1.00

Note: Some numbers were added or updated on the basis of data presented by the municipalities' websites as of March 2005. Some of these numbers are estimates only.

Sources: Data partially adapted from the Austin City Council report (2004).

organization, for example, to the Department of the Chief Information Officer. At the same time, working teams should also include experts from other departments. Recall in the case of New York City, the Department of Information Technology and Telecommunication was in charge of the 311 project. The department employees were already familiar with the entire infrastructure of the municipality and had established contacts with Accenture, which served as a major contractor. Single project ownership also increases the accountability of managers who assume sole responsibility for the outcome. Third, a phased implementation approach is recommended. The call centre should initially include several departments only. It may be expanded organization-wide at a later time. A majority of 311-enabled municipalities adopted this approach because it is difficult and risky to embrace all city services simultaneously. This point is especially important if several independent information systems are utilized for different municipal services. Fourth, interdepartmental collaboration needs to be encouraged while preserving departmental independence. The nature of 311 services requires close cooperation between previously dispersed or isolated departments. Indeed, citizen service representatives should have access to all organizational data in order to handle incoming inquiries. At the same time, the maintenance of previously established departmental structures eliminates the anticipation of downsizing, reduces uncertainty, and preserves political powers. Fifth, an attempt must be made to centralize all non-emergency government services in a single call centre; the 311 service should ideally embrace all municipal departments. This approach should be incorporated in a long-term vision for the organization. Finally, a marketing strategy must be prepared to inform and educate citizens. Recall that the two major challenges for citizens are the perception of threats to privacy and possible caller confusion. A comprehensive and effective marketing strategy should focus on both the promotion of 311 and the elimination of potential barriers to service adoption by the citizens.

Three-one-one projects have a very short history from which to assess their long-term social impact. The growing number of successful realizations of centralized public call centres demonstrates, however, that citizen relationship management is an important means of delivering high-quality services to citizens, making governments more effective, building constituent relations, and increasing the accountability of authorities. We can only hope that the Canadian government will adopt the best practices of U.S. municipalities to improve its services.

6 Mining the Nation's Intellectual Capital: Knowledge Management in Government

NICK BONTIS

Government organizations are facing critical challenges as they continue to evolve into an electronic working environment. Continually pushed by paperwork-reduction mandates, requirements to handle increased workloads with fewer personnel, and the rapid migration of taxpayers and citizens to electronic communication channels, governments are adopting new approaches to knowledge management (KM). Three significant trends are converging and are causing public sector organizations to look carefully at their knowledge management infrastructure: a widely anticipated turnover as the result of retirements; an acceleration of e-government initiatives; and a move toward enterprise-wide architecture. This chapter addresses these trends by examining how KM initiatives are being developed and implemented. The first section defines knowledge management, outlining practices and outcomes. Subsequent sections address the potential benefits of knowledge management in government while identifying conditions peculiar to the public sector. A sampling of Canadian government cases is then reviewed, with an assessment of the state of KM in the federal and Ontario governments.

What Is Knowledge Management?

Most scholars and practitioners agree that knowledge management may be defined as the process through which individuals and groups capture, accumulate, and use organizational knowledge (Bontis 1998). Organizational knowledge is often referred to as intellectual capital and consists of three primary domains: human capital – the tacit knowledge existing in the minds of employees and their capacity to solve organizational problems; structural capital – the infrastructure and knowledge embedded in technology, processes, and routines; and relational capital – the knowledge embedded in relationships established with the external environment, such as customers, partners, and suppliers (T.A. Stewart 2001). In the case of government organizations, relational capital consists primarily of relationships developed as part of electronic service delivery to citizens and, secondly, information-based exchanges with stakeholders and other levels of government. There is a growing understanding, however, that internal relationships are in many cases either non-existent or ineffective and that improved client service will not occur until there is a better standard of relationships within (Jones 2005).

The objective of knowledge management is to harvest the full potential of an organization's intellectual capital (Bontis 1999). This ideal outcome requires all employees to share knowledge and to be supported by an organization-wide culture that encourages collaboration, innovation, and knowledge re-use. The objective of knowledge managers is to facilitate activities directed towards the creation, development, control, and flow of knowledge within an organization. This, in turn, depends upon state-of-the-art technology, including next-generation databases, powerful browsers, full-functioning intranets, advanced search engines, turbocharged document-management software, information exchanges and auctions, data-mining algorithms, and even information agents with artificial intelligence capacity.

The need for robust hi-tech systems that harvest the full intellectual capital of firms is driving an expected increase in KM spending in both the public and private sectors. According to Dataquest, spending on KM is expected to grow 19 per cent annually, with the briskest business deriving from KM-related software maintenance and support. KM World reports that the global market currently stands at $12 billion, with governments accounting for about 30 per cent of that spending (KM World 2005).

Despite the focus on technology spending, some KM initiatives emphasize people as much as, if not more than, infrastructure. The main problem here lies with deciding which executive should drive the KM initiative. In business and government, it is often left to the CIO or IT department. This approach explains, in part, the traditionally strong focus on technology-related spending. It has been suggested, however, that a KM initiative driven by the HR department could counter the technical emphasis with a clearer focus on employees and the culture required for sharing. More and more, in fact, we are witnessing a shift from IT and HR to the corporate or organizational headquarters. Alternatively, KM is increasingly being driven by those responsible for strategy and associated business processes. This approach allows KM to be viewed from a strategic perspective and enables the value propositions to determine how responsibilities for KM are shared across the organization.

Ultimately, whichever department is the main sponsor, the results of KM should clearly be felt throughout an organization. According to Orlov (2004), a properly implemented KM initiative should

- Share solutions to customer/citizen problems by using software that captures and retains information on problem resolutions (see chapter 5 on 311 call centres as an example)
- Help groups or teams collaborate and share work by setting up environments where people can share ideas or lessons learned, provide each other with updates, keep document versions straight, and reuse prior work
- Locate people with specific skills and create online communities of practice so that individuals with specialized expertise can reduce the time spent solving problems, making decisions, taking action, or moving projects forward
- Manage unstructured content repositories by allowing desktop access to shared file systems that link workflow with document-related business processes in a Web-based virtual repository that can be meta-tagged and indexed for quicker access and reuse
- Provide customized access to existing data through information-retrieval technology that is linked to customizable portals
- Reduce corporate memory loss when key employees leave or retire by codifying process knowledge that is linked to applications, tasks, and databases
- Help to build an environment where continual learning, competency-development, innovation, and collaboration are simply the ways things happen

The Importance of Public Sector KM Initiatives

A survey of 132 central government organizations from twenty OECD member countries including Canada, France, Germany, Greece, Korea, and the United Kingdom yielded a startling increase in KM activity following the attacks of 11 September (Organization for Economic Co-operation and Development 2003). The analysis shows, however, that only 25 per cent of those organizations had an idea of how much they actually spent on all KM practices. The numbers on overall KM expenditures are thus not reliable. In terms of budget increases, almost 80 per cent of the organizations did state that the total budget allocated to KM practices (technology, organizational arrangements, personnel development, and transfer of competencies) had increased in recent years. Even so, the authors of the OECD report argue that government organizations lag behind their private counterparts and have been 'late comers' to the field (OECD 2003, 5).

In 2002, research analysts at IDC (an IT research think-tank) surveyed forty-four key KM decision makers in federal and local governments. Their top reasons for pursuing KM included enhancing internal collaboration, capturing and sharing best practices, and providing e-learning (Motsenigos 2002). Government respondents indicated, however, that they face significant obstacles in adopting KM, in particular a lack of executive-level buy-in and a lack of funding. Among those government respondents who had not yet adopted KM, the majority indicated that they were in the exploratory stage. Although KM is a high priority in government – as a result of the focus on information sharing as one way to tighten national security – many agencies struggle with implementation. In addition to buy-in and funding issues, government agencies are still in the early stages of determining how KM can be adopted within their functional area. A study by KPMG surveyed the top 500 organizations in Europe and found that on average 6 per cent of their annual budget was spent on KM-related activities. Many of these organizations, however, were not entirely clear on the link between KM and outcomes. They simply knew they should be pursuing KM (Jones 2005).

There are many reasons why KM initiatives should be implemented in the public sector, from the logistical to the visionary. In many developed countries, including Canada, the public sector generates up to half of the country's gross domestic product (GDP), financed largely though corporate and personal taxes. Although reduction of costs has rarely been a major driver of public sector projects, any reduction of expenses achieved through KM would allow governments to either decrease taxes or introduce new services for the public. Many public bodies face budget constraints, forcing them to improve service quality by increasing efficiency and further challenging traditional models of public sector management.

Governments are knowledge-intensive organizations. At the same time, public sectors in many countries have experienced a dearth of new talent for many years. Knowledge drain is also occurring as more government employees retire (Liebowitz 2004). Between 2000 and 2005, over half of the public sector workforce in the United States reached the age of retirement. According to the Canadian Advisory Committee on Senior Level Retention and Compensation, 80 per cent of senior-level public servants will be eligible to retire by 2010, creating a significant resource gap. A survey of federal and provincial deputy ministers in Canada conducted by the Institute of Public Administration revealed retirement, recruitment, and knowledge transfer to be among the top ten managerial issues facing Canadian public organizations over the next several years (Marson and Ross 2004), making KM practices a pressing necessity.

Knowledge management is also a critical factor in improving national security (Walker 2002). Only through the collaboration of different security departments can it be possible to prevent well-organized terrorist strikes similar to the 11 September attacks (Murphy and Murphy 2002). Independent, inward-looking security silos result in fragmented, incomplete, and dispersed knowledge that cannot be utilized efficiently for the benefit of the state. Knowledge management may also help countries deal with emergencies such as natural disasters by disseminating information to the appropriate government. But addressing knowledge needs is only part of the issue. While it is essential that there be a free flow of useful knowledge among partner organizations, there must also be a close coincidence – if not interoperability – between their systems and processes. Knowledge management can deliver results in all of these areas as a result of its focus on collaboration (Jones 2005).

With the implementation of new customer-relationship management approaches in the private sector (Kalakota and Robinson 2000; Peppard 2000), citizens now expect better services from not only commercial enterprises, but also government agencies at all levels, assuming that there will be greater accountability, transparency, and efficiency. People are aware of the high standards of the private sector, and they expect elected officials to be responsible for the implementation of effective citizen service approaches. Here, too, KM becomes an essential resource.

Most OECD countries have embarked on the realization of e-government plans. The goal is to connect independent departments electronically, provide e-mail and Internet access to employees, improve internal processes, facilitate efficient information access, and involve constituents in democratic processes. The implementation of e-government technologies, however, requires the recruitment of skilled personnel, a high degree of collaboration between dispersed public bodies, and the development of a common strategy for the entire government – all virtually impossible without a coherent set of KM practices.

Finally, the successful implementation of KM improves a country's position in the international arena. Knowledge management shapes all aspects of society: culture, education, health care, and democracy. It can help develop a highly competitive workforce in the public sector that is capable of fully exploiting a nation's intellectual capital (Bontis 2004).

KM in the Public Sector: A Distinctive Case

The challenges inherent in adopting KM force governments to develop proactive approaches towards the implementation of knowledge management. A possible solution is to borrow approaches utilized by private firms. There are, however, a number of key differences between the public and private sectors that government KM practitioners will need to consider when designing and implementing initiatives. These can be broadly defined as structural, functional, and cultural differences, with the first term encompassing differences in organizational structure and managerial constraints, the second differences in objectives, stakeholders and customers, outcomes and resources, measurement needs and social responsibilities, and the third differences in attitudes to risk and to knowledge sharing (Skyrme 2003).

To begin with the obvious: private and public sectors have different *organizational structures*. Governments operate at several distinct yet interconnected levels. Their activities embrace a disparate range of sectors such as health care, security, education, and justice. This range requires every public body to have its own structure, depending on its set of objectives. Many public bodies, such as municipalities, have highly fragmented organizational structures that are seen by citizens as a collection of independent institutions (Zaharova and Zelmene 2004). Many public agencies are also very large, are geographically dispersed, and serve large numbers of citizens. Public organizations tend to be more bureaucratic, to lack performance incentives, and to provide a higher degree of job security. Additionally, most information flows upwards, and senior managers are often reluctant or unable to send complete information to their subordinates (Beveren 2003). Public KM initiatives, therefore, need to connect isolated government bodies such as different departments and agencies, encourage collaboration, and facilitate the flow of information up, down, and sideways.

The implementation of such initiatives requires the support of managers at all levels whose goal must be to foster knowledge sharing by any means. At the same time, *managerial constraints* are substantially higher in the public sector because public administrators have little room to adjust the existing system of motivation and reward (Liebowitz and Chen 2003). Usually, very limited financial incentives may be offered, annual job performance reviews are judged on a 'pass/fail' basis, and promotions are based on tenure and power rather than knowledge-sharing proficiencies. Thus, the institutionalization of government KM practices needs to be accompanied by the elimination of managerial constraints and the development of performance-based reward systems.

Moving from structure to function, it is clear that in contrast to private companies, public sectors have multiple, intangible, and non-financial *objectives* that are more difficult to define, measure, and report on. Often their goals are ambiguous, conflicting, or wide-ranging, for example, improving the 'quality of life of the country' (Smith and Taylor 2000). Public sector objectives also encompass outcomes that have a much longer time frame. Most government managers believe they have little or no competition and that their survival depends on uncontrollable political factors rather than on organizational performance. This perception has two major implications. First, this vital distinction of the public sector affects the motivation, urgency, and audience for KM projects. Second, the KM models developed for private enterprises may not fully capture the uniqueness of the public sector. While out-of-the-box solutions may be equally applicable to internal business processes that are similar in both sectors, it is at the level of the strategic positioning of KM that the difference between the two sectors matters most.

The goal of commercial enterprises is to achieve a constant increase of value for shareholders, an increase that is directly reflected in financial performance. In the private sector, there are multiple and disparate *stakeholders* including taxpayers, private companies, governments of all levels, and lobby groups. It may be more difficult to address the unique and often conflicting needs of all stakeholders of public organizations. This point highlights the need to improve public administrators' awareness of stakeholders' preferences through information capturing and dissemination. In the private sector, one does what appeals to the largest number of customers and clients and annoys the fewest. In government, one letter of complaint can cause a whole business line to cease to exist (Jones 2005).

Governments' *inability to select their customers* also dramatically distinguishes the sectors. Recently, commercial enterprises have embarked on the implementation of customer-relationship management approaches aimed at identifying the most profitable market segments and ensuring that these customers receive service of the best quality. In contrast, governments are in a more vulnerable position since they may not select their constituencies or offer different levels of services (Parycek and Risku 2004). Instead, public agencies are expected to treat all citizens in a similar manner to ensure service consistency.

Governments are custodians of information on behalf of citizens; they do not collect or create information for profit, but rather to provide a service imposed by a legal commitment. When creating or sharing information, government organizations must be diligent and do so in accordance with enabling legislations. They must also protect that information from misuse or abuse. These restrictions protect, yet they may also discourage those seeking opportunities for knowledge sharing. A good understanding of the government environment will help separate what may or must be shared and what needs to be restricted. In a context of discovery – organizations in business and government are still learning – issues of knowledge sharing go beyond the simple willingness of employees to exchange information. Greater analysis is needed to determine the impact that 'sharing or not sharing' will have on the path that information may take.

The *nature of outputs* also differs between public and private organizations, necessitating a very different set of metrics. Government organizations distinguish themselves from the private sector by the scope of their mandate and their duty to serve. Government services touch upon every aspect of our society. Compared to those of privative companies, most outputs of government agencies are intangible, such as non-commercial services, policies, information, or regulation. The manufacturing of tangible products may be relatively easily analyzed in terms of costs, quality, or productivity through generally accepted metrics or performance indicators (Cinca, Molinero, and Queiroz 2003). The same types of metrics cannot always be directly employed to assess the intangible outputs of public sectors. Other methods are necessary. There is a rapidly emerging practice of performance measurement in the public sector that focuses on outcomes of public policy and programs, not just their outputs (N. Bedi interview 11 October 2005). Citizens are rightly concerned with the social, economic, and other results (*outcomes*) of the public sector, not merely the physical *outputs* that may centre on policy briefs, legislation, or the delivery of services. The task is considerably more complex than assembling performance metrics for a private sector organization and requires extensive knowledge and information.

Inputs or *resources* consumed by governments are also less tangible than those in the private sector. Public agencies utilize fewer raw materials, less machinery, and less equipment. At the same time, they require the qualified human capital, expertise, and knowledge that are integral parts of KM models (Cinca et al. 2003). In other words, governments exhibit a stronger need for knowledge managements. *Social responsibilities* also differ between public and private entities. Private firms generally view environmental concerns as an unwanted financial burden, whereas their management may be the key mandate of public agencies. Strategies for KM may vary depending on the accountability of the sector.

Important differences in organizational culture also distinguish the two sectors, with significant implications for KM initiatives. *Knowledge hoarding* tends to be more prevalent in bureaucratic public entities. The readiness to share information or expertise is a key driver of the success of KM implementations because members of organizations should have a certain degree of mutual confidence, trust, and respect (Bontis 1999, 2001; Ford 2003). In many government organizations, however, especially large, hierarchically structured and geographically dispersed ones, personal expertise represents an enormous source of power that public servants guard jealously and strive to exploit for personal benefit. Most government employees believe that 'if they give away their respective expertise and resulting competitive edge, they may be less likely promoted or rewarded, thus creating a counter culture to knowledge sharing' (Liebowitz and Chen 2003, 422). The unwillingness of public employees to share knowledge represents a major challenge for KM projects.

There is also an emerging phenomenon of managers hoarding knowledge from their subordinates. In a recent empirical research study, middle managers in the Canadian public service reported 'accessing information' to be a significantly more troubling problem than 'information overload' (Girard 2005a). In fact, accessing information – defined as knowing exactly where to find data or information, but not having the key to access it – was the number one concern of the respondents. In practical terms, this phenomenon occurs for many reasons. In some instances, it is simply a matter of unfortunate oversights: perhaps a manager knows that a document exists in a locked filing cabinet, but she does not have the combination to open it because nobody expected her to need to have access. The situation also occurs, however, when executives actually forbid middle managers access for a variety of reasons.

An oversight is an acceptable consequence of normal business and is easily resolved once the problem has been identified: the manager will be given the combination. Deliberately erected barriers to information pose a much more serious challenge and are often very difficult to eliminate. Failure to resolve this issue, however, would constitute a managerial breakdown of the greatest magnitude, with potentially devastating organizational implications. The prospect alone should serve as a wake-up call to government leaders. Public service middle managers must have immediate and unobstructed access to the information they require to perform their duty to their fellow citizens.

The destruction of unnecessary barriers to information is within the reach of management. There are few, if any, technological, legal, or organizational reasons to permit such barriers to exist. Sadly, anecdotal evidence suggests that virtually all stem from a culture of mistrust. If government executives would only trust their middle managers, who are the guardians of this national repository of knowledge, the problem would undoubtedly evaporate. Though a stroke of a pen would resolve this policy issue, executives appear reluctant to address the problem.

Finally, *attitudes towards risk* differ fundamentally between the sectors. Taking the necessary risks is the hallmark of successful entrepreneurs. In contrast, governments have generally been more conservative and public sector employees more risk-averse. The government approach to risk is rules-based, developed within the context of a complex enterprise, and managed through a prescribed, transparent process designed to address greater obligations and to sustain closer scrutiny. The consequences of failed risk taking in government can be far greater than in the private sector and can affect the health and safety of a nation (Boulet, interview 3 October 2005). Moreover, the punishment for a trivial mistake is often severe, while the reward for the introduction and completion of an important, innovative project is slight. The realization of new, unexplored KM initiatives is always accompanied by a degree of risk that may be deemed unacceptable by members of bureaucratic public agencies.

Influenced by the major disparities outlined above, private and public sector employees necessarily demonstrate different attitudes toward key dimensions of knowledge management (McAdam and Reid 2000). Public servants perceive knowledge capture and dissemination to be of particular importance, given present and future resource limitations as a result of budget cuts and retirements. They highly value knowledge construction through education and training as part of KM procedures and see the benefit of KM principles beyond simple information manipulation. Government employees believe that heir organizations capture more knowledge, and do so in a more structured manner, for example through formal discussions and meetings. At the same time, they lag behind private businesses in KM implementation.

The private sector has already accumulated a strong body of expertise on the implementation of KM practices, and this is often applicable to public agencies. Managers must be aware of the differences between the sectors, however, when they seek to implement knowledge management projects in the public sector.

Good Practice in Public Sector KM

A model of good KM practice in government must focus on attainable outcomes. These include improved efficiency, knowledge creation and transfer, knowledge retention, innovative workforce attraction, internal and external expertise location, enhanced decision making and evidence-based policy making, and timely dissemination of knowledge.

Improved efficiency of the entire organization is the most important outcome of the implementation of KM in the private sector and constitutes the major justification for KM investments. In a parallel development, the overall efficiency of public agencies also improves dramatically as the result of more expedient use of organizational resources, the exploitation of synergies among previously isolated bodies, and the elimination of work duplication.

Knowledge creation occurs when employees share their expertise and experience in a community during formal meetings, for instance, brainstorming exercises, and less formal discussions, such as storytelling. New proficiency also emerges when previous knowledge is reused and improved (Skyrme 2003). Given a strong collaborative culture, *knowledge transfer* occurs when employees share good practices with their colleagues, external government bodies, and even third parties such as suppliers and contractors. This improves decision consistency, teamwork efficiency, and the quality of government services.

Knowledge retention and the infusion of new talent through *innovative workforce attraction* are vital for the transformation of governments into responsive, adaptive, and learning organizations (Liebowitz 2003). To cite a particularly dramatic example, through downsizing and attrition, the National Aeronautics and Space Administration (NASA) experienced losses of critical skills that made it impossible to land a man on the moon again. In 2001, Matthew Weinstock wrote that knowledge depletion at NASA 'poses potentially serious problems for the safety and planned flight rate of future space shuttle missions' (Weinstock 2001). By 2002, NASA had published its *Strategic Plan for Knowledge Management* (National Aeronautics and Space Administration 2002) specifically to address its loss of intellectual capital and to provide a roadmap for their future KM plan. The chair of NASA's KM team, Jeanne Holm, observed,

> If we do not begin to manage our knowledge as an Agency, we will repeat our mistakes. Worse, we will be destined to never learn from our successes. The gauntlet thrown down before us is to either deliver our missions from silo'ed organizations ... or to invest the time and money to fly safely and successfully today while leaving a unique and irreplaceable legacy for the future of NASA and the Nation. (National Aeronautics and Space Administration 2002, 6)

Knowledge may also be retained by increasing the job satisfaction of public servants, and that achieved by introducing a sense of community among employees and by allowing them to utilize their talents fully, to take initiatives, and to be rewarded for both personal and organizational achievements. Knowledge audits may identify the most knowledgeable people, while planning for succession would capture the knowledge of employees before they leave the government.

The *location of internal and external expertise* is imperative for improving public sector efficiency. In contrast to most private enterprises, government organizations tend to collect information and document their procedures relatively well. At the same time, much of public employees' knowledge is tacit or silent (Skyrme 2003). Two dilemmas must therefore be addressed. First, employees who possess tacit knowledge that represents a vital organizational resource must be identified and their knowledge documented if possible. The documentation of tacit knowledge converts it into explicit knowledge that may subsequently be utilized by others. Second, expertise profiles need to be available for all organization members both within the department and throughout the government. Skills directories and Yellow Pages–like indices that contain information on the areas of expertise of all public employees help to identify individuals who possess unique knowledge in a particular field. Electronic document location systems may assist users in finding reports on similar tasks, further improving efficiency and reducing the risk of repeating past mistakes.

Implementations of knowledge management *enhance the decision making* and support the *evidence-based policy development* that are a government's key activities (Wiig 2002). These complex issues require administrators to have a high degree of awareness and certainty about past mistakes, the current state of an organization, changes in the external environment, and future trends in the area. Decision and policy making also involve the use of empirical evidence obtained through research. Meta-knowledge is particularly important here, since multiple viewpoints need to be reconciled. Political leaders may benefit from being more informed about the actual needs of their constituencies at a given time to make more conscious strategic decisions. Through the employment of KM, dispersed ideas may be aggregated, analyzed, and delivered to public administrators. Enabled to make more informed decisions, public employees may feel an empowerment that increases their sense of community, builds self-esteem, and fosters a knowledge-sharing culture.

The Tension between Sharing and Privacy

Governments operate in multiple sectors. For some of them, *timely dissemination of knowledge* is a prerequisite for their operation. To note a particularly pressing example: public health care faces at least three challenges. The first is the quantity of information involved, ranging from patient records to leading-edge scientific discoveries. The second is the timeliness of available information and knowledge. The third is the sector's high level of fragmentation, composed as it is of an array of independent institutions. To address the needs of citizens, health care professionals require access to all available current resources, access that is timely, effective, and efficient. Delays or human errors may cost dearly (Walton and Booth 2004). An increase in efficiency further results in cost savings and reduces the sector's need for ever-increasing government funding.

In recent years organizations that maintain databases on their clients and customers have come under greater scrutiny. This examination is largely the result of a series of unfortunate accidental disclosures and related or independent charges by clients that personal information is not being securely maintained, or is being used inappropriately, even sold to other organizations (Jones 2005). Generally, individuals consider health information to be the most sensitive, and it is, for the most part, held by government organizations. It is certainly the area that generates the greatest public attention and concern when a failure occurs. Clearly, there is a need for a multi-party trust relationship and strict legal, policy, procedural, and technical safeguards. Most importantly, there is a need for clients to understand and accept the risks associated with what most would agree is a more efficient and in fact safer way of providing health care – and likely other services as well (Jones 2005).

At the same time, the safety and security of personal information is emerging as one of the most significant structural impediments to enhanced information sharing and organizational collaboration. In some cases, such as that of the Canadian federal government, there are strict policy prohibitions against data sharing: information must be used only by the collecting organization for the purpose for which it was collected. Horizontal and vertical sharing and collaboration therefore become a major challenge. The growing emphasis placed by policy makers upon inter-agency collaboration is creating considerable pressure to share personal information about individuals, with the twin aims of improving the integration of services and the management of risks. (See P. 6 et al. 2005a for a detailed empirical description of this tension in the United Kingdom.)

The challenge is to promote sharing while protecting users of information from unintended abuses. According to Rose Langhout, head of information and IT for the Ontario Ministry of Government Services, 'To do KM well, you must have personal information (e.g., registration information for tax filers, drivers license, etc.), and privacy policy in your basic toolkit' (Langhout interview 11 October 2005). While government encourages citizens to adopt electronic channels, individuals will do so only if they have sufficient confidence in the security of the channels and in the protection of their information. Previously, the issue of privacy was canvassed primarily by lawyers. The Ontario Legislature's reappointment of Ann Cavoukian for a second term to 2009 as the province's information and privacy commissioner suggests it has now entered the political mainstream. Cavoukian's role is set out in three statutes: the Freedom of Information and Protection of Privacy Act, the Municipal Freedom of Information and Protection of Privacy Act, and the Personal Health Information Protection Act (Cavoukian 2005). For any organization in the Ontario government, KM planning must encompass the basic tenets underlying these acts. Cavoukian urges public agencies

> to go beyond the requirements of these Acts and to serve as a role model to the private sector by adopting robust and verifiable information management practices. These include a credible governance and accountability framework that strictly minimizes collection, use and retention of any identifiable data, attaches electronic audit trails and enforcement mechanisms to all data access and uses, and offers multiple opportunities for data subjects to be involved and to otherwise exercise a maximum amount of informed choice in the processes. (Cavoukian 2005)

Misuse of information may occur when data are collected in one database and then integrated with another. The litmus test must always be whether the information gatherer had the authority to do that a priori. Information gatherers must receive consent from the client for a specific instance of data collection prior to starting. Clients must also consent to their use.

The risks of data misuse are not always foreseeable. Consider the following: a municipal government office collects data on property holders that are typically stored in physical form at city hall, including information such as name, phone number, and the value of the home. City hall would like to appear more citizen-service oriented, so it decides to publish the information on the Web, making it searchable. Criminals then use this information in the commission of property crimes. Citizens who had previously benefited from 'practical obscurity' now suffer from the very e-service delivery designed to serve them (Langhout 2005). With the advent of electronic functionality such as online searching, what was once obscure has now become ubiquitous, and even dangerous, if it is in the wrong hands.

Canada recently passed the Personal Information Protection and Electronic Documents Act, which provides that, as a general rule, no private sector organization can collect, use, or pass on any personal information for commercial purposes without the individual's consent. On 1 January 2001, all federally regulated organizations based in Canada became subject to this rule, and by 2004, all commercial enterprises that collect and share personal information were required to comply, with the exception of activities within a province that has passed substantially similar legislation (Cavoukian 2005).

In addition to the conflict that can arise between inter-departmental information sharing and privacy, there is also the tension between the multiple roles the public sector plays. Government's role is to serve the public interest, assure transparency, and provide access to information. But it must also guard individual privacy by withholding access to information. Furthermore, it must consider the collection and synthesis of individual information that may be perceived as unacceptable from a privacy perspective, but is necessary for the broader public interest and security. This is a classic case of a conflict between the inherent rights of the individual and the rights of the state to serve the 'public interest' on behalf of the community (Riley 2004b).

Who Benefits from KM in Government?

The parties that benefit from the implementation of KM in the public sector include individuals, non-governmental organizations, and nations. *Citizens* benefit because KM facilitates the modernization of the government and encourages public bodies to think of citizens as customers. This approach may blur the line between the quality of service provided by private and public institutions. The transformation of public agencies into citizen-centred learning organizations dramatically improves users' satisfaction with services (Woods, Lantsheer, and Clark 1998). Interdepartmental and inter-organizational collaboration of government bodies at all levels empowers citizen-service representatives who have better quality and more current resources at their disposal. Public officials, in turn, become more responsive to the needs of citizens, and they are able to handle their inquiries immediately instead of referring them to other departments. Public agencies act within a legal environment, and their decisions affect the lives of their constituents. Knowledge management promotes consistency of government services and ensures that public administrators treat all citizens equally (Snellen 2003).

Document-management applications are a principal component of KM approaches. The purpose of these systems is to collect, store, and disseminate comprehensive information that may. include public records. Governments tend to accumulate vast amounts of information, and freedom of information laws allow constituents to access most public sources (Riley 2004a). Citizens or private organizations may easily obtain publicly available information if they are offered access to parts of those systems. In addition, this approach could facilitate self-service where interested parties may fulfill their information needs without contacting government agents. Records, Document, Information Management System (RDIMS) is a federal shared-system initiative providing the functionality to capture, manage, store, preserve, protect, and retrieve document-based information. Among many benefits, RDIMS is considered a key part of the infrastructure necessary for the Canadian government to go online, allowing departments to move towards an electronic-based document management system. It also shortens the government's business cycle dramatically and enables departments to meet information-related obligations in a more efficient manner, dramatically saving time and resources.

Citizens also benefit from knowledge management as a key facilitator of e-democracy, which it underpins in at least three ways (Riley 200c; Skyrme 2003; Xenakis and Macintosh 2003). First, it helps disseminate public information to voters through the Internet, information kiosks, telephone, Short Message Service (SMS), etc. For example, an e-voting portal may offer comprehensive information on all party candidates by serving as a single entry point. Personal identification numbers, passwords, and voting details may be delivered to citizens electronically. Second, information may also flow from individuals to the administration. Often politicians and authorities lack knowledge that ordinary citizens have. Knowledge management allows the aggregation of the results of surveys conducted both on- and off-line. Some individuals may also find it easier to contact their elected representatives and respond to surveys electronically. A real-time two-way interactive channel may be established between citizens and the authorities. Third, voters may form virtual communities to discuss current political issues, address their concerns, and offer advice to other members. These communities may become an important information source for political candidates and decision makers.

Other benefits of KM become manifest on the *national level*. Intangible resources constitute a significant portion of the wealth of the nation. The intellectual capital of each country comprises the hidden capacities of people, private companies, public institutions, and communities that are an important source of wealth creation (Bontis 2004). Better employment of intangible assets in the public sector enhances a country's ability to improve the well-being of the entire nation. Maximization of a society's knowledge-related benefits may be achieved through building competitive public intellectual capital capabilities and developing a knowledge-competent workforce (Wiig 2002). By becoming more innovative, efficient, and responsive to the needs of others – gains that we assume, based on the evidence, are achieved through the better management of information, knowledge, and technology – governments support innovation, facilitate foreign direct investments, and make the economy knowledge-focused rather than solely resource-dependent. Through the development of a knowledge-competent public workforce, governments may demonstrate to individuals and private businesses the value of education and expertise.

The benefits of knowledge management initiatives are unarguable. Government sectors in all countries, however, lag behind private enterprises in implementation of knowledge management (Cinca et al. 2003). On the one hand, many successful KM private sector practices may be highly relevant to public service organizations (Wiig 2002). On the other, public sectors encounter unique challenges that require the modification of existing approaches and the introduction of new (Bedi 2004; Skyrme 2003). What follows is a summary of several notable KM methods practised by Canadian government organizations. Each illustrates a key facet or principle of KM.

Knowledge Audit in the RCMP (Jones 2003, 2005)

The knowledge audit is a critical component of a KM strategy because it determines knowledge strengths, weaknesses, and flows in an organization. The goal of a knowledge audit is three-fold (Liebowitz et al. 2000). First, it helps to identify what explicit and tacit knowledge already exists in the targeted area, including potential sinks, sources, flows, and constraints. A knowledge map may be constructed representing the taxonomy of knowledge in a particular area. Second, the knowledge audit determines what knowledge is missing and who needs to fill the void. Third, it can generate recommendations for improving knowledge management.

The Royal Canadian Mounted Police considers KM a collaborative enterprise demanding learning, idea exchange, and cooperation to achieve overall organizational goals. Knowledge management is not viewed as an information-management tool or the second stage of information-management development. Indeed, information management may or may not become a part of the final KM strategy. Instead, KM is understood to be continuous improvement through strategic management of information and knowledge achieved by technical and non-technical methods, systems, and approaches. All are tightly focused on operational effectiveness in a knowledge-based, interdependent work environment.

Given the nature of the organization, the RCMP has a great variety of data and information at its disposal. In order to investigate how efficiently these resources are utilized, what knowledge exists, what knowledge is needed, and how knowledge flows relate to overall objectives, a 'knowledge audit' was initiated in 2003. Knowledge audits seek to identify key situations and issues so that desired outcomes can be defined and the activities and initiatives implemented that will support their realization.

Since no suitable knowledge audit methodology matching the RCMP's goals was found, an in-house methodology was developed. At the first stage, an examination of the RCMP mission, mandate, objectives, organizational structure, service distribution, and business processes was conducted. The results were compared with actual information and knowledge conditions and issues. This review was achieved through interviews with personnel in various functional areas and geographic locations, and at a variety of hierarchical levels. People were also asked about their views on up to thirty potential information and knowledge management activities in the RCMP. The objective was to gain a better sense of the organization – its current processes, challenges, directions, and opportunities – in order to focus on the most important and pressing issues. The process was thoroughly documented, making it possible to disseminate the results to senior managers and employees.

One of the risks of the initiative was the time lag between the actual survey and the generation of final results. The RCMP is a dynamically changing organization and it is important that findings be translated into activities in a timely manner. At the second stage, a number of knowledge management questions were incorporated into a previously planned employee survey that was delivered to half the workforce. Statistically analysable data were collected.

The process also generated a set of principles of good practice:

- Use business language.
- Speak of objectives and outcomes rather than processes and tools.
- Be realistic and avoid rash promises: organizational transformation is a long process.
- Develop a good understanding of a knowledge audit and be optimistic about the expected outcomes.
- Communication of both successes and failures to management and employees is critical.
- Design an annual plan that includes budget, and keep a long-term (three-year) plan in mind.
- Build bridges with other departments, especially with information technology and information management staff.
- Establish a network with KM colleagues through personal contacts and communities of practice.

The findings of the audit highlighted a number of critical issues. Personal knowledge emerged as knowledge of government laws, policies, partner mandates, procurement, and budget. Regarding sources of information and knowledge, the key issues were discrepancies between horizontal and vertical knowledge flows, knowledge quality, knowledge tools, and sharing versus hoarding. With reference to work plan development, the challenge lay in the translation of findings into activities defined and resourced to the appropriate level. One consequence, therefore, was that the knowledge audit outcomes focused less on long-term strategic initiatives and more on tactical plans that would enable the organization to accelerate knowledge flows as quickly as possible. More specific initiatives involved knowledge transfer and retention, just-in-time knowledge management, interdepartmental collaboration, and infrastructure leveraging. By applying 'just in time KM,' for example, it has been possible to help shape organizational activities that would otherwise have had a minor payoff, by a relatively low-cost intervention. This approach focuses on articulating quick-win investments that realize explicit and recognizable outcomes that can be translated to other parts of the organization, thus ensuring a wider impact. It appears that for this organization, at any rate, this KM methodology will be the one supported for the foreseeable future.

Technology is often considered a critical enabler of KM because it allows the implementation of knowledge repositories, intranets, virtual communities, and the like. The contemporary literature offers various techno-centric viewpoints on KM. The public sector KM community, however, believes 80 per cent to 90 per cent of KM is related to people, process, and culture rather than technology (Liebowitz 2003). The results of a survey of Canadian federal government managers revealed that 90 per cent of respondents agreed or strongly agreed that 'leadership' is an important enabler of knowledge management (Girard 2005b). As one respondent noted, 'Projects that start today have the distinct advantage of all the advances in knowledge management. However, the best tools available won't be any use if senior management does not recognize the value of knowledge management.' An intriguing discovery was that culture was seen to be as important as technology, though both were statistically less significant than leadership (Girard 2005b). Perhaps this is further evidence of the human focus of KM. And the implication seems clear. Successful KM implementations should be strategy driven, outcome-oriented, considered, and transparent rather than technology-focused.

Knowledge Sharing at National Defence (Girard 2004, 2005b)

The main tenets of knowledge sharing have been shaped over several centuries and have become part of the institutional culture and structure of military organizations. All defence functions from top to bottom are designed to transform data and information into knowledge, convert tacit expertise into explicit knowledge, and disseminate it throughout the chain of command (Chatzkel 2002; Lausin, Desouza, and Kraft 2003). It was in this sector that concepts such as 'lessons learned' and 'post-mortem review' were first developed.

The MAKE (Most Admired Knowledge Enterprise) award is given annually to organizations deemed world-class in KM initiatives. This prestigious award is judged by a global panel of Fortune 500 senior executives and internationally recognized KM experts. The panel rates organizations against a framework of eight key knowledge performance dimensions that are the visible drivers of competitive advantage and intellectual capital growth. The U.S. Navy was the first public organization to receive the MAKE award, for its ability to deliver superior performance. Experts in the U.S. Department of Defense believe that there are clear benefits to practising knowledge management (Sasser and Bartczak 2004). The Army and the Navy treat information technologies as an important service or enabler of KM rather than a prerequisite. They view their institutions as perpetual machines that are powered by and produce knowledge to achieve high-level objectives.

Canada's national defence organization has also spearheaded several KM initiatives. Knowledge management in the Canadian Forces dates back to 20 October 1871 when the Canadian Permanent Force officers met in messes in Kingston and Quebec. The concept of a mess[1] supports the notion of socialization, which is one of the pre-eminent processes of knowledge sharing (Nonaka and Konno 1998). A mess is a place where people meet to share their experiences, ideas, and viewpoints in a safe environment. Although the Canadian Forces have always been a knowledge-based organization, the institutionalization of a strategically based KM program is a more recent phenomenon, for a number of reasons. First, the forces now have a thinner organizational structure that is less suitable for tacit knowledge exchange, and the value of social spaces such as messes is often downplayed. Second, the forces are experiencing a major transformation from an industrial, hierarchical model to one of collaborative human networks. Third, technology has altered the way the organization works. On the one hand, it has advanced reconnaissance, surveillance, and intelligence services. On the other, many of the currently used electronic systems do not adequately support basic document filing or knowledge exchange.

The Canadian Forces embedded KM into their Strategy 2020 vision to reflect the Department of National Defence's long-term goal of becoming an innovative, learning, knowledge-based, and command-centric institution. There are three major guiding principles in their implementation of KM. First, it is driven by strategy and based on outcomes. The goal is to identify problems and solutions to obtain observable results, rather than to fit KM into the formal organizational structure: there is no knowledge management for knowledge management's sake. Second, KM responsibilities are decentralized, with KM approaches, activities, and teams clearly present across the organization. This decentralization permits functional groups and domain experts to decide on the best implementation strategies. Third, at the corporate level, the Directorate of Knowledge Management 'touches' KM themes horizontally across the organization through a recently created multi-disciplinary Knowledge Management Advisory Group.

An example of this decentralized approach is the Defence Research and Development Canada (Valcartier) organization, which helped the Canadian Army introduce an innovative system – known as the Army Lessons Learned Knowledge Warehouse – that supports the complete cycle of knowledge management (Defence Research and Development

Canada 2004). It represents a Web-based application that allows personnel to share observations and lessons learned during peace missions. Overall, it serves as an important learning tool, and it centralizes knowledge in a manner that decreases delays in gathering and disseminating information.

Virtual Networks and Forums of Practice in Canada

Communities of practice are defined as 'groups of people who come together to share and to learn from one another face-to-face and virtually' (American Productivity & Quality Center 2001, 8). Participants share a need to communicate their expertise, experiences, knowledge, reflections, best practices, insights, and tools. Communities build a knowledge-sharing culture in dispersed organizations, foster the acceptance of successful approaches, promote standardization of practices, and may ultimately lead to enhanced service to the public.

Employees have created communities of practice inside and outside of their organizations long before the emergence of KM and information-communication technologies. Now the Internet and e-mail offer a new channel for collaboration. For the past several years, public agencies have also embarked on the implementation of communities of practice.

The KM Network (http://www.kmnetwork.ca) was established in 2001 by a group of professionals in Edmonton, AB. It serves as a community of practice for managers of both private and public-sector organizations who are interested in knowledge management issues. Participants have diverse backgrounds and knowledge needs ranging from technical implementations to KM in educational settings. The website is employed to disseminate news and important documents. The actual knowledge sharing takes place during regular meetings where people tell stories and share their experiences. For this, monthly breakfast meetings are held, and two conferences have been organized.

The Interdepartmental Knowledge Management Forum (IKMF)[2] is a non-governmental function that represents a virtual community of practice for public sector KM professionals in Canada. Founded in 1999, it currently has 484 members who have established a productive dialogue (over 3400 messages thus far) on public KM issues in a knowledge-sharing environment. The goals of IKMF are to promote knowledge-leveraging culture, demonstrate the success of KM principles, and provide guidance for KM managers in the public domain.

Ontario's Ministry of Municipal Affairs and Housing:
Quick-Win KM Approaches (N. Bedi Interview 11 October 2005)

In an environment of multiple strategic priorities and limited financial resources, organizations able to launch quick KM initiatives with real outcomes tend to progress more effectively than those seeking an over-arching and comprehensive KM system.

Ontario's Ministry of Municipal Affairs and Housing is a heavily policy-oriented organization responsible for housing, land-use planning, local government, and urban and rural development in Ontario. Its policy agenda intersects those of many other ministries, is heavily intergovernmental, and involves a wide array of stakeholders and partners. In the last three years, the ministry has moved forward with a systematic approach to KM that began with an organization-wide needs assessment. The ministry used information gathered from focus groups and a ministry-wide KM survey to address needs identified by staff. Following an initial focus on 'quick wins' that could be implemented within resource constraints, the ministry then developed a KM strategy to include longer-term initiatives. The strategy's goals were to integrate KM initiatives into everyday business processes, resulting in better services to stakeholders, reduced costs, greater efficiencies, increased staff productivity through better use of time, greater innovation, and increased communication with other ministries in the Ontario Public Service. Knowledge management needs and approaches were identified around five themes: leadership and planning, awareness building, knowledge identification, knowledge capture, and knowledge transfer. Initiatives in each of these areas have been implemented or are under way. Particularly notable ones include an exit protocol; successful communities of practice; a staff key contact list; collaboration tools for business planning; extensive use of electronic approaches for interacting with citizens and stakeholders for policy development purpose; records and document management.

While KM initiatives across the government and elsewhere seem to take a back seat during times of fiscal constraint, the ministry has kept its momentum on the KM front by paying attention to a few factors. Firstly, it has embraced a balanced approach focusing on people, culture, and processes. Secondly, the 'stages of KM development' and adaptation have been implicit in its strategy. After a blitz of activity to raise awareness on the importance of KM, the ministry moved on to initiatives that deliver business value within operating constraints.

Finally, the ministry is moving forward by setting up metrics to measure the impact of its KM initiatives on strategic outcomes.

For a review of the KM initiatives at Industry Canada and the Alberta provincial government, refer to http://www.digitalstate.ca.

Assessment of KM in Government

A recent research project considered which KM strategy would likely be most successful in the Canadian federal government (Girard 2005c). Building on the seminal research of Michael Earl (2001), the project sought to solicit the view from the front, which in this case meant the middle managers of the Canadian public service. Specifically, the aim was to determine which of Earl's schools of knowledge would be most appropriate in curbing the organizational memory loss and taming the information anxiety that are so prevalent today.

The most interesting conclusion about KM strategies was that respondents opted overwhelmingly for a single strategy. Seven schools or strategies were described to the respondents, and yet a single school, the 'organizational,' surfaced as the strategy most likely to fit respondents' perceived needs. Emphasizing collaboration, Earl's 'organizational school' focuses on maximizing the use of social networks with a view to knowledge sharing. The 'commercial school,' which focuses on knowledge assets and commercialization, was rated the lowest, while the remaining five schools ranged somewhere in the middle.

The fact that a single knowledge strategy emerged as the clear preference of respondents suggests that it may be possible to develop a single knowledge strategy for government. It may be premature to announce such a definite finding, however, based on this exploratory research alone. Corporate experience suggests that a blended approach is worth consideration. Consider Honeywell's recently implemented system with an explicit goal 'to help knowledge flows across boundaries' (American Productivity & Quality Center 2003, 7), which could be described as Earl's 'engineering school.' The system, however, is also about 'connecting people across networks' (Earl's 'cartographic school'), enabling collaboration (Earl's 'organizational school'), and getting assistance (Earl's 'system school') (American Productivity & Quality Center 2003, 16). The lesson is clear: some KM implementations will be blended systems that span the boundaries of the schools espoused by Earl, and some will not.

That a single school was important to the respondents of the government survey demonstrates the importance of that school; it does not demand the exclusion of others. In order to alleviate knowledge loss in government, a system for creating and sharing organizational knowledge is essential, but this system may include components of various schools. The wise executive should consider the work of Earl with a view to determining which schools are most applicable to his or her organization. The Honeywell case demonstrates the value of considering a blended system. That said, if resource limitations permit only a pilot project or the implementation of a single system, then this research suggests the most advantageous school for a government organization is the 'organizational school' (Girard 2005d).

When assessing Ontario's knowledge-management initiatives, Rose Langhout of the Ministry of Government Services argues that there are three primary aspects of KM that the provincial government has been implementing well: awareness, common application of tools, and people-to-people connection or tacit knowledge flow (Langhout 2005). She feels that the Ontario government is among the leading provinces in KM implementation in Canada. And there are plans to move further by talking to practitioners and asking what they need for their day-to-day work leveraging what has already been done in different ministries, and tapping into KM expertise external to the Ontario government. Nilam Bedi of the Ministry of Municipal Housing and Affairs agrees with his colleague. He states that 'our big challenge moving forward is to move from awareness to practice ... to examine the most pragmatic solutions that require the smallest investments yet provide the quickest wins' (N. Bedi interview 11 October 2005). Bedi recommends that governments customize their KM initiatives to suit their own value propositions, as opposed to purchasing solutions that were developed for the private sector. He also warns to keep goals modest:

It's very tempting to charge on with quick wins without reflecting on the problems KM should address. Early successes are important for gaining acceptance, and this enthusiasm can only be sustained through a well-reasoned game plan that addresses objectives. There is a tendency to focus on the 'cookie cutter approach,' and the general approaches do work well, but those tend to be as a guide. You have to understand the dynamics of your organization. Avoid the tendency to go in with a huge shopping list of initiatives. It's often difficult to weave a large number of programs into the business strategy and demonstrate the value of all of them. Instead, develop a formal, written strategy with limited, realistic goals. That way, rather than scattering your efforts over a large number of projects, you can evaluate where efforts should be concentrated. (KM Review 2003)

David Jones, director of KM at the RCMP, notes that people often comment to him that KM seems to be just common sense. He agrees: 'While the language and methods of KM may be a little troublesome for people, it really is all about trying to cope with organizational development and management in the twenty-first century. It's about trying to get the right things happening and the right relationships working between people, processes and technology' (Jones 2005).

Conclusions

Public agencies are knowledge-based organizations that represent an important part of national economies. They face increasing competition with the private sector for human capital, rising expectations of citizens, and a need to improve efficiency. Most governments have realized that KM projects offer significant benefits for public organizations and stakeholders alike. There are, however, several challenges and potential pitfalls that KM managers need to be aware of.

First and foremost, most knowledge managers agree that the impact of KM projects is difficult to measure directly. In the public non-profit sector, this issue becomes more important because many financial principles employed by business do not apply to governments. Additional measures may be needed to evaluate KM successes objectively.

Second, the implementation of KM requires immediate financial investments. At the same time, visible outcomes may become evident only in the long term because knowledge-management success requires cultural changes. If a sound strategic plan that outlines future benefits in service quality, efficiency, or money is missing, KM projects may be difficult to justify. Another option when launching KM in a bureaucratic organization is to concentrate on highly visible short-term results that may demonstrate the viability and effectiveness of knowledge management to key decision makers.

Third, although the value of local KM initiatives is unarguable, organization-wide coordination of efforts is needed, as well as the support of the senior-level administrators who are responsible for the overall strategic planning within the government body. Without them, any advances made will be marginal at best.

Fourth, thorough consideration should be given to organization-wide involvement of employees in KM in terms of reward and recognition structures. Most systems of compensation within public agencies do not adequately support knowledge sharing and collaboration. Some private sector practices may be successfully adapted to embed KM into people's daily working habits. If KM practices are included in job descriptions, however, a new knowledge-intensive and knowledge-sharing culture may emerge over time, especially with the inflow of a new workforce.

Fifth, implementing and sustaining KM require a degree of expertise that the public sector may not necessarily have. In this case, the employment of external consultants should be considered who may have important skills to bring governments up to speed in knowledge management. A good option is to form KM teams consisting of both external independent consultants and full-time employees that may lead the activities at the initial stage.

Last but not least, public agencies should not focus on KM implementations only or devote all organizational efforts solely to KM. Other strategic, tactical, and routine activities need to be conducted to support the overall organizational objectives. Knowledge management should not be viewed as a substitute for other operations.

The public sector possesses tremendous intellectual capital. If leveraged properly, it may contribute substantially to the well-being of the nation. Many public organizations have practised knowledge management principles for years without identifying them as such. It is hoped that governments will be able to mirror the pioneering efforts of the private sector to make a difference in people's lives. What is needed now is the leadership of the major national, regional, and local political decision makers.

Notes

1 Currently, in the Department of National Defence a mess is referred to as 'meeting environment supporting socialization,' reflecting its purpose in terms of KM.
2 Available through Yahoo! Groups at http://finance.groups.yahoo.com/group/ikmf_figs.

7 Moving Beyond Politics as Usual? Online Campaigning

Compared to the impact of information technology (IT) on the structures, processes, and systems of government and on service delivery, little scholarly attention has been paid in Canada to the political implications of IT. The next two chapters of this book examine the political dimension of electronic governance by explaining the ways in which politicians exploit IT to enhance their electoral fortunes and fulfill their legislative roles. This chapter focuses on the former issue by examining politicians' use of the World Wide Web, with particular reference to the most recent federal and Ontario elections.

In the United States, the year 2000 has often been described as the 'Year of the Internet in politics' (Bimber and Davis 2003, 28), that is, the year in which online campaigning had a widespread and significant effect on the conduct of elections. Since the mid-1990s, online campaigning has become increasingly sophisticated and influential. By 2000, all of the major political parties and most political candidates at all levels of government in the United States had created websites as a means of enhancing their electoral fortunes. However, the extent of politicians' commitment to online campaigning ranged from a rudimentary symbolic website presence to positioning a high-quality website as an integral component of their campaign techniques. Many commentators have argued that online campaigning really came of age with the 2004 election campaign (see Hines 2004 for example). According to a Pew Institute study, the number of Americans who went online to obtain campaign information during the 2004 campaign doubled to more than 40 per cent from the 2000 campaign (Kerner 2004).

Among the milestones in the evolution of online campaigning, three events are especially notable. The first was the election in November

1998 of Jesse Ventura, a poorly funded candidate from a minor party, as governor of Minnesota. He made effective use of the Internet, including e-mail communication, to raise money, mobilize supporters, and respond to critics. Second, John McCain, a contender for the 2000 U.S. Republican Party presidential nomination, raised more than $10 million online, much of it in the form of small individual contributions. Third, outside the United States, Roh Moo-hyun, a relatively unknown politician in South Korea, used the Internet, beginning in 2000, to help him become president in December 2002.

These events, especially McCain's fundraising success, were important precursors to the widely publicized but ultimately unsuccessful campaign of Howard Dean, a candidate for the 2004 U.S. Democratic Party presidential nomination. He used the Internet in innovative ways to attract a large number of volunteers and to raise a huge sum of money. The major Dean website – http://www.deanforamerica.com – with its links to associated campaign sites, became the 2004 gold standard for online political campaigning.

Regardless of the debate on whether a particular year, election, or event constitutes the tipping point in the history of online political campaigns, it was clear by 2004 that these campaigns had become a significant feature of elections, not only in the United States but in several other countries as well. Thus, it is important for political actors and political scientists to assess the role and impact of online campaigning, not only in an absolute sense but in relation to other campaign techniques. The major arguments in this chapter are that the use of online campaigning has increased substantially during the most recent set of elections in Canada, that there is considerable variation in the quality and sophistication of websites from one party, one candidate, and one government to another, and that the development of online campaigning is still at an early stage. This book does not examine the related issue of electronic voting, since little advance was made in the use of this technology during the period under examination.

This chapter begins with a brief account of the 'Dean phenomenon' and other experiences with online campaigning in the United States. The second – and major – section of the chapter sets out a framework for analyzing political websites and applies it to a federal election, two federal party leadership contests, nine provincial elections, and a municipal mayoralty election, but with special attention to the federal and Ontario experience. The third section draws out the learning points on the evolution of online political campaigning in Canada.

While the focus is on the sites of the major political parties, this section also provides data and analysis from an examination of individual candidates' sites in the federal and Ontario elections. The 2006 federal election was held after the deadline for completing the manuscript, but a postscript has been added to the chapter.

The research for this chapter includes an online survey of the communications director and/or the webmaster for the Liberals, Conservatives, New Democrats, and Green Party for the 2004 federal election[1] (hereafter described as the Federal Website Study) and for the Liberals, Progressive Conservatives, and New Democrats for the 2003 Ontario election (the Ontario Website Study). The chapter also includes data from four Legislator Surveys that are explained in the methodology section of the next chapter, and from the 2004 Canadian Election Survey (CES). To save space in this book, tables 7A, 7B, 7C, and 7D are shown in full on the book website at http:www.digitalstate.ca/supp/ch7.html.

Online Campaigning in the United States

During the early years of the twenty-first century, Canada's federal government has been ranked first in the world in *e-government* maturity, that is, in the breadth and depth of online service offered to Canadians and in customer relationship management. In the maturity of online political campaigning, however, the United States, especially in the federal sphere of government, is the world leader. The United States is prominent also in any list of milestones of online campaigning.

Online political campaigning, especially in the United States, has given rise to a new vocabulary in political discourse, including 'open-source politics,' 'meetups,' and 'blogging.' It was by using such tools in innovative ways that Howard Dean emerged as a prime mover in advancing the art of online campaigning. The Dean campaign was the first to use open-source politics in the sense of a 'two-way campaign in which the supporters openly collaborate with the campaign to improve it, and in which the contributions of the "group mind" prove smarter than that of any lone individual' (Suellentrop 2003). The campaign encouraged Dean's supporters to organize and promote the campaign on their own, through such means as meetups.

A *meetup* is a local gathering of a group of people brought together online by a common interest and then meeting face-to-face in such places as coffee shops and pubs. Meetup.com, which was created in

2002, provides 'a technology platform and global network of local venues' to enable people with shared interests of any kind (Harry Potter fans, dog lovers) to combine online communication with offline meetings in local venues. The Dean campaign capitalized on the enormous political potential of meetups both as a means of bringing together supporters and potential supporters and of raising funds. Bruce Bimber, a leading scholar of e-democracy in the United States, has described meetups as 'the latest and greatest hope for the Internet, drawing citizens into democracy,' but with uncertain long-term prospects for transforming political campaigning (Bimber 2003).

Like meetups, *blogging* is a broadly based online innovation that has been adapted for use in political campaigning. A *blog* (short for weblog) is a website that is frequently updated and that is composed of posts in reverse chronological order. Blogs are often described as electronic diaries but, unlike diaries, they are publicly accessible, and many of them permit readers to respond. *Political blogs* are used by individual politicians to share their views on political events and campaigns, to seek or maintain political support, and to raise money through a large number of small donations. Many individual citizens have created their own blogs to support particular politicians, and there are blogs that provide opinions about or attack specific politicians, such as presidential candidates.

The Dean campaign not only made very effective use of meetups and blogging but also combined these tools with extensive use of e-mail, often described as the 'killer application' in electronic campaigning. E-mail provides politicians with an inexpensive way to send messages to a large number of individuals and to tailor the messages to specific audiences. The messages can serve such important purposes as soliciting donations and volunteers, inviting supporters to upcoming events, and getting out the vote. By June 2004, President Bush's campaign team had compiled a list of more than 6 million e-mail addresses (Boutin 2004).

Internet fundraising has several advantages over conventional approaches. Whether the donor is linked to the campaign through meetups, blogs, or one of the other innovative campaign tools, making an online donation is quick and simple. Moreover, online fundraising is more cost-efficient than such traditional techniques as door-to-door canvassing and direct-mail solicitations. For the 2004 presidential election Dean raised roughly $20 million (during the Democratic primary election period); Bush raised $14 million; and Kerry set an online record by raising $5.7 million in twenty-four hours and $82 million overall (PoliticsOnline 2005). It is notable that most of the money came from small donations.

The experience of Howard Dean and, to a lesser extent, John McCain, Bill Bradley, and many other U.S. politicians, has shown that innovative use of online campaigning is far from sufficient to ensure victory. Still, the use of the Internet and e-mail is now a major component of U.S. election campaigns and leadership contests. With the American experience as context, we turn now to an examination of online campaigning in Canada.

Online Campaigning in Canada

Background

Online campaigning in Canada continues to lag behind that of the United States. While the Internet played a modest role in the 1996 U.S. elections, it played a more prominent part in the 1998 campaigns and, by the 2000 elections, 'the Internet was firmly entrenched in the routines of American political campaigns' (Kamarck 2002, 85). By 2000 also, requests for donations and for volunteers had become popular features of most party and candidate websites. However, websites tended to take the form of electronic campaign brochures. There was little interactivity, and criticisms of political opponents were restrained, focused on issues, or posted on a separate site (Kamarck 2002, 89–98). While there was much optimism among political and technological experts about the potential impact of the Internet on future political campaigns, there was also considerable scepticism (Norris 2002).

Grant Kippen asserts that the first use of the Internet by a federal political party in Canada was by the Liberal Party in the 1993 campaign (2000, 36). By the 1997 campaign, he notes, all major political parties had an established presence on the Internet, which they used to disseminate information to voters and the media. Cynthia Alexander (2001) agrees that the major parties all had websites by 1997, but she contends that the Liberal and Progressive Conservative parties were following the lead of the Reform and the New Democratic parties, which had set up websites in the mid-1990s (460). She observes also that notable website uses during the 1997 election were the Reform Party's town hall Web design layout, the Progressive Conservative

Party's Star Trek galaxy–inspired site, and the New Democratic Party's information-intensive site. The Liberal Party 'paid scant attention to the web, posting a static bare bones site that was unimaginative and offered little interesting information' (463).

The parties' online presence took the form of websites containing such information as candidate biographies, press releases, and policy statements (Kippen 2000, 38). Very few individual candidates had personal websites by this date. Indeed, Kippen discusses the use of websites for campaign purposes as one of the next generation of campaign technologies, along with Web-TV, hand-held computing devices, and customer relationship management (2000, 42–3). A small survey by Elections Canada in 2000 suggested that skepticism about the importance of online campaigning was not confined to the United States. One respondent noted, 'The vast majority of voters and, in particular, the all-important undecided voters have little interest in seeking out campaign material or information.' Another respondent, while acknowledging that websites have enormous potential, predicted that 'the major parties will choose *not* to direct substantial time, funding or staff to the development of truly effective Web sites' (McMahon 2000, 2).

This scepticism was borne out by experience with online campaigning in Canada's 2000 federal election. The use of party websites as a campaign tool was not substantially more advanced than in 1997. Party strategists reported little confidence in the effectiveness of either party or candidate sites to attract undecided voters; there was little use of e-mail, except for internal party purposes; and websites resembled electronic brochures in their appearance and content (Marland 2003, 18–19). Attallah and Burton described the 2000 election as 'Canada's inaugural Internet election,' because all political actors were active online participants during the campaign. They concluded, however, that the websites of the major parties were 'lackluster, suggesting that they accept the reality of the new medium and the need to meet a bare minimum but that they have not fully thought through its true political utility or value' (2001, 227–9).

Two provincial elections, in Alberta and British Columbia in 2001, confirmed this skepticism. Harold Jansen's analysis of candidate websites (2004) for these two elections shows considerable variation in the quality and extent of online campaigning, not only between the two provinces but also between candidates from different parties within each province. Jansen found, in general, that the political websites functioned as online versions of campaign brochures, and that only a

modest effort (largely in Alberta) was made to attract donations or volunteers. There was very little multimedia content, and few sites
requested e-mail addresses that could be used to contact voters. Interactivity was limited largely to opportunities to contact candidates by
e-mail or Web-based forms. Only a few candidates permitted voters
to put questions to candidates, to participate in online surveys, or to
post messages. Despite the undeveloped state of these websites in the
2000–1 period, some of the 2003 provincial elections and the 2004
federal election provided grounds for more optimistic predictions
about the importance and efficacy of online campaigning.

Canada's 2003–4 Elections

The year 2003 was a remarkably busy year in Canadian politics. There
were elections in eight of the ten provinces: Quebec (14 April), Manitoba (3 June), New Brunswick (9 June), Nova Scotia (5 August),
Ontario (2 October), Prince Edward Island (29 September), Newfound-
land (21 October), and Saskatchewan (5 November). In the federal
sphere, a new leader of the Progressive Conservative (PC) Party was
chosen on 31 May, and a new leader of the Liberal Party was selected
on 14 November. National attention focused on the mayoralty election
in Toronto, Canada's largest city, which was held in conjunction with
the 10 November 2003 municipal elections across the province of
Ontario. In addition to these political contests, during 2004 the newly
created Conservative Party of Canada chose a leader on 20 March, a
federal election was held on 28 June, and the Alberta election took
place on 25 October.

The extent and nature of Internet usage in Canada suggest a possible
large payoff from political parties' and candidates' investment in websites and e-mail for online campaigning. The percentage of Canadians
who were regular Internet users in 2004 (63.41 per cent) was very close
to that in the United States (66.98 per cent) (Accenture 2004, 68), and
the percentage of Canadian Internet users who had ever visited an e-
government website (79 per cent) exceeded that of U.S. users (76 per
cent) (Accenture 2004, 104). However, the Canadian Election Survey
(CES),[2] a survey of Canadians' political attitudes and voting behaviour
in connection with the 2004 federal election, suggests that Canadians
did not make substantial use of the Internet compared to traditional
sources of election information. Respondents indicated that they got
most of their information about the election from television (52.2 per

Table 7.1
Internet use and general interest in politics

	Interest in politics (%)			
Internet use	Low	Medium	High	Total (%)
Low	96.9	90.7	81.6	88.9
Medium	1.9	6.2	10.1	6.5
High	1.2	3.1	8.3	4.6

N = 3840.
Source: 2004 Canadian Election Study.

Table 7.2
Internet use and interest in the 2004 federal election

	Interest in federal election (%)			
Internet use	Low	Medium	High	Total (%)
Low	98.4	93.5	81.7	88.9
Medium	1.1	5.2	9.8	6.5
High	0.4	1.2	8.5	4.6

N = 3842.
Source: 2004 Canadian Election Study.

cent), followed by newspapers (21.1 per cent), radio (11.7 per cent), family (4.7 per cent), friends (3.4 per cent), and, finally, the Internet (2.8 per cent).

The CES data in table 7.1 show that 8.3 per cent of respondents with a high interest in politics generally also paid a lot of attention to the Internet as a source of political information, compared to those with medium interest (3.1 per cent), or low interest (1.2 per cent). Almost 97 per cent of respondents with a low interest in politics also had little interest in using the Internet to obtain political information. Table 7.2 shows similar findings for the 2004 federal election in particular: 8.5 per cent of respondents with a high interest in the election paid a lot of attention to the election on the Internet, compared to 1.2 per cent of those with medium election interest, and 0.4 per cent of those with low election interest. Over 98 per cent of respondents with low interest in the election also paid little attention to the Internet as a source of election information.

There are several notable relationships between the characteristics of the respondents and their preferred source of information about the 2004 federal election. Table 7.3 shows the relative popularity of the

Table 7.3
Internet use and interest in the 2004 federal election, by age

Information source	Age				
	18–24	25–34	35–54	55+	Total (%)
Television	44.0	51.7	53.2	60.8	54.8
Radio	10.3	12.5	13.8	10.8	12.3
Newspapers	17.2	15.8	21.7	22.5	20.7
Internet	6.6	5.5	2.6	0.9	2.8
Friends/family/other	21.9	14.5	8.7	5.0	9.4

$N = 4220$.
Source: 2004 Canadian Election Study.

Internet for those persons in the 18–24 and 25–34 age categories (6.6 per cent and 5.5 per cent respectively), compared to those in the 35–54 and 55+ categories (2.6 per cent and 0.9 per cent respectively). These findings have implications for the audience to which political websites should be directed and, indeed, for the resources that parties should devote to websites as opposed to other sources of campaign information. Note for the 18–24 age group not only the relatively high Internet use but also the lower use of television and newspapers.

Political party officials and party website designers also need to assess the implications of such factors as education and income for media choice, and especially for website strategy and content. For example, table 7A (available at http://www.digitalstate.ca/supp/ch7.html) shows the diminishing importance of television and the increasing importance of the Internet and newspapers along the continuum from less than high school education to university graduation. Table 7B (available at http://www.digitalstate.ca/supp/ch7.html) suggests only a modest effect of higher incomes on Internet use for political purposes, but indicates the relative importance of radio and newspapers in the higher income brackets, and of television in the lowest income bracket. Finally, table 7C (available at http://www.digitalstate.ca/supp/ch7.html) breaks down intention to vote in the election by the respondent's preferred source of election information. A slightly higher percentage of those who are certain or likely to vote favour newspapers over television, radio, and the Internet.

The 2003–4 elections in Canada attracted unprecedented traffic to political party websites, but it is difficult to compare the extent of this traffic from one party to another. The number of daily 'unique visits' reported for three of the parties during the thirty-five-day federal campaign were 20,000 for the Conservatives, 15,000 for the Bloc Québécois (Bloc) and 8549 for the NDP (Nersessian 2004, 2). However, the NDP director of communications estimates that during the campaign the party's site received both more 'visits' (410,000 – about 11,700 daily) and more 'hits' (29 million) than during the entire year of 2003 (Lavigne 2004b). The Green Party site went from 10,000–100,000 daily hits in the immediate pre-election period to 500,000–1,300,000 daily hits during the campaign itself (Denis 2004). The Liberal Party webmaster has described 'hits' as an incorrect measurement and, instead, measured gigabytes of traffic: 180–200 GB of throughput for his party during the election period (Tierney 2004).[3]

Framework for Website Analysis

We turn now to an examination of the use of political websites for online campaigning. The analysis is divided into four categories: structure and navigation, information dissemination, mobilization of supporters, and interactivity. In the Canadian context, only limited data are available on some aspects of these categories, and it is risky to make predictions about the long-term impact of online campaigning. Even in the United States, where there is a large body of evidence on this subject, Michael Cornfield, an expert on online campaigns, concluded in 2004, 'It is still too early to mark any systematic or historical Net-related change in how Americans campaign and how they react and respond to campaigns' (2004, 199).

Website Design and Navigation

The beauty of a political website is to a large extent in the eye of the beholder. In addition, the range of beholders includes not only website designers and webmasters, but also communications directors and other party officials, the news media, party supporters, and site visitors in general. While there is considerable difference of opinion on the ideal design and navigation features of political websites, there is substantial agreement that certain fundamental features should be included and given a high profile. The home pages of national and provincial party sites normally contain a photograph of the leader and links to the leader's biography, the party's platform and policies, a 'Find Your Candidate' function, news and issues (including a 'What's New' link), a media page, donation and volunteer solicitations, and a

'Contact Us' invitation. Some sites include a search function, a site map and a blog section. The *location* of these features on the home page varies considerably from one party to another.

There are two broad models of website design. The *comprehensive* model provides a lot of information in relatively small fonts in a limited amount of space (for example, the Nunziata and Jakobek sites in the Toronto mayoralty election). The *portal* model uses larger fonts, empty space, and simple design to facilitate easy navigation to other pages (for example, the David Miller and John Tory sites in the same election). The Barbara Hall campaign used the comprehensive model for her main site but foreshadowed future approaches to online campaigning by permitting users of Internet-enabled cell phones and PDAs to switch to a text-only portal version of her site. In the federal election, the portal approach was taken by the Conservative site, which was widely praised for a clean uncluttered appearance that gave an impression of easy navigability. The Bloc site was decorative and colourful, but its comprehensive approach resulted in an extremely crowded home page that made it difficult for visitors to locate particular content links.

The priority for a home page is to create the right first impression. It must be aesthetically pleasing and must position important links to be clearly visible, making the site easy to navigate. The objectives are to encourage visitors to 'stick' or 'click through' –to go beyond the home page – and to enable them to do so by facilitating simple and rapid navigation from one page to another. Even a site's use of colour can affect the visitor's first impression and inclination to stick. One Web analyst noted that the federal NDP site, painted in bright orange and lime green, looks 'really bad' and 'the webmaster ... must be gnashing his teeth in frustration' (Richardson 2004). The party's director of communications explained that they 'wanted to use colours that help reinforce that the party has energy, that it's vibrant, fresh and new' (Lavigne 2004a). A common reason given for extensive use of graphics and a busy layout is to attract young voters. In the federal election, the Bloc home page provided a link entitled *'Interdit aux plus de 30 ans'* ('not for the over 30s') to a crowded Web page designed in part on the basis of focus groups with young people. A home page button – *'Écoutez la thème* – permitted visitors to see a group of young Bloc supporters singing the campaign's theme song.

The 2004 Federal Website Study, described above, showed that the central figure in website design for three of the parties was the webmaster, either working alone, with the communications director, or with more than one senior party official. The NDP site was designed by the party's advertising firm in consultation with the communications director. Compared to decisions on design, the parties' decisions on the initial content and on day-to-day changes in content were, in general, made by a broader range of party officials under the guidance of the communications director. Party leaders either provided occasional input or were simply kept informed of content decisions. The exception was the Green Party, where the party leader provided substantial input on content.

Political parties have become sensitive to the practical as well as the symbolic benefits of high-quality websites, both for the party as a whole and for individual politicians (Davis 1999, 15; Gibson, Nixon, and Ward 2003, 13). In Canada's 2003–4 elections, the parties often showed their website address on their television and newspaper advertisements. Many individual candidates included it on their campaign signs and brochures. During the federal campaign in particular, the news media ran several stories on the quality and content of political websites, including criticism of several incumbent politicians who neither had a site nor responded quickly to e-mail inquiries (Butters 2004). The Federal Website Study showed that all four parties conceptualized their website as a central component of their overall campaign strategy. The NDP reported, 'The website is an extension of the overall campaign. It is seen as a complementary component that adds, but does not replace, traditional aspects of political party campaigning. The look, feel and functionality of the site must be consistent and complementary to the overall campaign' (Lavigne 2004b). The Liberals reported that their website was one of the party's 'main communication tools. The website and mass emails were the key to a successful campaign. It was the reason we were able to release information as it came in' (Tierney 2004). Gibson and McAllister, on the basis of data drawn from the 2001 Australian Election Study, concluded that the use of political websites has a direct effect on the vote. They found that, except for the use of party workers, 'the overall importance of web utilization is about as important as all the conventional methods of election campaigning combined' (2003, 19).

In recent Canadian elections, there was considerable variation among politicians in the importance they attached to online campaigning and in the quality of their websites. In the Ontario election, 58 per cent of the candidates had a personal website,[4] with the Liberals at 89 per cent and the PCs and NDP at 45 per cent. A higher percentage of

Liberal candidate sites allowed donations to be made (76 per cent, compared to 49 per cent for the PCs and 36 per cent for the NDP) and provided sign-ups for volunteering (82 per cent, compared to 60 per cent for the PCs and 48 per cent for the NDP). Biographies were posted on 97 per cent of the candidate sites.

In the federal election, outside Quebec, most of the major party candidates had a personal website (85.19 per cent). The Bloc had no candidates outside Quebec. Within Quebec, only 13.33 per cent of Bloc candidates had a personal site. Only a few candidates of the other major parties had a personal site in that province. No NDP candidates in Quebec had personal sites, but the main party site provided links to a 'cookie-cutter' site for each candidate, that is, a site containing the candidate's biography set within the common elements provided by the central party organization to all of its candidates. The NDP communications director explained that the party

> provided a common local candidate web site template. Candidates were informed that links to the main site would be established for template sites or sites that were consistent in look. All messaging on template web sites that did not conform to the overall campaign messaging were removed immediately. The templates gave central control over local candidates' web sites, while permitting for local content. (Lavigne 2004b)

The other parties were much less committed to a common look and feel for the candidate sites.

The reason for the paucity of personal candidate websites in Quebec appears to be that individual candidates created and paid for their own sites. Candidates outside Quebec had more resources for this purpose than those inside the province. The NDP communications director explained that it was a resource versus a non-resource item, rather than a Quebec versus a non-Quebec one (Lavigne 2004b).

Table 7.4 shows the content of the individual candidates' sites for each of the major parties during the federal election. The most common elements of the sites, in order of the frequency of their inclusion, were contact information, the candidate's biography, an opportunity to volunteer or to obtain a lawn sign, information on a candidate's policies or positions, local news coverage of the candidate, and requests for donations. Updated press releases, photo galleries, and electronic newsletters appeared on roughly one-third of the sites. A little more than 10 per cent of the sites contained candidate endorsements.

Table 7.4
Content of candidate websites by party (2004 Canadian federal election)*

	Liberal		Conservative		NDP		Bloc	
	N	%	N	%	N	%	N	%
Candidates with personal site	187	80.3	180	77.3	203	98.0	10	13.3
Website content								
Contact information	184	98.4	174	96.7	202	99.5	8	80.0
Candidates' biography	183	97.9	175	97.2	182	89.7	8	80.0
Volunteering/lawn signs	141	75.4	132	73.3	193	95.1	3	30.0
Policies/positions	161	86.1	157	87.2	113	55.7	1	10.0
Local news events	145	77.5	113	62.8	89	43.8	5	50.0
Donations	66	35.3	87	48.3	154	75.9	0	0.0
Updated press releases	110	58.8	108	60.0	7	3.5	1	10.0
Photo gallery	118	63.1	71	39.4	16	7.9	4	40.0
Electronic newsletter	20	10.7	21	11.7	143	70.4	0	0.0
Endorsements	20	10.7	24	13.3	15	7.4	1	10.0
Bilingual option	18	9.6	8	4.4	22	10.8	0	0.0

Source: Examination of websites of individual candidates in 2004 Canadian federal election.
*The numbers for the three national parties are based on ridings outside Quebec.

Table 7.5
Importance of information technology in the last election

Response	MPs		MPPs	
	2003	2005	2003	2005
Not at all (%)	4.6	6.2	2.2	3.2
Of minor importance (%)	29.2	12.3	31.1	16.1
Somewhat important (%)	41.5	38.3	42.2	32.3
Important (%)	24.6	27.2	15.6	29.0
Highly important (%)	—	16.0	8.9	19.4
N	65	81	45	61

Note: The 2003 MP survey did not include a 'highly important' category.
Sources: 2003 MP survey, Kernaghan, Riehle, and Lo 2003; 2005 MP survey; 2003 Ontario MPP survey; 2005 Ontario MPP survey

Slightly fewer than 10 per cent provided bilingual coverage. There were substantial variations among the four parties in several website components, including policy/position statements, local news events, and requests for donations. A much smaller percentage of sites included such other components as a media section, coverage in languages other than French and English, the use of cookies, a riding map, polling information, a discussion group, an opinion poll, a blog, community Web links, a question and answer section, speeches, and television advertisements. While many of the candidate sites amounted to little more than electronic campaign brochures, a substantial number of them did go beyond the traditional campaign literature by providing such material as updated press releases, local news coverage, and electronic newsletters.

As depicted in table 7.5, the importance of IT for both federal MPs and Ontario MPPs in their last election increased substantially, with twice as many MPPs saying that IT was either important or highly important in 2005, compared to 2003.

When asked about the importance of IT by the time of their next election, MPs and MPPs both placed the greatest importance on the use of IT for building electronic databases, followed by voter registration/targeting, online campaigning, and online fundraising (table 7.6). For MPPs, the utilization rate for databases was almost 97 per cent. Aside from database use, there was little change in the importance that MPs attached to these online campaign activities, but MPPs envisaged considerably greater use of online campaigning and especially of online fundraising.

Table 7.6
Areas of importance by the next election

	MPs		MPPs	
	2003	2005	2003	2005
Voter registration/targeting (%)	63.6	57.3	66.7	71.0
Electronic databases (%)	72.7	85.0	95.6	96.8
Online fundraising (%)	28.8	28.8	20.0	41.9
Online campaigning (%)	48.5	51.3	44.4	55.7
N	66	82	45	62

Sources: 2003 MP survey, Kernaghan, Riehle, and Lo 2003; 2005 MP survey; 2003
Ontario MPP survey; 2005 Ontario MPP survey

Information Dissemination

The dissemination of information to political actors is the core function
of political websites. The layout and navigation features discussed
above are designed to facilitate the provision and diffusion of information about parties and candidates, their platforms and policies. Four
main questions provide a framework for examining information dissemination: What information? Information for whom? Dissemination
by whom? Dissemination by what means?

What Information?

We have noted that political party websites are quite similar in their
general content: they share several basic features and they highlight
these features on their home page. Among the most important content
features are leader and candidate profiles, itineraries and contact
points, platform and policy documents, press releases, advertisements,
and volunteer and donation links. Websites can differ enormously in
the relative emphasis placed on each feature and on the manner in
which the content is presented. In Manitoba, compared to elections in
other jurisdictions, the information on the three party websites was
sparse, even on party platforms. One party posted its full platform,
another posted only part of its platform, and still another posted neither the party platform nor even a detailed biography of the leader. By
way of contrast, in the Nova Scotia election, the Liberal and PC parties
published forty- and fifty-six-page platform documents respectively,
and the NDP, which had been criticized in the previous election for an

overly complex platform document, adopted a new approach of focusing on seven key commitments, each of which was elaborated in four hundred to five hundred words.

In general, the party websites for the 2003 Ontario election were considerably more comprehensive and expansive in their content than those for the other provincial elections held that year. Especially notable were the websites of each Liberal candidate. They shared a common integrated framework with all other candidate sites and also contained a boundary map and a demographic outline of the riding. In comparison, only five NDP candidates had personal websites linked to the central party site. The Liberal site permitted the party platform to be downloaded in five separate modules, each of which focused on a major policy area, unlike the NDP site, which required that the whole platform be downloaded (interview with Helen Burstyn, policy and platform chair, Ontario Liberal Party, 28 November 2003).

In the federal election, all party websites had substantially the same content in the form of candidate biographies, platform documents, and press releases. It is notable that the Bloc site contained descriptions for almost all candidates in a standard résumé format; very few Bloc candidates had a personal website. The Liberal and Conservative sites, in addition to highlighting a 'Candidate of the Day' on their main page, also highlighted a 'Volunteer of the Day' to encourage site visitors to volunteer. All parties had a page focusing on key platform promises and provided a copy of their entire platform. Press releases were updated daily and were used to respond to press releases from other parties. One notable flurry of press releases debated the public comments of Bono, U2's lead singer, who praised Prime Minister Martin for his work with third world countries. Beyond the standard fare, the Liberal website included answers to various FAQs about the election process (for example, 'What do MPs and Senators do?'), as well as the complete text of several of Mr Martin's speeches. Both Mr Martin and Stephen Harper, the Conservative leader, also included a daily blog, although Harper's blog was usually very succinct (for example, a fifty-word summary of the day's events). On the NDP site, leader Jack Layton's new book, *Speaking Out*, was prominently featured. Each party also provided links to websites operated by party associations, such as the party's youth wing, and to attack sites, discussed below.

According to party officials, the most popular parts of the websites during the federal election were the party platform, the video advertisements, and the 'Find Your Local Candidate' section. Also very popular for the NDP was the 'Ed's Back' video – a rapper-like presentation by a former leader of the federal NDP who returned to active politics.

Information for Whom?

There is a close connection between the choice of website content and the audience that the parties and candidates want to influence. The foregoing discussion indicates that the main audiences targeted by political websites are individual voters and the news media. The Ontario NDP described its site as being 'designed for the navigational ease of general users and media.' More specifically, its stated purposes were to

- provide a vehicle for showcasing the party platform
- provide information by topic to users
- convey daily updates and background research to candidates
- post daily itineraries, photos, and news releases
- encourage action and involvement in the party and the election (interview with Sheila White, communications director, Ontario NDP, 19 November 2003)

There is no consensus in the Canadian context on whether a site should be designed to influence individual voters who are already supporters of that site's party or candidate, or an effort should be made to attract and persuade the 'floating voter.' Expert opinion in the United States suggests that political websites should devote much more time, energy, and site space to reinforcing the support of their current or probable supporters than to wooing uncommitted voters or those committed to other parties (Bimber and Davis 2003, 144–5; Cornfield and Rainie 2003, 14–15, 22–3). The last two groups are unlikely even to visit the website. Moreover, Gibson and McAllister found for the 2001 Australian election that the value of a political website lay in giving the candidate a profile with the media and opinion leaders rather than in attracting voters to the site and changing their vote (2003, 20).

In the Ontario election, the Liberal website was aimed more at undecided than decided voters, but party officials 'went after a number of different segments (including women, youth and ethnic communities)' that research indicated 'were responsive to the change message and the Liberal brand' (Burstyn 2003). For the NDP, the main target was youth: 'Young people expect to see a website and, like any technophile, will not become engaged in politics unless one is provided' (White 2004). Websites are often designed to influence not only the general voter but also particular segments of voters. The home pages of some party sites, for example, provide links to pages – or even separate sites – aimed at such specialized audiences as youth and the elderly. During the federal election, the Bloc had a youth site, a seniors' site, and an 'assembly of the citizens' site linked to the main Bloc site but containing substantially different content.

Much of the information provided for individual voters is also useful for the media. However, most sophisticated websites – especially central party sites – make special provision for disseminating information to the news media in such forms as policy statements and press releases. The hope is to influence voters indirectly by persuading journalists to transmit this information to the general public.

Both on their media page and their home page, political parties often provide information in the form of press releases and online versions of television advertisements that are critical of their opponents. This material is supplementary to and often similar to television and radio 'attack ads' that are associated with the general phenomenon of negative campaigning. Early in the campaign, the parties tended to minimize attack material on their official websites and to run the attacks on separate sites. As the campaign moved into its final stages, attacks became a central feature of the party sites. The federal Liberal website included a set of thirty-second television advertisements that reflected the heavy use of negative advertising during the Liberal campaign as their polling numbers dropped.

The increase in number and virulence of negative press releases after the leaders' debate has become a regular feature of election campaigns. In the federal campaign there was an escalation of critical comments about the Conservatives by the Liberals and the NDP immediately following the leaders' debate and the widespread assertion that the Conservative leader had won. The NDP communications director explained that their strategy 'was to post our response as quickly as possible on debate nights. The speed with which our analysis was posted ... was paramount' (Lavigne 2004b). During the Quebec election, the morning after the leaders' debate, all three parties criticized one another openly on their respective home pages. The Liberal Party attacked the PQ for mismanaging public finances and the ADQ leader for abdicating his responsibilities. The success of the Liberal leader in winning the debate was widely ascribed to his use of an unsubstanti-

ated article from the Internet citing recent comments by former premier and PQ leader Jacques Parizeau, in which he blamed the 1995
sovereigntist defeat on 'money and the ethnic vote.' The current premier, PQ leader Bernard Landry, who had not been briefed by his staff
on the Parizeau story, appeared surprised by the reference and thus
out of touch.

While the four main federal parties all engaged in negative campaigning, the Liberals were generally credited with having the greatest
success in influencing voters' intentions. Liberal Party strategists
claimed that their television advertisements portraying the Conservatives as warmongers and anti-abortionists turned the campaign
around by heightening voters' concerns about the Conservative leader
(Winsor 2004). These advertisements were replicated on the Liberal
website, but it was likely that relatively few undecided voters sought
them out there compared to those who saw the televised version. The
2004 CES election data show that Canadians obtained little of their
election information from party websites, compared to television.

The Website studies showed that, in general, party officials found
their sites to be an effective medium for attacks on – or at least criticism
of – other parties and their leaders. The federal NDP described its site
as 'an excellent medium' for this purpose in that the medium 'is
quickly adaptive and allows for creativity at very low cost' (Lavigne
2004b). The Ontario NDP noted that while their online news releases
criticized the positions and claims of other parties, they preferred Canada News Wire for quick response and attack (White 2003). The Green
Party said that websites 'may be an effective medium for attacks,' but
'we wouldn't know as we aren't really interested in attacking other
parties or their leaders, just criticizing their policies and records while
advocating and defending our own' (Denis 2004). The Liberal webmaster said that he 'would not consider them necessarily attacks, but more
"reality checks." We were the first party during the campaign to add a
reality check section to the website. This was one of the key areas in the
site. The basics of it are another party leader makes a statement to the
press, and if it is not correct we would put up the "reality check" and
blast an email out to the media' (Tierney 2004).

Dissemination by Whom?

Aside from the mainline political parties discussed above, the three
other prime sources of information on election campaigns are minor or

fringe parties, separate groups often described as 'third parties,' and the news media. The media serve as both an audience for information posted on websites and a major channel for disseminating that information.

The Internet has been widely touted as a vehicle for enhancing democratic participation in general and the visibility of minor or fringe political parties in particular. Cyber-optimists argue that the Internet enables these parties to spread their message despite the absence of substantial media coverage and thereby helps to level the playing field for political parties. Many experts on electronic democracy, however, are pessimistic that the Internet will be of significant benefit to these parties compared to the larger, usually wealthier, and longer-established major parties. The federal election offers mixed evidence on this point. In addition to the main parties, eight other parties ran candidates and had websites: the Canadian Action Party, the Christian Heritage Party, the Communist Party, the Libertarian Party, the Marijuana Party, the Marxist-Leninist Party, the Progressive Canadian Party, and the Green Party. The first seven of these parties received negligible media coverage, and their websites were generally ignored. Taken together, these parties attracted a little more than 1 per cent of the total vote.

However, the Green Party, which moved as high as 7 per cent of the vote in election polls, ran candidates in every riding and received over 4 per cent in the election itself. While the party was not included in the televised leaders' debate, it received a substantial amount of media publicity, including references to its website that, according to party sources, received an unexpectedly large number of hits (Howell 2004). Newspaper stories included 'Web helps Green party gain political ground' and 'Greens cotton on to Web's populist power.' The party's leader noted that millions of people were going to bypass the media to visit the Green website 'because the media isn't giving equitable coverage, and they are going direct to the source' (Howell 2004). The party reportedly received almost half of its campaign funds through its website (Lin 2004). Table 7.7 shows the party for which survey respondents intended to vote, according to the extent of their Internet use for political information. There is a striking relationship between high Internet attention and the intention to vote for the Green Party: 13 per cent compared to 5.7 per cent for the Liberals, 5.1 per cent for the Conservatives, 6.8 per cent for the NDP, and 2.5 per cent for the Bloc Québécois.

'External' or 'third-party' sites have become increasingly numerous

Table 7.7
Internet usage and party vote intention

Internet use	Liberal (%)	Conservative (%)	NDP (%)	Bloc Québécois (%)	Green (%)	Other (%)	Don't know/ Refused (%)	Total (%)
Low	86.8	87.6	85.3	91.0	82.7	89.0	92.8	88.9
Medium	7.6	7.3	7.9	6.5	3.0	2.7	4.8	6.5
High	5.7	5.1	6.8	2.5	13.3	8.2	2.4	4.6

N = 3797.
Source: 2004 Canadian Election Study.

and prominent in disseminating information during Canada's online political campaigns. These sites are separate from partisan political sites and are usually run by organizations rather than individuals. The sites may simply offer factual information related to the campaign. They may provide both factual information and election analysis. They may represent particular groups and interests within the election context. Alternatively, they may attack one or more political parties, leaders, or candidates. Each of these categories is discussed in turn.

The Elections Canada website (http://www.elections.ca) is an excellent example of the first category, *factual campaign information*. This impressive site supplied detailed information on such matters as the registration of electors, electoral law and policy, election financing, electoral districts, and past election results. The site was organized by sub-pages specific to voters, young voters, the media, political parties, candidates, and others. The Youth site was particularly innovative, going far beyond typical educational resources to offer various election-oriented games, including election trivia, election crossword puzzles, and 'circle-a-word' election games. Although the actual impact of these games is likely minimal, they do attempt to leverage the Internet's capability as an interactive medium in an innovative fashion.

There was also a large number of election 'portal' sites with the primary purpose of collating links to election websites and news articles. Two notable examples of such sites are Canadian Political Parties (http://home.ican.net/~alexng/can.html) and Canada 2004 (http://www.nodice.ca/election2004).

In the second category of external sites, election *information and analysis*, the news media are the main actors. Almost every print and broadcast media website included a special section on the 2004 federal election. CTV, the CBC, and the Globe and Mail sites stand out for their depth of coverage and their use of the Internet's interactive capabilities. For example, CTV had a main page that featured links to election-related stories in user-friendly text and video formats. There was a large amount of content beyond simple coverage of election events, including extensive documentation on the Ipsos-Reid polls. A CTV mobile news bus followed the leaders, and the main site had a link to the 'Bus' sub-site. The 'Issues' section contained a point-by-point comparison of the election platforms of the major parties on sixteen major issues. Profiles of the leaders, links to party websites, and archived videos were also provided. On election night, this site not only showed the results as they were announced, but also allowed the results to be broken down geographically, included a list of notable winners and losers, and provided a photo gallery, historical information on minority governments, and free access to streaming video of CTV's television coverage.

A large number of online media polls were conducted on election matters. Media sites included such questions as 'Which group of election issues should take priority? National security and tax cuts or health care and social programs?' (http://www.nationalpost.ca); 'How much do election promises influence your vote?' (http://www.ckco.ca).

The third category of external sites involved in information dissemination is a very large one that can usefully be divided into two subcategories: sites targeting *broad segments of society* (such as youth, seniors) and sites hosted by specific *interest groups*. A large number of sites during the federal campaign were dedicated solely to mobilizing the youth vote.

- *Rush the Vote* (http://www.rushthevote.ca/), a site sponsored by a non-profit organization to foster political awareness among Canadian youth through art, music, and education, provided a program that included a series of 'Rush the Vote' concerts held during the election. This bilingual site was heavily animated with the use of Flash and background music to create a youthful feel.
- *Student Vote 2004* (http://www.studentvote2004.ca/) involved high-school students in the democratic process in an innovative way. Elementary schools registered online to receive non-partisan instructional materials for use in classes. On election day, schools received election kits containing ballots and ballot boxes to allow them to hold a mock election in their 'riding.' On election night, the CBC

website published the results. Two hundred and sixty-five thousand students participated.

- *Great Canadian Job Interview* (http://www.jobinterview.ca) offered a bilingual, non-partisan televised forum with Canada's federal party leaders, broadcast live on CBC Newsworld. Young Canadians aged 18–34 were encouraged to submit questions online at the website, which were then posed to the candidates.

The websites of many special *interest groups* had some election-oriented content, ranging from a simple press release to substantial election coverage. The sites of groups in the latter category had very similar content features: daily news, analysis of party platforms on issues relevant to the group's concerns, an electronic newsletter, a media section with links to articles and videos, information on how to vote, and a discussion board. Such diverse organizations as the Canadian Islamic Congress, the Arthritis Society of Canada, and the United Church of Canada set out their election concerns on their websites. The website of the Canadian Union of Public Employees focused primarily on providing information in support of public services. The site featured daily news commentary, an e-mail newsletter, campaign materials such as downloadable posters, candidate responses to 'Questions of the Day,' and a list of reasons not to vote Liberal or Conservative.

The final category of external sites, *attack sites*, includes those created specifically to criticize and undermine particular parties, candidates, or ideologies. Some of the sites were linked to the main party sites, but others operated outside of official party sanction and control. In the Ontario election, the Liberal and NDP sites provided formal links to several anti-PC sites. The sites linked by the NDP included the Ontario Electricity Coalition, Ontario Tenants, Trust Me: A Chronicle of Ernie Eves and His Tory Contortions, and Tom Tomorrow comics (a satire on Conservative policy). Another anti-PC site, to which neither the Liberal nor New Democratic party sites provided a link, was that of the Ontario Secondary School Teachers Federation (OSSTF).

During the federal election, a 'humorous' site entitled 'Whack the PM!'. (http://www.whackthepm.com/whack.html) attacked all the party leaders in a roughly even-handed manner. The use of humour to make a political point is more common on third-party sites than on political-party sites. Posting humorous content on a party site can generate substantial traffic, but it is risky because it can elicit groans as well as laughs. For example, opinion was likely to be divided on the effectiveness during the Nova Scotia election of the premier's weekly top-10 list dealing with such topics as 'John Hamm's Top 10 Fun Things To Do with Lawn Signs after the Campaign.' A safer approach is to disseminate humorous messages by e-mailing them to one's supporters, or including them in blogs, rather than featuring them on the home page.

Dissemination by What Means?

Among the major means of disseminating information are the use of multimedia (text, photographs, graphics, video, audio, and Flash animation), Intranet sites, multi-lingual sites, e-mail messages, and blogs. Each of these approaches is discussed in turn.

Most party sites have a multimedia link on their home page to facilitate easy access, especially by the news media, to material that could be used to advance the party's electoral fortunes. In the Manitoba election, the PC Party made extensive use of multimedia tools, including twelve photographs, four radio clips, five television advertisements, and nine televised speeches, in addition to hundreds of campaign pictures from the daily log. Providing multimedia access to information, especially in the form of videos and Flash animation, slows the loading and navigation process and can be particularly irritating for visitors relying on dial-up rather than broadband access to the Internet. Flash animation can be effective if used sparingly – as on the Conservative Party home page for the federal election in which the campaign theme 'Demand Better' was followed by flashing and changing tag lines such as 'Vote Conservative' and 'Tax Relief.'

In addition to serving the information needs of individual voters and the news media, political parties provide campaign information to party officials and party workers on *intra*net sites. These password-protected sites constitute an online toolkit for party activists by providing information intended for candidates and supporters who are involved in the campaign. The sites are geared to helping party workers attract support for their local candidates, reinforce the commitment of supporters, and get out the vote. Typically, the sites contain campaign materials (for example, letterhead, leaflets), fundraising guidelines, as well as an election-day manual and 'talking points' on campaign issues. The NDP site contained talking points on more than a dozen issues, including advice on the question of whether the NDP would prop up a Conservative minority government.

Another effective means of disseminating information is to make the website available in more than one language. The need for this service varies from one jurisdiction to another. The Nova Scotia parties provided only English; the PC Party was the only Manitoba party to provide both languages; and the New Brunswick, Quebec, and federal parties (except for the Bloc in the federal election) made their sites available in both official languages. In Ontario, the Liberal and PC parties reached out to minority communities by providing summaries of their platforms in several languages other than English or French. The PCs' summaries appeared in fifteen languages.

During the federal election, the Liberals, Conservatives, and NDP provided their main site in both English and French. The Bloc site was available only in French, except for the party platform, which was provided in both languages. There were problems with unintended impressions of tokenism. The party sites with bilingual content appeared to have been created as English-language sites that were then translated into French. For example, the French version of the Liberal multimedia site had videos in English, without subtitles, and all of the advertisements were in English. The parties did little to tailor the content and strategy used for their English sites to appeal to a French audience.

An extremely important means of disseminating information is collecting e-mail addresses of committed and potential supporters through the website and then using those addresses to send e-mail messages. A U.S. expert who argued that e-mail is the single most valuable channel of communication for online campaigners noted, 'Where politics is concerned, a flimsy e-mail list will outperform a sterling Web site ninety-nine days out of one hundred; the hundredth day being an event like the day after a leaders' debate' (Cornfield 2004, 26). The CES data on the 2004 Canadian election show that the extent of e-mail contacts with voters was small compared to the traditional modes of contact. Table 7D (available at http://www.digitalstate.ca/supp/ch7.html) shows that 2.4 per cent of the respondents had been contacted during the campaign by a political party by e-mail, compared to 23.9 per cent by phone, 14.4 per cent in person, and 42.8 per cent by regular mail.

Most political websites have at least one mechanism to obtain the e-mail addresses of site visitors. The resulting e-mail list can then be used to disseminate information to targeted audiences for such purposes as responding to attack ads, reinforcing voter support, and getting out the vote. The federal NDP had a dedicated staff person to track all incoming messages and send them on to the appropriate party official. 'E-mails from members of the public were treated as very, very important. Response time was vital' (Lavigne 2004b). In the federal election, all four major parties had a highly visible home page feature inviting visitors to provide their e-mail addresses to obtain the party's newsletter. The newsletters took the form of e-mail messages highlighting the parties' virtues and their opponents' deficiencies. Creating a specific e-mail list of media outlets is also extremely important in that it enables campaign officials to communicate their message to journalists both more quickly and less expensively than through telephone or fax messages.

During the federal campaign, many candidates, party officials, and journalists made frequent and effective use of text messaging through PDAs, especially the BlackBerry, to communicate quickly with one another. A duel of press releases over the NDP leader's comment about the Liberal leader killing the homeless by cutting the budget was conducted over BlackBerrys. The equally controversial Conservative press release entitled 'Paul Martin Supports Child Pornography?' arrived on the BlackBerrys of journalists, who then rapidly disseminated both the original release and the responses to it from other parties.

Information, in the form of facts, analysis, and opinion, is increasingly disseminated through blogs. BlogsCanada (http://www.Blogs Canada.ca), a site created by Jim Elve of Waterford, ON, supports Canadians wishing to send and receive information and ideas on a wide variety of topics. Most political blogs are written by non-candidates. At the time of the federal election, the BlogsCanada website listed fifty-nine political blogs. A few of these were written by journalists (for example, Paul Wells of *Maclean's*, Andrew Coyne of the *National Post*), but most were created by a disparate group of people and carried such intriguing titles as 'Ranting and Roaring,' 'The Armchair Garbageman,' 'Small Dead Animals,' and, to be expected, 'My Blahg.' Bloggers emerged as significant actors during the U.S. presidential campaign, leading to competition and criticism between bloggers and mainline journalists. A selected group of bloggers was permitted to attend – and blog – the Democratic and Republican conventions, and political bloggers were credited with exposing as fakes the CBS-reported documents on President Bush's military service.

While blogging has had a much lower profile in Canadian elections, the websites of several party leaders and a small number of individual candidates contained blogs. Most of these blogs were poorly devel-

Table 7.8
Advertising preferences ranked

Rank	MPs		MPPs	
	2003	2005	2003	2005
1	Personal meetings/rallies	Personal meetings/rallies	Personal meetings/rallies	Personal meetings/ rallies
2	Newsletters/householders	Lawn signs	Lawn signs	Lawn signs
3	Print media	Direct mail	Direct mail	Direct mail
4	Television advertising	Print media	Radio messages	Radio messages
5	Websites	Websites	Print media	Print media
6	E-mail and e-mail lists	Radio	E-mail and e-mail lists	E-mail and e-mail lists
7	Radio	E-mail and e-mail lists	Websites	Websites
8	Outdoor advertising	Television	Television	Television

Note: Newsletters/householders asked only in the 2003 survey.
Sources: 2003 MP survey, Kernaghan, Riehle, and Lo 2003; 2005 MP survey; 2003 Ontario MPP survey; 2005 Ontario MPP survey.

oped and managed, but they at least signalled politicians' awareness of the potential value of this new campaign technique. Blogs can be especially effective in reaching young voters. However, they risk alienating these voters if they are used largely as another form of press release, replete with political spin and rhetoric (such as the blog on the federal Conservative site) rather than personal musings and reflections.

None of the blogs on the main party sites during the federal election permitted the posting of comments – a practice that can involve a genuine and mutually beneficial exchange of views but that can also be manipulated by party supporters and party critics. Jack Layton, the NDP leader, wrote a regularly updated diary containing personal musings on the election. Paul Martin's personalized blog on the Liberal site was not updated from October 2003, when it was used during the Liberal leadership convention. Stephen Harper's blog on the Conservative site was an anonymously written and succinct summary of the day's events. Notable among the individual candidates' sites were the personalized blogs of the NDP's Ed Broadbent, who observed that blogging 'engages people in the computer age in a way they would not otherwise have been engaged' (Broadbent 2004).

It is important to examine the use of websites and e-mail in relation to other campaign techniques. Table 7.8 shows the ranking attached to these techniques by individual federal MPs (not by parties) for 2002 and 2005. There is a striking difference between the relative value of these techniques to MPs and the evidence in table 7.3 on the main sources of election information for Canadians. While television, radio, and newspapers rank highly as sources of political information, individual politicians favour the use of such techniques as personal meetings and rallies, newsletters/householders, and lawn signs. The importance of television advertising, e-mail, and e-mail lists declined between 2003 and 2005.

Mobilizing Supporters

The means used to disseminate information can also be used for *mobilization* in the broad sense of recruiting volunteers, obtaining financial contributions, reinforcing voter support, and getting out the vote (GOTV). While these functions are performed largely through traditional campaign techniques such as direct mailing, canvassing, and telephoning, the Internet has become an integral part of mobilization. Enabling online volunteering and donations can, for example, be an effective means of identifying supporters – and their e-mail addresses – for GOTV.

The home pages of most party and candidate websites feature highly visible links inviting visitors to assist the campaign through voluntary work or financial contributions. Some jurisdictions and some parties are more advanced than others in their mobilization efforts. In the New Brunswick campaign, all parties accepted online donations, but none provided an online option for volunteering. In the Manitoba campaign, all parties solicited both volunteers and money, but the NDP site made more elaborate provision for seeking volunteers. Only the Liberal site facilitated 'cyber volunteering' by providing users with a 'Tell a Friend' option and the opportunity to print campaign buttons via an e-Media tab. In the federal election, all parties provided means for supporters to campaign online. The NDP site had the most extensive set of e-campaigning functions: it allowed supporters to collect pledges and to forward e-mails to friends, and news clippings and press releases to potential supporters.

The Ontario and federal campaigns were comparatively sophisticated in their online mobilization efforts. In the Ontario campaign, all three major parties offered several opportunities for participation, whether through 'live events' – the traditional campaign activities – or by electronic means. The NDP recruited volunteers with a simple request for basic contact information and an indication of interest in telephoning, policy development, riding association participation, election-day assistance, and fundraising. The PCs requested much more detailed information, including language fluency and dates and times of availability, and outlined more specific options such as canvassing, joining the youth team, entering data, and delivering lawn signs. In the federal campaign, the Liberal and Conservative websites contained a picture and profile of a 'Volunteer of the Day.'

Motivated in part by Howard Dean's success in raising millions of dollars online in the months preceding the Ontario election, all three parties solicited online contributions. All parties also solicited funds by selling party memberships online. The PC Party site offered an innovative 'Cornerstone Club' membership package for $500, which provided exclusive access to the leader at social events. The site also offered an online 'Tuck Shop' in which supporters could purchase PC-branded memorabilia such as shirts and coffee mugs.

In the federal campaign, all party websites allowed visitors to purchase party memberships and make donations. In all cases, party memberships simply required responses to a basic set of personal questions, accompanied by payment by credit card. All parties included information on tax credits for political contributions. Here the similarities ended. Only the Bloc site had a server security certificate (from GeoTrust). Only the NDP permitted donations by cheque and the option of making monthly donations. Only the Liberals required contributors to indicate that they were at least eighteen years old, were citizens or permanent residents, and were paying with a personal rather than a corporate credit card. While hard data on the cost of creating and maintaining websites and on the amount of funds raised are scarce, the federal NDP has noted that it cost $100,000 to build and maintain its site and $2000 to host it for the election period. During the campaign, the party raised $158,000 online and attracted an unspecified number of volunteers (Lavigne 2004b).

All political websites are designed in part to reinforce the party's or candidate's appeal to current or likely supporters. Obtaining supporters' e-mail addresses is important to reinforcing the vote through newsletters, providing information and requesting volunteers and donations. These addresses are also important for GOTV. The day before the federal election, the NDP sent a letter from its leader to all 'friends' of the party emphasizing the critical need, especially in such a close election, to translate support into votes. Readers were invited not only to vote, but also to take friends and family members to the polls with them, and to work with the local campaign office to get people to the polls (Layton 2004). Near the end of the Ontario election, then premier Ernie Eves sent a personal e-mail message seeking support – in the form of votes, volunteer work, and donations – to 55,000 people (according to PC party officials) or as many as a million and a half people (according to Liberal sources) (Smith 2003). The fact that the message was sent to many people who were not PC supporters illustrates the potentially counterproductive nature of unsolicited e-mail messages that some recipients may view as political spam.

The Federal Website Study revealed that the party sites were used to capture such information about site visitors as IP addresses, language preferences and postal codes, the number of visitors, the number of page views, and to what extent various pages were being accessed. In accordance with the parties' privacy policies for website usage, no personal information was collected.

Interactivity

Website interactivity is important both for disseminating information and mobilizing support. Reference has already been made to means by which voters, party and candidate supporters, and the media can interact with political websites. Among these means are e-mail LISTSERVs, online donations, volunteer signups, blogs, and downloadable video clips (online versions of television advertisements).

Bimber and Davis (2004, 27) note that during the 2000 U.S. elections, interactivity was more illusory than real in that voters could send e-mail messages to candidates, but responses were uncommon. In recent Canadian elections, not only were such exchanges rare but so was the use of bulletin board postings, chat rooms, and virtual town hall meetings where voters and candidates could interact and where voters could exchange views. In the United States, however, the approach of the Dean campaign described above and the 2003–4 initiatives of the Bush and Kerry campaigns show a vigorous movement in the direction of much greater website interactivity. Their sites facilitated meetups of their supporters and provided campaign blogs. In addition, they 'offer[ed] videos free of TV news producers. They enlist[ed] allies in petition-writing skirmishes on issues of the candidates' choosing. And ... they also ask[ed] for cash' (Information Week 2003).

Although Canadian websites, especially when compared to those in the United States, are not very interactive, there has been evidence in recent campaigns of greater emphasis on interactivity and even some use of open-source politics. In the federal election, the New Democratic Party had an 'e-Campaigner' tab on the home page inviting visitors to 'join the NDP e-Campaign today and we'll start you off running for your own personal online campaign to collect pledges and rally support for the NDP.' The e-Campaign Web page contained a letter from the party leader describing the e-Campaign as 'Canada's first online election community that puts you in charge of your own personal campaign to raise money and bring new voters.' In the Ontario election, the Liberal site had an e-Campaign feature that enabled volunteers to create their own mailing lists and then to mail out material drawn from an inventory.

The use of e-mail has become an increasingly common campaign instrument. During the federal campaign, all party sites contained feedback forms inviting visitors to send electronic messages to the parties, and a subscription service for electronic newsletters. These newsletters exploited the Internet's multimedia capabilities by sending not only text messages but also pictures and links to sites and articles. The Liberal website, in addition to its electronic newsletter, invited visitors to subscribe to *Newswatcher*, a news e-mail service that forwarded media articles to subscribers at no charge. All party sites included a function allowing visitors to provide comments or ask questions. Among the most publicized of these was the Youth Text initiative, which allowed youth to engage in two-way text messaging with the party headquarters of different political parties. All party websites contained Youth Text Web links. The Conservative site promised that a response to questions or comments sent to the party leader by text messaging would be sent to the sender's cell phone within forty-eight hours.

The use of political meetups in Canada has been insignificant, both in numbers and impact, in comparison with that of the United States. The CEO of Meetup.com announced that in the United States, meetups would be created by early 2004 for every candidate in approximately five hundred races at the presidential, Senate, House, and gubernatorial levels ('Capitol Advantage and Meetup.com,' clift@publicus.net, 18 December 2003). In the Canadian federal campaign, Meetup.com was not linked to the main site of any of the parties, though it was used to set up some meetings of the party faithful. Meetups received little media attention, with the exception of a Bloc adaptation of the meetup concept called 'Rendez-vous.' A prominent section of the party's home page invited young supporters to get together on 2 June in seven locations across Quebec for informal meetings – 'Échanger et prendre une bière' ('To chat and have a beer').

During the 2003 Conservative leadership campaign, an independent third-party site called Torydraft featured two controversial interactive features. The first was the use of online 'unscientific' polls on matters of interest to the conservative movement in Canada, including voter intentions on the leadership contest. The second feature was a 'News and Gossip' section that posted not only news on the leadership candidates but also gossip items about them for which the source was not always clear.

Online interactivity in the narrow sense of direct two-way communication between a voter and a party or candidate site has been uncommon in Canadian elections. Especially rare has been an actual exchange of information and opinion, for example, when there is an exchange of e-mail messages involving a candidate responding directly to a particular voter's concern. There has, however, been frequent communication in such forms as a voter e-mailing an opinion to the site and later receiving a copy of a widely distributed newsletter. It is understandable that candidates, both in Canada and the United States, should strive to exercise strict control over the content of their websites so as to prevent manipulation of the sites by political opponents.

Conclusions

The evolution of online campaigning in Canada before 2003 tended to support the cyber-pessimists' view of the potential impact of the Internet on electoral politics. Before turning to the grounds for cyber-optimism, we can summarize the pessimistic view as follows:

- *Supplementary, not transformative.* Websites and e-mail communications are supplementing rather than replacing traditional campaign techniques. Online campaigns have not supplanted candidates' traditional activities of media relations, fundraising, speeches, and rallies. Candidates continue to rely heavily on traditional paid media advertising.

- *Preaching to the converted*. Political websites appear to be less effective in attracting support from the 'floating voter' than in attracting persons who are already committed to the parties and candidates sponsoring the sites, and who are reinforced in their voter choice and are mobilized for campaigning and voting.
- *Limited fundraising potential*. In general, notwithstanding the success of U.S. politicians such as Howard Dean, George W. Bush, and John Kerry, political websites in Canada are only modestly successful in raising money.
- *Reinforcing traditional campaign activities*. While more Canadians are volunteering online to assist political campaigns, they are volunteering for traditional campaign efforts such as getting out the vote.
- *Technologically timid*. The great majority of individual candidate sites amount to little more than electronic campaign brochures, with little use of multimedia and interactivity.
- *Behind the (U.S.) curve*. Online political campaigns in Canada have made relatively little use of such U.S. innovations as meetups, blogging, and open-source politics.

A more optimistic view of the potential impact of online campaigns on electoral politics in Canada can be drawn from this chapter's analysis of the 2003–4 elections, especially from lessons learned during the federal campaign. The Federal Website Study drew out several lessons from that election. The lesson on which there was the most agreement was that much more attention should be given to both the design and the content of the party website before the election writ is dropped. The NDP would have 'launched e-campaigners earlier in the campaign. Uploaded our flash movie earlier. Started the election site even earlier that the writ drop day' (Lavigne 2004b). Among major success factors, both the Conservatives and the Green Party mentioned website design and layout. The Green Party was happy with 'the general look and feel (graphics, organization, navigation)' and 'provision of multiple and easy methods for visitors to contribute to the campaign and contact local campaigns.' The site was successful 'because it was not conceived and designed as an advertising vehicle but as an information resource and two-way communications medium' (Denis 2004). The Liberals highlighted the success of their site's 'Reality Checks' section and the videos. The NDP singled out its fundraising success but lamented the lack of public involvement beyond financial contributions.

Other parties might learn from the NDP's observation that site visitors respond as positively to 'fun items' as they do to policy. Moreover, in their experience, basic information (easily finding your candidate) was just as important as more sophisticated information (the party platform). The Liberals learned that e-mail communications were more important than they had anticipated. Both the Liberals and the Green Party mentioned an unexpectedly high volume of traffic. For the Green Party, the traffic was at least 'two orders of magnitude higher than anticipated during the campaign and an unknown amount higher still on election day' (Denis 2004).

The Federal Website Study demonstrated that at least the senior media and communications officials in Canada's political parties now believe that online campaigning has become an important campaign technique. The Green Party asserted that the Internet 'is like no other medium and is quickly becoming the most effective and accessible technology for political organizing and campaigning' (Denis 2004). There is no doubt that online campaigning is becoming – and for many parties and candidates has already become – an integral part of election campaigns. Yet online campaigning is still at an early stage of development. A survey of individual federal and Ontario legislators discussed in the next chapter showed that they value most of the traditional campaign techniques (such as personal contacts, print media) over the use of the Internet and e-mail. At the same time, the great majority of legislators reported that they viewed use of the Internet as an important political technique, and that it was likely to become more important in the future.

There are additional grounds for optimism:

- *Now a standard campaign technique.* Political parties and candidates are increasingly incorporating use of the Internet and e-mail into their political campaigns. Websites have become a standard feature of these campaigns, both for elections and party leadership contests. It is at the very least symbolically important for parties and individual candidates to have a viable website.
- *More website traffic.* An increasing number of citizens are visiting party and candidate websites for political information, especially during election (and leadership) campaigns.
- *Increased e-mail usage.* Parties and individual candidates are making increasing use of e-mail communications to solicit and reinforce political support.

- *Volunteer volume up*. More Canadians are volunteering online to assist in political campaigns.

While the United States is the world leader in online campaigning, we need to remember, when making comparisons between Canada and the United States, that the nature of elections in the two countries is very different. Since the United States has fixed-term elections, the date of elections is known well in advance; political campaigns are much longer; the electorate and therefore the market for political websites is much larger; comparatively huge amounts of money are spent on elections; and the media are more continuously involved in covering political campaigns. Nevertheless, in part as a result of learning and borrowing from U.S. experience and innovation, the *websites* of Canada's major parties and political leaders are not substantially behind those of the United States in their quality and sophistication. By 2004, the Canadian sites were more advanced than the 2000 U.S. sites in the availability of policy materials, video capability for replaying speeches and advertisements, the provision of media rooms, and the use of attacks. However, in overall use of websites and e-mail in innovative ways for a variety of political purposes by a large number of people, the U.S. political system is well ahead of the Canadian one.

Despite the major role played by the Internet in the 2004 U.S. elections, several U.S. commentators have argued that Internet use in U.S. politics is still in its infancy (Darr 2004). Phil Noble, founder and publisher of PoliticsOnline, predicts the development of 'more "peer-to-peer" communications: ordinary citizens talking to one another online about politics and public policy and an expansion of blogs, those Web pages devoted to opinion-molding by persons not necessarily associated with traditional media' (Darr 2004). The webmaster of Canada's Green Party has observed, 'There are no experts [in online campaigning], just other explorers who have also only recently set out' (Denis 2004). The Green Party's enthusiasm for political use of the Internet has not yet been matched by Canada's *major* political parties. The extent to which the major parties will devote additional resources to online campaigning in the next cycle of elections is difficult to predict. The parties have little hard evidence that shifting resources from traditional campaign techniques to online campaigning will have a substantial payoff in political support. Michael Cornfield, a leading U.S. expert on Internet campaigning, concluded that U.S. campaigners had learned a lot from the 2004 elections 'about how to use the Internet to attract and aggregate viewers, donors, message forwarders, volunteers and voters' (2005, 1). He concluded also that 'Internet use made a difference in the 2004 Presidential race' in that 'the most successful campaigns relied on it to gain advantages over their competitors' (6). While Canada's parties are likely to adapt some of the U.S. lessons to their future Internet campaigns, they are far behind the United States in the use of such innovations as news-pegged fundraising appeals, meetups, blogging, online referenda, decentralized decision making, and political comedy.

Postscript on the 2006 Federal Election

The second federal election within nineteen months was held on 23 January 2006. Given the Liberal minority government that emerged from the 2004 election, political parties and candidates had good reason to expect a new election at almost any time and, therefore, to expedite their website planning. In the runup to the 2006 election, as in 2004, assessments of the party websites differed substantially (Babble 2005), even among informed observers (Ingram 2005; Watkins 2005), thereby supporting the argument made earlier in this chapter that the beauty of a website is to a large extent in the eye of the beholder. The primary focus in this postscript is on differences in the 2004 and 2006 online campaigns and on some politically costly errors in website use.

In website design, only the Liberal site had a splash page – to permit visitors to choose the English or French version of the site. The garish green and orange used on the NDP's 2004 site were considerably reduced and muted. The Conservative home page again made extensive use of Flash technology, including a Flash banner and pictures that changed every few seconds, while the Liberal home page had a continually changing account of the size of the budgetary deficit that would allegedly result from implementing the Conservatives' promises. The design of the Conservative home page was similar to that of the Republican National Committee website in the 2004 U.S. election. The 'Action Centre' section listing such essential links as donating and volunteering was well positioned for visibility and easy navigation. The high level of technological sophistication on this site was not universally welcomed, since the site took longer to load for dial-up visitors, and some visitors did not have Flash technology installed on their computers.

The parties made some additions to the kind of information they had disseminated to site visitors in 2004. The Liberal, Conservative, and NDP home pages used a 'fact check' or 'reality check' link to rebut their opponents' claims. Only the NDP site contained endorsements. These were in the form of a home page link entitled 'Our Record' leading to a sub-site on 'What They Are Saying,' which listed favourable quotes by the media and opinion leaders.

Compared to the 2004 election, this time the major parties disseminated more 'information' in the form of attack ads. In 2004, the Liberal party made very effective use of attack ads that were simultaneously posted on its website and shown on television. In 2006, as in 2004, the Liberals launched strong attack ads to counter a surge of support for the Conservative party in the latter stage of the election. Two weeks before the election, the Liberal party released twelve ads that were widely criticized for their virulence. One of the ads, which distorted a Conservative policy on locating more soldiers near Canadian cities, was quickly withdrawn, but not before it had been circulated to the news media and posted on the Liberal website. Almost every day during the second half of the campaign the Liberal site featured an attack item (usually aimed at the Conservatives).

On the day before the election, the Liberal home page featured a large unflattering picture of Mr Harper, the Conservative leader, above a link entitled 'What's Stephen Harper Got to Hide?' followed by several attack items. The Conservative home page also featured a picture of Mr Harper, but against a background sprinkled with the word *integrity* above the message 'Vote for Accountability' that was followed by two rebuttals of Liberal allegations. The comparatively short NDP home page highlighted links to four of the party's television ads and to an e-card site that permitted visitors to send a message to persons thinking of voting for a party other than the NDP. The Bloc featured positive stories on Mr Duceppe and negative stories on Mr Harper down the middle of a lengthy home page.

Individual candidates, as well as party officials, have to keep in mind that even comments made off-line can be rapidly circulated online and adversely affect their electoral fortunes. A Liberal ad used a politically controversial quote from a 1997 speech by Mr Harper that was found on the website of the Council for National Policy, a right-wing U.S. think tank. Égale, a gay and lesbian rights organization, searched the websites of thirty-four new Conservative candidates to see if the sites contained any reference to the candidates' reported opposition to same-sex marriage (Chase, Galloway, and Clark 2006). A widely publicized Internet-related error involved Michael Klander, executive vice-president of the Ontario wing of the Liberal Party, who used his blog to make offensive remarks about the NDP leader and his wife, who was also a candidate in the election (Brautigam 2005). This case shows the inherently risky nature of blogs and the difficulty that parties face in controlling those who speak – or purport to speak – on their behalf. There can be substantial benefits from party supporters communicating with one another through blogs, but political opponents can mine these communications for embarrassing material. Blogging by journalists and individuals, as opposed to party officials, featured more prominently in the 2006 election. In one case, Liberal candidate Sarmita Bulte was criticized, initially by several bloggers across the country and then in the mainstream media, for aligning herself too closely with the recording and movie industries on the issue of copyright. This controversy was widely viewed as having contributed substantially to her defeat.

While the overall level of interactivity on the party sites was modestly higher than in 2004, the use of blogging was not significantly greater. Only the Bloc's 'blogue' was ostensibly written by the party leader. There was very little interactivity in the form of dialogue between voters and the parties or between the voters themselves. Only the Bloc site posted some visitors' comments. One remark that appears to have been posted unintentionally said, '[My wife and I] think that your party is pathetic ... You are taking our people of Quebec down the road to civil war.' Several candidates had their own blogs, and some of these (for example, Paul Summerville, Garth Turner, Gary Gervais) posted responses.

All four parties used Really Simple Syndication (RSS), which allowed them to feed headlines, links, and article summaries from their websites to the computers, PDAs, and cell phones of supporters, party workers, and the news media. In addition, the Conservatives had a prominent home page link inviting visitors to sign up for podcasts, and the NDP site had a similar invitation on its multimedia page. In 2006, the parties made more frequent use of e-mail messages seeking donations, campaign workers, and votes. None of the parties used online polls.

The quality of the 2006 party websites can be assessed by comparing them not only to the 2004 sites but also to party sites in the most recent U.S. and U.K. elections. Hillwatch, a government relations firm, concluded that the 2004 party websites were little more than virtual lawn signs (2004) and that the 2006 sites were 'still virtually lawn signs' (2006). The detailed analysis provided earlier in this chapter suggests that this assessment is unduly harsh for the 2004 election. It is an overly severe assessment of the 2006 election as well. The 2006 Hillwatch report did draw attention to ways in which the Canadian party sites lagged behind the U.S. and U.K. sites. Unlike the Canadian sites, the U.S. and U.K. sites targeted communities and regions. All that the Canadian sites had were home page links to youth sites (with the Liberals also targeting Aboriginals). Moreover, whereas the Canadian sites had little content aimed specifically at the country's several regions, the U.K. Labour Party site, for example, informed visitors about what the government had done for certain areas. Unlike those of both Canada and the United Kingdom, the U.S. parties made effective use of open-source politics (such as meetups) to promote the parties' fortunes at the local level with little or no involvement from the parties' central offices.

The Canadian party websites made relatively little use of humour. The NDP site offered 'the Great Paul Martin Credibility Hunt' promising a free trip to one of the countries of which Mr Martin's ships had flown 'flags of convenience.' The challenge was to prove that Mr Martin's values were 'more than convenient.' The blog on the Liberal site, written by Mr Martin's speechwriter, made an effort to be entertaining, but was described by a University of Toronto professor as 'very lame,' 'absolutely shameful,' and 'so sophomoric and giggly [as] to be embarrassing' (Ohler 2005). The caveat expressed earlier in this chapter about the prudent use of humour bears repeating here.

In general, the major parties made slightly more sophisticated use of websites and e-mail for the 2006 campaign. However, the overall conclusions drawn earlier in this chapter about the state of online campaigning in 2004 apply to the 2006 campaign as well.

Notes

1 Despite several invitations, the Bloc Québécois failed to respond to either the French or the English version of the study's questions.
2 Data from the 2004 Canadian Election Survey were provided by Neil Nevitte of the University of Toronto. The survey was funded by the Social Sciences and Humanities Research Council of Canada (SSHRCC) and was completed for the 2004 federal election by the 2004 Canadian Election Sur-

vey Team made up of Nevitte et al. Neither the University of Toronto, the SSHRCC, nor the Canadian Election Survey Team is responsible for the analyses and interpretations presented here.

3 Stephen Brooks, webmaster for the federal Conservative Party, demonstrates the technical nature of the issue of what constitutes a 'hit' when he explains that a hit 'is one request by the client (the visitor, or, more specifically, the visitor's browser) for a resource on the server. As such, one web page may result in many hits. The client may not only request the .html file, but may request any embedded GIF or JPEG image files, or any other elements, thus generating more than one hit' (Brooks in e-mail communication 18 August 2004).

4 The term *personal website* refers here to a site that is developed by the candidate (or that tailors a party's template to the candidate's personal needs) and is specifically designed to attract political support. This type of site should be distinguished from the MP and MPP sites discussed in the next chapter that are used to serve the members' constituents and are financed from public funds.

8 Making Political Connections: IT and Legislative Life

KENNETH KERNAGHAN

Once online campaigning has come to an end and the election results have been announced, the new and re-elected legislators turn their attention to their legislative and representative roles. Legislators play a central legislative role through their work in the *chamber*, *committees*, and *caucus*. They also play an important representative role, in large part by providing service to their *constituency*. Increasingly, these roles involve the use of IT to connect legislators to other legislators, party research offices, interest groups, public servants, constituents, and staff in constituency offices.

An analytical distinction can be made between IT usage by the legislature as a whole to facilitate legislators' involvement in debates, in legislative committees, and in consultations with members of their own party, and IT usage by individual legislators to serve their constituents. This chapter examines these two major categories in turn. The term *legislature* is used broadly to refer to both the federal House of Commons and the Ontario Legislative Assembly.

In October 1999, a major report entitled *Building the Future* outlined future requirements for Canada's Parliamentary Precinct (the House of Commons, the Senate, and the Parliamentary Library). The report asserted that 'IT has become a utility, as important to the functioning of the House [of Commons] as heating, plumbing and electrical systems – enabling Parliamentarians to carry out their work' (Canada, House of Commons 1999, 38). The importance of effective exploitation of IT goes beyond this utility function to the heart of democratic government. A common theme in contemporary studies of parliamentary democracies is the decline in the role of legislatures as representative institutions and in voter turnout at elections. Many advocates of increased use of

IT believe that it can significantly increase public participation in politics. They argue that online campaigning (discussed in chapter 7), combined with more rapid and frequent connections between legislators and citizens, will enhance public confidence in Canada's governments, including the legislatures. Many other observers believe that the use of IT in these ways will do little to enhance participation in Canada's political life or to invigorate the country's democratic institutions. This chapter informs the debate by examining the current and anticipated impact of IT on legislatures and legislators.

IT and Legislatures

The Federal Parliament

Among notable milestones in the history of IT in Canada's federal Parliamentary Precinct are the following:[1]

- In 1867, the year of Confederation, electric (battery-powered) call bells were installed in the original Centre Block, with separate systems serving the House of Commons and the Senate.
- In 1877, the year after the telephone was invented, the first commercial telephone call in Canada was made by Prime Minister Alexander Mackenzie from the West Block to the residence of the governor general.
- In 1928, James Malcolm, the minister of trade and commerce, made the first trans-Atlantic telephone call from the Centre Block to Cardiff, Wales (5600 km away) to make a speech to the British Empire Exhibition.
- In 1957, when the Canadian Parliament was opened for the first time by a reigning monarch, the opening ceremonies were broadcast for the first time; this was also the first time that the Queen had used live television to address her subjects in any commonwealth country.
- In 1977, regular television and radio broadcasts from the chamber of the House of Commons began (Canada, House of Commons 1999, 38–9).

From the late 1970s to the mid-1980s, the distribution of radio and television programming throughout the precinct was increasingly complemented by the distribution of computer data. Personal computers were first installed in 1981, and the Office Automation Systems and

Information Services (OASIS) network that was introduced in 1985 supported the distribution of computer data. In the early 1990s, substantial improvements in IT services included a commitment to ongoing investment in IT infrastructure, consolidation of IT support groups into the House of Commons Information Services Directorate, initiatives to ensure 'consistency, compatibility, connectivity and security' of the computers and software applications needed to support legislators in the four lines of business noted above, and the creation of longer-term plans for both system and service improvement (Canada, House of Commons 1999, 40–1).

By the late 1990s, the offices of federal legislators had been outfitted as small 'business centres,' and computer-based tools had changed the way legislators fulfilled their duties (Canada, House of Commons 1999, 41). They now enjoyed such IT services as remote access from their constituency offices, Internet services, and electronic access to the Library of Parliament and the Senate. It was apparent in the early 2000s, however, that legislators had become increasingly computer literate and expected better IT services than their predecessors had enjoyed. The *Building the Future* report recognized that these increased expectations were only the beginning of greatly expanded demands for IT infrastructure and that as much provision as possible should be made for these future requirements during the renovation of the parliamentary precinct.

In response to this burgeoning need for enhanced IT, the 1998 House of Commons Business and Technology Strategy, as updated in 2000, focused on six major projects:

- Examination of the technology needed for the three components of the Commons' architecture – desktop, server/back office, and network
- Development of an integrated security system for the precinct
- Implementation of a multimedia vision for Parliament, including new infrastructure for committee rooms and Web broadcasting of Parliament's proceedings
- Implementation of the Constituency Communication Network (CCN), which provides secure remote access services through high speed connectivity in the constituency offices
- A long-range architectural plan to develop an effective IT infrastructure and technology network to enable the sharing of solutions across the precinct
- Development of PRISM – a technology system to support MPs in their work in Chamber and in committees by delivering information

and parliamentary publications. The three principles underpinning PRISM are data integrity and consistency, retention of historical records of events, and movement from a document-centred organization to a knowledge management one. (Bard 2003; Canada, House of Commons Administration 1999)

The House Administration is responsible for implementing such projects. It is headed by the clerk of the House, who reports to the House speaker. The clerk is also the secretary to the Board of Internal Economy, which is the governing body of the House and is composed of members from each political party. Among the five major service areas of the House Administration is the Information Services Directorate, which provides advice, support, and strategic information on information technology. The directorate's several service units comprise, among others, a Multimedia Services unit, which provides information services (for example, the parliamentary websites), and an Information Technology Operations unit with such responsibilities as planning, designing, managing, and supporting the precinct networks (for example, broadband, Ethernet).

The six projects adopted in 2000 were implemented over the next few years. By early 2004, considerable progress had been made in the use of IT to support Parliament's four lines of business: Chamber, committees, caucus, and constituents (Canada, House of Commons 2004). In addition, plans and priorities had been set for further initiatives (Canada, House of Commons Administration 2004b). By the end of 2004, IT improvements affecting all business lines had been implemented, were in progress, or were planned (Canada, House of Commons Administration 2004a, 2004c). Some of these improvements cut across more than one line of business. For example, continuous enhancements were made in the PRISM application/infrastructure to the benefit of both the Chamber and committees (for such purposes as improving the capacity for research and retrieval of parliamentary proceedings). In general, however, IT progress and planning can be examined separately for each of the four business lines. As a basis for this examination, it is helpful to provide first a brief description of the parliamentary website.

The Parliament of Canada Website

A new and much improved opening page for the website was launched in September 2004 (http://www.parl.gc.ca), created and maintained jointly by the Senate, House of Commons, and the Library of Parliament. Each of these three components of the Parliamentary Precinct manages its own content, however, and the separate branding on the site is obvious.

The main menu on the home page (as of June 2006) provides links to information on Chamber business, committee business, bills, senators and members, Chamber and committee webcasts, and inter-parliamentary affairs, as well as a connection to a virtual library maintained by the Library of Parliament. Two central features appear prominently in the left column. The first is 'Today in Parliament,' which provides links for the current day to Chamber business (for example, Senate and House of Commons Order Paper and Notice Paper), bills (on the day's agenda), and committee business (such as schedule of meetings, webcasts). Then there is an A to Z index (from Addresses of parliamentary secretaries to Women) that is a treasure trove of information on almost every conceivable topic related to Parliament. The centre column highlights 'Current Parliamentarians,' including a find-your-MP function, followed by such features as 'Learning about Parliament' and 'Visiting Parliament Hill.' The right column focuses on 'What's New on the Site?' This website is central to the effective conduct and visibility of Parliament's business.

Parliament's Business Lines

This section focuses on the impact of IT on legislators' four main lines of business.

Chamber

By the summer of 2003, all members' desks in the House had been equipped with electricity and connectivity to the House of Commons network/Internet. Members are now permitted to use laptop computers and BlackBerrys in the House for such purposes as constituency work, communicating with their staff, and doing research. By early 2005, the majority of members had BlackBerrys (Janice Hilchie, e-mail communication 12 May 2005). The use of cell phones in the House is prohibited, and the use of cell-enabled Blackberrys is regulated by the House speaker.

On 2 February 2004, the Parliament of Canada website launched ParlVU, a service that brings Parliament to the computers of Canadians by providing a live webcast of the televised parliamentary proceedings from the Chamber of the House of Commons. The service is available with English, French, and Floor sound choices. An audio service is also available for committee meetings not being video recorded/broadcast. This service had been made available almost a year earlier on IntraParl, the House's internal communications network.

Two additional innovations were requested by the Special Committee on the Modernization and Improvement of the House of Commons. The first, a portal for the *electronic filing of notices of motion and written questions*, was developed and launched in April 2005 together with a security procedure to verify authenticity. The second was a mechanism by which Canadians can create and submit *online petitions*. Only a few governments in the world permit online petitions, and Canada's House of Commons receives not only a comparatively high number of petitions (an average of 2000 per year over the 1989–2004 period) but also 'more conceptual kinds of petitions' relating, for example, to 'certain pieces of complex legislation' (Canada, House of Commons 2005). Some development work has been done on e-petitions and has been presented to the Standing Committee on Procedure and House Affairs for its consideration.

It is notable that while no decision has been taken to implement a system of electronic voting for members, the cabling infrastructure to support such a system is available at members' desks in the House. More work is required, including decisions from members on procedures, the type of system, and potentially the installation of buttons and screens. Finally, as noted, a 'Today in Parliament' feature has been added to Parliament's website to provide easier online access to all pertinent information bearing on Parliament's business on a particular day. A 'Today in the House' project was under way in mid-2005 to refine that access further.

Committees

While the Parliament of Canada website has gradually been transformed since its creation in 1994, the committee websites have undergone little change until recently. Redesigned committee websites came into operation in September 2004 with such new features as links to information on committee members; the committees' terms of reference, structure and history; and committee studies and reports. There is also a subscription service for those who want to receive information about the committees' work electronically, and a search tool leading to information on committee witnesses. Part of the incentive for these enhancements is the need for a more informed basis for future citizen involvement in committees' electronic consultations, as well as preparing the technical infrastructure that could support such consultations. ParlVU provides live *video* webcasting of the televised House proceedings to the two committee rooms that are wired for this purpose and delivers live *audio* webcasts to the other committee rooms.

Caucus and Constituency

The caucus responsibilities of members involve not only the discussion of strategic and policy issues but also the direction of the work done by the parties' research bureaus. Since the mid-1990s, several IT initiatives have been undertaken to provide members with full and secure connections between their parliamentary offices and their party research bureaus, as well as between their parliamentary offices and their constituency offices. Through a high-speed communication network, all the constituency offices have access to House services through the IntraParl website by such means as Internet and wireless communications tools. The House Administration has also improved the management and security of the e-mail system.

The Ontario Legislative Assembly

In Ontario, as in the federal sphere, the important implications for the Legislature of advances in IT had been formally recognized by the mid-1980s.[2] In 1985, a unit (now a branch) of the Ontario Legislative Assembly called Legislative Information Systems (LIS) was created to support installation of a new information and communications system for MPPs. This system, which was completed in 1986, replaced typewriters in MPPs' offices with state-of-the-art resources in word processing, spreadsheets, contact databases, and calendar management tools. It also enhanced communications between MPPs' offices through the use of e-mail.

A major step forward was the implementation by the LIS over the next several years of the 1986 Global Strategic Plan containing more than fifty initiatives. The plan's major purpose was to coordinate the use of IT in the Queen's Park and constituency offices of members, the

Office of the Legislative Assembly, and the three party caucuses. On the basis of the Strategic Plan, the 1987–8 Operations Plan for Information Systems focused on such matters as improving training and user support, identifying the best way to enhance the use of IT in both sets of MPPs' offices, and implementing connectivity between the members' system and other Assembly systems.

In the 1990–1 fiscal year, each MPP's Queen's Park and constituency office was provided with a personal computer for the first time (a decade later than in the federal sphere), and e-mail communications were enabled between MPPs and the Office of the Assembly. The society-wide explosion of Internet use at this time was reflected in the subsequent creation of an external Internet site for the Legislative Assembly that contained House publications, Hansard, committee publications, and lists of members and services. An intranet for internal communications was also created for such items as a draft Hansard, news, and research papers. By the end of the century, the Assembly was able to provide better service less expensively than in the past, since all users of the system were using the same hardware and following the same software standards.

Measures in information technology taken early in the new century included a Procedural Precedents database linked electronically to Hansard and Journals documents, an inventory database for Interparliamentary and Public Relations (IPRB), Web access for IPRB tour bookings, and implementation of spam-control hardware and software. In addition, LIS plans to implement an enterprise anti-spyware solution, to upgrade systems infrastructure to support major Assembly initiatives, and to provide a security awareness program for all Assembly staff.

Still other measures are in progress. An Administrative Services System begun in 2004 will replace technologically outdated systems for finance, human resources, purchasing, payroll, and asset management with systems that will eliminate duplication and inefficiency. A Status of Legislation component is being added to the Members Database that is available on the Assembly website. A multi-year Information Infrastructure project has been adopted to improve the creation, storage, management, and distribution of Assembly information. Finally, discussions have begun on the recommendation of the Standing Committee on the Legislative Assembly that Assembly staff be authorized to use technology that is appropriate to the conduct of their business in the House.

Four main actors are involved in determining the use of IT in the Queen's Park Precinct. The Speaker heads the Office of the Legislative Assembly and chairs the Board of Internal Economy (BOIE). The clerk of the Assembly, who is the office's administrator, reports to the BOIE and is responsible for the overall direction and management of the Assembly, including IT matters. The deputy clerk chairs the Information Technology Advisory Committee (ITAC), established in 2001 to approve, coordinate, and oversee all significant IT/IM projects and to set project priorities. The director of the LIS Branch provides the secretariat to ITAC.

The BOIE is composed of MPPs from all political parties with official party status and is responsible for approving initiatives and funding for the Office of the Assembly. The Standing Committee on the Legislative Assembly advises the Speaker and the BOIE. Responsibilities of ITAC include developing and then annually reviewing a Corporate Information Technology Strategy and Plan; reviewing strategic and cost-benefit considerations of current IT projects and setting priorities; reviewing major IT projects each year to ensure that they are aligned with the Corporate Plan; and providing advice on IT matters, including policies, standards, and guidelines. A Web Management Team reports to ITAC. There is also a Standards Committee, composed of representatives from all divisions of the Assembly as well as the systems administrators from each party caucus, which determines hardware and software standards for all Assembly users. Among the responsibilities of LIS are the purchase and installation of new hardware for both the Queen's Park and constituency offices of MPPs and the provision of Helpdesk support, Internet connection, and firewall, anti-virus, and anti-spam protection.

The Assembly Website

Compared to its federal counterpart, the Assembly's home page has an uncluttered 'bare bones' appearance. The main feature, taking up more than half the page in the centre, is a picture of the Chamber. The right column is blank space and the left column has links to such pages as a site map, a French version of the site, visitor information, and a glossary of parliamentary terms. At the top of the page are links to pages containing information on members, bills, House business, Hansard, committees, and the library. Unlike the House of Commons website, the Legislative Assembly site has no search, quick links, or 'Contact

Us' functions, no equivalent of the federal 'Today in Parliament' feature, and no need for a webcast link, since webcasting to the public is not available. The Web Management Team is considering a revision of the Assembly website that could include a refocusing of its content according to theme; improving its educational objectives to appeal to a broader range of users, including school children; launching a photo gallery; expanding the glossary with hyperlinks; and adding 'How Do I?' pages and FAQs.

The Assembly's Main Business Lines

Unlike the federal House of Commons, the Ontario Legislative Chamber is not wired. It is important to keep in mind, however, that the wiring of the House of Commons was facilitated by a major renovation of the parliamentary precinct as a whole. In Ontario, MPPs' desks are not connected to a Legislative Assembly network or to the Internet, and there is no provision for electronic voting in the Chamber or from MPPs' legislative offices. Moreover, MPPs are not permitted to use electronic devices in the Chamber. Neither laptop computers nor cell phones are permitted. The Speaker, who is responsible for enforcing this prohibition, accepted advice from a legislative committee that members would not object if he tolerated the passive and unobtrusive use of BlackBerrys. The Speaker has, however, threatened to crack down on the addictive use of 'crackberries' (*Toronto Star* 2004), in view of such unacceptable usage as an MPP reading a statement from her BlackBerry during a debate.

Since 1986, the Assembly has had its own broadcast facility called the Ontario Parliament Network, with a television service known as Ont-Parl. The House proceedings are available across the country through cable television and satellite receivers, and throughout the Assembly and adjoining government buildings on an internal closed circuit cable service. The proceedings of House committees are also available, for the most part on a recorded basis for replay.

There is no Ontario equivalent to the federal ParlVU system that provides a live webcast of parliamentary and committee debates to the public, and no provision has been made for electronic filing of notices of motion and written questions or for online petitions. However, in mid-2005, one committee did webcast its proceedings, and the webcast was linked to both the home page of the Assembly Internet site and to the committee's own website. Members can receive real-time video streaming of legislative debates in their legislative offices over the precinct LAN. In addition, when the Legislature is not in session, streaming coverage of committee proceedings from the one committee room with full television service is available on the in-house streaming network.

Since 2000/1, constituency offices have been connected to the Queen's Park networks through a secure Internet connection. Cabinet ministers, parliamentary assistants, and their staff whose offices are in ministries outside the Queen's Park Precinct have a direct network connection to Queen's Park.

The extent to which the federal and Ontario legislatures will make greater use of IT depends largely on the demand for IT-related services by the legislators themselves. It is important, therefore, to understand legislators' current and probable future use of IT to carry out their legislative and representative roles.

Legislators' Use of Information Technology

There has been much speculation, but little empirical research, on the impact of IT on Canadian legislators. To help remedy this deficiency, this section provides baseline data on legislators' general use of IT and their more specific use of IT for dealing with constituents and other political actors. This chapter is informed by an examination of federal and Ontario legislators' websites described respectively as the federal MP website analysis and the Ontario MPP website analysis. This chapter is informed also by four legislator surveys consisting of two surveys of federal MPs and two surveys of Ontario MPPs (see Methodology section at end of chapter). Note that in both the federal and Ontario jurisdictions, an election held between the first and second set of surveys brought a substantial influx of new legislators. The 2004 federal election resulted in a greatly reduced number of seats for the governing Liberal Party, and the 2003 Ontario election resulted in a change of government from the Progressive Conservatives to the Liberals.

As noted in chapter 7, political candidates are expected to have a website for campaign purposes, and most of them do. Similarly, successful candidates are increasingly expected to have a website that enables them to connect with constituents and other political actors *between* elections. A Crossing Boundaries National Council study showed that by mid-2002 only 58 per cent of federal legislators had functional websites (2002). Table 8.1 shows that this percentage had

Table 8.1
Status of MP websites, 2005

Party	Functional	No site	Functional (%)
Liberal	101	32	75.9
Conservative	92	6	93.9
Bloc Québécois	20	33	37.7
NDP	16	4	84.2
Independent	4	—	100
Total	233	75	75.6

Source: Federal MP website analysis (2005).

Table 8.2
Status of Ontario MPP websites, 2005

Party	Functional	No site	Functional (%)
Liberal	58	13	81.7
NDP	4	4	50.0
Conservative	17	7	70.8
Total	79	24	76.7

Source: Ontario MPP website analysis (2005).

risen to 75.6 per cent by mid-2005. The Conservative Party had the largest online presence at almost 94 per cent of its MPs, while the Bloc Québécois had the lowest online presence at 37.7 per cent – a participation rate that lowered considerably the overall percentage of MPs with functional sites. Table 8.2 shows that in mid-2005 the percentage of Ontario MPPs with websites (76.7 per cent) was almost identical to the federal sphere (75.6 per cent).

The 2002 Crossing Boundaries study divided the content of MPs' websites into two major categories: 'Most Common Features' and 'Advanced ICT Tools.' Table 8.3 compares the occurrence of the most common features for MPs in 2002 and 2005. While a biography and contact information remained the most popular features, there was an enormous increase in the use of press releases and a substantial increase in the inclusion of links, communication with constituents, a welcome message, and riding information. In 2005, the content of MPP websites was similar to the MPs' sites.

Table 8.4 shows the prevalence of advanced IT tools and, for MPs, the change in usage between 2002 and 2005. The rate of adoption was slower than that for the common features. Use of the online feedback

Table 8.3
Common features of political websites (2002, 2005)

Feature	MP websites (%)		MPP websites (%)	
	2002	2005	2003	2005
Biography	94	97.4	—*	96.1
Contact info	92	97.4	—	97.4
Links	78	92.2	—	88.3
Press releases	2	81.9	—	81.8
Communication with constituents	56	81.9	—	87.0
Welcome message	64	77.7	—	87.2
Riding info	64	75.0	—	81.8
Speeches	62	57.8	—	36.4
Functional website	58**	76.0	—	77.0
N	171	233	—	79

* The 2003 Centre for Collaborative Government study did not include an analysis of MPP websites.
** The Centre for Collaborative Government had three categories of websites (functional 58%, under construction 19%, and no site or immediate plans 23%). The 2005 survey reduced these categories to either functional 77% or non-functional 23%.
Source: 2003 data from the KTA Centre for Collaborative Government MP website study for Crossing Boundaries; 2005 federal website analysis; 2005 Ontario MPP website analysis.

Table 8.4
Advanced IT features of political websites (2002, 2005)

Feature	MP websites (%)		MPP websites* (%)	
	2002	2005	2003	2005
Online feedback or comment form	37	33.6	—	49.4
Online survey or poll	8	13.0	—	5.2
Subscribe to newsletter	11	15.9	—	14.3
Site search	1	13.4	—	3.9
Audio/video clips	12	6.5	—	1.3
Community bulletin board	1	2.0	—	—

* The Centre for Collaborative Government study did not include an analysis of MPP websites.
Source: 2002 MP data from the KTA Centre for Collaborative Government MP website study for Crossing Boundaries; 2005 MP website analysis; 2005 MPP website analysis.

or comment form, which is by far the most commonly used advanced tool, declined slightly during this period. In 2002, the use of online surveys, newsletter subscriptions, and audio or video clips hovered around 10 per cent. By 2005, there had been a modest increase in the use of online surveys and newsletter subscriptions, but a decline in the use of audio or video clips. In general, there was little use of interactive tools. In 2005, while MPPs' use of the online feedback or comment form was considerably higher than that of MPs, the MPs' use of all other advanced features exceeded that of MPPs. Note that neither MPs nor MPPs are permitted to link their personal websites to the brief biographical entry for each of them that is contained on the main legislative site.

Information on legislators' websites regarding their voting records tends to be highly partisan, incomplete, intermittent, or non-existent. This deficiency may have been remedied in the federal sphere by the launch in May 2005 of an external-to-government non-partisan website entitled How'd They Vote (http://www.howdtheyvote.ca/). This site, which was created by Corey Horner, a twenty-four-year-old engineering graduate from British Columbia, provides the voting records on major bills for every MP as well as such information as MPs' attendance record, the number of speeches they have made in the House of Commons, and quotations from each of those speeches. This initiative demonstrates how IT can be used to assist voters to hold elected representatives accountable for their legislative performance. Media coverage of the site contained explanations from several MPs as to why their performance was below the norm (Bailey 2005, A9).

To help elected officials make more effective use of IT for constituency service, members of the Crossing Boundaries National Council's Private Sector Committee (Bell, CGI, and Microsoft) launched a pilot project in December 2004 called The Wired Elected Official (now called Wired Officials, http://www.crossingboundaries.ca/wired-officials-en.html?page=wired-officials&lang_id=1&page_id=159). The five tools developed for this project were dynamic websites, case management (to enhance management of constituents' issues), personal information management (to assist with meeting and event planning), an e-consultation tool (to obtain citizen input on policy issues), and remote access (to connect the official to citizens from any location). These tools were delivered to two provincial officials: Jody Carr of New Brunswick and Doreen Hamilton of Saskatchewan. In part because of heavy marketing of the tools, constituents used them extensively to obtain information, access to services, and opportunities for consultation. The intention is that this project will help elected officials across Canada improve their use of IT.

Are elected officials a receptive and competent audience for this assistance? The Legislator surveys suggest that federal and Ontario

Table 8.5
Reported computer literacy rates of MPs and MPPs

	MPs (%)		MPPs (%)	
Self-reported skill level	2003	2005	2003	2005
Not at all	13.6	4.9	13.0	6.3
Know the basics	51.5	40.2	43.5	34.9
Use computer with confidence	27.3	46.3	37.0	44.4
Very competent	7.6	8.5	6.5	14.3
Total	100.0	100.0	100.0	100.0
N	66	82	46	63

Sources: 2003 MP survey, Kernaghan, Riehle, and Lo; 2005 MP survey; 2003 Ontario MPP survey; 2005 Ontario MPP survey.

Table 8.6
MP age and computer literacy (2005)

	Age of MP			
Self-reported skill level (%)	26–46	47–54	55–58	59+
Not at all	—	4.7	10.0	4.5
Know the basics	15.8	42.9	45.0	54.5
Use computer with confidence	57.9	47.6	45.0	36.4
Very competent	26.3	4.8	—	4.5
Total	100.0	100.0	100.0	100.0
N	19	21	20	22

Sources: 2005 MP Survey; House of Commons Parliamentary website.

legislators are gradually becoming more active and more skilful IT users. There has been a substantial improvement in the past few years in the computer literacy of both MPs and MPPs (table 8.5). Almost 95 per cent of both MPs and MPPs have at least a basic level of computer literacy.

In the federal sphere, the percentage of respondents who described themselves as using computers with confidence or being very competent rose from 34.9 per cent in 2003 to 54.8 per cent in 2005. The percentage of those who were not computer literate declined from 13.6 per cent to 4.9 per cent.

An analysis of the computer literacy of federal legislators in relation to age and gender suggests that age is a more influential determinant. Table 8.6 shows that the reported computer literacy rate of MPs declines with age. MPs in the 26–46 cohort are much more likely to use

Table 8.7
MP gender and computer literacy, 2003 vs. 2005

Self-reported skill level(%)	2003		2005	
	Male	Female	Male	Female
Not at all	16.0	6.3	6.2	—
Know the basics	44.0	75.0	43.1	29.4
Use computer with confidence	30.0	18.8	41.5	64.7
Very competent	10.0	—	9.2	5.9
Total	100.0	100.0	100.0	100.0
N	50	16	65	17

Sources: 2003 MP survey, Kernaghan, Riehle, and Lo; 2005 MP survey; 2003 Ontario MPP survey; 2005 Ontario MPP survey.

computers with confidence (57.9 per cent) or to be very competent (26.3 per cent) than even the 47–54 cohort (47.6 per cent and 4.8 per cent respectively). The most pronounced difference is that 26.3 per cent of the 26–46 cohort describe themselves as very competent, compared to less than 5 per cent of the other cohorts. The fact that almost 85 per cent of the youngest group of MPs but only 41 per cent of the older group use computers with confidence or are very competent suggests that, over time, newer legislators will bring greater computer skills to Parliament and will be inclined to make more effective use of IT.

There are differences between the computer literacy of male and of female MPs in all four categories shown in Table 8.7. About 85 per cent of male MPs compared to 95 per cent of female MPs either know the basics or use computers with confidence. Female MPs are less likely than their male counterparts to have no computer literacy or, at the other extreme, to be very competent. The overall higher computer literacy of female MPs cannot be explained by reference to age. Although younger MPs are more computer literate than older ones, the average age of all female MPs (53.7) and of the female survey respondents (55.9) is higher than that of their male counterparts (51.7 and 52.1 respectively).

Since 2003, MPs and MPPs have become more frequent users of the *World Wide Web* (table 8A) and, especially, of e-mail (table 8B). (Both tables are available in full at http://www.digitalstate.ca/supp/ch8. html). In 2005, 92.6 per cent of MPs and 95.1 per cent of MPPs used e-mail either daily or more than once a day, whereas 80.8 per cent of MPs and 87.3 per cent of MPPs used the Web this frequently. While

Table 8.8
Internet activity comparison

Internet activity (%)	MPs		MPPs	
	2003	2005	2003	2005
Conducting research	83.3	91.4	71.1	79.4
Connecting with constituents	63.6	70.4	64.4	77.8
Doing committee work	45.5	28.4	11.1	15.9
Online surveys	13.6	16.0	13.3	11.1
Newsgroups	30.3	23.5	17.8	14.3
Electronic mailing lists	25.8	29.6	33.3	38.1
Electronic discussion forum	—	6.3	—	7.9
Online townhall	—	3.7	—	4.8
Maintaining personal website	—	53.1	51.1	65.1
Online chats	—	4.9	—	1.6
E-mail	75.8	88.9	82.2	95.2
I do not use the Internet	6.1	2.5	11.1	1.6

Note: Electronic discussion forum, online townhall, maintaining a personal website, and online chats were not options in the 2003 MP survey.
Sources: 2003 MP survey, Kernaghan, Riehle, and Lo; 2005 MP survey; 2003 Ontario MPP survey; 2005 Ontario MPP survey.

e-mail has been described as 'the killer application' in online campaigning, it is acquiring a similar status for legislators' activities between elections. There has also been a large increase in the percentage of legislators who themselves use the Web and e-mail rather than relying on their staff to perform these functions for them.

What activities do legislators engage in when spending all this time online? Table 8.8 provides a detailed breakdown of the use that MPs and MPPs make of IT. The most popular uses – conducting research, sending e-mail, and connecting with constituents – have all increased in recent years. There has been a considerable expansion in the use of online surveys, but very little change in the use of such interactive mechanisms as online chats, discussion forums, and town hall meetings. This finding is consistent with the results of the website survey reported above and with the use of websites for campaign purposes discussed in chapter 7. The emphasis has been on improving approaches to 'broadcasting' rather than on interactive two-way communication. The Crossing Boundaries III Political Advisory Committee noted in 2002 that not only were too few federal MPs making use of new IT, but those who were using it were in 'send' and not 'receive' mode (14). This was still the case in 2005. There are notable exceptions, however. Federal MP Carolyn Bennett has experimented with consultative techniques, not only to serve her constituents but also to seek public input into the policy deliberations of a parliamentary committee (the subcommittee on the status of persons with disabilities). Similarly, Reg Alcock, a federal MP until the 2006 election, monitored and served his constituents through such IT applications as a large database about his constituency and video-conferencing from his Ottawa office.

While it is reasonable to expect that legislators with high levels of computer literacy would make greater use of interactive mechanisms, the legislator survey results contained in table 8.9 do not support this expectation. These data show that MPs, regardless of their computer competence, focus on the most popular activities of research, e-mail, connecting to constituents, and maintaining a personal website. The data suggest also that as legislators become more computer literate, there may be only modest movement in the direction of using such mechanisms as discussion forums, online chats, polls, and town hall meetings. The perceived lack of a political payoff may trump legislators' technical capacity to use interactive approaches.

In their responses to an open-ended question on the ways in which IT can improve or reduce the effectiveness of legislators, most MPs and MPPs stressed their greatly increased capacity to communicate quickly and efficiently. The comment of a federal MP was typical: 'IT can improve the speed at which issues are dealt with. It reduces the cost of movement of information. It allows the filing, retention and administration of correspondence, information and communication. It provides a protocol for contact with constituents that is efficient, timely and personal.'

Many respondents saw IT as a mixed blessing. With respect to the use of e-mail, another federal MP commented, 'You can get answers to questions quickly and you can give quick …responses to requests. However, this is a two-edged sword. I swear that some constituents e-mail and then sit by their computer waiting for the answer, so any response more than an hour is considered slow service, and it is seldom possible to respond that quickly.'

Overall, the legislator surveys offer comfort to those who believe that increased use of IT will help legislators connect more effectively, not only with constituents but also with citizens in general – and thereby foster public trust and confidence in politicians. Table 8.10 shows that, since 2003, the use of Internet technologies for connecting with constituents has become important or highly important for more

Table 8.9
2005 MP online activities by computer literacy

Type of Internet activity (%)	Not at all	Know the basics	Use computers with confidence	Very competent	Combined
Online survey/poll	—	15.2	18.4	14.3	15.9
Online town hall	—	6.1	2.6	—	3.7
Connecting to constituents	25.0	69.7	76.3	57.1	69.5
Maintaining a personal website	25.0	57.6	52.6	42.9	52.4
Electronic mailing lists	—	33.3	28.9	28.6	29.7
E-mail	50.0	87.9	89.5	100.0	87.8
Electronic discussion forum	—	6.1	7.9	—	6.1
Online chats	—	6.1	2.6	14.3	4.9
Doing committee work	—	24.2	13.0	28.6	28.1
Using newsgroups	—	24.2	34.2	—	23.2
Conducting research	75.0	87.9	92.1	100.0	90.2
I do not use the Internet	25.0	3.0	—	—	2.4
N	4	33	38	7	82

Source: 2005 MP survey.

Table 8.10
Value of Internet technologies as a way to connect with constituents

Reported importance (%)	MPs		MPPs	
	2003	2005	2003	2005
Highly important	18.2	46.3	45.7	44.4
Important	56.1	40.2	43.5	46.0
Neither important nor unimportant	25.7	9.8	8.7	7.9
Unimportant	—	3.7	2.2	1.6
Total	100.0	100.0	100.0	100.0
N	66	82	46	63

Sources: 2003 MP survey, Kernaghan, Riehle, and Lo; 2005 MP survey; 2003 Ontario MPP survey; 2005 Ontario MPP survey.

Table 8.11
Value of Internet technologies for more frequent and broad consultation with citizens

Response (%)	MPs		MPPs	
	2003	2005	2003	2005
Yes	47.0	57.5	62.2	66.7
No	7.6	16.3	4.4	7.9
Uncertain at this time	45.5	26.3	33.3	25.4
Total	100.0	100.0	100.0	100.0
N	66	82	45	63

Sources: 2003 MP survey, Kernaghan, Riehle, and Lo; 2005 MP survey; 2003 Ontario MPP survey; 2005 Ontario MPP survey.

than 85 per cent of MPs and MPPs. For MPs, there has been a notable increase in the 'highly important' category from 18.2 per cent in 2003 to 46.3 per cent in 2005.

In addition, table 8.11 suggests that an increasing percentage of legislators believe that Internet technologies *should* be used for more frequent and broad *consultations* with citizens. The growth since 2003 in support for electronic consultation with citizens has been somewhat greater in the federal sphere (from 47.0 per cent to 57.5 per cent) than in Ontario (from 62.2 per cent to 66.7 per cent), but the overall level of support is higher in Ontario. The level of uncertainty on this issue has diminished slightly, but one-quarter of legislators in each jurisdiction are still undecided. Nearly all e-consultation initiatives to date have been taken by political executives and public servants rather than by legislators or legislative committees. These executive/public service initiatives are examined at length in the next chapter.

The trend toward increased connectivity with constituents and greater support for the idea of consulting citizens provide modest grounds for optimism among advocates of democratic renewal through citizen engagement. However, as explained above, improvement in the computer literacy of legislators may not substantially enhance their use of such interactive IT applications as e-consultation. There is reason for concern that the influence of legislators in the policy process will decline relative to that of public servants.

Shortly before Paul Martin became prime minister, he suggested that MPs could help reduce the 'democratic deficit' by using electronic avenues to pursue policy consultations with Canadians in general and constituents in particular (Chenier and Peters 2003). Table 8.4 indicates that federal and Ontario legislators engage in very little electronic consultation with constituents. Moreover, little effort has been made by legislative committees to consult citizens on policy. As mentioned earlier, a notable exception in both areas is the work of federal MP Carolyn Bennett (Stewart 2004, 83–5) who, in addition to using several traditional techniques for consulting her constituents, has a website containing her personal blog, important dates and events, contact information, and links to other information sources. The site also includes a feedback link. In addition, in her capacity as chair of a Sub-Committee on the Status of Persons with Disabilities, Dr Bennett led a pilot project in 2003 that sought to inform and consult Canadians through an interactive website dealing with the Pension Plan Disability Program. Three interactive tools were used: issue polls to obtain input on particular issues, permission for citizens to share their stories and experiences about government processes online, and opportunity for citizens to present solutions. The issue poll attracted about 1500 people, 135 stories were posted, almost 30 people proposed solutions, and over 90 per cent of the participants said that they would participate again. Following the consultation exercise, participants were invited to a national round table to comment on the officials' draft report.

This reportedly successful e-consultation project required careful planning and sizeable human and financial resources. Dr. Bennett's conclusion was that 'e-consultation can provide a rich new input into our work by allowing us to gauge whether or which policy or program recommendations resonate with the values of Canadians they are intended to serve' (Chenier and Peters 2003).

Table 8.12
Daily importance of Internet technologies

Reported importance (%)	MPs		MPPs	
	2003	2005	2003	2005
Highly important	42.4	48.8	45.5	54.8
Important	45.5	34.1	38.6	29.0
Somewhat important	10.6	11.0	9.1	14.5
Of minor importance	—	2.4	2.3	—
Not at all important	1.5	3.7	4.5	1.6
Total	100.0	100.0	100.0	100.0
N	66	82	44	62

Note: The 2003 MP survey and the 2005 MPP survey did not include the category 'Of minor importance.'
Sources: 2003 MP survey, Kernaghan, Riehle, and Lo; 2005 MP survey; 2003 Ontario MPP survey; 2005 Ontario MPP survey.

Ontario legislative committees have promoted electronic citizen participation by using video conferencing. On many occasions, committees have permitted witnesses in remote locations to testify from their home community, thereby saving substantial travel costs. Similarly, committees are able to avoid the costs of travelling to communities where they have learned that only one or a few people want to testify on the topic under consideration. In 2005, the Standing Committee on Social Policy webcast its complete set of hearings on the Accessibility for Ontarians with Disabilities Act. This initiative included the provision of closed-captioned simultaneous interpretation for the hearing impaired, ASL sign language interpretation, and large print agendas for the visually impaired. The webcasting provided access for those unable to attend the hearings or without access to OntParl, the parliamentary television channel. In addition, meetings held throughout the province were filmed and then broadcast on OntParl and webcast.

Both federal and Ontario legislators strongly affirmed the importance to their work life of Internet technologies such as e-mail, the World Wide Web, and the BlackBerry (table 8.12). A substantial majority believed that the importance of these technologies would increase over the next two years (table 8.13). These data show that Internet technologies already occupy a central place in the work life of legislators and suggest that the importance of these technologies is likely to increase.

Table 8.13
Change over the next two years in the importance of Internet technologies to work life

	MPs		MPPs	
Response (%)	2003	2005	2003	2005
Yes – increase in importance	66.7	65.4	69.6	72.6
No – stay the same	6.1	18.5	13.0	12.9
Uncertain	3.0	7.4	8.7	11.3
A member of my staff undertakes this function on my behalf	24.2	8.6	8.7	3.2
Total	100.0	100.0	100.0	100.0
N	66	82	46	62

Sources: 2003 MP survey, Kernaghan, Riehle, and Lo; 2005 MP survey; 2003 Ontario MPP survey; 2005 Ontario MPP survey.

Canadian legislators, like those in the United States (Congressional Management Foundation 2005; Johnson 2004), are becoming increasingly overloaded with e-mail messages, many of which are from non-constituents. An Ontario MPP explained in 2005 that there have always been a few constituents who telephoned the constituency office regularly but now some of them 'send 8–15 messages daily. In the past, when they would have to buy a stamp for each message, such people would send only to their own MPP. Now, once they have saved the list of MPPs, they can send their opinions to every MPP without cost. This overburdens the IN Box of even the most patient staff of an MPP.'

Another MPP noted that the staff resources now devoted to responding to e-mails could be devoted to community outreach or research.

Table 8.14 depicts the differences between MPs and MPPs in the types of e-mail messages they receive. Twenty-three per cent of MPs' messages are individually written messages on policy issues, compared to 13.8 per cent of MPPs' messages. However, MPPs receive more requests for assistance (24.4 per cent) than MPs do (14.7 per cent), probably because provincial governments provide more services than the federal government does. Legislators in both jurisdictions also receive a large number of what they consider 'useless' messages (such as spam, junk mail).

A quarter of the e-mails received by both MPs and MPPs are form e-mail messages on policy issues. A federal minister noted that efficiency is reduced 'by interest groups and non-constituents blocking up e-mail inboxes with form letters that are sent to all MPs regardless of constitu-

Table 8.14
Types and frequency of electronic messages received by legislators

Message type (%)	MPs		MPPs	
	2003	2005	2003	2005
Individually written messages on policy issues	—	23.0	13.7	13.8
Form messages on policy issues	—	23.7	16.8	23.2
Constituent requests for assistance	—	14.7	31.6	24.4
Miscellaneous but useful messages	—	13.3	9.8	15.6
Useless messages	—	23.6	26.7	22.3
Total	—	98.3	98.6	99.3

Note: Question not asked in the MP survey 2003. Respondents were asked what percentage of electronic messages fell into the above categories. Categories do not add up to 100% because MPs and MPPs self-selected the frequencies of certain types of electronic messages they received.
Sources: 2005 MP survey; 2003 MPP survey, 2005 MPP survey

ency.' Another federal respondent viewed form letter messages as spam. He lamented, 'Spam is a problem. Our one rural office had 1400 emails today from lobbyists.' An Ontario MPP noted, 'Mass mailing ties up staff time trying to identify constituents.'

Conclusions

The previous chapter, which dealt with online campaigning and voting, provided support for both cyber-optimists and cyber-pessimists. Similarly, this chapter shows considerable advance in the use of IT by both legislatures and legislators, but this advance has not been as extensive as some IT advocates have anticipated. Among the grounds for a pessimistic view of future IT usage are these:

- *One-way flow.* Most MP and MPP websites focus on such one-way communication features as a biography, contact information, and press releases. Very few sites contain advanced IT features like online surveys and video clips. The use of interactive features such as online chats is rare and may not increase significantly with increased computer literacy.
- *E-consultation not for everyone.* More than one-third of both MPs and MPPs are opposed to, or uncertain about, the use of IT for more frequent and broad consultation with citizens.

- *IT not so important.* About one-quarter of both MPs and MPPs do not believe, or are uncertain, that the importance of IT to their work life will increase over the next two years.
- *Excessive e-mail.* Both MPs and MPPs are suffering increasingly from e-mail overload, including form-letter messages from lobbyists and non-constituents.
- *Better connections needed.* In Ontario, MPPs' desks in the Legislative Assembly are not connected to the Internet, MPPs are not allowed to use laptop computers or cell phones in the Chamber, the use of BlackBerrys is restricted, the Assembly website is relatively unsophisticated, and live webcasting of committee proceedings is very limited.

Among considerations supporting an optimistic view of IT usage are these:

- *Computer competence on the rise.* The computer literacy of MPs and MPPs has increased substantially in recent years, and more legislators are themselves using the World Wide Web and e-mail rather than depending on their staff for these activities.
- *Improved connections with citizens and constituents.* The great majority of both MPs and MPPs believe that the use of IT for consulting with constituents is important or highly important, and a majority of them believe that IT should be used for more frequent and broad consultation with citizens.
- *Increasing importance of IT.* A large majority of MPs and MPPs believe that Internet technologies are important to their work life, and two-thirds of them believe that these technologies will become even more important over the next two years.
- *Enhanced IT resources.* The federal Parliament and, to a lesser extent, the Ontario Legislative Assembly have gradually increased the use of IT in their four main business lines – Chamber, committees, caucus, and constituents – and have plans to enhance IT usage further. Both jurisdictions are providing legislators with the basic IT resources needed to perform their legislative and representative roles. The federal Parliament's website has been much improved, and plans are under way to improve the Ontario Legislative Assembly site.
- *Well-connected legislators.* The House of Commons desks of federal MPs are equipped with electricity and connectivity to the House of

Commons network and the Internet, and MPs are permitted to use laptops and BlackBerrys in the House.

- *Better websites.* More than three-quarters of MPs and MPPs now have personal websites, and the overall quality of these sites is gradually improving.

Canada's Crossing Boundaries National Council has focused much of its attention on enhancing politicians' use of IT. The data provided in this chapter support the council's assertion that many politicians are realizing that IT has become a critical tool for doing their work. The council warns that politicians who do not use IT effectively will suffer in the performance of their legislative and representative roles (Crossing Boundaries 2002, 13). Among Crossing Boundaries' proposals to improve the performance not only of individual legislators but also of the legislatures themselves are a new horizontal committee system, electronic voting (especially for referenda), and a 'digital commons' for promoting citizen engagement (22–4). While Canadian politicians are likely to give an increasingly sympathetic hearing to such proposals, the evidence provided in this book indicates that reforms are likely to be slow in coming.

Chapters 7 and 8 of this book have examined politicians' increased use of IT in recent years both in election campaigns and in the federal and Ontario legislatures. This heightened use of IT has had a substantial effect on political parties, political candidates and campaigners, voters, legislators, and legislative officials. Several of the trends noted in these chapters, moreover, suggest the likelihood of an even more substantial impact over the next few years. The extent of this impact will depend on whether changes in the political system and culture foster and facilitate expanded use of IT. The belief that IT will revitalize Canada's representative institutions through such means as electronic voting and electronic engagement seems unduly optimistic about Canadians' interest in both online politics and politics in general. However, IT does offer opportunities to *help* renew democratic institutions by permitting political actors to communicate and deliberate with one another more efficiently and more frequently.

APPENDIX: METHODOLOGY

The main data source for this chapter, and an important source for the previous chapter as well, were four legislator surveys consisting of a

Table 8.15
Response rate of surveys

	MP surveys		MPP surveys	
Sample	2003	2005	2003	2005
N	66	82	46	63
Response rate (%)	22.0	26.6	44.6	61.2

Sources: 2003 MP survey, Kernaghan, Riehle, and Lo; 2005 MP survey; 2003 Ontario MPP survey; 2005 Ontario MPP survey.

survey of federal MPs in 2002–3, a survey of Ontario MPPs in 2003, and surveys of both MPs and MPPs in 2005. For the first federal survey, the data were collected between 27 November 2002 and 8 January 2003 by Nancy Riehle of the Crossing Boundaries (CB) project at the KTA Centre for Collaborative Government. To facilitate comparative analysis, the questions used in the CB survey were determined largely through CB's collaboration with Peter Chen in connection with his 2002 survey of Australian legislators (Chen 2002). The CB survey consisted of twenty-three questions, of which twenty-one were multiple-choice and two were short-answer. The survey questions for all four surveys were designed to examine five major themes: general Internet usage, dealing with constituents, electronic campaigning, e-mail usage, and the impact of technology.

The CB survey was distributed through e-mail messages to all MPs inviting their participation. Follow-up inquiries were made by telephone to MPs' offices. The survey was administered online through a website and was available in both official languages. To ensure authenticity and avoid multiple responses, each respondent was required to enter a unique user name and password to access the questionnaire. The data were analysed by researchers outside the CB project but were reported in a CB publication (Kernaghan, Riehle, and Lo 2003).

Table 8.15 shows the response rate for all four surveys. The much higher percentage of returns for Ontario MPPs reflects the increasing problem of survey fatigue among federal MPs in particular. Nevertheless, the sample of members in each survey is itself small and, as explained below, the sample for each survey is generally proportionate to the composition of the legislatures. The response rates compare favourably with similar surveys of IT usage by legislators. A 2002 survey of federal MPs by Jonathan Malloy had a response rate of about 11 per cent (7).

To facilitate comparative analysis, the second federal survey and the two Ontario surveys used substantially the same questions as the CB survey of federal MPs. The 2003 survey of Ontario MPPs was conducted between June 1 and 15 August. A copy of each survey, along with a self-addressed envelope and a cover letter, was sent by regular mail to each member's constituency office and was also e-mailed to that office. The surveys were addressed individually, allowing researchers to track the respondents. To encourage a maximum rate of response, follow-up calls were made four weeks later to the office of each MPP who had not responded. The survey instrument consisted of seventeen closed questions and two open-ended ones designed to facilitate easy response and comparability with the 2003 federal survey. The return rate was almost 45 per cent (46 of 103).

The survey instrument for the 2005 surveys was virtually identical to the 2003 Ontario one. This similarity permitted comparative analysis over time and across the two jurisdictions. The second Ontario survey was conducted between 11 May and 1 August 2005 and the federal survey between 1 June and 1 August. For these two surveys, the questionnaires were sent by regular mail to each member's legislative office as well as to his or her constituency office. On the same day as this mailing, an e-mail message was sent to all members to alert them and their staffs that the survey would arrive shortly. This e-mail message also permitted members to complete the questionnaire by means of an electronic survey form that was attached as a Word document. Initially, little use was made of this electronic option, but it became the popular choice for those members who responded positively to follow-up requests.

Within three weeks from the first mailing, each Ontario MPP who had not responded received a telephone follow-up request. Those members or their assistants who showed interest in completing the survey received a personally addressed e-mail message accompanied by yet another copy of the questionnaire. For federal MPs, who greatly outnumber their Ontario counterparts, the follow-up telephone and e-mail contacts were more limited and were determined in part by the need to create a representative sample of respondents. A larger number of MPs than MPPs declined to participate, citing either survey fatigue or a policy of not responding to any surveys.

An important caveat in interpreting the data is that a substantial number of the surveys were completed on behalf of members by staff in their legislative or constituency offices. Permitting this option facilitated a higher response rate and recognized that most correspondence directed to members is filtered through staff assistants. In the 2003 CB survey only 34.8 per cent of the surveys were completed by the legislators themselves, compared to 52.2 per cent for the 2003 Ontario survey, 51.2 per cent for the 2005 federal survey and 41.3 per cent for the 2005 Ontario survey.

The respondents to the four surveys were generally representative of the composition of the legislatures. Compared to the House of Commons, the 2003 CB survey under-represented the Bloc Québécois and the Province of Quebec and slightly under-represented the Liberal Party. Women, the Canadian Alliance, non-rural ridings, Western Canada, and Ontario were slightly over-represented. In the 2003 Ontario survey, the Liberal Party, the New Democratic Party, and urban ridings were somewhat over-represented.

The returns for the 2005 federal survey over-represented Ontario, Alberta, and Prince Edward Island, but substantially under-represented Quebec. All political parties, except the Bloc Québécois, were slightly over-represented. The Bloc was considerably under-represented, despite repeated efforts through French-language communications to secure their participation – a problem encountered by other political scientists (Docherty 1997, xvii). The 2005 Ontario respondents were representative of the composition of the Legislative Assembly, except for the over-representation of women.

Notes

1 For information on the Parliamentary Precinct, we are indebted to Louis Bard, chief information officer of the House of Commons, and Janice Hilchie, principal clerk, Information Management, Procedural Services, House of Commons.

2 For information on the Ontario Legislative Assembly, we are grateful to Todd Decker, clerk of journals and procedural research, and Lyn Center, client communications and liaison.

9 E-Consultation: Technology at the Interface between Civil Society and Government

SANDFORD BORINS AND DAVID BROWN

In this chapter we discuss the impact of IT on public consultation, a key component of policy-making. The previous chapter dealt with the use of IT by legislators; in this chapter, our focus shifts back to the executive branch, in that the consultations we discuss were conducted either by public servants or by ministers acting in their departmental capacity. As in other chapters, we apply a channel choice framework; thus, online consultation is seen as an alternative to other forms, for example, written communications or attendance at public meetings or hearings chaired by legislators or regulators. We deal mainly with citizen consultation, which involves government receiving information about citizens' views, and less with citizen engagement, in which government enters into deliberative dialogue and shared decision making with citizens (Democratic Renewal Secretariat 2005). We do so because most of what we have observed was consultation, rather than engagement, and also because we see the former as a prelude to the latter. We begin with six short case studies of recent consultations – three in Ontario and three at the federal level.[1] We then discuss five common themes that emerge from the cases: the creation of organizational capacity for consultation, relationships between websites and portals used for consultation, coordination and timing of consultation initiatives during a government's mandate, consultation and channel choice, and the potential to move beyond consultation to more intensive citizen engagement.

E-Consultation in the Federal Government

While never central to its policy process, the federal government has historically made use of public consultation tools – most notably royal commissions and white and green papers – to solicit input on major public policy issues. Consultations became more common in the early 1990s: for example, the Mulroney government's Green Plan included an extensive public consultation exercise in 1990 (Gale 1997). In the early Chrétien years, then finance minister Paul Martin made frequent use of public consultation in developing budget measures to reduce the deficit, and the Department of Finance was an early adopter of the Internet to publish and obtain feedback on budget documents. In 1996, a requirement to consult stakeholders and Canadians in general became part of a major reform of the government's regulatory process. A fundamental element of all consultation has been the requirement, based on the Official Languages Act, that they be equally accessible in all channels in both English and French.

The emergence of the Internet in the early 1990s and the launch of the Government of Canada website in 1995 were paralleled by several experiments with online citizen engagement. By 2000, the Privy Council Office (PCO) Communications Secretariat had taken an interest in online consultation and began to partner with Public Works and Government Services Canada (PWGSC), which had initiated some of the earlier experiments, to sponsor the development of online methodologies and an e-consultation community of practice within the federal government to put them to use. An important step was the establishment in PWGSC of the On-line Consultation Technical Centre of Expertise, headed by Elisabeth Richard, a pioneer in government use of the Internet (Debbie Cook, interview 26 April 2005; Elizabeth Richard, interview 18 April 2005).

The idea of establishing an online consultation portal was first considered in 2000 in discussions led by Debbie Cook at the PCO. In 2001, she spent six months on exchange in the British Cabinet Office studying the Blair government's approach to online consultation, which was then a prominent feature of its official website. Subsequently, Heritage Canada took the lead in launching a pilot public consultation portal, in 2003, and then in developing a business case for a permanent portal (Stephanie Ashton, interview 15 April 2005). The deputy minister of heritage, Alex Himelfarb, became cabinet secretary in 2002 and was an important supporter of the initiative in both positions. In December 2004, the Treasury Board Government Communications Policy was revised to include a section on consultation and citizen engagement. This mandated a permanent Consulting with Canadians portal (http://www.consultingcanadians.gc.ca), which went live on the Canada Site in

April 2005. The policy required that all public consultations be publicized on Consulting with Canadians and set out procedures to be followed when the consultations are online, including ensuring that public feedback is adequately processed. At the same time, it was decided to give the Consulting with Canadians portal a low profile, with access through the 'What's New' button on the Canada Site home page rather than on the home page itself (Luc Gauthier, interview 27 April 2005).

While most of the impetus for these developments came from the public service, they were backed by Cabinet Secretary Himelfarb and Prime Minister Martin, who declared his support for online consultation at a Crossing Boundaries Conference in April 2003 (Martin 2003). The policy changes also required endorsement by two Cabinet committees: Treasury Board, which provides funding and sets the policy framework for federal government communications and consultation, and Operations, which oversees the government's communications.

Consultations are generally considered to be related to three areas of public policy development: major national policy issues, regulations, and service delivery (Richard interview 2005). The first two in particular engage ministers, while the third is largely the domain of officials. The most fully prescribed area is the development of regulations. The *Canada Gazette*, the official government newspaper published by PWGSC, has online and paper editions, both legally authoritative. The government's Regulatory Policy, administered by the PCO, requires that all draft regulations be pre-published in part 1 of the *Gazette* for 'timely and thorough consultation with the interested parties,' using the channel of the public's choice. The final texts must be published in part 2, showing the results of the part 1 consultations (Carol Kennedy, interview 19 April 2005).

Three cases illustrate the federal government's experience with e-consultations. Two illustrate uses of e-consultation in policy development – the 2003 foreign policy review with the sponsoring minister actively involved, and the spam task force that worked at the level of officials and stakeholders. The Spike TV case, which is quite different, deals with e-consultation in the regulatory context. A second regulatory case, involving non-steroid anti-inflammatory drugs such as Celebrex, Vioxx, and Bextra, is posted at http://www.digitalstate.ca/supp/ch9.html.

Dialogue on Foreign Policy

On 22 January 2003, Foreign Affairs and International Trade Minister

Bill Graham announced a Dialogue on Canadian Foreign Policy, based on a public discussion paper and an extensive program of public consultations that continued until 1 May 2003. The process ended with a *Report to Canadians* from Graham dated 27 June 2003. The consultations were based on the philosophy that 'foreign policy must be informed by public advice fully representative of our country's diverse population and regions' (Graham 2003). They involved an intensive range of activities, including fifteen townhalls across Canada (in-person events complemented by advance online notice, simultaneous webcasting, and online posting of the results), nineteen expert round tables, a national Youth Forum, meetings with the provinces, and parallel activities by the House of Commons Standing Committee on Foreign Affairs and International Trade.

Technology-based methodologies were integral to the process. Consultation documents were available online, and some 28,000 copies of the discussion paper were downloaded. Over 3400 responses to the paper's five themes were submitted online in English and another 378 in French. A bilingual, moderated online discussion forum was available for each of the five themes, and attracted almost 2000 participants; the townhalls were webcast and the documents from the expert round tables were posted on the consultation site along with video interviews with participants and weekly summaries of the round tables and the online forums. All was supported by an extensive consultation website on the DFAIT site containing numerous information resources (Graham 2003).

Foreign Minister Graham was actively involved in the process, participating personally in all fifteen townhalls, and five of his Cabinet colleagues also participated. This involvement undoubtedly stimulated public interest in the process and raised expectations about the outcome. The use of the website was seen by DFAIT as one of the innovative aspects of the consultation, and there was a conscious effort to expand the traditional array of consultative tools, including considerable care to establish proper rules of conduct for participation in the online discussion forum (Foreign Affairs and International Trade Canada 2004). This added dimension clearly broadened the reach of the consultation by providing an accessible and accurate source of information about the process and a record of what was being said. It is unlikely that such extensive consultations could have been carried out in three months without the website and online tools. Multi-channel approaches to individual events such as townhalls made them more widely accessible and gave them greater depth.

In the end, however, the consultation can be considered an 'artistic success' but a political failure. Coming at the end of the Chrétien government and for practical purposes feeding into a policy-making vacuum, Bill Graham's *Response to Canadians* was essentially a personal statement, in which he could only assert that the results of the consultation would inform his discussions with Cabinet colleagues (Graham 2003). In any event, he was moved to the Defence portfolio when Paul Martin came into office in December 2003. Martin chose to launch a completely new process for reviewing foreign policy, which by the end of his time in office had still not moved beyond an international policy statement written by officials without any further public consultation.

Spam Task Force Online Forum

Spam, or unsolicited commercial e-mail, is an artefact of the online environment. In May 2004, Lucienne Robillard, then minister of industry, created a Special Task Force on spam to oversee implementation of a comprehensive plan to reduce its volume. The task force brought together experts and stakeholders representing Internet service providers, businesses that use e-mail for legitimate commercial activity, and consumers. The action plan was itself the product of earlier consultation, and the ten members of the task force were asked to consult through implementation working groups in each of the action plan's five areas.

The full task force met nine times over six months, issuing its report in May 2005. Each working group hosted an online forum in which the public was invited to comment on a discussion paper and other task force documents, with the promise that comments would be taken into account by the task force. This yielded 171 postings on the online bulletin board (which was not, however, carried on the Consulting with Canadians portal). In addition, there was a webcast stakeholder round table discussion and a private online forum for the members of the task force and working groups (Industry Canada 2005).

The exercise was sponsored by the branch in Industry Canada that had supported the Information Highway Advisory Council in the mid-1990s and later efforts to consult the IT-related business community. The online element was considered to be one part of the larger task force effort. The public forum was judged to have introduced a wider range of views and to have been more conversational. The stakeholder discussions were more expert but less lively. The private forum turned out to be an effective method of disseminating information and documents to task force participants, but not as strong as more traditional means such as e-mail and list-serves for group discussion among them. While both the internal and the public online forums involved some initial costs to construct, they required limited resources to run. In the final judgment, the online element was considered worthwhile and would probably be used again in appropriate circumstances (David Charter, interview 20 April 2005).

Distribution of Spike TV: Call for Comments

In March 2004, the Canadian Radio-television and Telecommunications Commission (CRTC) issued a call for comments on a request from the Canadian Association of Broadcasters (CAB) that Spike TV be removed from the list of non-Canadian programming services that could be carried by Canadian cable and satellite distribution companies. The consultation, which was posted on the Consulting with Canadians site, was open to all interested parties, including the general public. It was conducted entirely online, and the posted submissions formed the basis of the commission's decision – to reject the CAB application and approve Spike TV for distribution in Canada – issued in January 2005.

The issue arose when the Nashville Network (TNN), based in the United States, was taken over by Viacom in August 2003 and re-branded as Spike TV, a 'men's lifestyle' programming service. The CAB, representing Canadian-based television networks, including pay and specialty channels, argued that the programming changes were so extensive that Spike TV was no longer covered by the previous approval for TNN and that it posed a competitive threat to Canadian broadcasters and distributors.

The CRTC consultation lasted two months and generated 219 submissions, of which 184 were opposed to the CAB submission. Submissions – from individuals, corporate stakeholders, national associations, and several MPs – were sent by mail, e-mail, or fax. All were posted on the CRTC website in a downloadable form and were also available in paper form for consultation in CRTC offices across the country. The CRTC made it clear that its decision was based solely on this material, combined with its own internal staff work (Canadian Radio-television and Telecommunications Commission 2005).

This case illustrates the use that a regulatory agency can make of the online medium in addressing a relatively straightforward and non-technical issue with a wide range of public and stakeholder perspectives. The input and discussion was entirely in writing, as an alternative to public hearings, but the focal point of that exchange was the postings on the CRTC website. The chosen medium does not seem to have been controversial, perhaps helped by the fact that the participants in the consultation could be expected to be reasonably technologically oriented. (The demographic profile of the Spike TV target audience – males aged between eighteen and forty-nine – is also among the highest users of the Internet.) It seems likely that this will become a standard part of the public consultations toolkit for the CRTC and perhaps other regulatory agencies.

E-Consultation in Ontario

The Harris government, elected in 1995, believed that by winning power on the basis of a detailed election manifesto – the Common Sense Revolution – it had ipso facto consulted the voters, and its obligation was to enact the provisions of that manifesto. Premier Harris had little enthusiasm for extensive public consultation about particular pieces of legislation and saw elaborate consultation exercises as simply giving the government's political enemies a platform. His more pragmatic successor, Ernie Eves, took the first steps in e-consultation. Some low-key e-consultations were initiated by individual ministries, such as Municipal Affairs and Housing's province-wide consultation on 'smart growth' and Transportation's consultation on aggressive driving. The most significant central e-consultation dealt with the 2003 Throne Speech, which was posted on the government's home page and linked to a website designed to facilitate response to the speech. There were 9100 visitors to this website, and 2700 of them completed an online questionnaire (Steven Green, interview 16 June 2005).

The government's IT organization, based in the Management Board Secretariat, was responding to the politicians' emerging interest in e-consultation. Corporate Chief Strategist Joan McCalla hired Melissa Thomson to do background work on e-consultation.[2] Thomson had entered the Ontario Public Service (OPS) through its internship program, which is geared to attracting talented recent graduates. Thomson established a staff-level working group that met monthly to compare departmental experience in and plans for consultation. However, without strong political support, public servants were reluctant to do much more. That political support came when the McGuinty government took office. One of the six themes in the Liberal election campaign was 'strengthening democracy,' and included in it were commitments to mandatory public hearings for major legislation and the use of citizens' juries (Ontario Liberal Party 2003).

We have included three case studies showing the diversity of consultations launched in the McGuinty government's first year – the first two were central initiatives, while the last involves six consultations initiated by the Ministry of Municipal Affairs and Housing – as an example of consultations undertaken by the different ministries.

Ideas Campaign

The Liberals' campaign document included a commitment to a valued public service, and it was to this commitment that the McGuinty government first turned. In a letter e-mailed to all public servants the day he took office, Premier McGuinty wrote, 'Our team is excited about working with you to implement real, positive change. Ontario is fortunate to have a public service that is second to none' (McGuinty 2003). McGuinty asked the OPS for ideas about ways to improve the quality, delivery, and efficiency of public services.

The Ideas Campaign was launched by Premier McGuinty on 18 December 2003 – less than two months after he took office – and used an intranet site available to all public servants on a common desktop platform, a call centre, and group brainstorming. By the time the Ideas Campaign concluded on 31 January 2004, Ontario's 62,000 public servants made a total of 11,500 suggestions, 92 per cent of which were submitted over the intranet site. A response of this magnitude was far greater than expected. The popularity of online submission indicates that Ontario public servants are comfortable with this technology and also that the software employed was user friendly.

In a sense, the Ideas Campaign was too successful. So many ideas were received that it required considerable time and effort by committees of middle managers to categorize and evaluate them. Ideas that made it through the initial assessment were then sent to the relevant ministry – though it often took time to determine which ministry that was – and some have been implemented. In many cases, public servants suggested things the OPS was already doing. In addition, given the ultimate decentralization of the exercise, the government has not attempted to produce a global list of the top ten or twenty ideas emanating from the campaign (Joyce Barretto, interview 8 April 2005).

2004 Budget Consultation

As discussed in chapter 3, the Eves government had forecast a budget roughly in balance in the 2003–4 fiscal year, and all three parties used this forecast in developing their platforms. The Liberals promised many new initiatives that would be funded by expected revenue growth and the cancellation of some proposed Conservative tax cuts. During the campaign, however, independent analysts began to forecast a deficit approaching $5 billion, and, during the transition period, a former provincial auditor confirmed the pessimistic view of the analysts. Consequently, the key issue that faced the Liberals upon taking office was how to deal with the large and unexpected deficit as well as its implications for their election platform.

The McGuinty government could have made the spending cuts and tax increases necessary to balance the budget unilaterally, and blamed the Eves government. Instead, it launched a public consultation on priorities for budget cuts and speed of eliminating the deficit. In effect, it was attempting to renegotiate its mandate with the electorate. The public consultation was conducted by a full panoply of traditional approaches – travelling legislative committee meetings, meetings between representatives of the Ministry of Finance and interest groups, and townhalls chaired by MPPs – as well as new ones, such as citizens' juries and an online questionnaire. Citizens' juries and meetings heard from a total of 2500 individuals and 540 interest groups or organizations. The online consultation was established at a new site (http://www.townhallontario.gov.on.ca), then located just below the premier's site on the Government of Ontario home page. It used the slogan 'delivering change' and a graphic of diverse faces – both reminiscent of the Liberals' campaign website. The consultation site was visited by 14,000 people. It contained a comprehensive policy paper laying out deficit projections and policy alternatives, such as new taxes and user fees, spending cuts, and asset sales. The paper was followed by a questionnaire that asked for preferences among these alternatives and priorities for government spending. A measure of interactivity was provided, in the sense that respondents could see the distribution of responses to date, including their own. The questionnaire was completed by 1500 people, only 10 per cent of those who visited the site, suggesting that it was too long and complicated.

The budget focused on health care and elementary and secondary education as the two key priorities, set out a three-year schedule for eliminating the deficit, introduced a progressive tax earmarked for health care spending, and increased a variety of user fees, but did not attempt to raise revenue through asset sales. All of these directions were broadly consistent with the results of the public consultation.

The health tax became a source of controversy because, during the election campaign, McGuinty had made a high-profile commitment not to raise taxes. His critics, in particular the media and taxpayer groups, argued that McGuinty was well aware of the province's deteriorating fiscal situation during the campaign but, cynically, promised new programs he knew he would not be able to deliver without raising taxes. The McGuinty government had not anticipated these attacks and did not respond effectively.

The view in the Premier's Office, Cabinet Office, and Ministry of Finance was that the 2004 budget had established clear fiscal directions for the government's mandate, so the objective of the 2005 budget was to implement those directions. The people had been consulted in 2004 and they had spoken, so it would appear indecisive to launch another full-scale consultation (Karen Rosen, interview 31 May 2005). Thus, the e-consultation on Town Hall Ontario for the 2005 budget was simply a paragraph outlining the government's approach to tackling the deficit and asking for suggestions on where to cut spending and on how the federal government – which, by the province's estimate, receives $23 billion more in taxes from Ontario than Ontario receives in return – should help solve the problem. There was no longer any interactivity: those who responded did not see any other responses or even a summary of them.

Ministry of Municipal Affairs and Housing Consultations

The Ministry of Municipal Affairs and Housing (MMAH) was the most active of all ministries in consultation, launching consultations on six topics: rent reform, protection of the greenbelt surrounding Toronto (in two phases), planning reform, rural planning, and a review of the Municipal Act. In addition to public meetings and facilitated stakeholder consultations, all had an online component that included consultation documents and online surveys. Only the three most significant consultations – greenbelt protection, rent reform, and planning reform – were linked to the Town Hall Ontario website. The expertise for this work was found internally in the Technology and Business Solutions Branch and Communications Branch. The latter developed and managed the Web pages and questionnaires for the different branches of MMAH that had overall responsibility for each consultation. Content management software already in use by the ministry was employed. The incremental cost of adding an e-consultation component to each consultation was approximately $22,000, consisting mainly of software modification, server testing, and staff time (Louise Simos, interview 15 April 2005).

The balance between online and paper questionnaires varied from consultation to consultation, depending largely on how the two alternatives were promoted to target groups. In the second phase of the greenbelt-protection consultation, 90 per cent of approximately two thousand surveys were submitted online, while in the rent reform consultation, the ratio was 50:50. In the case of rent reform, concern about the digital divide prompted an emphasis on, and widespread distribution of, postage-paid paper questionnaires. One instance of an entirely online component was the display of detailed maps of the greenbelt on the MMAH website. It was considered too expensive to publish and distribute paper maps. Landowners in the greenbelt area were intensely interested in how greenbelt-protection policies would affect them, and as a consequence the map pages had 62,000 visits (Simos interview 2005).

Seeing the Big Picture

The objective of this section is to develop a 'big picture' of consultation in the federal and Ontario governments, based on the smaller pictures of the six cases. Electronic consultation is relatively new to the federal and Ontario governments, and its development has largely paralleled the general evolution of their use of technology in dealings with the public, moving from a marginal to an increasingly central role in combination with other more traditional channels. With the development of the Internet, there has been a systematic effort in the federal government at the working and middle management levels, encouraged by the central agencies and a few key senior managers, to explore and entrench e-consultation tools and activities. While it was not adopted as a government-wide priority by the Chrétien government, e-consultation was gradually taken on board by individual ministers and in particular as part of the regulatory process where there were clear advantages for arm's length decision making. Under the Martin government, e-consultation moved to a more structured institutional environment and was cautiously linked to efforts to address the democratic deficit. The Harper government has given no early indication of its approach to e-consultation, although the regulatory process remained in place.

In Ontario, there was also interest in e-consultation at the level of individual ministries. At the political level, the Harris government's lack of interest in consultation of any kind was replaced with greater receptiveness by Eves. The McGuinty government took office with a strong commitment to consultation, which led to both central initiatives and a much more receptive climate for ministerial initiatives.

The themes presented below are the components of a bigger picture of practices that both governments have been developing to manage e-consultation.

Organizational Capacity

The federal government's organizational capacity to use e-consultation has gradually matured over a ten-year period. From the outset, a priority for the PCO Communications Secretariat and PWGSC – the public service leaders in this area – was to understand the nature and implications of the technology and its potential applications. At early stages, this primarily involved facilitating the emergence of a 'community of practice' among interested departments and bringing in outside expertise. With the establishment of the Centre of Expertise on On-line Consultation Technologies at PWGSC, a permanent source of technologically oriented but policy-sensitive advice became available. The Treasury Board Secretariat's Chief Information Officer Branch and Government Communications Policy office have supported these developments without actively promoting them.

The 2004 changes to the Government Communications Policy provided the backbone for the current federal approach, in particular the recognition of the Consulting with Canadians portal as the permanent government consultation site and a requirement to obtain PCO approval for all consultation initiatives and to post them on Consulting with Canadians. The policy also requires departments engaging in online consultation to develop a capacity to deal with the input that is provided electronically. The policy changes were approved by two Cabinet committees; combined with the ongoing role of the Operations Committee and Prime Minister Martin's known interest, this provided a basic level of collective ministerial support for the growing adoption by individual portfolio ministers of e-consultation.

The biggest challenge has been to embed the use of e-consultation in the ongoing processes of government. E-consultation is by its nature a multi-disciplinary function, linking program managers, policy makers, the public communications community, and the information management community – not a natural alliance. Part of the continuing evolution has been that there is no standard model for locating the lead responsibility for e-consultation within departments, and in different parts of the government it can be found in any of these areas. Similarly, e-consultation requires new combinations of public service skills that are still relatively scarce. A key element of the 2004 Communications Policy change was creation of a more formal role for the directors-general of communications, whose responsibilities include media relations, publishing, advertising, and polling on behalf of their ministers. This group had previously been cautious about e-consultation because of concerns about managing public expectations and potentially large volumes of input. The policy change ensures that any e-consultations will be managed, but does not by itself bring the methodology into the policy and decision-making mainstream (Gauthier interview 2005).

Regulations constitute a distinct subset of federal e-consultations. The starting point is policy requirements for public consultation in the early stages of the regulatory process. The seven major regulatory departments (Agriculture, Environment, Finance, Health, Industry, Justice, and Transport) each have a regulatory coordinator and are extensive users of the Consulting with Canadians portal. The PCO Regulations Secretariat provides an overview of the regulatory process and supports the Cabinet Operations committee, which processes orders-in-council and considers draft primary legislation and the government's legislative strategy among its varied functions. The secretariat in turn has a close working relationship with the *Canada Gazette*, as the government's newspaper of record, and with the legislative drafting office in Justice.

E-consultation has also been indirectly supported by Government On-Line (GOL), Ottawa's initiative to deliver government services electronically. At its outset in 1999, GOL excluded initiatives in policy 'services,' including e-consultation. There is no doubt, however, that the general success of GOL has strengthened the institutional environment and technology infrastructure for e-consultation and created a considerably higher level of awareness and support for electronic tools among government program and information managers.

The situation in Ontario was somewhat different. Without comparable maturity of ministerial capacity for consultation, with fewer central agency resources devoted to supporting ministerial initiatives, and with several central consultation initiatives as an immediate priority, the McGuinty government moved quickly to create capacity in the Consultation Projects Office (CPO). The office was led by Lee Allison Howe, an associate deputy minister with a background in communications, and Joyce Barretto, a senior manager with a similar background, and was staffed by a handful of younger public servants who were or had recently been in the OPS's internship program (Barretto interview 2005). The CPO worked hard to get the Ideas Campaign and budget consultation underway within eight weeks and to run them simultaneously. One of the consequences of the success of the Ideas Campaign is that the office was bogged down for several months after the campaign deadline of 31 January 2004 analysing and evaluating submissions.

While the CPO handled the centrally launched initiatives, other ministries showed that they did have the capacity to manage consultations, including those with an online component. As a result, Cabinet Office decided to wind down the CPO, and it closed in April 2005, with its staff all reassigned to Cabinet Office, its original home, or to other ministries. Though Cabinet Office moved away from active engagement in consultation, the CIO's office moved back into the area. In fall 2004, it established a small e-Citizen Engagement Support Office with a mandate to support consultation and citizen engagement in other ministries, to develop guidelines for e-citizen engagement, to undertake pilot projects such as public access terminals in libraries in several rural communities, and to chair a committee in which ministries can share consultation experiences (e-Citizen Engagement Support Office 2005; Glen Padassery and Barbara Swartzentruber, interview 14 April 2005).

Websites and Portals

Even though public consultation fell outside the formal scope of GOL, the citizen-centred philosophy and the well-developed infrastructure of the Canada Site made it natural to look at taking a similar portal-based approach. The two-step approach of an initial pilot sponsored by a department, with central agency encouragement, followed by the embedding of the e-consultation site in the Canada Site was also consistent with the GOL approach. The major debate has been the profile to give to Consulting with Canadians. When it was relaunched on the Canada Site, access was provided through the 'What's New' button on the Canada Site home page, rather than being listed on the home page itself. Departments were given six months from the relaunch in April 2005 to list all their consultation activities on Consulting with Canadians. Central agency officials considered that it could take two or three years before the level of activity was sufficient to warrant placing the Consulting with Canadians link on the home page itself. Even then, Consulting with Canadians is not a consultation site as such but a listing of consultations; actual online consultations are found on the departmental sites concerned (Gauthier interview 2005).

In the early days of Consulting with Canadians, the majority of the listed consultations were related to regulatory activity. In addition to linking to the departmental sites, Consulting with Canadians linked to several other sites that also bear on regulations, including the PCO Regulatory Affairs and Orders-in-Council site, which sets out the policy framework, the *Canada Gazette*, which is the authoritative source of proposed and existing regulations, the Department of Justice site, which lists the Statutes of Canada and legislative drafting guidelines, and House of Commons sites related to the legislative process (Kennedy interview 2005). Curiously, the Regulations Cluster, which is linked to the Canada Business Service Centre on the Canadian Business Gateway, was not linked to this network, even though its purpose was to help the private sector navigate the regulatory maze (Kennedy interview 19 April 2005).

In the case of Ontario, the most significant development was the spectacular rise and fall of the Town Hall Ontario portal (http:// www.townhallontario.gov.on.ca). The portal was started shortly after the 2004 budget consultation was launched, and it was given a prominently located button on the right sidebar of the Government of Ontario home page, just under the button for Premier McGuinty's site. Soon a number of consultations were posted on Town Hall Ontario, and, as we discuss below, there were so many consultations happening that Cabinet Office started to decide which would be posted on Town Hall Ontario and which would be left to ministerial home pages. When the intense consultation that characterized the first year of the

McGuinty government came to an end, Town Hall Ontario's role was greatly diminished. It has been removed from the right sidebar on the Government of Ontario home page and now serves mainly as an archive of completed consultations (Green interview 2005).

A number of factors contribute to this history. The rise of Town Hall Ontario coincided with the McGuinty government's intensely consultative first year. Having a portal provided two advantages in that context. When members of the public search online for a particular consultation, they are likely to be led to it through the portal, which facilitates searching and also exposes them to other consultations that may be of interest. The portal also created a place where public servants conducting a consultation could see the other ongoing consultations, so it supported a developing community of practice (Rosen interview 2005).

When the McGuinty government reduced the pace of consultation, there was less new business appearing on Town Hall Ontario. Individual ministries have mixed views of Town Hall Ontario. While they were happy to have a link to it, they preferred to publicize the consultation pages they had built on their own sites, such as MMAH's http:// www.greenbelt.ontario.ca. The Ministry of Municipal Affairs and Housing wanted to create a Web presence directly related to their issue – greenbelt protection – rather than an indirect link to a general purpose portal (Simos interview 2005). When the greenbelt consultation was a top priority for the government, it had its own link on the Government of Ontario home page. Similarly, the Premier's Office has preferred to create separate websites for new initiatives and to display them initially as buttons on the Government of Ontario home page. For example, in mid-July 2005, in addition to the buttons for the premier's page and premier's kids zone, which are ongoing, there were buttons for major policy initiatives (the 2005 budget, Results Ontario) as well as buttons for flavours of the month: Fair Share – Strong Ontario (Ontario's case for greater federal funding), tsunami relief, consultations about the new City of Toronto Act, and the Shared Air Summit held on 20 June 2005. Over time, these buttons will change, but the point to recognize is that the Premier's Office has used the government's home page, rather than a consultation portal, for its major consultation initiatives.

Ontario's recent experience does raise questions about the future of consultation portals. A consultation portal is intrinsically different from a service portal. In the latter, individuals approach the government for service, and are encouraged to do so through a portal struc-ture that will ultimately lead them to the right door. In the case of the consultations, it is the government that is approaching individuals and groups to encourage them to comment. However, citizens are less likely to be interested in consultation in general than in consultation about issues of concern to them. Citizens are therefore unlikely to go to a consultation portal to see if there is something there they want to comment on; rather, they need to be informed that there is a consulta-tion happening on an issue of concern to them. In addition, from the point of view of the ministry or ministries doing the consultation, the best way is to frame the consultation in terms of that particular issue. If this were the case, then the most a consultation portal could do would be to serve as a back door to help individuals who saw an ad for a spe-cific consultation but forgot the URL, to find their desired consultation. Portals may, however, be more useful to institutional users and indi-viduals who regularly participate in specific areas of public policy, such as regulations.

Consultation, Coordination, and a Government's Mandate

In the early years in particular, the impetus for developing an e-consul-tation capacity in the federal government came primarily from inter-ested officials in central agencies and in departments that had a history of public consultation. It was not driven by either top management or politicians, and for some time had a 'below the radar' quality. This hes-itation had several elements, including concerns by politicians that direct online contact between public servants and the public would risk creating competition with the roles of MPs and ministers, and con-cerns by the communications community that e-consultations would create unmanageable expectations and resource pressures. These con-cerns were gradually assuaged by the gradualist approach adopted by PCO and PWGSC, an accumulation of experience with the e-consulta-tion medium, and the movement of electronic channels into the main-stream of government interaction with the public. Because the central agencies were involved from the outset, albeit not always enthusiasti-cally as institutions (as opposed to leading roles played by individu-als), it was a natural step for e-consultation to be embedded in central agency policy and coordination machinery. Less clear is whether a sin-gle model will develop in departments – leaving aside the regulatory process – given the number of different disciplines involved. The fact that PCO, in support of the Cabinet Operations Committee, signs off on new consultation initiatives whether or not they have an online component, ensures that departmental ministers are also involved (Dave Thompson, interview 25 April 2005).

To date, the impact of the electoral mandate cycle at the federal level is also unclear. The final year of the Chrétien government saw at least two ministerially led public consultations, on foreign policy and on a national identity card, but both turned out to reflect personal agendas of ministers expected to leave their portfolios and did not lead to changes in government policy. The Martin government, which came to office at the end of a mandate cycle, did not launch major public consultations, although it did strengthen the policy and institutional framework for consultation, in particular online. The election of minority governments in 2004 and 2006 rendered the issue of planning for a five-year mandate cycle irrelevant. In addition, a minority government, in its uncertain and likely short tenure, will probably focus on implementing its election platform.

The McGuinty government's case is completely different, since it was elected with a strong majority and has the luxury of planning for a full cycle. In its first year in office, it started numerous consultations. In addition to those discussed above, there were consultations about waste diversion (Ministry of the Environment), sustainable development of the Great Lakes Water Basin and provincial parks (both Ministry of Natural Resources), post-secondary education (Ministry of Colleges and Universities), mandatory retirement (Ministry of Labour), and conservation (several ministries). The Liberals came to power with ambitious plans and a deficit that was higher than anticipated when the plans were made; thus, consultation is a way of realigning plans and fiscal realities. Some of the McGuinty government's plans were vague, and consultation may have helped to bring precision. Finally, the McGuinty government believed that democracy demands consultation and that the Harris government's disinclination to consult was undemocratic.

Launching so many consultations at the same time could lead to consultation overload, and Cabinet Office had to play the role of 'air traffic controller,' coordinating consultations to set priorities and to ensure that ministries were aware of each other's efforts. Thus, Cabinet Office allocated space on the Town Hall Ontario website, restricting it to the most high-profile consultations.

A second aspect of coordination regarding consultation involves inter-ministerial coordination within a specific consultation. In most instances, the consultations were conducted by one ministry, which had lead responsibilities. In some instances, such as greenbelt protection, the lead ministry consulted with other ministries that were affected by its initiative (Michael Bunce, interview 13 April 2005). The one instance that involved extensive inter-ministerial coordination was conservation. Starting a consultation about a broad theme necessarily brought a total of fifteen ministries with different pieces of the theme to the table, and got them all involved in developing a common document to publish in hard copy and post online (Baretto interview 2005).

The pace of consultation has now slowed; ministries have completed their consultations and are now drafting legislation or regulations and will be implementing them. Thus, the government has moved from the policy-development phase that would characterize the first year of a first mandate to a program-development phase and ultimately a program-delivery phase (David Guscott, interview 20 April 2005). In the run-up to the election scheduled for 4 October 2007, the McGuinty government hopes to focus the voters' attention on the results it has achieved, so additional consultations would be a distraction (Rosen interview 2005).

Consultation and Channel Choice

The federal government's 2004 consultation and public engagement policy makes it clear that consultations should as a rule be conducted through a range of channels. Unlike transactional services to the public, there was little serious suggestion that consultations should be conducted only electronically. Discussions of e-consultation methodology had highlighted the importance of recognizing that participants in online consultations do not necessarily fully represent the population, although they can represent defined – and often geographically dispersed – communities of interest. Electronic consultations were generally seen as supplementing other channels, as it was judged that there was not a clear business case indicating that electronic tools and channels will on their own significantly expand the reach of public consultations or realize major cost savings (Cook interview 2005).

The foreign policy review case study, however, did demonstrate that electronic tools can be effectively combined with more traditional methodologies such as public meetings and written input to provide a process that is richer overall. Indeed, other case studies suggest that there may be dimensions of public consultation where the electronic channel is the central element. The spam task force found that electronic tools facilitated the work of the task force and its working groups. The CRTC's Spike TV consultation used the website as the vehicle for making available a definitive compendium of submissions, including those originally submitted in written form, and the CRTC used its online process as an alternative to a public hearing. While the spam task force judged that its online input was at times less expert than in-person discussions, all three cases accepted the public online input as a legitimate contribution to the process, and the online vehicles were a key means to make available the documents of record that formed the basis for the consultation.

Ontario's deficit meant that considerations of channel choice were more strongly affected by cost considerations. In this analysis, the two main alternatives are face-to-face consultation (the spoken word) and written consultation. Two types of face-to-face consultation are facilitated workshops (for example, citizens' juries) and public meetings. Facilitated workshops involve fewer people but greater depth of engagement, while public meetings can accommodate a larger number of people, but often with little engagement. Both are relatively expensive in terms of design work done by either staff or consultants, travel and accommodation for speakers or facilitators, and facilities and equipment rental (Ministry of Municipal Affairs and Housing 2004; Simos interview 2005).

For written consultation, four alternatives are written submissions, paper surveys, online surveys, and telephone polling (the last defined as written because its final product is in written form). Written submissions provide substantial engagement for the writer; their impact, however, clearly depends on who reads them. On the basis of its considerable experience with surveys, MMAH estimates that online surveys are substantially cheaper than telephone polling or paper surveys (Simos interview 2005). Telephone polling is labour intensive and cost has in recent years been driven up by the high percentage of people refusing to answer. The advantage of telephone polling is that, despite the high percentage of refusals, it attempts to be representative of the population. The online survey is less expensive than telephone polling because it eliminates the individuals doing the surveying and less expensive than paper surveys because it eliminates manual data entry. This was a distinct advantage for MMAH, which came to online surveys without substantial resources (Simos interview 2005). The concern with online surveys is representativeness; to the extent that widespread diffusion of the technology erases the digital divide, this problem will diminish.

Simos also observed that, if both paper and online surveys are used, the balance between the two may depend on how aggressively each is marketed. For example, a ministry could choose mass distribution of paper questionnaires to the group it wants to consult, or alternatively it could display a URL prominently in media advertising about the consultation. One of the other advantages of online consultation is that it is less expensive for government and more convenient for an increasingly large proportion of the population if consultation documents are posted online. An example was MMAH's posting of over one hundred detailed maps of the greenbelt online, while publication would have been much more expensive and would have taken much longer.

One distinction between the spoken word and written consultation is that written consultation leaves a paper trail, which is subject to freedom of information requests, while the spoken word, unless official notes are taken, is not. This distinction may explain a greater willingness on the part of politicians to engage in face-to-face consultation. In addition, at least some politicians believe that the art of representation involves assessing the views of citizens in face-to-face meetings, and that this art cannot be replaced by the written word, whatever its form (Perri 6 2004a).

Beyond Consultation to Citizen Engagement

The 2004 consultation section of the federal government's Communications Policy recognizes citizen engagement as a component of public consultation, without providing a very precise definition. Government departments have experimented with citizen engagement, working with organizations such as the Canadian Policy Research Network and the Public Policy Forum to pilot methodologies such as deliberative polling. It was also suggested in interviews that consultation – and in particular e-consultation – was a way to provide a role for citizens between elections. More generally, e-consultations were seen as a potential means of addressing the democratic deficit that is a growing concern to many politicians, in particular that of new and younger voters who have been raised in a networked environment. The continued emergence of new technologies such as text messaging and wireless ensures that the issue will always have an open-ended dimension

(Cook interview 2005).

The McGuinty government's experience to date has been primarily with e-consultation, in which individuals submit their views to government. Rare instances approached genuine interactivity: in the Ideas Campaign participants were able to see one another's views with minimal moderation, and in the 2004 budget, consultation participants could see the numerical totals for the questionnaire. In contrast, the face-to-face approach has been fully interactive, for example in the use of facilitated workshops for some consultations, a stakeholder task force for the greenbelt protection consultation, and a citizens' assembly for a planned consultation on electoral reform (http://www.citizens assembly.gov.on.ca). Are we to conclude that the electronic channel is the best for written questionnaires but that face-to-face is the way to provide interactivity? Is there a place for greater online interactivity in the Ontario government's consultations? There appears to be interest at two levels. Individual ministries have young, computer-savvy Web developers who will want to push this envelope (Simos interview 2005). There is also interest at the political level in exploring online discussion forums (Green interview 2005).

Ultimately the move towards more systematic, online citizen engagement in the policy process will depend on the willingness and ability of politicians to include citizens in a domain that has traditionally been assigned to the institutions of representative democracy. However, it will also depend on citizens themselves – on their willingness to have public institutions evolve in this manner, to participate in these new institutions, and to accept the result.

Conclusion

The case studies illustrate that e-consultation can provide an effective input into policy development, including provision of a more visible, accessible, and effective policy deliberation, and reduction of its costs. At their best, e-consultations constitute online conversations, preparing and supplementing face-to-face deliberations but not replacing them (Cook interview 2005). The nature of the policy issues may also be a factor. The federal government's spam task force addressed an issue arising from the 'new economy,' which lent itself to using new economic tools. Similarly, the Spike TV consultation drew the attention of two groups – media institutions and males aged eighteen to forty-nine – that are known to be more oriented to the Internet than the mainstream of the population. In contrast, the provincial government's e-consultations have been on broader issues (the budget, urban development, and conservation) directed at the entire population. Experience with e-consultation in the both the federal and Ontario governments has been positive enough to launch and sustain electronic channels as a permanent feature of the policy development landscape. Both governments have been working out issues of how to manage e-consultation, and, as technology evolves to provide greater opportunities for citizen engagement on the electronic channel, we expect them to continue working on these management questions.

Looking in more detail at e-consultation, we have a number of specific findings:

- The federal government slowly developed an e-consultation portal and is allowing experience to determine the role it will play. The McGuinty government quickly developed and just as quickly abandoned its portal, instead providing access to individual consultations through the government's or individual ministries' home pages. This suggests that the value of a consultation portal will depend on a government's overall approach to public consultation and policy deliberation.
- It is now well within the ability of communications branches of individual ministries to develop and manage e-consultation. The role of central agencies is now to enforce policy and priorities, provide endorsement and technical expertise, and to serve as a focal point for developing a community of practice. They also provide a vital link to the government's political agenda and its operating style.
- In a majority government with a normal five-year mandate, the primary time for consultation is early in the mandate. Nevertheless, specific issues may arise throughout the mandate necessitating consultation, and end-of-mandate consultation can help departing ministers develop their political legacies or raise their profile before the coming election. The life of a minority government is too short and uncertain for such timing considerations to be relevant. The regulatory process, in contrast, exists independently of the electoral mandate cycle and drives consultation at any time.
- While electronic consultation has begun at a minimal level of engagement, with governments making documents available online and asking for responses which are not posted, both the federal and Ontario governments have moved toward greater engagement,

through such steps as posting responses online, moderated discussion forums, video posting online, and webcasting of in-person town hall discussions. It appears that there is an appetite in both governments for greater experimentation, as part of the progressive integration of online tools into the larger process of public policy consultation and decision-making.

• At the same time, both governments have been much more aggressive in developing online capabilities in providing services to the public than in the policy-making process. It will bear watching whether this is simply a case of policy making lagging behind service delivery – but eventually catching up – or whether there is an inherent tension developing within the triangle formed by the political system, service delivery and policy making that will have longer-term implications for how government and society interact.

Notes

1 There have been a growing number of e-consultation exercises at the municipal level, which, as a result of space constraints, are beyond the scope of this book. One example is a consultation incorporating an online component that the City of Saint John, NB, launched in 2002 to deal with a budget deficit (Culver and Howe 2004). For a discussion of the mobilization of the online community in the United States to oppose the Communications Decency Act in the mid-90s, see Pal (1998).

2 Thomson is profiled in chapter 10.

10 Digital Leadership: The Human Face of IT

SANDFORD BORINS AND DAVID BROWN

Introduction

The arrival of digital technology in the public sector can be seen as a wave sweeping areas of government such as service delivery, consultation, and campaigning to a greater or lesser degree. The discussion in previous chapters, like that of much of the literature, attributes the penetration of digital technology to impersonal factors such as comparative channel costs and other aspects of service provision significant to both users and governments.

The literature on innovation reminds us that some individuals and organizations respond to these impersonal factors sooner than others do, and consequently attempts to explain differences between early and late adopters. Research on the application of IT to government in the 1980s and 1990s has implicitly focused on those in the vanguard. This was a period when a variety of new technologies (GIS, smart cards, electronic kiosks, e-mail, the Internet) were being introduced into the public sector, and researchers were interested in who were the first to adopt them and why. Borins (1998) found that the typical early adopter was a middle manager or front-line worker who was already familiar with the technology – perhaps having learned about it from the children – and who had both the foresight to understand how it could improve the performance of her operation and the leadership skill to communicate this realization to colleagues and superiors whose support was necessary.

The focus on the vanguard misses something that became increasingly important as IT became more pervasive in both government and the rest of society. Early adopters' main concern is launching IT in their own organizations. In the private sector, this is an appropriate consideration, because technology provides a competitive edge. Similarly, in the public sector, their initial focus was on getting the technology established in their own organizations. However, as awareness of the technology increased, the early adopters found growing interest by their colleagues in other departments. Consequently, they began to devote more effort to replication.

Central agencies also became more interested in IT, with the objective of achieving consistency of practice across departments and ensuring political support, or at least political acquiescence, for the changes that were being introduced at a dizzying speed. Although the central agencies took initiatives of their own to introduce IT, much of their leadership came through the use of their standard tools: influencing budgetary decisions, establishing government-wide policy frameworks, and providing direction to the community of IT specialists in government. The central agencies' ability to call meetings, set the agenda, and command public servants' attention gave them considerable influence on the environment in which the front-line leaders did their work. They also played a critical role in interpreting technical issues for non-expert decision-makers. Through their ability to recognize issues and accomplishments in speaking to the politicians and the public, central agencies shaped expectations and incentives. However, perhaps their most important role was to give digital leaders in departments the room and the backing to do their work.

In this chapter, we focus on digital leaders: public servants or politicians who have influenced the spread of IT throughout government. Some may be early adopters who have then encouraged their colleagues in other departments, and others may be those who have attempted to set common standards and ensure consistency across government. Some led through their personal initiative and energy, others by playing traditional roles in new ways. Digital leadership can operate at both the bureaucratic and political levels. At the bureaucratic level, digital leadership is often provided by an early adopter who works through formal or informal networks and communities of practice to help colleagues in other departments. Digital leadership at the senior level involves the development of the government's IT organization, as well as common standards, practices, and infrastructure.

Digital leadership at the bureaucratic level also entails addressing conditions unique to the digital world, or at least accentuated by it. In addition to the technical understanding involved – in an inherently non-technical environment – most digital applications are multidisciplinary, bringing together people with expertise from all corners of IT and well beyond its boundaries. Networked communications cut across hierarchical lines and challenge traditional lines of accountability. Much of the work is done through group collaboration, often self-empowered and driven by individuals who are seeking to unlock the potential of the technology without too much concern for bureaucratic niceties. In the federal government, the Gateways and Clusters initiative, which was powered by collaborative work teams, illustrated the potential of such an approach. At the same time, the teams were operating in a forest of committees that required considerable skill to navigate.

At the political level, individual politicians can be digital leaders by being early adopters, for example, MPs or MPPs who were among the first to establish their own websites or, more recently, blogs. Digital leaders also include ministers in portfolios with responsibility for the IT organization and the application of technology throughout government. At the federal level, Reg Alcock epitomizes both contexts, in that he was an early adopter of technology as a public servant in Manitoba and then a backbench MP from 1993 to 2003, and exercised a key responsibility for overseeing the IT organization as president of the Treasury Board in the Martin government.

This chapter will begin by using the case study approach to learn more about digital leadership. In this instance, the cases are individuals who have exercised or continue to exercise digital leadership. We became aware of these individuals during the research for chapters 2 and 3. We see them as exemplary within the federal or Ontario governments. Yet in a sense, they are also typical: similar individuals could also be found in other jurisdictions. If, however, a jurisdiction is at the leading edge, it is likely to have a critical mass of such individuals and to be able to integrate their efforts coherently. At the bureaucratic level, our sample includes both front-line and senior level digital leaders. Those at the front line include a creator of websites, a policy analyst with a strong interest in e-consultation, and a program manager with a longstanding commitment to improving service delivery. Those at the senior level include three corporate CIOs, one of whom was Ontario's first, and an agency head who serves as a government-wide digital champion. Finally, we discuss Reg Alcock as a politician who spanned both the early adoption and portfolio responsibility aspects of digital leadership at the political level. Space constraints have required us to post several profiles on our website http://www.digitalstate.ca/supp/ch10.html. These are mentioned at the appropriate point in the text.

Front-Line Digital Leadership

Steven Green: Creator of 'Eye-Candy' Websites

As manager of creative services and new media in the Ontario Cabinet Office, Steven Green is personally responsible for the premier's website and Cabinet Office sites – in effect for communicating the government's key messages in cyberspace. Thus, in the transition period he developed options to give Premier McGuinty's site a more contemporary look and more interactivity than Premier Eves's, and during this mandate developed sites devoted to new priorities such as Strong Ontario and Results Ontario.

Green's educational background includes a degree in mass communications and political science and an MBA. He has a strong technical and new media background, having taken a computer apart while in high school and having learned HTML and Mozilla in the early 1990s. He founded a Toronto-based interactive agency in the early nineties and, after the dot-com interlude, he joined the public service.

In the McGuinty government, he sees his website development work as setting up 'eye-candy websites' that use visual appeal to reinforce the messages Cabinet wants to communicate about its policies. He is in frequent contact with staff in the Premier's Office, in particular in the communications and media areas. He is occasionally in touch with Premier McGuinty himself, who has his own views on how to make the websites more effective and user-friendly. It is a point of pride for Green that the websites are developed internally and, consistent with the McGuinty government's emphasis on using existing resources, he counts over $1 million in savings relative to outsourcing since the government has taken office. He is active in the webmasters' community of practice and also teaches courses on communication and new media topics in the Ontario Public Service (OPS).

One of his dissatisfactions in Web development work is the nature of support offered by the Cluster system in the Ontario government. He feels it is unresponsive when it comes to supporting new media products, is cost-ineffective, and provides services typical of the late 1990s. Because he needs sites with advanced features established immediately, Green has reluctantly used external technologies for key parts of the premier's site. Looking ahead, Green's interest is in realizing the potential of IT in citizen engagement, direct democracy, and increased government transparency, and he is now pursuing research on establishing online discussion forums featuring cabinet ministers.

Melissa Thomson: Tech-Savvy High Flyer

Melissa Thomson's brief career in the OPS appears certain to be on the fast track. Where she differs from some others on this career path – or is perhaps representative of an increasing number of them – is that IT forms a key component of her résumé. Thomson does not have the technical background of a Steven Green. Rather, she is skillful at using technology to gather and disseminate information and understands the value of technology as an enabler of innovation.

Thomson joined the OPS after graduate studies in political science at York University. With an interest in social justice and experience in Citizens for Local Democracy – a group that opposed the creation of the Toronto megacity – she looked to the provincial government as a place to work within the system. She was recruited into the OPS internship program in 1999, and moved to the office of Corporate Chief Strategist Joan McCalla in 2001 to work on citizen engagement. Thomson saw this interest as being at variance with the approach of the government of the day, and she stayed below the radar. She devoted her efforts to the analysis of democratic reform while gathering and disseminating information about innovative approaches in other jurisdictions. McCalla supported her initiative to establish an inter-ministerial working group on consultation and also asked her to prepare a policy paper on citizen engagement and democratic reform. Thomson emphasized a strong and clear message: 'Information travels fast, and people organize quickly. Government can either ignore it or get with it.'

Thomson's moment came with the election of the McGuinty government. During the election campaign and transition period, she was asked by Management Board Secretary Kathryn Bouey to work out the implications of the Liberals' platform on democratic reform. When the new government decided to launch its Ideas Campaign and budget consultation, Thomson was an obvious choice to be seconded to the Consultation Projects Office (CPO). The work there was extremely demanding, as the office had few people, little money, and tight deadlines. She worked closely with Brainbank, the Montreal firm that supplied the software for the consultations, and the Central Agencies

Cluster, which adapted it. She also had a good deal of contact with the Premier's Office and the premier himself, as the politicians were clarifying their own priorities through public consultation. Thomson took great satisfaction that CPO 'delivered': the consultations ran smoothly, the software worked, and the government received considerable input from public servants in the Ideas Campaign and the public at large in the budget consultation. The CPO received a team award and Thomson a personal contribution award. She describes her involvement with the CPO as 'an incredibly powerful leadership learning experience.'

After six months at CPO, Thomson could see that it would inevitably wind down, and she began looking for something else. She was seconded to Cabinet Office, as a senior policy adviser, responsible for reviewing Cabinet submissions and brokering policy analysis among ministries. She jokingly observed that, after the intensity of the Ideas Campaign and budget consultation, she was the only person ever to move to Cabinet Office to enjoy a lighter workload. After eighteen months in Cabinet Office, she accepted a new position as executive assistant to Michelle Di Emanuele, deputy minister of government services. She remains on secondment from Joan McCalla's office and stays in touch with the emerging community of practice on consultation. A key conclusion she draws from experiences with e-consultation is that technology is supporting a general cultural shift towards decentralization and consultative decision making.

Michèle McLeod: Leader of Collaborative Work Teams

For most of the life of the federal Government On-Line (GOL), Michèle McLeod was director of Gateways and Clusters in the GOL office. A long-time advocate of improving service and process, she led a team-based, horizontal approach to implementing the most innovative part of GOL.

Trained in psychology, McLeod started working in the federal government in Unemployment Insurance in the early 1970s. From the beginning, she was interested in improving services to clients and streamlining processes in local community offices. In an early management job, she implemented self-directed work teams in a local office to empower the staff to examine their work processes and identify greater efficiencies and to help a deeply backlogged office recover and meet their service delivery standards. With these lessons in hand, she relocated to national headquarters where she developed a methodology and process for integrating and streamlining fourteen services for unemployment insurance recipients, thus improving service while freeing Human Resources Development Canada (HRDC) staff to focus on the more complex cases. This work led to her being asked to look at a replacement strategy for the network of HRDC electronic kiosks, in anticipation of the Y2K millennium bug. A key question was how Canadians accessed government information on the newly emerging Internet. In the late 1990s, she contributed to the development of an early integrated portal, Employer On-Line, on behalf of Industry Canada and HRDC (which included the employment service), an early Web-based Cluster for employers. When GOL was announced in the Speech from the Throne, McLeod was asked to contribute to the government-wide discussion of Gateways and Clusters and to develop recommendations on HRDC's role in GOL, eventually developing support and leadership for five Clusters that HRDC had agreed to lead. Thereafter, she was recruited by the CIO branch at the Treasury Board Secretariat to head the Gateways and Clusters unit in the GOL office.

McLeod's proudest accomplishment was building and leading the Gateways and Clusters community. Self-consciously anti-bureaucratic, the multidisciplinary teams established horizontal and collaborative problem-solving approaches, developing and abiding by principles such as avoiding duplication in the design and operation of the Clusters. The fact that such a rule and the terms of its application were the product of extensive community discussion made them much more powerful than if they had been promulgated by the Treasury Board. The full maturing of the approach came when deputy ministers delegated to the Gateways and Clusters network authority to allocate annual GOL funding for the Gateways and Clusters. One result was that, of the $95 million allocated to Gateways and Clusters from the GOL fund, there were few lapsed funds, unlike in other areas of GOL, where lapsing funds was an issue.

Part of the grassroots success of the Gateways and Clusters was the insistence that all of the stakeholders should be involved in brainstorming and decision making. This approach often involved McLeod in lengthy and sometimes frustrating meetings, which became easier as the community learned to work together. Another part of the success of Gateways and Clusters was the ability of its participants to harness the creative energy and enthusiasm of front-line workers, often people who were frustrated by traditional working environments. McLeod notes that it may not have been totally coincidental that the CIO and head of the GOL office were also women, as were all of the first generation of Gateway directors and many of the Cluster managers.

At the same time, the Gateways and Clusters stayed in touch with senior management and in particular, the committee of deputy ministers that oversaw GOL (the Treasury Board Secretariat Advisory Committee Information Management Sub-Committee, or TIMS). Rob Wright, then commissioner of the Canada Revenue Agency, and also chair of TIMS, acted as the original champion for Gateways and Clusters. He saw his role as removing roadblocks to innovations emerging from the working level as well as promoting the Gateways and Clusters concept among his deputy ministers and ministers. Ministerial engagement with GOL and support for funding were both essential. Our profile of Wright can be found at http://www.digitalstate.ca/supp/ch10.html.

As the citizen-centred approach spreads more widely across government, one big challenge, in McLeod's view, will be to ensure that program managers and staff take ownership for it without feeling that they have to reinvent the wheel. Another will be to deal with the fatigue after several years of intense activity. Two major priorities that she would like to see for the development of the Gateways and Clusters are measures to strengthen information as a service – perhaps the introduction of a knowledge gateway – and greater collaboration with the provinces in redesigning citizen-centred multi-channel service delivery. With the completion of the GOL initiative, McLeod moved to the Government of Canada Marketplace office in PWGSC to help apply the Gateways and Clusters governance model to e-procurement reform.

A digital leader with experiences somewhat similar to Michèle McLeod is Elisabeth Richard, who was also present at the creation of GOL, and who has more recently been involved in public consultation and information management. Her profile can be found at http://www.digitalstate.ca/supp/ch10.htm.

Digital Leadership at the Senior Level

Scott Campbell: Architect of Ontario's IT Organization

Scott Campbell was the OPS's first corporate CIO and the key architect of the province's IT structure. He was not brought in from the outside, but was a professional public servant whose career path took him into the management of technology.

After completing an MPA in the early 1970s, Campbell entered the OPS as a program analyst in the then Ministry of Government Services, and soon moved to the Management Board Secretariat as director of organizational policy. In 1983, he was asked to manage the implementation of a mobile radio network for the Ontario Provincial Police, a technology project that had no clear control and had gone over budget. In the early 1990s, he became chief administrative officer for the Ministry of Health and, as was the case in most ministries at that time, its IT unit reported to him. He returned to the Management Board Secretariat in 1996 as assistant deputy minister for its Services Division, with its IT policy unit reporting to him. In this position, it became apparent to him that the OPS had no clear IT strategy.

He won a mandate to develop an IT strategy, working with both an internal team and external consultants. The strategy would require a new IT organization, and he attempted to avoid what he considered to be the federal government's failing – that its CIO was a 'toothless tiger, relying on moral suasion.' He wanted Ontario's corporate CIO to have multiple levers of control over ministries, including mandates to develop IT policy and to assess the IT implications of submissions to the Management Board, as well as control over senior IT appointments in the ministries. The strategy envisaged a government-wide IT organization, rather than twenty-two departmental organizations, with seven Clusters to serve ministries with common issues and problems. He also saw the Cluster structure as enabling ministries to take advantage of economies of scale, hence doing work of higher quality than the 'technology islands' present in many ministries.

The strategy was approved by Cabinet in spring 1998, and $110 million in additional funding was provided to implement it. In the interview, Campbell described his bureaucratic and political tactics to win approval for the IT strategy: 'Meetings should have no surprises if all the homework has been done beforehand.' Campbell linked the IT strategy to the Harris government's key priorities such as increased internal coordination and greater efficiency. He got support from external experts, some with Conservative Party credentials and others with international reputations, and from central agency deputy ministers, for example, Cabinet Secretary Rita Burak and Management Board Secretary Michele Noble. Campbell considered himself fortunate in having a supportive minister in Management Board Chair Chris Hodgson, who was in his mid-thirties and technology-savvy.

Campbell was appointed corporate CIO in 1998 and stayed until his retirement from the OPS in 2001. He counts as his major achievements developing the strategy and having it funded and implemented, leading the implementation of common IT infrastructure, sponsoring all senior IT appointments, and generally putting IT on the government's political radar screen. His two disappointments were that the OPS did not have the necessary infrastructure to successfully manage complex public-private partnerships and that one of the seven initial Clusters, Health and Human Services, was too large and complex.

Greg Georgeff: Advocate of Improved Service and Greater Efficiency

Greg Georgeff was Ontario's second corporate CIO. He solidified the IT organization that Campbell built, initially pursued a vision of improving service on the electronic channel, subsequently shifting focus to increasing efficiency in the operation of the IT organization.

Georgeff began his career after college as a COBOL and Assembler programmer at the Ontario government's northern data centre in North Bay. He moved to Toronto as a computer operator for the Ministry of Education and developed an interest in data communications. He then moved to the private sector and ultimately into consulting, working on large-scale network integration. In 1990, one of his clients, Noranda, hired him full-time to deal with network issues, and he stayed there for a decade as CIO. He considers his major accomplishments there to include increasing the role of IT, firmly entrenching it in the organization's culture, and convincing executives to use e-mail and personal computers.

Scott Campbell recruited Georgeff back into the OPS in 2000 as CIO for the economic development Cluster, promising him many opportunities to launch major IT projects. Georgeff replaced Campbell as corporate CIO in 2001. In a sense, Campbell had played the same role for the OPS that Georgeff had played at Noranda, and Georgeff's challenge was to advance the IT organization Campbell had established.

Having worked in both the public and private sectors, Georgeff sees some clear contrasts. In the private sector, the criterion for deciding whether to undertake projects is simple: return on investment. At Noranda, the minimum acceptable rate was 12 per cent, but Georgeff's IT projects promised returns of at least 40 per cent and were always funded. Once a project was funded, the executive in charge had the responsibility to deliver it, with little hindrance from fellow executives, and was judged on the results. In the public sector, there is no comparable unidimensional investment criterion. Making a business case is difficult because there are no commonly accepted cost metrics, nor is there standard costing of fundamental activities. Departments tend to be protective of their own turf and skeptical of other departments' ideas. Because there is a need to secure the agreement of many players who have differing agendas and differing metrics, decision making is slow and arduous. The attraction to senior IT positions in the public sector is the variety of issues that must be dealt with.

Georgeff enumerates many achievements during his four years as corporate CIO. The Ontario government went from offering 10 per cent of government services electronically to 80 per cent. Efficiency was increased by consolidating infrastructure to take advantage of economies of scale and by starting to reduce IT spending even before the McGuinty government's cost reduction exercise. In human resources, he felt that he made the CIOs into a close-knit executive team, oversaw the shift from consultants to staff, and supported recruitment, such as the establishment of an IT group within the Ontario government's internship program.

Georgeff also played a major role in the broader Canadian e-government community. He was a guiding spirit in the Lac Carling Congress and the Canada-wide Public Sector CIO Council, both of which are designed to foster cooperation among governments. Ontario's IT organization has worked on methodology and common standards in areas such as authentication and information management, so as to lay the groundwork for integrated electronic service across Canada. Canada, he feels, is too small a country for each jurisdiction to do its own development work, and he was determined to have Ontario be the traditional leader.

Georgeff's termination without cause in September 2005 (discussed in chapter 3) followed private sector practice, differing markedly from the expected norm in a career public service. Deputy ministers attempt to put in place the most effective team of assistant deputy ministers. If one does not work out, the deputy minister will look for someone who is a better fit, in the first instance within the public service, but sometimes outside. If someone new were brought in, an attempt would be made to find another position for the displaced senior executive – perhaps a transitional appointment as a senior adviser to Cabinet Office. This was not done in Georgeff's case. One interpretation provided by OPS insiders is that Georgeff, despite being a full-time employee at the top of the OPS's IT executive scale, was not perceived by the Senior

Appointments Committee as a career public servant, but rather as an IT specialist. Consequently, there would be no other jobs in the OPS that would match his interests and aptitudes. In addition, with a 2004 salary of $249,000, Georgeff was by far the highest paid Ontario public servant. (For example, several senior deputy ministers were being paid approximately $185,000.) Thus, a transfer to a deputy minister or especially an assistant deputy minister–level position would have involved a sharp reduction in salary. The implications for senior IT executives within the public service are discussed in the section of this chapter providing reflections on digital leadership.

Helen McDonald: The Driver of Transformation

Helen McDonald was the Treasury Board Secretariat assistant secretary responsible for GOL during most of its lifetime. For the fifteen months before we interviewed her, she had been the acting CIO. In both capacities, her focus was on sustaining the transformation of government administration and services.

McDonald had no technological background when she went to work in the early 1990s as a strategic planner for telecommunications in Industry Canada. This position brought her into contact with issues relating to the Internet, including privacy and security in electronic commerce. She oversaw preparation of discussion papers on those topics for the Information Highway Advisory Council and led the teams that developed the Personal Information Privacy and Electronic Documents Act. McDonald went on to set up the Industry Canada GOL office and a strategy to promote the Business Gateway, which became an early foundation for Gateways and Clusters.

She was then recruited by Michèle d'Auray, the new CIO at the Treasury Board Secretariat, for whom she had worked at Industry Canada, to work on GOL. At TBS, she led the development of a government-wide approach to achieving the 2005/06 GOL targets and the related strategy of targeted investments.

For McDonald, the most difficult task has been achieving genuine service transformation through rethinking, streamlining, and integrating programs and services, and not simply applying IT to existing programs. A major challenge has been creating the incentives to encourage departments and programs to partner in a client-centric and whole-of-government approach. The GOL funding was used to get Clusters focused on citizen requirements and to support catalytic projects such as My Account, where citizens can see their accounts and conduct transactions with government departments, with privacy and security assured.

As CIO, McDonald's organization delivered three horizontal reviews as part of the effort launched by Reg Alcock to improve the efficiency and effectiveness of government administration. These dealt with IT services to government, corporate administration, and external service delivery, and all three suggested opportunities for savings through a whole-of-government approach. The reviews supported the arguments being made for Service Canada and were the basis for the decision to move to shared administrative services. Her other priorities included developing integrated service to business, strengthening cyber-security, advancing information management, and enhancing project management.

McDonald's perception was that much of the leadership for GOL and service transformation, at least in the early days, came from the community of departmental CIOs, which is beginning to include people with non-IT backgrounds. She noted that the role of the departmental CIO was evolving, and believes departments should review how they are selected and evaluated. She pointed to the key role that the new Service Transformation Advisory Committee (STAC), chaired by the secretary of Treasury Board, will play in guiding transformation and change management, as compared with the more technology-oriented mandate of TIMS, which it replaced. The committee will need to drive citizen-focused, whole-of-government approaches – recognizing common clients and common policy outcomes, and using a common architecture and language – while ensuring clear accountabilities and an appropriate incentive structure. This approach will require the key ministers – the president of the Treasury Board and the minister responsible for Service Canada – to keep pushing towards a new model of horizontal governance and expenditure management.

Ian Wilson: Champion of Information Management

Ian Wilson is the pre-eminent Canadian archivist of his generation and has become the federal government's most senior advocate of improved information management.

Wilson began his career at the Queen's University Archives in the mid-1960s, becoming university archivist in 1970. He moved to Saskatchewan in 1976 as provincial archivist and then back to Ontario in

1986, also as provincial archivist. While in Toronto, he was an adjunct professor in the Faculty of Information Studies at the University of Toronto. He was appointed national archivist of Canada in 1999. Wilson's background is not technical; rather, he is interested in the impact of technology on his profession, for example, the potential of the new technologies for preserving the Canadian documentary heritage. Information technology has played a significant role at several important junctures of his career. He began his term as archivist of Ontario in a classic turnaround, coming to an institution that was ignored, under-resourced, and demoralized. One aspect of his turnaround was simple office automation, moving from typewriters to word processors and introducing scanning.

When Wilson came to Ottawa in 1999, one of the issues he faced was the relationship of the then National Archives and the National Library. The two shared a location and common administrative support. He and then national librarian Roch Carrier realized that the public thinks of the government's information holdings as a whole, and does not draw distinctions between two separate institutions. They also recognized that there would be potential synergies in combining their operations. Consequently, Wilson and Carrier advocated a merger and full integration of the collections and services. Legislation was passed in May 2004, and Wilson was appointed the first librarian and archivist of Canada. Mergers of government agencies are uncommon, even more so when the initiative for the merger is internal and voluntary rather than imposed. Wilson and Carrier developed a vision of a new knowledge-based institution, reflecting discussions they had held across the country. They jointly challenged the two institutions and the associated professions to look outward to the needs of Canadians, rather than protecting traditional professional turf.

One of Wilson's key initiatives at the archives and now in Library and Archives Canada has been extending its reach by enhancing its online presence. He points out that, as a consequence of the Internet age, the archives went from having 35,000 in-person visitors per year to 3 million online visits, making it one of the top ten federal government websites. Wilson describes one of his objectives as librarian and archivist as creating an informed citizenry, able to participate intelligently in public debate; hence he does not endorse the conventional wisdom that transactional capacity is the primary objective of government online initiatives.

Wilson's perspective on information technology and management goes beyond the library and archives. He is a member of the federal government's deputy minister–level committee on IT and was designated the government's information management champion. He has become an internal advocate for improvements in the federal government's performance in information. He sees the Treasury Board Secretariat's CIO Branch as having concentrated on GOL and Public Works and Government Services Canada on IT services, overlooking the fundamental importance of effectively managing the government's information resources.

He cites a variety of failures in information management in recent years. In his view, Y2K marked a systemic failure of the public service. The problem was entirely foreseeable decades in advance but huge urgent expenditures were finally required because the basics of good information management had been ignored. One of the areas of savings mandated by the Program Review of the mid-1990s was records management, with the consequence that the quality of record-keeping in the federal government declined. In the transition from paper to IT systems, the basics of record-keeping for audit and accountability were forgotten, thus contributing to Human Resource Development Canada's problems in tracking grants and contributions (Good 2003) and the recent sponsorship scandal. Wilson comments that, after millennia of experience, public servants should be able to keep records!

Wilson outlines a long list of challenges the federal government now faces in information management. Electronic records, from e-mail and document management systems to websites, present special challenges for their maintenance across many generations of software and hardware. Library and Archives Canada is seeking solutions as it copes with the e-mail records from the Prime Minister's Office during the Chrétien and Martin governments, graduate theses in electronic form, and its new mandate to acquire websites of continuing value to Canada. Paper has not disappeared, however, and a recent study suggests that the government currently stores over fifty thousand cubic metres of paper at an annual cost of $250 million. Audits and enquiries regarding First Nation land claims, residential schools, and the use of herbicide on military bases highlight the importance of good historical records.

Wilson is making the case that these problems are escalating to a crisis in information management requiring a major initiative, comparable to GOL. Its solution will involve considerable upfront investment, some of which could be recouped by efficiencies in dealing with 'the paper mountain' and new models for delivering information services across departments.

Wilson has a long track record of success as a bureaucratic entrepreneur. When President Bush visited Ottawa in 2004, he and then U.S. ambassador Paul Cellucci – both of whom are married to librarians – made a stop at the Library and Archives Canada preservation centre. According to Cellucci, the president loved the tour, was impressed by the building's structure and layout, and said that it furthered his thinking about his own presidential library (Cellucci 2005, 188). The president's reaction drew the attention of official Ottawa to the international interest generated by the merger of the National Library and Archives. Perhaps for Ian Wilson the stars are now in alignment.

Digital Leadership at the Political Level: Not Just the 'Minister of Shiny New Things'

Reg Alcock's first exposure to IT was as the director of the Seven Oaks Centre for Youth in Winnipeg in the early 1980s. The centre had a Radio Shack TRS80 computer, and Alcock used it to create an information file on the kids passing through the centre. He soon started to understand the flow dynamics of this population, for example, that 82 per cent of the children stayed fewer than three days. A few years later, he became director of child welfare for the province, and attempted to repeat his success by contracting out the creation of electronic records for all 3000 children in the system. This project failed, however, because there was no ability to integrate data from different sources.

These contrasting experiences left Alcock aware of the complexity of holding and managing information across domains. He went to the Kennedy School at Harvard to take a master's degree in public policy, with a special interest in technology and its impact on organization. Alcock returned to Manitoba, entering provincial politics in 1988, and was first elected to the House of Commons in the Liberal sweep of 1993.

Alcock spent a decade as a backbencher. As a techno-enthusiast at the time the Internet was becoming widely accessible, he undertook several initiatives. He built the first political website in Canada (http://www.digitalcommons.ca) and used it to post the Liberal campaign platform, to put his draft statements about policy issues online to elicit constituents' comments, and to show a narrated House of Commons tour. He also had a video-conference facility installed in his office, so he could complete his constituency service on weekday evenings, and give him more time to spend with his family on weekends. Not expecting to be appointed to Jean Chrétien's cabinet, he spoke his mind frequently; when GOL was announced in the 1999 Throne Speech, Alcock told the media it was a nice idea but would not work because of the extensive re-engineering of back-office functions that would be required. Alcock was also interested in management issues, and helped create – and served as the first chair of – the Standing Committee on Government Operations and Estimates.

When Paul Martin took over the government in December 2003, Alcock was appointed to his dream job: president of the Treasury Board. Martin has joked that Alcock is 'a proponent of shiny new things,' but Alcock's concern is not just with technology per se, but with improved management. We interviewed Alcock in his office immediately after a two-hour cabinet meeting in which he had presented the Treasury Board's wide-ranging set of proposals for improving management in government (Treasury Board of Canada 2005). Alcock was delighted because Cabinet had been willing to devote two hours to a discussion of the public service when its agenda is usually dominated by politics or policy. Beyond that, the proposals were well received. Alcock's responses to our questions showed that he viewed technology as part of a larger management reform agenda. Shared services, by establishing common administrative support systems for the entire government, would finally make it possible quickly to answer questions such as whether the demographic makeup of the public service is reflective of the country. Establishing Service Canada is a departure from the traditional departmental structure in which operations are subservient to policy, and it creates a strong new department whose sole responsibility is service delivery. He is also confident that a high-quality service department will generate a great deal of valuable information for policy ministries to use.

Alcock views IT as responsible for three deaths: those of time, distance, and deference. Deference will die because technology makes it easier for the public to obtain information, and harder for politicians or public servants to suppress it. Alcock accepts the death of deference as inevitable and hence is a proponent of proactive disclosure, which, he feels, will change bureaucratic behaviour. As an example, he believes the recent decision requiring politicians, political staff, and senior public servants to disclose their travel and hospitality expenses is leading to greater frugality. Information made available to the public should not just be in read-only PDF files, but in a form that can be analysed more readily. He wants information to be generated quickly and robustly, thus counteracting debate dominated by myths. While he did not use them, the words that come to mind are those attributed to Daniel Patrick Moynihan: 'Everyone is entitled to his own opinions, but not his own facts.'

Alcock espouses a radical theory of change. First, a crisis is an essential lever to achieving major management change in a huge organization, and he refers to the Gomery Commission as 'the wind beneath my wings.' Second, he believes that, if you try to change one or two things in a big system, the system will reassert itself and nullify those changes. Consequently, he prefers to risk system overload by introducing a long change agenda all at once. Alcock realizes that, politically, his interests are unusual. The public generally does not talk to ministers about management, so ministers are usually not interested in management. Alcock is interested in management because he sees government as having no alternative but to embrace the technology that is causing the deaths of time, distance, and deference, with the resulting increase in citizen expectations. In a world where business operates at the speed of thought, government cannot afford to be much slower.

Reflections on Digital Leadership

These sketches of digital leaders in the Ontario and federal governments suggest five areas in which the members of our sample can be compared: their technical expertise, role as educators, visions of technology, ability to collaborate across organization boundaries, and response to the political context. Following that, we shift to factors that appear unique to each of front-line leaders, senior public servants, and politicians.

Technical Expertise

Two of our sample, Greg Georgeff and Steve Green, began their careers as programmers. Green remains involved in a hands-on way by continuing to create Web pages. Both have a deep and detailed knowledge of the use and capabilities of a variety of technologies. None of the others has comparable expertise. Some (Scott Campbell, Ian Wilson, and Helen McDonald) have sufficient knowledge of technologies that they have a good understanding of how their application would affect operational cost and organizational structure. Others, such as Melissa Thomson, are deeply involved in IT-based communities of practice. A decade or two ago, the early adopters matched Georgeff's and Green's profiles more closely. The fact that the more recent digital leaders come from broader and less technical backgrounds is evidence of the growing pervasiveness of IT in the public sector. At the same time, all of the leaders interviewed acknowledged that a major challenge continues to be how to bring technical issues into the non-technical decision-making realm so that government can make informed decisions about new technologies.

Digital Leaders as Educators

Many in the sample of digital leaders are, in some sense, educators. Some have taught at a university (Ian Wilson at Toronto) or continue to teach in executive development (Steven Green). Others, such as Melissa Thomson, reflect on their experience and make best practice presentations to their communities of practice. Michèle McLeod emphasizes the experience to be learned from the communities of practice themselves. The CIOs (Campbell, Georgeff, McDonald) frequently spoke at conferences and made presentations to delegations from other governments. Alcock has also made speeches to conferences about technology in government (Alcock 2005). Digital leadership intrinsically involves communication of what one has learned as a practitioner.

A Variety of Visions of Technology

The sample of digital leaders expressed several visions of technology. Some (Alcock, Wilson) emphasized the importance of using technology to increase the amount of information available to the public. Alcock put his emphasis on increasing transparency of government through proactive disclosure of administrative practices or retroactive disclosure of performance, and hence influencing public servants and ministers. Wilson's focus is on the ultimate mission of Library and Archives Canada, preserving and communicating Canadian experience. Others (particularly Campbell, Georgeff, and McDonald) emphasize increasing the ability of government to provide transactions electronically to a public grown increasingly comfortable and familiar with e-commerce. A third focus, emphasized by Thomson and Elisabeth Richard, is on using IT for consultation, and ultimately increasing the sophistication and interactivity of consultations that can be conducted over the electronic channel.

The sample was attuned to the potential of technology for reducing the cost of government, albeit in a variety of different ways. Georgeff and McDonald see themselves as providing digital leadership by promoting common platforms and standard infrastructure and applications. Georgeff has often emphasized his responsibility as CIO to reduce the cost of technology and to use technology to reduce the cost of government. Efficiency is a key virtue to him, putting him somewhat at variance with the stereotype of public servants who are much more concerned about other values – political support, bureaucratic empire-building, or representativeness – than efficiency. Reg Alcock also sees common applications such as shared services or integrated service delivery as providing efficiency gains, and as the minister who introduced these common applications, he has had to deal with the objections. Ian Wilson makes cost-savings one of the components of his call to action in information management.

The IT-based innovators (for example, Green and Thomson) see themselves as saving money by undertaking IT-based initiatives on the cheap: Green developing websites internally rather than contracting them out, and Thomson adopting private sector consultation software. A similar case is that of the Ontario Ministry of Municipal Affairs and Housing's consultations, which used its existing content management software, rather than a more elaborate and expensive alternative provided by the IT organization (Simos interview 2005). These cases signal an ongoing source of tension. The IT organization will provide solutions that are sized to fit all, or at least as many as possible, and the innovators will likely be uncomfortable with common approaches and therefore look for something unique. They will continue to fly below the radar and to use applications that are not in the common suite.

Collaborating across Organization Boundaries

Information technology creates strong incentives to collaborate across organizational boundaries to deliver client-focused service and to take advantage of economies of scale. These incentives conflict with the vertical accountability structure of traditional government, and digital leaders must mediate this conflict if they wish to make progress on service transformation, e-consultation, or infrastructure. The digital leaders we have profiled do this in a number of ways. Michèle McLeod led the Gateways and Clusters initiative, which was essentially an alliance of interdepartmental working groups. Helen McDonald's role as the federal government's CIO included not only oversight of the Gateways and Clusters initiative, but managing whole-of-government approaches to service delivery and internal support services. Rob Wright used a committee of deputy ministers to promote such approaches among senior officials and to support innovation at the front line. Ian Wilson initiated a merger of the National Library and the Public Archives to enhance service to users. The information management initiative he now champions will need widespread support within government to go forward. Greg Georgeff played a key role in the Canadian e-government community, for example fostering co-operation among governments in the Public Sector CIO Council, and having Ontario take the lead in working on common technical problems. Operating on the front line, Melissa Thomson developed an inter-ministerial community of practice in e-consultation, and her work on the Ideas Campaign and budget consultation required close cooperation with external consultants and the government's technology organization.

Inter-organizational collaboration, while essential to making progress, also has its challenges, in particular its pace. McLeod spoke of lengthy and sometimes frustrating meetings within the Gateways and Clusters community and Georgeff of the difficulty of collective decision making when organizations defend their own turf and have differing agendas and metrics. Effectiveness in this context involves patience and diplomacy to induce parties to come on board, as well as the ability to develop and communicate common visions that create urgency and momentum and to create incentives for collective effort. The necessity for inter-organizational collaboration suggests that soft skills are becoming increasingly important relative to the technical prowess that originally characterized digital leaders.

Responding to the Political Context

The public servants are aware of, and responsive to, their political context. For Wright, political support was crucial to the success of Government On-Line, while McDonald and her predecessors as federal government CIO were able to obtain statements in Throne Speeches and budgets endorsing GOL at key stages in its development. In other cases, public servants recognized that the political environment was not favourable, leading to a strategy of moving slowly and staying below the radar, for example, Thomson's quiet advocacy of e-consultation during the Harris-Eves government. On other occasions, they realized that the political winds had changed to become more receptive to their ideas, for example, the McGuinty government giving Green a mandate to increase the sophistication of the websites for the premier as well as major government initiatives, and encouraging Thomson and others in the OPS consultation community of practice to push e-consultation forward.

There are also cases of public servants attempting to win the broad support needed for major initiatives. Scott Campbell recounts the importance of building a political and bureaucratic coalition to support the new IT strategy he developed. He found external experts who were acceptable to the Harris government, and he emphasized the major role the private sector would have in implementing the strategy, which was also consistent with the Conservatives' ideology. Ian Wilson is trying to do in Ottawa now what Campbell did at Queen's Park in 1998, in his case building a bureaucratic and political coalition to support a major initiative in information management.

Front-line Digital Leaders: Increasing Visibility

When politicians are interested in using technology as a key component of their initiatives, as is clearly the case with the McGuinty government, front-line digital leaders are called upon to implement the technology-based aspect. Senior IT managers do not have the time or the technical competence to do this work, so it necessarily falls upon younger front-line public servants who are often the most up-to-date on the latest technology. If the political initiative involves the creation of a Web page, the politicians may well be interested in the look, feel, and content of the page itself, and this interest creates a direct line between the politician and the creator of the page. Thus, Green's stewardship of the premier's page and Thomson's work on the Ideas Campaign and budget consultation brought them into contact with the premier and his political staff. In many such cases, the work is limited in scope and individual contributions can be clearly identified. If the front-line public servant is perceived by politicians to have done a good job, or to have 'delivered,' that perception may be communicated to senior public servants, with the result that an individual's career can be fast-tracked. In addition, the fast track need not be restricted to the

IT area. Thomson, who moved from her success at the Consultation Projects Office to a policy position in Cabinet Office and then an executive assistant to a deputy minister, appears to exemplify this progression. Michèle McLeod has also attracted attention because of her digital leadership, which focused on harnessing the creative energies of front-line staff, but has chosen to stay in middle management.

The Senior Digital Leader: Not One of Us?

Senior digital leaders face much greater challenges than their front-line colleagues, assuming responsibility for many outcomes they can influence but not directly control. These include the performance of large-scale projects and the integrity of the IT system against outside attacks or unwarranted invasions on individual privacy. Given the pervasiveness of IT, an increasing number of government problems are seen as IT problems. In this context, it is often difficult to look good.

A second area of difficulty for senior IT executives is with their bureaucratic colleagues. As argued in chapter 1, IT-enabled government involves the creation of integrated service delivery and shared services, two trends that reduce the scope and size of line ministries. Deputy ministers in line ministries may resent this restructuring for a number of reasons: centralized service delivery reduces the visibility of their ministers, centralized support services may reduce flexibility, and the loss of both service delivery and support services shrinks their bureaucratic empires. They also complicate the accountability picture by separating policy and program development, on the one hand, from implementation and technological support, on the other. This distinction does not always hold up well in the face of criticism in the legislature or the media. Because these changes are facilitated by IT, it is the IT executives who bear the brunt of their line department colleagues' resentment.

Greg Georgeff's termination may have been a result of both blame for project failures and resentment at IT-based centralization. In addition, it sharply raises the issue of how IT executives are regarded within the senior bureaucracy. As discussed above, despite having begun his career in the OPS, by virtue of having worked in the private sector for two decades, Georgeff was regarded as an IT expert rather than a career public servant. Georgeff's successor, Ron McKerlie, was also recruited from the private sector. The federal public service has also recruited a large number of senior executives from the private sector, but, rather than hiring them as career public servants, it has recruited them through an executive exchange program with the Information Technology Association of Canada serving as their nominal employer (Leblanc 2005). This arrangement has facilitated paying them salaries that exceed the federal public service scale while reducing the tension between their expertise and the career system.

Senior IT executives in government now seem to occupy a high-paying job ghetto. Their off-the-scale salaries make them likely to stay there as opposed to moving to other areas of the public service. This stasis of course feeds the belief by other senior public servants that senior IT executives are different and not quite as attuned to the public service culture. Ideally, the public sector's front-line digital leaders would rise to the top of the IT function and, from there, move to other areas, including both operating departments and central agencies. To some extent, both the federal and Ontario governments have made progress in that direction, in that a considerable number of IT executives just below the most senior level have come up through the ranks.

Political Digital Leaders: Managing the Risks

We can distinguish between digital leadership by backbench MPs and cabinet ministers. The data in chapter 8 make it clear that the comfort level of parliamentarians with IT is increasing as a new generation, already familiar with technology, is entering politics. There will be more legislators who want to innovate in their use of technology, as Reg Alcock and Carolyn Bennett have already done. To an extent, the improved level of IT infrastructure in the legislature will support them. They will, however, face an electronic version of the traditional constraints on backbenchers. Parties try to enforce discipline in cyberspace by providing a free website template for backbenchers, forcing those who want individualized sites to pay for them privately. Similarly, the bureaucracy has taken control of e-consultation, as discussed in chapter 9, although to a considerable extent it has filled a gap left by ministers and their advisors. Therefore, the question facing backbenchers is whether there are outlets for any inclination they might have to be at the digital leading edge. A few who are particularly independent-minded about policy, for example, Conservative backbencher Garth Turner in the Harper government, have taken the step to develop a personal website and use it for blogging and policy consultation with constituents.

Ministers in IT-based portfolios can play a larger role than back-benchers in advancing the IT agenda. Public servants can provide them with plans and proposals, but it is ministers who make the ulti-mate decisions whether to accept the proposals. In addition, they face some of the same risks and pressures that senior IT executives face. They are accountable to the legislature for the performance of projects, breakdowns in system integrity, and invasions of privacy. They face resentment from Cabinet colleagues if their initiatives reduce the pro-file of ministerial portfolios, the ability to support regional employ-ment, or politically motivated procurement choices. Ministers in IT-based portfolios must also understand a variety of technical issues suf-ficiently well to make policy choices and explain them to the public. Some measure of expertise is thus desirable. As the percentage of MPs comfortable with IT increases, it should be easier to find ministers with such expertise.

Conclusion

This chapter has provided a human face for our discussion of the man-agement of IT in the federal and Ontario governments. It profiles a group of individuals who see themselves as innovators in government, advancing an agenda of change through the application of technology. They take pride in their achievements thus far, but also see that there is much more to be done in applying technology to government. While many of these individuals chose to be at the leading edge of change, they recognize the necessity to bring their colleagues along. While these stories are told by individuals, they are all stories of collective effort, where that effort involves collaboration among departments within one government, collaboration across governments, or collabo-ration across organizational levels, involving ministers, senior officials, and front-line public servants working together. Ultimately, these are not stories about the revolutionary capacity of new technology, but rather stories about leadership: leaders inspiring, persuading, or cajol-ing large organizations to embrace new technology.

In the next two chapters, our focus shifts to a comparative perspec-tive in which we discuss progress made in the United States and United Kingdom by political parties and governments applying tech-nology in their dealings with citizens and in their internal operations.

11 Evolution or Revolution? E-Government in the United States

FRED THOMPSON

In this chapter, I look at two recent encounters with e-government in the United States: the 2004 presidential election and the American military's development of a worldwide information grid. We selected these cases because they are at the leading edge of e-government worldwide, as a result of their scale and the resources lavished upon them. As extreme cases, they may help to illustrate the transformative potential of information technology.

Theoretical Considerations: The Economics of Organization

About ten years ago, Gil Reschenthaler and I (1996) argued that information technology (IT) was revolutionizing organizational architecture and design and would ultimately make over government as well, fundamentally altering its processes, its size and scope, its strategies, and its tactics. In so reasoning, we were in effect turning an argument made by Alfred Chandler in *The Visible Hand: The Managerial Revolution in American Business* (1977) on its head.

According to Chandler, the rise of big business in the nineteenth and twentieth centuries and implicitly big government as well was driven by technological changes, which created overwhelming economies of scale and scope. Our position was that information technology had reversed this process, reducing the comparative advantage that accrued to hierarchy and bureaucracy and increasing the efficacy of market-like, self-organizing governance mechanisms relative to centralized coordination and control. Like Chandler's, our position was grounded in the logic of the new economics of organization. The basic idea behind the new economics of organization is that the comparative advantage of governance mechanisms boils down to a question of information or transaction costs and to the ability and willingness of those affected by information costs to recognize and bear them (Coase 1937). Hence, the circumstances that create market failures – public goods, natural monopolies, externalities, moral hazards, and adverse selection (the problems that justify government action in a capitalist economy) – are all fundamentally information failures. Markets could deliver public goods, for example, if information technology existed that would permit free riders to be profitably excluded from enjoying them. Monopolies could be compensated to behave like competitors if information costs were lower. In addition, bargaining between self-interested individuals could eliminate externalities, without the intervention of government, if transaction costs were zero. Much the same logic applies to the choice between organizations and markets, and the kinds of governance mechanisms used within organizations.

A corollary to this basic Coasian insight is that information costs – typically search, bargaining, logistics, and/or enforcement costs – can be reduced by carrying them out through formal mechanisms of governance: organizations rather than markets, or government rather than private organizations. Reduction does not imply elimination, however. This fact implies a second, perhaps less obvious corollary to the basic Coasian insight: the conditions that wreck markets also impair organizations and governments. Consequently, as Robert Gibbons (2003) explains, the organizations we observe tend to be less efficient than the markets we observe, even when they are more efficient than the markets they replace; the government agencies we observe tend to be less efficient than the private organizations we observe, even when they are more efficient than the private organizations they replace.

The 2004 Presidential Campaign

Electoral campaigns may seem a trivial test of our thesis. However, American presidential campaigns involve millions of volunteers, thousands of professionals, and billions of dollars. Moreover, for many elected officials, campaign leadership is the only executive experience they ever get. Lacking other executive experience, what they learn on the campaign trail strongly influences administrative practices in office. Political campaigns are also endowed with certain of the characteristics that facilitate the adoption of information-based architectures: a clear focus and shared sense of purpose, open commu-

nication throughout the organization, and bright, intrinsically motivated participants.

A survey of candidates' websites in the presidential primaries
clearly demonstrated that most simply used the Internet as an alter-
nate channel for information available through other media. Use of this
channel undoubtedly facilitated communication with the 10 per cent to
12 per cent of the population that relies on the World Wide Web for
news, and with reporters, who tend to be fairly Internet savvy. Many
reporters find it easier to take information from press releases on the
Internet than from faxes and to use the Web to search through position
papers for inconsistencies and to compare and contrast the stances of
the candidates. There were two salient exceptions to this generaliza-
tion, however: Howard Dean's use of the Web to identify likely supporters and to ask them for money, and the Bush campaign's use of the
Internet to get out the vote on Election Day.

The Dean campaign was remarkable for its ability to raise funds
from small donors (less than US$250). Democrats have customarily
relied more heavily on very large donors – wealthy individuals, trial
lawyers, and teachers' unions primarily – and federal matching funds
than have Republicans, who have relied on direct mail campaigns to
raise funds. The Dean campaign was so good at raising money that it
could afford to forgo federal matching funds (along with the spending
limits they entail) and eventually announced that it would no longer
accept large individual and corporate donations. While the Dean campaign failed (many of its IT workers were recruited for John Kerry's
presidential campaign, where they substantially contributed to the
Democrats' success in raising and spending more than the Republicans
during the presidential campaign),[1] Howard Dean was later elected
chairman of the Democratic Party. Under Dean, the Democratic Party
has raised two dollars for every three raised by the Republicans,
despite the incumbency advantage of the latter. Dean's successes have
relied on precisely the same organizational and IT know-how that carried him to a surprise lead early in the race for the Democratic nomination for the presidency. Openness has been one of the keys to Dean's
success in the use of the Internet for campaign purposes. The Republicans, and initially the Kerry campaign, merely solicited e-mail
responses to their press releases and position papers. Most messages
received an automatic reply appealing for support. In contrast, Dean's
campaign network classified and posted the comments to the Web, and
invited responses from viewers. They also asked viewers to copy com-

ments to friends and to invite them to link to Meetup.com. This had the effect of creating an extensive community of online participants. Over 13,000 people participated in Meetup.com in April 2003, 61,000 in July, and 110,000 in October. Meetup.com's participation peaked in February 2004, with 189,000 participants (Samuel 2004).

Furthermore, potential supporters identified themselves through their willingness to participate in the online community. Only after people were involved in the Dean campaign did it solicit their financial support. This is also the approach that experienced fund-raisers (for example, those who work for universities and other charities) take. Not surprisingly, the response rate to Dean's solicitations was between four and ten times higher than his competitors'. Of course, this meant that the Dean campaign organization had to mobilize and train a large number of individuals to monitor traffic on the Web, identify potential supporters, and tailor appeals for support to them. It also meant that the campaign had to use its computers to chart volunteer activities and communications traffic so that it could afford to pass the exercise of judgment down in the organization to the volunteers communicating directly with the other members of the online community. As Democratic Party chairman, Dean has installed this same system. Perhaps its most astonishing feature is that most volunteers supply their computers and work from their own homes, schools, or offices.

The Republican effort to get out the vote on Election Day was every bit as fascinating. The problem both parties face is ensuring that likely supporters actually vote. Both parties maintain extensive databases on registered voters, paying special attention to party members and independents, especially identified supporters and those with characteristics that would predict their support at the polls. They also try to determine who has voted and who has not and to encourage those who have not to do so. This approach means reminding voters with absentee ballots to mail them in, monitoring polling places to identify those who have not voted, and phoning or visiting the laggards to persuade them to vote. In presidential elections, special attention is usually given to potential supporters who vote intermittently in by-elections.

Forty years ago, this process relied heavily on local organization and local knowledge. Data, which are now typically supplied in digital format by county clerks and are frequently updated, often in real time, and warehoused by the national party organization, were laboriously coded by hand on notecards maintained at the precinct level. While a few well-organized patronage machines could rely on street-level adherents to know their constituencies so intimately they could predict not only who would vote but also how, most simply maximized turn-out, leaving it to the fates to sort things out. The electoral advantages that accrued to large-scale, centralized database management trans-formed this process. When voter data were combined with modern political/market research and the use of giant call centres, national campaign managers could determine which voters to target to maxi-mize the vote count in their favour, given the resources available. This had the result of reducing overall turnout relative to earlier times, but of increasing the predictability of outcomes. It also resulted in the cen-tralization of the process.

In 2004, the Democrats relied on this basic process, although they executed it with exceptional competence and zeal. As Matt Bai reported (2004), the Democrats focused on 'hard yeses': 'They found stalwart Democratic voters – the base – and pounded them with mail, phone calls and visits to make sure they went to the polls.' The masters of modern field organizing, the Democrats 'dismissed the Republican effort as an exercise in self-delusion, insisting that volunteers could never build a turnout model to compete with professional organizers.'

In contrast, the Republicans used the Internet to transform the pro-cess. Using information from the phone banks and polling places, the Republicans made data on voters, their intentions and their propensi-ties, available to local volunteers, and relied upon the volunteers to interpret the data and use the Internet to coordinate their own efforts. To participate in this process, all interested volunteers had to do was enter their zip codes on a Web page: the system provided a targeted list of neighbourhood voters, a map showing the locations of their resi-dences, estimates of the time required to visit them, and a set of talking points. The rest was up to the volunteers. In other words, the Republi-cans used the Internet to distribute information and decision-rights to front-line personnel and depended upon them to figure out how to leverage the resources available locally. Consequently, Republican vol-unteers were consistently faster off the mark and responded more appropriately to the emerging situation than their more centrally directed Democratic counterparts.

The final result was the largest voter turnout in numbers of any American election in history. As a percentage of the potential electorate (the voting eligible population), it was the highest since 1968 (turnout levels were exceptionally high by historical standards during the 1950s and 1960s). Fifty-five per cent of the voting eligible population voted for a presidential candidate, versus 50 per cent in 2000 and 48 per cent in 1996 (see United States Elections Project, http://elections.gmu.edu/voter_turnout.htm). In addition, while this is by no means certain, many serious analysts now attribute the Republican margin of victory to success in getting out the vote on Election Day. According to census figures, closeness influenced turnout. Minnesota, one of the most closely contested states, for example, had the highest turnout rate. Hawaii, which the presidential candidates ignored until late in the campaign, had the lowest. In the fifteen states with the closest presidential races, 60 per cent of the voting eligible population voted for president versus 47 per cent in the fifteen least competitive states. (The figure of 60% is an improvement over 2000 (55%) and 1996 (45%).) Moreover, Republican success at getting voters to the polls evidently reversed what started out to be a clear win for the Democrats (Bai 2004).

Zack Exley, director of online communication and organization for Kerry-Edwards 2004, was subsequently reported to have said in reference to the Republican voter mobilization campaign, 'The right is beating the left at what used to be our game: grassroots politics, real democracy. Ironically, we were a little more "command and control," which doesn't really reflect the way the Democratic Party works' (Potier 2004).

Another manifestation of this difference is that the Democrats were far more concerned with security than their Republican counterparts. Not only did they have a strong preference for partisan Web-campaign firms, they worked hard to keep Republicans out of their system. Despite the fact that my research assistant was a former Democratic Party county central committee member and had the necessary URLs and passwords, he couldn't access the login page for the Democratic presidential get-out-the-vote campaign, evidently because his IP address wasn't pre-registered. In contrast, he easily accessed the Republican volunteer system.

It is, perhaps, not entirely irrelevant to our story that one of the legs of the modern Democratic Party remains firmly rooted in the industrial age. Mass production helped create the mass politics in the twentieth century. Mass production allowed unskilled assembly workers to reap substantial economic gains – a 40 per cent reduction in working hours and a twenty-five-fold increase in wages. In the English-speaking world, unions enforced artificial scarcity to win supra-competitive wages for their members. In the social-market economies of Northern Europe, workers did even better. Coordinated wage setting between national associations of employers and national labour organizations, usually led by blue-collar unions, achieved both high wages and considerable income equality, almost without strikes.

Ultimately, the ability of unskilled manufacturing employees to gain and hold supra-competitive wages depended upon their political power. By the 1950s, the rise of mass production had made them the largest single group in every developed country. Already organized by their employers, they mobilized easily on behalf of their own interests. In every developed country, labour unions emulated the organizing principles of big business – hierarchy and bureaucracy – and emerged as the best-disciplined and often the most powerful political force in the nation. Their preferences were reflected not only in labour laws, but in public policy generally. They were the architects and chief supporters of the postwar Keynesian welfare state, with its goals of full employment, social security, and income parity.

Information technology has profoundly altered this equation. In the first place, it has greatly reduced economies of scale and scope, as mass production has been replaced by flexible production. Consequently, average firm size has been falling for the last twenty years in most developed countries. Information technology has also given rise to new modes of internal organization, which emphasize multidisciplinary teams, whose members work together from the start of a job to its completion, in part because modern information systems and expert systems make it efficient to push the exercise of judgment down into the organization, to the teams that do an organization's work. Nowadays, single-product organizations are often organized as virtual networks or self-organizing systems, and multi-product organizations are alliances of networks, with everyone in the organization playing the part of customer or provider, depending on the transaction, and entire plants transformed into a network of dyads and exchanges.

Virtual networks require numerate and literate workers, capable of a high degree of self-direction. As a consequence of the shift from mass to flexible production, the number of unskilled industrial workers in the developed world has been falling for nearly thirty years. Decreased numbers have led to political decline. First, unskilled labour lost its leading role in the union movement. Then, union influence in general waned.

Today, the public sector is one of the last bastions of hierarchy and bureaucracy in America. It is not surprising that its employees are the bulwark of its union movement; nor is it surprising that public-employee unions now play a leading role in the Democratic Party. The interesting question is whether IT will transform the public sector in the same way that it has the private.

Global Information Grid

Donald H. Rumsfeld's main goal as United States Secretary of Defense has been the transformation of the American military into a leaner, nimbler, more affordable, but still dominant force (Rumsfeld 2002).[3] The use of IT to increase the agility of combat forces and the speed and effectiveness with which the military is deployed to achieve political ends without combat plays a central role in what has been described as a revolution in military affairs (RMA). Indeed, it can be argued that the backbone of the RMA is the integration of the Department of Defense's communications and computer systems into the Global Information Grid, or GIG.

The GIG is easily the most ambitious IT initiative being undertaken anywhere. It is a distributed network designed to spread processing power across a network of thousands of processors, servers, and routers located around the world. The diverse computers that make up the network will be linked together by a communications system that automatically routes and relays information from source(s) to destination(s) through any available medium or node. The GIG's communication system will use technologies pioneered by the Defense Advance Research Projects Agency's packet radio project as well as land lines, both of which rely on the Internet's open-systems standards and protocols to facilitate interoperability among its component elements. This communications network will allow the computers in the grid to exchange information, share workloads, and process information to provide users with information about local operating conditions[4] and to help them determine what they need and to get it when they need it. Information and related services will be available to any and all 'net-ready' users, meaning those connected to the GIG, with an adequate interface to enable the acquisition and presentation of information.[5] When the GIG is complete, everyone in the American military will be able to communicate with everyone else. The architecture of the GIG will eliminate the need to channel information, thereby eliminating the trade-off between information richness and reach – or so its advocates claim.

The grid is designed to be scalable to several levels or tiers of networks. At the highest level, it will comprehend all sensors, information processors, and users, from satellites in geosynchronous orbits on down – all the military's processors, servers, and routers, the communications grid, and stored data and metadata registers and catalogues. (Metadata describe and classify the information to which they are appended, including its source, description, intended use, pedigree, and security classification. Hence, they allow users to convert data into useful information.) The next tier might be a wide-area network comprehending a regional command, the next a medium-area network comprehending all the combat and support teams conducting operations in an area, and finally a local-area network comprehending the participants of a combat team or rapid reaction force.

Like most high-tech organizational architectures, the GIG will rely on quasi-market mechanisms to link customers and providers (sensors, weapons platforms, and intelligent agents, as well as people), and to ensure that users have access to the information and services (bandwidth, etc.) that they want when, where, and how they want it. Depending on the transaction, a user may be either a customer or a provider. Department of Defense policy envisions that users will post all of the information they collect or produce so that it can be immediately available to those who need it. In addition to tracking the progress of transactions and providing management for the system of exchange, the GIG's infostructure will supply

• Metadata posting and collection
• Searchable catalogues advertising the availability of services and information on the GIG (these catalogues will contain information that describes the capabilities of the service, the necessary inputs to use the service, and the outputs of the service)
• Discovery mechanisms to locate and identify information to support user tasks, including flexible access-control mechanisms to facilitate information visibility and availability (while hiding information where there is an explicit need for security beyond that afforded by the network)
• Agent-based mediation services to translate, fuse, and aggregate data elements into information to meet the needs of diverse users ranging from individuals to teams and organizations, and to sensors and/or weapons systems

These software agents will use metadata to package information for users. They are supposed to filter and deliver the right information to the right user automatically. That is to say, these agents will be made aware of the user's situation and information needs to provide relevant information without a specific user request. Software agents are intended to multiply the resources available to users by gathering and transforming raw data into actionable information to support operations, in the same way that users would, were the agents unavailable, thereby freeing them from routine information-processing chores and allowing them to devote their attention to operations.

The GIG relies on workload sharing and packet switching for resiliency. The grid will operate reliably despite the destruction of many of its components or communication nodes, because data and workloads can be stored and processed throughout the network, and information is automatically routed through its undamaged nodes by surviving radio transmitters and landlines. Moreover, according to David Alberts and Richard Hayes (2003, 197), automatic packet-switching network protocols and algorithms could protect communications nodes in ways never before conceived through cover, concealment, and deception. For example, network-level protocols could make every node look the same (in a traffic analysis) as every other node, thereby limiting an adversary's ability to identify and target high-value nodes such as command and control centres. Similarly, network-level protocols could, if the system detects an attack, change its waveforms to mimic a radar site or even the radio signals of an enemy unit.

From the first, Rumsfeld's aggressive pursuit of RMA met with resistance from the military services. Some of this opposition can be described only as reactionary. Substituting information and precision for mass and firepower threatened a wide array of vested interests. These ranged from the fear that Rumsfeld would cancel pet projects, cut force structure, or close facilities, to the certainty that doctrinal, organizational, and technological change would depreciate the value of hard-won individual knowledge and skills. At the same time, the kind of organizational architecture required to exploit modern IT – flatter, decentralized, horizontally linked task forces, capable of rapid improvisation and self-organization – threatened the military's deeply held belief that the best results come from centralizing authority, a carefully delineated chain of command, and exhaustive staff planning.

Iraq was for Rumsfeld merely another battle in his war against military bureaucracy. For eighteen months beforehand, he bullied his officers into writing war plans that reflected the doctrinal, organizational, and technological principles he espoused. He saw to it that America invaded the country with around one-third of the soldiers that his top generals wanted and without preliminary air attacks. This approach was followed partly to demonstrate the efficacy of the RMA and to give his uniformed subordinates no alternative but to rely on speed and improvisation to carry out their assigned missions.

Rumsfeld's confidence in the rightness of his cause was supported by events in the Balkans and Afghanistan. Those conflicts seem to confirm that minimum muscle, precisely deployed, 'will convince our enemies that resistance is futile – by showing them that they will always be beaten to the punch, outsmarted, outmaneuvered, and out-killed – and, thereby, reduce superfluous destruction, shorten conflict, and minimize harm to the innocent' (Rumsfeld 2002, 31).

The results of the most expensive war game ever conducted by the U.S. military, the Millennium Challenge, evidently further reinforced Rumsfeld's resolve to force his commanders to substitute agility and precision for mass and firepower. The game was played in 2002 against 'a rogue military commander' in the Persian Gulf. The military's top brass expected that the United States, with its overwhelming force, its superior intelligence-gathering capabilities, its total informational superiority, and its carefully delineated leadership structures, would crush the enemy. Instead, they were humiliated by their opponent, played by retired Marine Corps Lt Gen. Paul Van Riper, a fervent advocate of doing away with traditional command-and-control structures and of giving decision makers in the field the freedom to act on their own initiative (Van Riper and Hoffman 1998).

There is now widespread agreement on what Rumsfeld got wrong: providing too few troops to restore order afterwards. But he really had no alternative. The decision to pursue the RMA at all costs left the American military without the resources to put sufficient boots on the ground. Even if Rumsfeld had wanted to send four hundred thousand men to Iraq, he could not have.

Instead, RMA assigned foot-slogging policing to America's more backward allies. But problems of inoperability in the Balkans and Afghanistan, the inability of the allies to keep up or even to keep out of the way, persuaded many in the Pentagon that most allies were more trouble than they were worth and that America and the United Kingdom were better off going it alone, in the initial stages of the fighting at least.

From this perspective, disbanding the Iraqi army, scattering three hundred thousand armed and unemployed men into the population, was an especially egregious error. Restoring order called for a broken windows strategy, which implies a lot of policing and, therefore, a lot of police. The Iraqi military were the only trained force that could conceivably have supplied the necessary personnel. The allies lacked the personnel to seal the borders, let alone stop visible crime and looting. Consequently, the situation soon went from bad to worse. Clearly, if Rumsfeld had thought seriously about the problem of restoring order afterwards and the need for allied help, the United States might not have gone to war, at least not without the promise of that broad allied support.

Nevertheless, according to most contemporary press coverage, the Iraq War itself represented the apotheosis of the RMA. A more balanced discussion of events, written by Joshua Davis, appeared in *Wired Magazine*.

> The war was a grand test of the netcentric strategy in development since the first Gulf War. At least, that's the triumphal view from the Pentagon briefing room. But what was it like on the ground? ... I tracked the network from the generals' plasma screens at Central Command to the forward nodes on the battlefields in Iraq. What I discovered was something entirely different from the shiny picture of techno-supremacy touted by the proponents of the Rumsfeld doctrine. I found an unsung corps of geeks improvising as they went, cobbling together a remarkable system from a hodgepodge of military-built networking technology, off-the-shelf gear, miles of Ethernet cable, and commercial software. (Davis 2003)

Nevertheless, Davis was favourably impressed with the system cobbled together. Known as 'Geeks' to the soldiers in the field,[6] the system tracked every friendly unit, weapons platform, and soldier in the theatre and plotted their positions in real time on a digital map, together with all known enemy locations, plus a lot more: battle plans, intelligence reports, maps, online chats, radio transcripts, photos, and video. Soldiers accessed this system through a portal known as the Warfighting Web, which ran over the military's Secret Internet Protocol Router Network in much the same way as the public Internet.

Geeks facilitated the major operational innovation of the Iraq War: swarm tactics. In the earlier Gulf War, coalition forces advanced in a traditional linear formation, with each unit assigned sole responsibility for a specific portion of the front or held in reserve. Coordination was achieved and fratricide avoided through careful attention to the boundaries assigned the attacking units. Then, as each unit advanced, it would sweep its assigned corridor clear of adversary forces. If it met with unexpected resistance, higher command could redeploy neighbouring or reserve units to overcome or in some cases seal off an exceptionally obstinate foe. Unfortunately, maintaining a continuous front is costly both in manpower and equipment. Resources must be spread out all along the line and in echelon behind it. Moreover, units advancing in linear formation often cannot move any faster than their slowest element; they sometimes have no option but to engage forces blocking their assigned line of attack, battling on the periphery rather than going for the heart of the enemy's defences; and they are easy to locate and, therefore, attack.

In the Iraq War, allied units were spread out like polka dots over the battle-space and charged with the destruction of enemy command, communications, control centres, and supply lines. When allied units encountered strong fixed defensive positions, they often merely noted the locations and bypassed them. Dangerous enemy offensive units were engaged and – through self-coordination of local air, land, and sea forces – overwhelmed. This approach was possible because Geeks allowed soldiers to keep track of each other, even when they were out of one another's sight, and to come together rapidly and stealthily from all directions. Of course, dispersed attack formations avoid many of the drawbacks of a linear formations: forces are much more likely to be used to good effect, thereby saving on resources; the swarm can move forward as fast as its fastest elements – speed and surprise tend to degrade the efficacy of an adversary's response (Coram 2002); dispersed forces are hard to attack and nearly impossible to attack successfully when they move faster and concentrate firepower more accurately than their opponents.[7] The allied swarm used Microsoft Chat to coordinate the action – concentrate, attack, and disperse, combine and recombine – of myriad, dispersed, combat units. When a problem developed, a soldier would radio a Tactical Operations Center, where the problem would be typed into a chat session and addressed by anyone online – from experts at the Pentagon to the AWACS overhead or combat teams nearby. According to Davis, not only did technology change the way allied forces manoeuvred, it also changed the way they thought.

On the negative side, several observers have noted that allied forces lacked a system of systems (Boyne 2003; Cordesman 2003). Many of the information systems available at the outset of the Iraq War remained service-specific. As a consequence, a network had to be quickly improvised from these systems under difficult circumstances. Not surprisingly, this improvisation worked best between the highest levels of command. The net was probably weakest at the battalion level and below. However, even platforms that were relatively well integrated into the net – U.S. Air Force fighter planes and bombers – had problems with interoperability, communications, and data flow, as well as in procedures and computer support. These problems often showed up in an inability to redirect aircraft in mid-flight away from targets that had been destroyed or to surviving targets in a timely manner.

Network communications problems also sometimes hindered the ability of logistical units to synchronize their movements with the combat teams they supported, causing delays in re-supply. Indeed, orders from higher commands often simply outran the ability of lower-level combat and support units to interact and coordinate with each other. These problems were evidently due to doctrinal and training failures as much as to technological and equipment failures, although Davis noted that one Army analysis of information problems during the Iraq War focused on the need for improved energy sources to replace batteries.

The GIG is supposed to provide the information and telecommunication services needed to fix these problems (well, perhaps not battery life). It will enhance the ability of soldiers to make sense of the situations they find themselves in and support collaboration – capacities that are essential to promote a high level of shared awareness and to create the conditions needed for effective self-synchronization. However, the GIG won't fix what Cordesman (2003, 280) describes as the tendency of bandwidth creep 'to push information to virtually all potential users and to centralize decision making and review.' He concludes,

> It is far from clear that today's problems are truly bandwidth problems as distinguished from a failure to create efficient systems that limit the need for bandwidth, and equally unclear that careful review has been made of where the flow of information should stop, of how much information can really be used, and of the need to delegate and limit information flow. (280)

The champions of the RMA within the defence establishment go much further in denouncing existing military systems of command

and control, and affirming the need for fundamental changes. They argue that the military's culture, architecture, decision-making processes, and basic operating routines must be transformed to exploit IT's promise. In turn, these changes – expanding lateral information flows; increasing connectivity and interoperability, collaboration, and experimentation, forming and deploying small, agile, specialized teams; and devolving much (but not all) command authority downward – call for equally fundamental changes in the way military units are configured, trained, and equipped.

One of the key change agents in this process is the defence department's Command and Control Research Program, currently directed by David S. Alberts.[8] The Command and Control Research Program has produced a series of reports dating back to the mid-1990s outlining the changes the military must embrace to enter the information age. The most recent report in the series, *Power to the Edge: Command ... Control ... in the Information Age* (Alberts and Hayes 2003), reiterates the conclusions of its predecessors but goes much further in emphasizing the importance of flattening command hierarchies and of devolving power down to combat and logistic teams.

To those who have learned about the U.S. military from old war movies, this looks like an impossible stretch. To those more familiar with the modern military, however, Alberts and Hayes can be understood as saying merely that the armed forces as a whole should look more like the Special Operations Command, with its joint headquarters, exercises and training, tactics and doctrine, its relatively high degree of interoperability and equipment standardization, and its tailored task forces, composed of units that are brought together to accomplish a given mission or accomplish specified objectives, and are then reorganized or reconfigured to take on new responsibilities. Furthermore, Alberts and Hayes's combat and logistics units would look like special forces units: relatively small, highly skilled, multidisciplinary teams, with a lot of rank, but not many levels of command. This would still be a big stretch, but almost by definition not an inconceivable one.

At the same time that Alberts and Hayes call for the devolution of power to the edge, they are cognizant that authority and accountability are essential features of any system of command and control. Organizations that fail to allocate responsibility for performance, to align responsibility with authority, or to hold individuals accountable for the exercise of responsibility and authority are predestined to muddle and to pursue sectarian interests. Their point is that it is possible to move from a 'concept of command that is tied to an individual commander to a concept of command that is widely distributed' (Alberts and Hayes 2003, 18).

Rather than issuing detailed orders about what to do, when to do it, where to do it, and how to do it, or even specifying objectives each unit is to achieve and leaving the details of when, where, and how to the units, Alberts and Hayes would have headquarters assign missions to the units involved, but leave decisions about how they are to be achieved to the units involved to work out for themselves – they refer to this decision-making process as self-synchronization. They assert that effective self-synchronization requires headquarters to provide a clear and consistent understanding of command intent, appropriate rules of engagement, and sufficient resources. These measures would guide but not dictate details to subordinates. In addition, effective self-synchronization requires quality information, shared situational awareness, competence at all levels of the task force, and 360-degree trust – in information, subordinates, superiors, peers, and equipment.

To get from here to there, Alberts and Hayes make two critical assumptions. The first is that GIG will be constructed pretty much on time and on schedule. The second is that the American military will continue to experiment with RMA; that its basic principles will be vindicated; and that this vindication will lead to consensus on which practices matter, the recognition that these practices must be adopted together, as part of a complementary system, and, ultimately, to the willingness of people at the top of the uniformed services to share authority.

So far, development and deployment of the GIG is pretty much on schedule. This success largely reflects the military's willingness and ability to lavish resources on what is essentially an unproven concept. Few, if any, other organizations could afford to be so extravagant. The one area in which the GIG is admittedly behind schedule is in protecting the space-based segment of the GIG from attack, especially its resiliency in the face of an information attack. This is not now primarily a money problem. Rather, it seems that the military has so many platforms under development that there simply are not enough skilled aerospace systems engineers to go around. Since many of the platforms under development for the military reflect the assumptions of an earlier era, one might conclude that this constraint is a harbinger of more serious conflicts to come.

My point here is that the defence department's resource allocation, like most government budget processes, is incremental. It is better at preserving the human, material, and technological capacities of existing institutional arrangements and functional communities than at creating new ones. That conclusion holds a fortiori where it is necessary to scrap the old to bring into being the new. For the next few years, the American military can continue to pursue parallel tracks to the future, what Alberts and Hayes refer to as the modernization track versus the transformation track, but at some point, migration paths from one track to the next must be put in place. The Air Force, which has thought long and hard about the need to make the transition to a space and air force, still has not figured out how to change its resource allocation process to make it actually happen (Barzelay and Campbell 2003). What Alberts and Hayes propose looks a lot harder.

Moreover, reasonable people might conclude that the GIG and the vision of RMA it reflects misconstrue the basic security problems of the twenty-first century. Low-intensity or asymmetric combat looks more like policing than it does the conventional wars the RMA was designed to fight. This fact has become increasingly evident in Iraq in the period following the defeat of Saddam Hussein's conventional military forces. British units in Iraq during the occupation have been much more effective in the areas under their administration than have American. Moreover, American efforts to apply the IT practices utilized by some metropolitan police forces to control crime in the United States have not met with success. Perhaps this is because the problem in Iraq is now more like Chicago's policing problem, which is dominated by criminal activities carried out by organized gangs,[9] than New York's, which is dominated by disorderly individuals. Gang control requires the cultivation of community support and a great deal of human intelligence. Those are not the kinds of skills the United States military has cultivated.

Conclusions

Technological development is not a coldly rational, self-regulating economic process, proceeding automatically along a singular path. Even if one sets aside the contested nature of efficiency, the evolution of social constructs is precisely analogous to natural selection, a process that is inherently path dependent.[10] Human agency intervenes at every stage to order arrangements to suit felt needs and wants. We shape economic arrangements, social relationships, and technological developments at the same time that they shape us.

In turning Chandler upside down, we ignored this fact. Perhaps the key lesson of his work is that governance mechanisms had to be designed and tested and adapted before large-scale organizations to exploit industrial-age technological innovations could be built. Where the exploitation of IT is concerned, this process is still in its infancy.

E. Brynjolfsson and L.M. Hitt (2000) provide compelling evidence that computers can dramatically increase performance: where both are compared to industry averages, an 8 per cent increase in IT assets is associated with a 1 per cent increase in productivity. They emphasize, however, that the payoff to IT investment varies substantially across firms, even in the same industries.

In explaining this phenomenon, Brynjolfsson and Hitt stress the manner in which systems are implemented and deployed. They argue that if we want the high productivity that IT promises, it is not sufficient to invest in computers and software; our organizations must also adopt a specific relational architecture, set of processes or routines, and culture.

Brynjolfsson and Hitt refer to this pattern of practices as the digital organization. They insist that IT and digital organization are complements: organizations that simultaneously adopt the digital organization and invest more in IT have disproportionately higher performance. They note that the power of digital organizations to transform productivity was evident first in the computer industry. Many of the characteristics of digital organizations were already common practice in this industry and, as a result of their technological expertise, its leaders were themselves well positioned to grasp IT's inherent possibilities and to figure out how to reconfigure basic business processes to take advantage of them, although actually doing so often took many years. Table 11.1 shows Brynjolfsson and Hitt's digital organization reconfigured to represent a military organization.

Five of the characteristics of Brynjolfsson and Hitt's digital organizations are often found in high-performance organizations, especially those operating in hazardous environments that call for high reliability from their members (Weick and Sutcliffe 2001). These organizations consistently maintain focus and communicate goals, foster information access and communication throughout the organization, link incentives to performance, hire the best people, and invest in human capital (Pfeffer 1998; see also Ichniowski and Shaw 2003).

Table 11.1
Characteristics of industrial age and information age organizations

Mass military	Net-centric military
Centralized expertise and coordination	Dispersed expertise and self-coordination
Vertical integration and channelled communication	Horizontal integration and extensive communication
Large formations	Small formations
Many layers	Few layers
Specialized functional units	General-purpose units
Extreme division of labour	Extensive cross-training
Narrow skill requirements	Broad skill requirements
Low training requirements	Very high training requirements
Mass and firepower	Speed and precision
Ponderous	Flexible, agile
Sequential action and manoeuvre	Continuous action and manoeuvre
Heavy reliance on resources held in reserve to deal with the unexpected	Capacity to redeploy quickly
Limited situation awareness	High degree of shared situation awareness
Formal relations with subordinates, supporting units, and suppliers	Long-term, trust-based relationships
Low emphasis on social learning and information sharing	High emphasis on social learning and information sharing
Slow to adapt	Quick to adapt

Source: Brynjolfsson and Hitt (2000).

Moving from analog to digital processes[11] and distributing decision-rights to front-line personnel are the practices that truly distinguish the digital organization from more traditional bureaucracies. The first is inconceivable without computers; the second is a recipe for disaster where people lack a clear sense of mission and the motivation, capacity, and information needed to accomplish their missions. Digital processes include the following principles (Hammer 1990):

- Jobs should be designed around missions and goals rather than functions (functional specialization and sequential execution are inherently inimical to efficient processing).
- Those who use the output of an activity should perform the activity; the people who produce information should process it, since they have the greatest need for information and the greatest interest in its accuracy.
- Information should be captured once and at the source.

- Parallel activities should be coordinated during their performance, not after they are completed.
- The people who do the work should be responsible for making decisions and operational control built into their job designs.

Can government copy the digital model, organizing itself into alliances of networks, sharing top management, core competencies, and a common culture, and using computers to chart activities and operational flows? Can it use real-time information on operations made possible by modern IT systems to pass the exercise of judgment down into the organization, to wherever it is most needed, at service delivery, in production, or to the client? Can government abandon its hierarchies, its need to push operating decisions to the top of the organization, or its stove-piped functional organizations? Can it consistently maintain focus and communicate goals, foster information access and communication throughout the organization, link incentives to performance, hire the best people, and invest in human capital, as well as computers and software?

Adopting the digital organization remains problematic in several ways, two of which are crucial: lack of understanding that certain practices matter and that these practices must be adopted together, as part of a complementary system, and the unwillingness of the people at the top to share authority. The benefits are there, but so too are the costs. Nothing involving technology is inevitable.

Notes

1 In 2000, the only fund-raising category in which Democrats beat Republicans was $1 million plus donors. They remained ahead in this category in 2004 and caught up with them in other categories. U.S. law limits individual contributions to candidates, parties, and political action committees to a biennial maximum of $101,400. There are no real limits on soft money contributions – where donors spend their money to support a candidate or issue directly, rather than donate to a party or one or more of its candidates. Small donations are worth more than an equivalent number of large donations because the federal matching rate decreases with the size of contributions. During presidential primaries, for example, the federal government matches only the first $250 of an individual's contributions to eligible presidential candidates. On campaign finance in the United Sates, see the mini-

symposium on the Bipartisan Campaign Finance Reform Act of 2002 in the summer 2005 issue of the *Journal of Policy Analysis and Management* (Malbin 2005).

2 The natural log of margin of victory in the presidential race explained 10 per cent of the cross-sectional interstate variance in the log of voter participation in 2004, 1 per cent in 2000, and 7 per cent in 1996, with slope coefficients of -3, -1.3, and 1.9, respectively (the first of the coefficients can be interpreted to mean that a 1 per cent increase in the vote margin resulted in a 3 per cent decrease in voter turnout, while the slope coefficient for 1996 could be interpreted to mean that closeness doesn't always count in elections). However, the 1996 election was not expected to be close. Other contests probably influenced turnout in that election more than the presidential race. Demographics and weather are also significant determinants of turnout. Author's analysis.

3 One might be inclined to scepticism. Military organizations have earned a reputation for conservatism. In part, this is a necessary consequence of their need for resiliency and reliability in the face of combat attrition. Moreover, Fountain (2001, 167–92) has described the failure of an early experiment carried out by the U.S. Army's 9th Mechanized Division (HiTech) at Fort Lewis, WA, with a network-enabled information system. The failure of this experiment was at least partly due to the unwillingness of its senior officers to abandon hierarchy or to push operating decisions down into the organization. Nevertheless, Thomas Hughes (1998, 5) reminds us that the very first digital organization may well have been the Defense Advanced Research Project Agency's ARPANET project. Started in the late 1960s, the project was characterized by 'a flat, collegial, meritocratic management style as contrasted with a vertical, hierarchical one; the resort to transdisciplinary teams of engineers, scientists, and managers in contrast to reliance on discipline-bound experts; the combining of diverse, or heterogeneous, physical components in a networked system instead of standardized, interchangeable ones in an assembly line; and a commitment by industry to change-generating projects rather than long-lived processes.' For Canadian treatments of this revolution in military affairs, see Directorate of Land Strategic Concepts (2003) and Richter (1999).

4 For example, status information on the enemy, friendly forces, and neutrals, and terrain and weather information. Information is supposed to be supplied by users, and local and regional sensors, and to be processed by intelligent agents.

5 For example, a rifleman's processor could be a thin client dedicated to supporting a human-computer interface (with voice recognition, heads-up dis-

play, speech synthesis, and communications). It need not have its scarce computing capacity tied up providing other information-related services. Computing resources to support a user can reside anywhere on the grid.

6 *Geeks* refers to the network set up to fight the war. It is not an acronym but a nickname for the Operation Desert Freedom Theater of Operations Command, Control, and Communications Grid. However, its operators called it the G3C system, which might have suggested the nickname.

7 The worth of dispersed formations in desert warfare is not a new discovery. General Erwin Rommel used dispersed formations and swarm tactics against the British in North Africa during the Second World War, typically taking personal command at the most decisive spot of the operation. Although his tactics were unquestionably effective, visitors from the German General Staff were nevertheless often appalled by Rommel's flagrant disregard for sound principles of war.

8 Alberts is director, Research and Strategic Planning, Office of Assistant Secretary of Defense for Networks and Information Integration. Before taking this position, he was the director of the Center for Advanced Concepts and Technology and the School of Information Warfare and Strategy at the National Defense University.

9 Interestingly, the term *network* has been applied to guerrilla, revolutionary, insurgent, and terrorist forces for nearly a hundred years. Al Qaeda, for example, fits the definition in terms of lateral information flows, specialized teams, and devolved authority. Regardless of the success or failure of the GIG and any organizational transformation it inspires, military formations will undoubtedly tend to become more like those of their foes.

10 Paul David (1985) defines path-dependence in the following manner: 'A path-dependent sequence of economic changes is one of which important influences upon the eventual outcome can be exerted by temporally remote events, including happenings dominated by chance elements rather than systemic forces' (332). In other words, economic arrangements are partly a function of systemic change, but they are a function of random, fortuitous events as well. Moreover, systematic forces include culture, position, and power – people, institutions, and competing values – and not merely payoffs.

11 Moving from analog to digital processes means reconfiguring processes to exploit the power of IT to perform a variety of tasks rather than merely using IT to perform steps in existing processes. This is not a new problem, nor is it necessarily an easy one. First, the technology must be ready. Then someone must grasp its full potential and discover how to configure work to extract every advantage from it. Here, the early history of the moving

assembly line in the American automobile industry is instructive. Its development required two fundamental technological advances that took decades to achieve: tougher metals, which were needed to make jigs and bits for high-precision cutting, turning, boring, milling, and stamping machines, and small-scale electric motors, which were needed to run them. High-precision manufacturing machines were needed to produce truly interchangeable parts and small-scale motors to liberate workflow from the tyranny of a single central source of motive power and the need to transmit it by belts, shafts, and gears. These were necessary, but not sufficient, conditions for the invention of the moving automobile assembly line. Both were put in place when Ford Motor's Highland Park plant was designed in 1910. It wasn't until 1914, however, that its managers and engineers fully grasped the potential of interchangeable parts and machines run by small-scale electric motors and reorganized automobile manufacturing accordingly, doubling the plant's productivity at a stroke. The actual reorganization took only a few months. Recognizing the possibilities inherent in the new technologies and figuring out how to take advantage of them took years. It then took additional decades for the processes pioneered by Ford to become widespread throughout the automobile industry and to be adopted in other industries. Given this story, it is, perhaps, no surprise that the industry that has most fully exploited the power of IT is the IT industry itself.

12 Don't Try This at Home: Lessons from England

PERRI 6

This chapter offers a second contrast with the Canadian experience, and one that presents a quite different perspective from that offered by the examination of the situation in the USA. The rationale for the comparison is explained in the opening section. Next, some key drivers of e-government policy and programs are explained, as well as some of the most important generic problems faced. The empirical discussion examines first democratic and then governmental activities. Trends are described and analysed in online political campaigning, websites run by politicians and the legislature, and initiatives in online consultation before summing up the country's limited achievements in cultivating a vibrant online democratic life. New data are reported on the political parties' websites during the course of the 2005 general election campaign. The review of e-government initiatives is confined to central government programs. Changes in the central machinery of oversight for e-government are examined together with developments in the government's main Web portal, before reviewing the history of major project fiascos. This section considers the tension in e-government programs between supporting greater collaborative working and sharing of information from client records between agencies on the one hand, and respecting client confidentiality on the other. The concluding section sums up the performance of the U.K. government in England, before speculating about the prospects for the foreseeable future.

Contrasts

England[1] provides a useful contrast to the Canadian case. Because of its parliamentary system, its policy and decision-making processes resemble those of Canada more than those of the United States. As a country with a large sector of international information technology companies working with the public sector but based in the USA, the position of its government in relation to the major contractors has some structural similarities with that of Canada.

Moreover, English officials would claim that they often pay more attention, when looking for e-government ideas to borrow from other countries, to developments in Canada than in the United States. The recent creation of a role of chief information officer for central government has sometimes been presented as an example of learning from Canada, and officials would also claim that the design of the central government Web portal, http://www.direct.gov.uk,[2] has reflected lessons drawn from successful Canadian approaches. In its behaviour and achievements, England provides an important contrast with the Canadian case. Successive governments in England have had to report a much longer list of major failures, delays, cost overruns, abandoned initiatives, and scandals in the recent history of their major e-government projects and programs than has the Canadian federal government. Digitalization of politics is much less developed in England than in North America generally: individual politicians' and local party chapters' websites are not typically sophisticated by international standards; in particular, the Web presence of the legislature, the House of Commons, is grey and technical. Hitherto, the country has yet to see an equivalent of Howard Dean's approach to campaigning; and its armed forces, sophisticated as they are by European standards, do not yet boast information systems of the complexity of those of the United States. In civilian public services, England has a track record of attempting very large-scale and ambitious projects, seeking to make major transformations in the quality of services, the nature of the service offering, and the ways in which providers work simultaneously and in relatively short periods. On the other hand, the Canadian federal government has generally pursued more modestly scaled projects.

Some would argue that socio-demographic and geographical differences have something to do with this difference. Canada has about three-fifths of the population of England, but scattered over a vast area; England's nearly 50 million people are relatively concentrated. Moreover, British government in England is much more centralized than is Canadian federal government, and the latter has less direct responsibility for health care. Perhaps, though, organizational differences matter much more still. Despite the lip service, project management as a discipline is weak in the British public sector and programmatic knowledge management still embryonic. These facts suggest that it is worth considering how far the underachievement of the United Kingdom can be explained by the organizational weaknesses, and therefore whether the similarities of constitutional order and the effect of British 'benchmarking' of Canadian achievements tell us anything about the scope for, and the limits of, lesson drawing between countries.

Improving Services

Previous chapters have explored the consequences for e-government in Canada of a strongly felt imperative to enhance the quality of consumers' experience of government services. Central government's services in England are already highly visible. The centre administers most taxes, provides most cash benefits, manages a nationalized near-monopoly health care system, and – perhaps more important – authorizes and so tightly regulates, inspects, and sets limits to the financing of local services such as education and policing. Electronic service delivery has been the field of e-government in which most effort and investment have been put in England (see Bellamy 2002), although, as we shall see, the results have been mixed. Although a recent European Union study ranked the U.K. e-government service offering third highest after Sweden and Austria in a league table of sophistication, the country performed less well in getting services fully online (Directorate-General for Information and Media 2005). Comparatively few citizens actually use e-government services in England; Accenture (2005a, 29) reports just over 40 per cent of households surveyed in the United Kingdom had ever used an e-government service, making the country fourteenth in its league table of twenty-two developed and developing countries.

Managing Risk

Imperatives for improving the consumers' experience of public services are by no means absent from British e-government policy. In the 1990s, indeed, it could be argued that under both the Conservative governments and, from 1997, the first term of the Labour government, this was one of the most important drivers of e-government policy.

But another, of growing importance, has been the commitment of policy makers of both the left and right to enhance the capability of state agencies effectively to manage risks presented by particular groups within the citizenry, ranging from acquisitive or violent crime through tax or benefit fraud to risk in such fields as child protection and mental health, truancy control, conditionality in welfare, and so on. Of course, governments always have to be concerned with enforcement as well as provision, but in the late 1990s and early 2000s, risk management came to be the more important concern. It focused investment priorities and the attention of politicians and managers on e-government programs for capturing and analysing information about citizens and service users, and on predicting their behaviour and tracking their movements through systems and services. In turn, it has required intense focus on redesigning, connecting, and integrating back-office processes and client record-management systems. To some degree, this has been at the expense of the earlier focus on developing service provision and handling transactions over the Web or, better still, digital television as it becomes an increasingly important potential channel. To be sure, investment continues in, for example, plans for parts of individuals' health care records to be available for secure viewing by the patients online, in improving the facility for filing tax returns and making tax payments on the Web, and Web-based applications for licences and permits. Government continues to be concerned with improving the quality of, for example, online forms (National Audit Office 2003a). Yet the political priorities have shifted markedly since the late 1990s toward major projects for the integration of data systems throughout the criminal justice system, the development of a comprehensive and integrated database on all children, bringing together social services, education and law enforcement systems, and, most controversially and ambitiously, a population register for a bio- metric identity card. It would be a mistake to think that such aspirations were unimportant in British policy making before the attack on the World Trade Center. The conjunction of the advent of the international 'war on terror' with rising domestic pressures – highly publicized deaths of children, homicides by paranoid schizophrenics who had lost touch with public services, rising public concern about violent crime and about less serious anti-social behaviour – has concentrated policy makers' minds hugely on the need for information sharing and integrated data-management systems to orient interventions in these fields toward the control of risks.

Making Savings

A third imperative has recently become increasingly central to the Labour administration's strategy for e-government. If enhanced customer service provision was the dominant imperative in the 1990s and risk management became pre-eminent by the 2000s, then from 2003 onwards, budgetary and fiscal considerations have become increasingly central and are likely soon to come into direct conflict with those of risk management.

Since 2001, the Labour administration has increased public expenditure very significantly, especially in health care, primary and secondary education, and law enforcement, and this direction is planned to continue until 2008. In the run-up to the 2005 general election, the government felt especially vulnerable to criticism about the extent to which the additional expenditure committed was producing improvements in services that were visible to service users. The vulnerability was made worse by the fact that so much e-government investment had been in back-office systems. Moreover, the less benign economic climate and reduced expected tax yield raised a question about the sustainability of the policy. The political scope for further tax increases is, however, generally thought to be rather limited. Therefore, the chancellor of the exchequer commissioned Sir Peter Gershon to produce a report on how efficiency savings might be achieved, with a specific brief to look at e-government. After thirty years' experience in the computing, telecoms, and defence industries, including managing the merger of GEC and British Aerospace, Gershon was appointed chief executive of the Office of Government Commerce in April 2000. Principally, efficiency in this context means cuts in staffing, supposedly made possible by the substitution of automated e-government systems for human labour, across the public services might be achieved consistently with reform of services, enhancement of the visibility of service improvements, and redirection of effort to front-line services.

The recommendations (Gershon 2004) were accepted by the chancellor. This completely changed the context for public service reform generally and for e-government specifically. Gershon offered the prospect of very large savings of over £20 billion each year (very roughly equivalent to 2.5 per cent of annual total public sector expenditure or about 1 per cent of GDP) and reductions in staffing of more than 84,000 civil service posts by 2008, to be achieved principally through the substitution of IT-capital-intensive systems for labour-intensive ones. Particular proposals included

- large-scale amalgamations of back-office systems between public sector agencies, which raised questions about the extent of the real autonomy of agencies and of local authorities from each other and from the centre, as well as about confidentiality of information provided to single functions
- large-scale overhauling of procurement toward e-auctions
- much greater automation of case decision-making, which raised questions about the appropriate role of professional judgment in some services
- reduction in availability of traditional channels of delivery with the hope of finally eliminating them in a few years for many services, which raised questions about adequacy of access for groups with less access to or less confidence in the use of computers or interactive television channels

Following Gershon, departmental and agency targets have been realigned toward the development of e-government systems designed to substitute capital for labour wherever possible, in order to achieve targets for staffing reductions and efficiency savings. Great skepticism greeted these recommendations among journalists, pundits, academic commentators, and public sector trades unions, which was based on the long history of public sector IT programs failing to achieve either major efficiency savings or significant substitutions of capital for labour. Yet ministers claim to be undeterred. It remains to be seen how far this program can be implemented successfully, however, and just how radically it might change the balance of the e-government program (see the discussion of new strategy below). Just as open to debate is the question of how far the cost-control imperative behind Gershon can be made consistent with the risk management and service enhancement agendas.

Capability

Arguably, the fourth key factor that has shaped e-government in England has been weakness of capability. The country now has a long history of major e-government projects being abandoned altogether, being delivered years late and wildly over-budget, or installed but providing scandalously poor quality of performance and contributing to major service failures. Some of the best known cases are discussed briefly below. The debate about how this litany of failure is to be explained has generally pointed to weaknesses in procurement and project management capability on the client side (National Audit Office 2004), but recent academic work has argued that the more important problem is a structural one, that the British government is too dependent on a small cluster of major international IT companies operating in a rather oligopolistic manner (Dunleavy et al. 2004). The English approach to IT projects has often been extremely ambitious: projects tend to be devised that are very large in scale, that are not incremental but require major changes in staff working patterns, and that tend to be subject to political pressures to add extra goals and functions in midstream. These are all factors that project management wisdom advises are likely to lead to disaster, even when procurement and client-side project management capabilities are strong, which they are often not in English public authorities. In response, the centre has attempted to specify in much greater detail the procurement procedures, project management methods, and standards to be followed in such projects, including those run by local authorities. It has also created a central project authorization and procurement support system for central government bodies in the form of the Office of Government Commerce, working in tandem with the e-Government Unit.

Before examining e-government in detail, this chapter provides a brief overview for the English case of the issues of online politics, public online participation, policy making, knowledge management, service delivery, and project management.

E-politics, E-democracy

E-voters?

The significance of the Internet in English party politics remains limited, if we confine the measurement to the most visible, 'front-office' functions. Although 56 per cent of households are believed to have Internet access at home, 36 per cent to have broadband, and 57 per cent to have digital television in 2005,[3] few people use these resources for political or democratic purposes. The exit poll following the 2005 general election conducted by the survey house MORI found that very small proportions of the population had used the Internet to gain access to information about candidates or parties. Table 12.1[4] shows that there has been significant growth in these figures from the position in the 2001 general election, but from a very low base.

A Hansard Society study carried out by NOP, asking a slightly different question, was able to report fully 15 per cent getting some kind of election-related information online.[5] However, for MORI, numbers fall significantly when people are asked whether they visited a party's own website during the campaign (table 12.2).

Because the parties use their databases to concentrate their communications upon swing voters in marginal constituencies, many people indeed report receiving e-mail contacts from parties; in fact, MORI's data suggest that more people may have received videos from the parties than were e-mailed.[6]

The significance of the parties' sophisticated databases of swing and potential voters in marginal constituencies was highlighted during the 2005 election campaign. Complaints were made to the Information Commissioner (the data-protection legislation regulator), regarding claims that Labour Party[7] activists and ministers and Scottish Nationalists[8] were 'cold calling' voters targeted in this way, despite their having signed 'opt-outs' from such marketing techniques. If MORI's exit poll data are accurate, then Labour was probably not calling any more people, in absolute numbers, than the other parties; if anything, the other parties were scaling up their telephone calling to match Labour's activity in this area.

The Hansard NOP study found that 13 per cent of respondents sent or received e-mails about the election in 2005, compared with 5 per cent in 2001; that 22 per cent visited a media organization's site for election information, up from 11 per cent in 2001; and that 18 per cent claimed that the Internet had helped them make an informed choice, again up from 6 per cent in 2001.

NOP also found that only 3 per cent expected to have any contact with their MP at all after the election. If recent trends are anything to go by, those who can reasonably expect to make contact by e-mail will be even fewer: a Telewest Business survey found that only 1 per cent of respondents had ever contacted their MP by e-mail.

Longer-term trends, however, suggest that the Internet has been important in political mobilization in recent years, at least among those less readily attracted to conventional politics: Gibson, Lusoli, and Ward (2005) find support for this hypothesis in an analysis of 2002 NOP survey data. Other research by the same team suggests that the

Table 12.1

Responses to survey question 24/25: ... used the Internet to access information on candidates or parties?

	Yes, any party (%)	Yes, Conservative (%)	Yes, Labour (%)	Yes, Liberal Democrat (%)	Yes, other (%)	Yes, don't know party (%)	No (%)	Don't know (%)
24–30 May 2001	2	1	2	0	0	0	98	2
5–10 May 2005	7	4	5	4	2	—	92	—

Table 12.2

Responses to survey question 22/23: ... visited a political party's website?

	Yes, any party (%)	Yes, Conservative (%)	Yes, Labour (%)	Yes, Liberal Democrat (%)	Yes, Other (%)	Yes, don't know party (%)	No (%)	Don't know (%)
24–30 May 2001	2	1	1	0	0	0	98	0
5–10 May 2005	4	2	2	1	1	—	96	—

prospect for the Internet significantly to enhance the capacity of main-stream British parties to recruit members seems limited (Lusoli and Ward 2004), and generally the Internet tends to attract those already committed to work a little harder (Ward, Lusoli, and Gibson 2005).

Parties Online

There have been what North American readers know as 'campaign finance limits' in the United Kingdom for many decades. These are set as maximums for each candidate; in addition, returns are scrutinized by the Electoral Commission. No special allowances are given for the use of any particular technology; however, the effect has presumably been to limit investment to levels below what can be expected in countries with no such laws or less restrictive ones. Donations to political parties are not restricted, but those greater than a certain periodically revised threshold must be registered and publicly declared; public funding is restricted to support for parliamentary work. Figures on the parties' expenditure on major IT systems are not available.

A study of twenty-two websites run by political parties in England, Scotland, and Wales[9] during the 2005 general election conducted for the present study,[10] from the last week of January to the week after the election in May, confirms the general trend already noted toward rather limited interactivity in English online politics, by comparison with what can be discerned in some strands of U.S. politics on the Web, such as the Howard Dean campaign discussed in chapters 7 and 11.

Most parties organized their sites around the activities they expected their visitors to carry out – signing up for information, joining, donating, registering to volunteer, etc. The Conservatives in England, however, organized their site by policy areas; initially the Liberal Democrats in England organized their site by press releases, but soon switched to a visitor activity-based structure.

There were some differences in the tendencies of particular parties to highlight local issues on their websites. In general, in England, the centre-right parties were more likely to do so in 2005 than were the centre-left ones, but Scottish and Welsh parties across the left/right division were equally more likely to highlight local issues than were their English counterparts. The Conservatives were slightly more likely to run attack copy on their sites, and again the Scottish and Welsh sites of all the main parties were more vituperative than were their English sister organizations' sites.

None of the larger parties' sites ran any kind of open opinion polling on site visitors (perhaps their private sites for members did so); typically, they offered no more than opportunities to become a member or donate; the larger parties offered a link to official sites on which one could register to vote or apply for a postal vote. During the course of the election campaign, Labour in England added a facility to ask a question online and receive an answer privately, although the Conservatives in Scotland withdrew theirs.

Party size, measured by electoral representation in Westminster, is associated with some important aspects of website design and functionality. As one would expect, the larger parties highlighted policy positions on more issues than did smaller ones, and they also had the resources to use the site to respond to each day's or week's issues in the press. The smaller parties did not run distinct youth sites.

Interestingly, size is *not* well correlated with technological sophistication. Although the largest parties provided some interactive maps, downloadable video, and software, and the mid-sized Liberal Democrats offered an interactive organization chart, the somewhat smaller Green Party offered downloadable wallpaper, music, and logos, and also offered the facility for site visitors to send e-cards. Smaller parties of the right also showed significant technological sophistication: the far right British National Party offered downloadable software and audio, while the anti-European parties Veritas and the UK Independence Party offered several of these categories of interactivity. Green and centre-right parties tended to be more likely to offer facilities to sign up online for e-mail lists and to volunteer than were centre-left ones. No party publishes information on the donations yield from its website, and it is not known whether they even collect donation information in this way; the Electoral Commission requires registration of donations over a certain amount, but does not ask for information about channels of solicitation.

Most sites were oriented mainly to promoting their own host parties. Rather little effort was devoted to attack, although initially Labour ran some attack posters on its site, and over the course of the campaign, the Conservative Party site shifted more to attack. Smaller parties tended to devote less space to attack coverage than the larger ones, presumably because they had few seats to defend and because their supporters are more likely to be disillusioned with all the major parties rather than any particular one.

Broadly, and with some exceptions, the left of centre parties were more likely to highlight local issues on their sites than were the centre-right or even hard right parties, but all the Scottish and Welsh parties were more likely to give space to local issues than were their English counterparts.

The tendency to limit interactivity or facilities for deliberative activity is reinforced by a marked weakness in accessibility. As one would expect, Plaid Cymru offered their site in Welsh as well as in English. Surprisingly, the only other party to offer any material in minority languages was the Scottish Conservative party. As the 2005 election came to a close, the consultancy firm Cimex published a report on the main political parties' websites, which found that none met the standards of accessibility to people with sensory disabilities derived from their reading of the Disability Discrimination Act.[11]

If they did undertake any major redesigns of their websites for the general election, then nearly all the parties had completed them before the period of observations: certainly, their basic layout and structure were retained throughout the campaign, although Flash initial pages were changed by the larger parties that used them, and, of course, the larger parties changed the policy issues highlighted according to their campaign issue of the day or in response to press attention on a particular area.

E-Politicians?

The available evidence from England suggests that the country's politicians have yet to demonstrate innovation on a wide scale or any great commitment to use of the Web or e-mail for new deliberative and democratic purposes. A recent survey of MPs' websites found that most were cautious in content, relatively static, and offered few opportunities for interactivity (Ward and Lusoli 2005). Although an earlier Hansard Society report (Coleman 2001) was more optimistic, finding evidence of some local opinion polling, online consultation, and deliberation, the scale was certainly modest.

Some British MPs love gadgets at least as much as their Canadian counterparts, but the BlackBerry was probably adopted by politicians generally rather later in England than in Canada. Surprisingly, it was not until February 2005 that the speaker of the House of Commons issued an order banning their use in the chamber itself; such bans – issued, for example, for pagers and mobile telephones in the past – are usually a sign of near ubiquitous use.[12] Interestingly, the Welsh assembly has issued these devices to all members,[13] a decision that may well reflect a rather rapid change, because a mid-2002 survey found very few MPs even using e-mail from conventional computers.[14]

There has been a marked growth in 'blogging' by British politicians: some have very active blogs, either on their own sites or on dedicated blog sites. Little is known, however, about who reads them, how regularly they read them, or what they read them for. Certainly, there is no English politician yet whose blog has become a regular 'must-read' item, even for professional journalists and pundits, although of course some are more successful than others in using the conventional media to promote their blogs. Given the survey evidence quoted above about the limited voter interest in conventional politics online, there is no reason to think that as yet any MP can seriously imagine that her or his contribution to the 'blogosphere' is critical to her or his career. A Hansard Society study on political blogging in England followed several political blogs as case studies over several months, including some written by politicians. None offered much by way of interactivity, feedback, or deliberation for readers, beyond a basic commenting facility, which, when used, seemed to elicit little response either from the bloggers or other readers (Ferguson and Howell 2004).

Experts on e-democracy in England tend to regard blogging by people not seeking election as more interesting. Coleman (2005), for example, has become prominent in the English debate with his argument that the development of political blogging in England by individuals in a variety of social movements shows significant democratic potential.

The English experience of limited voter use of the Internet for electoral purposes, of timidity in Web presence among politicians, and a weakly developed pattern of blogging all reflect the continuing dominance of national broadcast and print media in what remains, in media terms as in political and legal ones, a highly centralized country. The contrast with Canada and the United States could hardly be more marked.

E-Consultation

Some of the earlier incarnations of the British government's portal site made a virtue of the effort to run online consultations. The http://www.ukon-line.gov.uk site offered an integrated listing of currently live consultations by departments and agencies, and offered a general e-mail facility for making comments. This feature has disappeared

from the face of its successor, http://www.direct.gov.uk. Most major
departments of state's websites do offer a list of current consultation
papers with closing dates, either from a 'consultations' button on the
home page (for example, Health, Education and Skills, International
Development) or else by searching for 'consultations' in the site A–Z
index. The typical pattern is to present live consultations chronologi-
cally, which is not generally the easiest way to search them. Those who
go straight to a topic may find a link to a live consultation paper if
there is one. But it could not be said that these sites make it a priority of
their design, layout, and appeal to attract comment on policy. Few
make available an open and deliberative facility, even subject to the
kind of moderation that would be required of any government-hosted
site. One exception is the Department for Work and Pensions site for
people with disabilities, which provides, for those prepared to register,
a forum to make their views known to civil servants and to exchange
views with other registered persons (https://secureonline.dwp.gov.
uk/dis-consult/).

Online consultations by political parties remain few. In 2001, as
part of its general election campaign, Labour launched http://www.
thebigconversation.org; although the site is still maintained, it
attracted rather limited interest (most topics have attracted under fifty
comments in the eighteen months prior to the time of writing in
December 2005), and there is little evidence that responses made to it
had any significant influence upon government policy.

Not So Democratic

For the political parties in England, new IT is of critical importance. Yet
the particular manner of its importance is interestingly congruent with
its prevailing role in the executive. Most of the main parties' investment in IT is directed toward their back-office systems for tracking
members, activists, and, above all, potential and swing voters, using
very finely grained demographic profiling tools and data mining and
matching techniques, which are deployed to support the tightest possible targeting of their communications. Their websites are, by contrast,
competently maintained and, for the most part, attractively presented,
but they are not really expected to become the major vehicles either for
narrowcast communication to members or broadcast contact with the
wide public, nor are they yet mission-critical instruments for fundraising and volunteer recruitment. The exit poll data from the 2005 general

election (summarized above) are reliable, and show that Web and e-mail contact with parties and candidates has grown since the 2001 election, but remain singularly unimportant in the overall mix; the main parties may be judging that there remains little likelihood in the short-term at least that this will change. Moreover, only a small proportion of the information held by the political parties about individuals or households or analysed at postcode level, is sourced through the party websites or private e-mail communication. In politics as in government, in recent years, back-office functions for IT have become more important than Web presence.

Although in the late 1990s, the British government's early efforts in developing online consultations and a Web presence for the House of Commons were praised as pioneering, today the democratic and participative elements of the Web presence of either the executive or the legislature are not, by international standards, especially impressive, nor is the country a leader in e-voting. The leading commentator, Professor Stephen Coleman, has been critical of the weak fulfilment of its democratic potential of the House of Commons Web base, suggesting that even the online consultations in which he was involved were less successful than they could have been, not least because of the limited commitment of parliamentarians to greater online participation (Coleman 2004).[15] The limited democratic profile of executive sites is certainly not unique in the developed world (Chadwick and May 2003), but it is consistent with the general pattern of the development of e-governance in England.

E-Government

Management

In the last years of the Major administration and in the early years of the Blair governments, reasonably senior ministers were given responsibility for the oversight of e-government activity. In 1996, Roger, now Lord, Freeman, as Conservative chancellor of the Duchy of Lancaster (Cabinet Office minister with Cabinet rank) issued the strategic green paper *government.direct* (Chancellor of the Duchy of Lancaster 1996). In the first years of the Blair administrations, strategic government-wide responsibilities for central government online programs were held by Ian McCartney, an important figure in the party with a Cabinet-level post, and later by Stephen Timms, a rising figure in the junior ministerial ranks with a record as an early adopter of the Web for political communication. They held the informal sobriquet of 'the e-minister.' At the time of writing, however, only a junior Cabinet Office under-secretary, Jim Murphy, holds this responsibility, but only as one in a long list of briefs. The government would justify this choice on the ground that now that the main areas of development are once again in the hands of the spending ministries and agencies, such a strong central political direction is no longer appropriate. Yet it is not clear that the argument is entirely compelling. McCartney's major contribution was to develop procedures to reduce the number of project fiascos (Cabinet Office 2000). E-government strategy has rarely engaged the attention of the prime minister or of the chancellor of the exchequer for long. Although 'modernization' of government was a key slogan for the first term and included e-government as a priority, by the second term, attention shifted from information management to service 'reform,' meaning more fundamental marketization, re-regulation, and performance management.

Recent years have seen a series of reorganizations in the central agencies charged with management and leadership of the e-government program in England. From the Conservatives, Labour inherited a Central Information Technology Unit (CITU) with a policy role but few real levers to corral departments, as well as an arms-length technical support body, the Central Computing and Telecommunications Agency (CCTA). Labour created a new role and office in the core executive, called the e-Envoy, charged with both championing IT generally and bringing leadership to the e-government program in particular; the inherited agencies reported to the e-Envoy. In 2001, in a further reorganization, the Office of Government Commerce (OGC) was created, also in the Cabinet Office, and given responsibility for the oversight of all major government procurement systems and procedures; CITU was formally incorporated into the Office of the e-Envoy (OeE), and the CCTA was brought into the OGC. The OeE and the OGC together exercised control over initial authorization of major new IT projects. In early 2004, on the departure of the second e-Envoy, the OeE was again reorganized. The incoming chief, Ian Watmore, was appointed head of e-Government, central sponsor for Information Assurance, and head of profession for Government IT. His role was officially described as being equivalent to that of a private sector chief information officer (CIO), although that title was used only informally for him. In December 2005, it was announced that, after less than two years in post but very shortly after having published a new strategy for e-government (for which, see below), Watmore left the role to take up a post as head of the prime minister's Delivery Unit, responsible for the oversight of policy implementation across government quite generally; his successor is John Suffolk, the former director general of Criminal Justice IT.

The e-Government Unit (http://www.cabinetoffice.gov.uk/e-government) has responsibility for the portal http://www.direct.gov.uk, the 'Government gateway' (http://www.gateway.gov.uk), a central portal for online transaction-based services with the central government still under development, for the management of '.gov.uk' domain name registration, for the Knowledge Network program to support interdepartmental knowledge management, for the development of common standards and guidelines for procurement and for technical specifications, and for the development of both a public-sector-wide IT profession and skills program, and of government-wide IT strategy.

Below this level, the organizational structure for management and leadership of e-government programs differs markedly among departments, agencies, and functions. Despite Labour's series of reorganizations and the attempts to give the core executive greater control over departmental and agency programs, significant discretion remains with the spending departments. For example, in the field of criminal justice, the Police Information Technology Organization (PITO) provides the management and procurement of most of the main national police data systems, but – despite the concern of the Home Office – local police forces continue to maintain and develop independent local intelligence data systems, and police intelligence data have yet to be fully integrated at the national level. By contrast, in the National Health Service (NHS), an agency has been specially created to be responsible for the procurement, management, and delivery of one of the largest new public sector IT programs anywhere in the world, and has effectively begun to force local health bodies to abandon their local systems in favour of the new national one. This agency, recently renamed Connecting for Health, is headed by former Deloitte consultant Richard Granger (who played a key role in implementing the London traffic congestion charging system). This highly ambitious program is intended to provide a comprehensive electronic patient record spine for the whole NHS in England, an integrated support system for patient choice of hospital and online booking for family physicians, a comprehensive searchable medical knowledge base for evidence-based practice, electronic prescribing, and a fully electronic internal payment management system for commissioning, all on a new dedicated broadband infrastructure for the NHS.

In education, local schools and even local education authorities continue to be able to exercise significant independence in their IT procurement. The government's decision to require the creation of a comprehensive database on all children, irrespective of whether they are known to any service to be at risk, will bring together local social services and local education authorities' information. Presumably, over time, it will bring pressure on schools to adopt systems that are fully compatible with the national register. Although the decision was justified on child protection grounds, it will affect many children who never face risks who would require the attention of the police and social services. The Department for Education and Skills has no equivalent of Connecting for Health. Consistently with its limited direct responsibility for schools or local education authorities, the DfES directorate for e-delivery has a largely internal orientation; the many specific DfES programs for a lifelong learning number, National Pupil Database, and the young people's database and card, Connexions, etc., are consequently correspondingly less integrated with each other than are the applications that will make up the Connecting for Health system.

Web Presence

Much of the public sector's e-government activity was driven in the first few years of the decade by efforts to achieve the targets set by the prime minister that all services be available online by 2005. Although the final statistics are not available, at the end of 2004, the e-Government forecast that by the end of 2005, 96 per cent of government services would be able to be classified as at least partly 'e-enabled';[16] however, care needs to be taken with both the definition of the scope of 'government services' and the standards required to be classified as 'e-enabled.'[17] In practice, a rather modest Web presence has sufficed in some cases to meet the criterion; certainly, neither seamless integration with other services nor sophisticated instant, securely identified transaction completion was required. Nor indeed was entirely digital back-office processing required for material submitted electronically. For example, in advance of the implementation of the Connecting for Health program, much of the NHS continues to use paper records, and many of the research councils that insist on online submission of grant applications then print out the applications to process them through refereeing and committee approval. The pressure applied to achieve the targets has certainly had an effect, although not necessarily the one that government might have wanted. In an October 2004 interview on taking up the role of chief information officer, Ian Watmore acknowledged that the priority was now to reduce the 'glut' of government information to fewer and better targeted services.[18]

Knowledge Management

In British government parlance, 'knowledge management' still lacks a stable meaning. It is often used to cover customer-relations management systems, document tracking and profiling tools, police intelligence data-management systems, quantitative data-analysis tools (for example, in crime mapping), modelling (for example, economic modelling in the Treasury), and even simple portals for thematically related documents. Rather rarely in civilian government is it used with reference to the practices and disciplines of explicit capture, classification, codification, and deliberate, targeted transmission of tacit knowledge to defined personnel; however, there are a number of such initiatives in the armed forces.

Since 2004, most central government departments have developed programs for electronic document and record management. The program is supported by the Public Records Office (see, for example, 2001), now part of the National Archive, which provides and manages much of the infrastructure. Some of the imperative for this initiative has come from the passing of freedom of information legislation. These programs produce very extensive metadata on all documents generated within government (Roberts and Bretschneider 2005).

A major central government initiative in digital support for knowledge management has been the creation of the Knowledge Network, managed by the e-Government Unit. This is a system, some parts of which are available, depending on their individual authorizations, to the 55,000 civil service users of the Government Secure Intranet (GSI) of linked intranets, extranets, databases, applications, and document libraries to support information sharing among civil servants. It has no presence on the public World Wide Web. It has developed from a policy briefing database built in the late 1990s and based originally on an idea borrowed from a small-scale experiment within the Department of Health, but it also includes a system to support collaboration between government lawyers, the OGC's IT projects database including lessons learned, a system to support departmental relations with the Treasury on public expenditure monitoring, and communications platforms for secure contact with other governments. A good deal of the development work has required the specification of standards for information supported and of authorization procedures for role-based access. No comprehensive evaluation of the network or of its levels of usage appears to be in the public domain. Anecdotal information suggests that the system is not as widely used as was originally hoped, and that commitment to the government-wide system beyond the Cabinet Office and in the spending departments remains limited.

Fiascos

Many major IT projects commissioned by central government in England have gone seriously awry (Cross 2005). Many of the delays, cost overruns, acute service breakdowns, and chronic long-term underperforming systems have become national scandals that have dominated press headlines for weeks. And the series of such failures did not come to an end with the McCartney report of 2000 on how problems could be avoided in future, the centralizing reform of commissioning in 2001, or the response to the National Audit Office report, although it is fair to say that many of the current crop of worst cases are in fact longstanding problems and at least some, though by no means all of the problems, can be dated back to the late 1990s. Indeed, in July 2001, the parliamentary ombudsman's annual report showed that problems caused by government IT systems were responsible for a large proportion of a steep year-on-year rise in citizens' complaints. In 2003, the Parliamentary Office of Science and Technology (2003) reviewed a long list of IT project failures and at least hinted that the new procedures had yet to reduce their likelihood. The following are a few of the most infamous cases of project failures:

- *Abandonment*. Libra, the system to support the magistrates' courts, was the subject of a damning National Audit Office report (2003b); by then, it had been largely scaled back and subsequently the program was, with a face-saving formula, put on ice in favour of a new more modern integrated system to be procured soon. Poor specification in procurement, disputes with contractors, and poor client-side project management explained a ten-year delay and an unacceptable overspend.

- *Late and over-budget.* The Swanwick air traffic control centre and system opened fully six years late and cost more than double the original estimate.
- *Acute service collapse.* In June 1999, headlines were dominated by queues outside Passport Agency offices around the country as the newly introduced computer system led to huge delays and backlogs of hundreds of thousands of cases, and to many people being unable to travel. The problem was solved, but only at great expense. A few weeks later in the same year, the Student Loans Agency was hit by similar problems with a new IT system, which resulted in major delays. The Criminal Records Bureau, having finally (after a delay of six months) gone live in March 2002 with a software system to handle checking of everyone working with children, quickly ran into problems that created a vast backlog of cases, and there were many false positive and false negative errors, so that many agencies were faced with impossible dilemmas about either employing unchecked personnel or closing services. Although the National Audit Office considered that, by 2003, its performance had improved, the cost of turnaround ran into hundreds of millions, and the agency was expected to be in deficit until 2006. In 2003, Inland Revenue's system failed, and the result was chaos in the payment of tax credits. Subsequently, EDS (formerly Electronic Data Systems) finally lost its contract with Inland Revenue to handle payments. In November 2004, a major crash in the Department of Work and Pensions computer system required emergency manual procedures to be activated to ensure that tens of thousands of people received benefit payments to which they were entitled. A system allowing people to make online claims for tax credits had to be shut down in December 2005 because the tax authorities realized that it had come to be regarded by organized criminals as comparatively easy to defraud using false identities.[19]
- *Chronic long-term failure.* The Child Support Agency represents one of the most serious long-term failures. Introduced in 1993 to replace a failing system by which women were expected to sue deserting fathers for maintenance money for their children, the agency has never successfully got on top of its delays, errors in payment amounts, errors in calculating entitlements, and inability to trace some men and to collect money from them. Its backlogs are now legendary. As a result, the government has been unable to introduce the tough new penalties for defaulting men that it would like to. The

agency is in continuous dispute with its suppliers. Successive chief executives have resigned. Ministers have admitted that the service is unacceptable. The problems with the computer system have been the subject of a stream of inquiry reports. Huge delays remain in transferring cases to the new system, and some journalists report these to be growing. Staff cuts have made some problems still worse, although the government claims that two recent software upgrades have made a positive contribution. The agency is now to be abolished.

It is a matter for debate just how much worse the English record is than that of other comparable countries. Canada has had problems with its gun licensing agency, and Florida's child welfare system, commissioned in 1994, was expected to go live in June 2005 some eight times over budget. Private sector projects too can fail, although it is easier for commercial companies to avoid publicity for their failures. In the United Kingdom, however, private sector projects seem more likely to be subject to delays, while public sector ones seem more often to come in over-budget.[20] Yet the concentration of cases in a state characterized by high dependence on the IT industry and weak in-house capability, the common factors in poor procurement and project management suggest a malaise peculiarly severe in England (Cross 2005; Dunleavy et al. 2004).

Of course, some projects have been completed successfully. The successful ones have tended to be smaller in scale, be less subject to political interference, and have a simpler range of functionality. For example, the National Archive is a major program of digitization of public records and provides much of the infrastructure for the rest of government to comply with the recently enacted freedom of information legislation, and its program has been completed successfully. The Universities and Colleges Admissions Service (UCAS) manages a very large number of online applications for university places for first degrees; this compilation involves extensive electronic transfer of applications, qualifications data, awards, etc., annually, and it was until recently regarded as a very successful, if very tightly defined, system (Bellamy 2003). The latest software for online applications seems to be causing some problems.[21] London's congestion charge system was put in place on time and has operated so far without serious glitches. The Ordnance Survey is now one of the most sophisticated GIS providers in the world, and is both a commercial success and a major example of government infrastructure services with strong capabilities for handling e-government projects; indeed, ministers have sometimes asked its managers to provide guidance to counterparts in agencies struggling with IT problems.

Yet the British government continues to pursue extremely ambitious projects. The Connecting for Health program is one of the largest in the world. There has been a steady stream of critical comment about the lack of involvement of and by the staff who will use the system. Although it is too early yet to say whether it is likely to run into huge problems, recent reports suggest that key elements such as the hospital choice and appointment booking system Choose and Book are already expected to be a full year overdue.[22] The comprehensive databases on children have, at the time of writing, yet to be fully scoped, but will also present major challenges. The most ambitious project so far is the planned national population register and biometric identity card scheme, which could also present the additional problem that it could be an obvious target for terrorist attack (Perri 6 2003).

Sharing, or Not

A central element in the Labour government's program, especially in its first term, was the ambition to achieve 'joined-up government' (Perri 6 et al. 2002; Sullivan and Skelcher 2002), meaning greater collaboration, coordination, and integration horizontally among agencies, departments, functions, and services. It became clear by the late 1990s that deepening such collaboration would in many cases require the sharing of personal information from client records between agencies, and that this might well raise issues of privacy and confidentiality, where citizens believed that they had provided information to a single body on the basis that it would not be disclosed to others. The Performance and Innovation Unit, later to become the Prime Minister's Strategy Unit, published a major report in 2002 (Performance and Innovation Unit 2002) on the relationship between privacy and information sharing, which recommended specific legal authorization for a number of particular types of information to be shared, as well as a new general power. On further consideration, the Department for Constitutional Affairs (DCA), which was charged with oversight of subsequent policy process in this area, decided against new primary legislation, taking the view that existing legal powers, when correctly interpreted, sufficed for most of these purposes, and issued guidance to that effect (Department for Constitutional Affairs 2003).

The movement toward greater sharing, and especially electronic sharing, of client information has been driven in England more by the risk management imperative than by aspirations for service enhancement. Although there have been experiments in, for example, a single online change of address facility that is intended to update a person's records with all the public services with which he or she has contact, these initiatives have been much less important than those to address problems of coordination in law enforcement, child protection, mental health, and care for older people.

In a number of fields, however, major e-government initiatives continue to feel the need to worry away at the issue (Perri 6, Bellamy, and Raab 2005; Bellamy, 6, and Raab 2005). After two Cambridgeshire schoolchildren were murdered by a man who had obtained a job as a school janitor and who, it subsequently transpired, had previously been investigated by the Humberside police force for sexual assaults upon young girls but never prosecuted, a major inquiry was undertaken to understand the reason for the failure to share information among police forces (Bichard 2004). The Humberside force claimed that their decision to delete their records reflected their understanding of their duties under the data protection (privacy) legislation – an interpretation of the law not upheld by the information commissioner (the regulator under the act) or by any reputable privacy lawyer, and indeed, not one consonant with the Association of Chief Police Officers' own code. The national scandal that followed resulted in greater pressure on the police to retain and share 'soft' information, and in a revised code of information management. The former permanent secretary Sir Michael Bichard, who carried out the inquiry, has said publicly, however, that he remains to be convinced that his recommendations have been implemented to the point that one could be confident that no such tragedy could occur again for that reason.

More generally and quite apart from considerations of confidentiality, blockages to the sharing of information arise from inter-professional and inter-organizational problems. Another national scandal that resulted in major shifts in policy was the death from neglect and abuse of a child, Victoria Climbié, which led to a major national inquiry that found, as every such child death inquiry has found for fifty years, that failures of agencies in touch with the household to share information effectively, and to make use of information that was shared, bore a significant part of the responsibility for the child's death (Laming 2003). None of the agencies cited confidentiality as a reason for its information practices. Following the inquiry, however, even the government's flagship e-government initiatives in joint child-protection information systems, called Information Sharing and Assessment projects, have sometimes been held up by local authorities seeking legal opinions on the legality of sharing clients' personal information required.

Research undertaken from 2003 to 2005 in health and social care as well as in crime and disorder agencies at the local level has found that many front-line professionals continue both to doubt that they and their colleagues are following prescribed procedures under information sharing protocols and confidentiality codes and to avoid sharing if they consider that, in their personal professional judgment, confidentiality is at stake (Perri 6 et al. 2005a, 2005b). Detailed protocols often lie unread, but are in any case necessarily incomplete and leave many decisions to be made on the basis of professional judgment.

Any hopes that government could resolve these tensions with a combination of additional regulation of professional practice and new software systems that might discipline professionals to share information in prescribed ways or provide for sharing by default now seem greatly overblown. Yet for at least some policy makers, these hopes seem to have been rather important in shaping the character of e-government initiatives in recent years in England.

Conclusion

Although HM Treasury does not break down public expenditure statistics in ways that would enable one to construct figures for the amounts spent on IT – and indeed it would now be difficult to disentangle in any non-arbitrary way what is e-government and what is simply government activity that is, more or less inevitably, carried out using some kind of IT – it is clear that the British government is spending very large sums indeed in England on e-government programs of many kinds. Kable, the British consultancy firm specializing in public sector IT, estimates that by 2007 the public sector IT market will be worth between £14 billion (Kable, cited in Transformational Government Strategy Project Team 2005) and £16 billion (Kable, cited in Simpson 2004)[23] – figures actually smaller than the savings expected by the government from implementing the Gershon program. The political parties are also spending significant sums to invest in IT infrastructure, within the limits of the election expenses laws and their rather parlous finances.

By international standards, the UK is not regarded as among the worst performers in e-government. In the Accenture's 2004 rankings, its 'overall maturity score' was tenth in the league table of countries, significantly behind Canada and the United States (Accenture 2004); by 2005, it was still ranked joint tenth but achieved a lower absolute score (Accenture 2005b, 11). Accenture's 2005 report noted the 'tepid' enthusiasm of the British public for the public services made available online, but the general tenor of their report was that one should wait to see whether the ambitious programs for Connecting for Health, the biometric identity card, and other initiatives could be brought off successfully, and to see whether the 'Transformational government' strategy to be unveiled in the autumn of 2005 (see below) would provide the clarity and coherence that Accenture believes still to be required. Democratic development is not the most important criterion in Accenture's method, whereas for a majority of the academic commentators who have written about the English case, it is probably the most important reason for their criticism. By contrast, journalistic and business comments on the country's e-government performance, as well as some academic analysis, have focused on the series of project fiascos.

The priority for back-office processing and data collection and the less participative and outward-looking styles of design do not only reflect the limited incentives upon politicians in such a highly centralized polity with a markedly more autonomous central state than is found in Canada or the United States, although these structural factors are important. More urgently, the e-government program is squeezed between imperatives for risk management and cost control that redirect service enhancement toward designs that require less labour-intensive human responses to citizen communications and that focus and reduce the number of channels and the number of communications from citizens that are not standardized and amenable to automated responses.

The prospects for e-government and e-politics in England are mixed. At least after 2008, if not before, at least the rate of growth in public spending will probably have to be curbed, limiting scope for innovation in e-government. The national biometric identity card and underpinning national population register are likely to cost much more than the official estimates, and may well soak up many of the resources available for major projects, apart from the Connecting for Health program. In the aftermath of the London Underground and bus bombings of July 2005, the risk management agenda is likely to be entrenched as an overriding priority for data systems and for data integration programs. In that context, it seems reasonable to expect redoubled efforts from the core executive to avoid repetitions of the worst problems of project failure with which the country's e-government program has been dogged in recent years.

Probably the major priorities will be greater focus on fewer and better targeted online services as hinted at by Ian Watmore, the former central government CIO, in his October 2004 interview. In November 2005, the e-Government unit published, for consultation, a new government-wide strategy document for e-government, called *Transformational government* (Transformation Government Strategy Project Team). Its promises include

- 'customer group directors' for each priority target group in the population
- a public-sector-wide Service Transformation Board with operational responsibilities (suggesting greater central oversight of local government programs)
- rationalization and pooling of central and local government call centres, payment facilities, back-office functions, and infrastructure (perhaps centralizing them)
- reduction of the number of government websites from the present 2500
- more mobile-accessible services
- more online subject access to personal records
- encouragement for citizens to use cheaper channels and a phasing out of more expensive ones
- reduction of facilities for paper form filling and filing
- a common identity management system based on the ID card and its underlying database
- from the centre, additional IT project financial oversight, new systems of portfolio and program management, new support for the IT profession in government, and greater oversight of suppliers' performance

Some of these aims are ambitions that have been set out in several previous policy statements going back to the 1996 *government.direct* green paper, through the 2001 *Modernising Government* white paper, and the 2002 Performance and Innovation Unit report, *Privacy and Data Sharing*. For example, the aspiration of organizing services around 'customer groups' is a variant of longstanding aspirations, now disappointed several times, of developing clusters around 'life events' and 'clienteles'; improved identity management has been promised in programmatic statements for many years. Officials insist that, unlike previous initiatives, this one has much greater commitment from the permanent secretaries (chief executives of the departments of state), that it is fully aligned with the public expenditure commitments and the Gershon savings, that the identity card program is already under way and will provide critical infrastructure, and, finally, that the government now has better systems of procurement and project management. If all the objectives of this ambitious strategy were met, then perhaps England might outperform Canada in e-government in some years' time. But it seems more prudent to pay attention to the track record of under-achievement in implementation before drawing such inferences. It will hardly be possible to assess how well founded such optimism may be before, at the earliest, 2011 or 2012, when the identity management system might – if plans are implemented smoothly – be in place and another full public spending cycle should be complete.

In the area of e-politics, even if the present gentle rate of growth in Internet, digital TV, and mobile usage for political purposes peaks – as the argument of this chapter has suggested it probably would, at a level below what can be expected of wealthier and more decentralized, federal countries such as Canada and the United States – then the net in all its different channels can nevertheless be expected to play a significant part in the orientation of political communication.

The English experience certainly offers lessons for other countries, but hardly a model. The thing that one might have thought would have been an advantage – a relatively powerful central government structure – has in many ways been the source of problems in the e-government program, for it has led both to excessive ambition in project size and to poor project oversight, and may well be connected with the weakly developed democratic aspects of the country's e-government capability. Moreover, the tension between risk management and cost control that runs through much of the program may reflect particular exacerbations of these problems in a country dominated by a political climate in which managing risks has become increasingly central across the public services, but where there is limited room for fiscal manoeuvre, yet limited experience of being able to use e-government to realize either of these basic goals. Hence the advice to readers outside the United Kingdom are given in the title of this chapter – 'Don't try this at home.'

Notes

1 This chapter is concerned with England, not with the United Kingdom: since the 1998 devolution, Scotland and Wales show markedly different trends, and Northern Ireland is a special case anyway. Confusingly for outsiders and very irritatingly for Scots and Welsh people, the Westminster government is still referred to as the 'British government,' even in relation to its functions in England. Constitutionally, there is still no such thing as the 'English government': even Westminster and Whitehall's operations purely within England cannot be referred to in this way. This convention is followed here because it would be tedious, if correct, always to write 'British government policy *in England*.'

2 This is the successor to http://www.ukon-line.gov.uk and, prior to that, http://www.open.gov.uk, and intended to be easier both for public service users and citizens to use, and less oriented to professionals and public servants.

3 http://www.ofcomconsumerpanel.org.uk/publications/english_key_findings.pdf

4 The source for the following tables is http://www.mori.com/polls/2005/post-election.shtml.

5 http://news.bbc.co.uk/1/hi/uk_politics/4654243.stm

6 However, the difference is within the margin of error for the survey sample.

7 http://news.bbc.co.uk/1/hi/uk_politics/4395195.stm.

8 http://news.bbc.co.uk/1/hi/uk_politics/vote_2005/scotland/4426815.stm.

9 Labour England, Labour Scotland, Labour Wales, Conservative England, Conservative Scotland, Conservative Wales, Liberal Democrat England, Liberal Democrat Scotland, Liberal Democrat Wales, Green England and Wales, Green Scotland, Scottish Nationalist Party, Plaid Cymru, UK Independence Party, Unity Coalition, British National Party, Scottish Socialist Party, Pro-Life Party, Pensioners Party, Islamic Party, Veritas, and Official Monster Raving Loony Party.

10 The observations were conducted, and data were recorded and analysed in detail by Heather Wilson, then of the University of Toronto. I am grateful to Heather for her extensive and careful work on this research project.

11 http://www.usabilitynews.com/news/article2394.asp.

12 http://news.bbc.co.uk/2/hi/uk_news/politics/4254271.stm.

13 http://www.wales.gov.uk/assemblydata/N0000000000000000000000000000030350.html.

14 http://www.theregister.co.uk/2002/08/16/mps_shun_email/.

15 See also http://news.bbc.co.uk/1/hi/technology/4596533.stm.

16 http://www.cabinetoffice.gov.uk/newsroom/news_releases/2004/
    041213_on-line.asp?ID=53

17 The official definition, buried in a Cabinet Office Technical Note on the per-
    formance management targets for the Office of the e-Envoy, is as follows:
    '"Capability" in this context is the capability to deliver e-enabled services
    (this is not limited to on-line delivery, but may include e-enabled call
    centres, digital TV and kiosks).' The inclusion of call centre access presum-
    ably allows scope for some telephone-based services to be counted as part
    of the achievement of the target, at least if the call centre service has a
    website attached with some e-mail contact facility: see http://www.
    cabinetoffice.gov.uk/reports/service-delivery/sda4.asp#target3

18 http://news.bbc.co.uk/1/hi/technology/3739684.stm

19 http://news.bbc.co.uk/1/hi/business/4493008.stm

20 For a short review of studies on private sector IT project failures, see Huber
    2003.

21 http://news.bbc.co.uk/1/hi/education/4343324.stm

22 http://news.bbc.co.uk/1/hi/health/4396256.stm

23 The £16 billion figures comes from Kable, Central government market pro-
    file, cited in Simpson 2004. The lower figure of £14 billion in 2004 also
    comes from Kable, and is cited in the *Transformational government* workfile
    (Transformational Government Strategy Project Team 2005, 15, para 34),
    where it is calculated as representing 1.2 per cent of GDP and rising in real
    terms over the last decade. That workfile also cites Kable as the authority
    for the estimate that about 25 per cent of expenditure is devoted to new
    projects, and the remainder to servicing legacy systems.

13 Is IT Transforming Government? Evidence and Lessons from Canada

SANDFORD BORINS

Is IT transforming government? To those who study the impact of IT, the question is inescapable. It shapes the discourse, whether as implicit premise, utopian promise, dystopian threat, or disputed paradigm. It is the question that has motivated this study and the longitudinal research design that structures it. We believe that this book has demonstrated how complex the question continues to be. The answer clearly depends on what is meant by *IT*, an ever-expanding set of practices as well as tools, both increasingly diverse and increasingly pervasive. It depends still more on what is meant by *transformation*.

Narratives of technological innovation have always used transformation as a major theme (West 2005). From gaslight, to telegraphy, to automobiles, each new advance has been celebrated, and deplored, as an agent of irrevocable change. In the case of IT in government, there are a variety of definitions, and no clear consensus, about what is meant by *transformation*. Based on his study of the content of public sector websites, West conceives of transformation as a 'gradual secular change that unfolds slowly but surely over time' (7) and believes that transformational change will have occurred when government websites, in addition to providing information, transactions, and integrated online services, display a capacity for interactive democracy through public feedback and discussion. Similarly, Barney (2005) evaluates government IT on the basis of whether it facilitates decision making that is more responsive, inclusive, and participatory. In contrast, Fountain (2001; with Osorio-Urzua 2001) looks inside government for transformation, as evidenced by substantial cost-savings and significant change in organizational structure.

If we draw an analogy from the individual, it is clear that sudden, total conversions are rare. Change comes more usually in waves, affecting different aspects of experience at different times, overlapping and coexisting through longer or shorter periods of transition, manifesting itself as much in alterations of perspective as of action. Often it is only in retrospect that the extent or nature of change can be grasped, while its implications remain to be lived out. Change generated by information technology within the public sector, we believe, should not be expected to be any less varied, asymmetrical, or asynchronous in its effects, or any less elusive in its consequences. However, that does not mean we should not be looking for – or at – it now.

Technology generates its own genealogy, across a span of three overlapping 'generations.' There is the 'pre' cohort, which never really either adopts or adapts. There is the 'post' generation, which, having grown up with the technology, has little memory of, or identification with, a time before. In addition, there is the 'hinge' group, whose experience extends from a period before a technology's widespread dissemination up to a more or less willing embrace. In our study of digital leaders (chapter 10) we profiled a number of members of the 'hinge' cohort, believing them to be representative not just of the human factor in Canadian public sector IT, but also of the transitional moment at which the IT function in Canadian governance now stands. The penetration of IT into the public sector is clearly irreversible, yet it is by no means complete. Furthermore, there is an awareness, by practitioners and observers alike, of gains and losses, benefits and disadvantages, that may well lose its force as IT becomes increasingly inseparable from government's daily workings. This sense of being at, or very near, a threshold makes it all the more imperative not only to attempt to answer the question with which we began, but to weigh the implications of that answer. There may never be a more critical time to ask.

We start this concluding chapter by reviewing developments in the use of IT in both the federal and Ontario governments between 2000 and 2005, identifying key trends and themes as they have emerged in the course of the book. However it is accomplished, the core work of politics remains getting elected and setting policy, and the core work of bureaucracy remains implementing policy and delivering service. Our focus is on the work experience of politicians and public servants.[1]

We then look from a broader perspective at the nature of the changes that can be deduced from these developments to consider whether they are, or may be, beneficial. There is a tendency within the literature to assume that greater use of IT is always and self-evidently 'a good thing,' offset by a correspondingly categorical school of dissent. We avoid both extremes, positioning ourselves as techno-realists, recognizing the inevitability of mixed results and consequences yet to unfold. This leads us to look ahead to speculate about IT-based developments that might ensue in the next five years. Finally, we propose lessons – essentially for practitioners – from the Canadian experience we have documented.

Progress in the Last Five Years

This section summarizes progress made from 2000 to 2005 in implementing IT in three aspects of Canadian government: the electronic workplace, the electronic citizen, and the electronic client. Each corresponds to an aspect of the model of IT-enabled government presented in chapter 2: the electronic workplace to internal government organization, the electronic citizen to the political and policy development interface, and the electronic client to the service delivery interface. The summary is based on the evidence regarding the federal and Ontario governments presented in earlier chapters, with occasional references to other governments in or outside Canada.

The Electronic Workplace

By 1999, networked personal computers, the Internet, and e-mail had become close to ubiquitous among public servants in the federal and Ontario governments. By 2005, they *were* ubiquitous. At the political level, after a slow start, there have been substantial increases in the use of IT, and by 2005, 90 per cent of the federal MPs and Ontario MPPs we surveyed said they used the Internet or e-mail at least daily. In addition, a majority of the legislators surveyed described themselves as either very competent or at least confident in their use of computers. At the senior levels of the bureaucracy and in the political world, the BlackBerry had become the device of choice for ubiquitous and continuous e-mail and Internet contact, and it is commonly seen on the floor of both the House of Commons and the Ontario Legislature (as well as the U.S. Congress and U.K. Parliament). Considering the legislature as a workplace, by 2003, the federal House of Commons had been wired for laptop connectivity, but the Ontario Legislature had not been wired by 2005.

The government's IT organization plays a key role in building and maintaining technological infrastructure. Both governments saw changes in where their IT organization was positioned in the larger structure of government. The federal government's CIO and CIO Branch have remained within the Treasury Board Secretariat for the entire period, working under a decentralized, leadership-based model in which the CIO has had limited formal authority but considerable influence through access to ministerial decision making and control of an investment budget. When Prime Minister Martin took office in December 2003, however, the Government On-Line initiative was moved out of the CIO Branch to Public Works and Government Services Canada (PWGSC). Ontario's corporate CIO and his organization were located in the Management Board Secretariat until June 2005, when they were moved to the Ministry of Government Services. The corporate CIO continues to advise cabinet on IT policy and major projects.

In 2005, both governments undertook major IT-supported initiatives in integrated front-line service delivery and integrated support services. In its February 2005 budget, the federal government established Service Canada as an agency responsible for providing services to individual Canadians on behalf of a range of departments.[2] With the sunset of Government On-Line in spring 2006, the component dealing with individuals (the Canadians Gateway) has moved from PWGSC to Service Canada. The February 2005 budget also saw PWGSC given greater power to establish shared support services for departments as well as serve as a government-wide procurement agent.

Ontario had begun work on providing shared support services in the late 1990s, and during the last five years has been deepening its efforts in that area. Both the Ministry of Consumer and Business Services and the IT organization were working on integrated front-line service initiatives. In June 2005, the McGuinty government established the new Ministry of Government Services to include front-line service delivery (the former Ministry of Consumer and Business Services), shared support services and procurement, and the IT and human resource management organizations. As such, it creates the most ambitious integrated service delivery and shared support organization in Canadian government today. It also links the IT organization more closely to its principal clients.

One key way in which IT organizations support these integration initiatives is through major projects. During 2000–5, the federal government has been reasonably successful with its large projects and has avoided publicly embarrassing cost overruns or performance short-falls, with the notable exception of the firearms registry (Canada, Office of the Auditor General 2006). In contrast, Ontario has seen one high-profile project terminated without having delivered promised results (the Integrated Justice Project), another major project sharply criticized by the provincial auditor (Ministry of Community and Social Services Business Transformation Project), and a third quietly termi-nated (the Bell Canada transactional services project). These projects have given public sector IT in Ontario a partisan edge as the Liberals, while in opposition, attacked the projects initiated by the Conserva-tives and now, as the government, reduced the extent of collaboration with the private sector and established an external task force to review the management of major projects.

Another way the IT organization can support integration is through knowledge management initiatives. By 2005, both the federal and Ontario governments had established communities of practice in knowledge management. There have also been a number of initiatives undertaken on a ministry or agency basis with the encouragement, but not leadership, of central agencies. Examples at the federal level include projects in the Department of Defence, RCMP, and Industry Canada.

Electronic Citizens

The use of IT in the political arenas of campaigning and policy consul-tation has both supply and demand aspects, in that political parties create capacity on the electronic channel for campaigning, and govern-ments create capacity for consultation, but it is up to citizens to decide how much and in which ways to use the electronic channel rather than the traditional channels.

On the supply side, by 2005, most of the federal and provincial par-ties had built sophisticated websites that included a press room for communication with the media, the party platform, facilities for dona-tions and volunteering, and downloadable ads originally presented on radio and television. The press room components of the sites, as well as BlackBerry-enabled e-mail, were commonly used for timely communi-cation with the media. The 2004 election was the first time that attacks on other parties, as well as media attack ads, found a prominent place on party websites. Most individual candidates, with the exception of those of the Bloc Québécois, had personal websites that used templates and content provided by the party. The federal campaign of 2004 and provincial campaigns of 2003–4 were the first time that parties displayed the URLs of their websites prominently in their advertising and in other media.

On the demand side, the sites of the major federal parties as well as the Greens were registering 10,000 to 20,000 unique visits per day during the 2004 campaign. Three per cent of all voters, but a higher percentage of younger voters, said that the Internet was their main source of information about the campaign. Approximately 20 per cent of the electorate visited party sites, and journalists for other media were frequent visitors. While all parties and many candidates had a facility for online fundraising, only the Greens appear to have raised a substantial percentage of their donations online. By the 2004 federal election, there was substantial online political activity originating outside of the parties, including news sites, attack sites, commentary by interest groups, blogs, and a variety of sites encouraging younger Canadians to register and vote.

The second context for electronic citizenship is consultation. The federal and Ontario governments demonstrated different patterns of consultation, both traditional and e-enabled. At the federal level, consultations were undertaken at the departmental level, with those directed at technologically sophisticated communities putting greater emphasis on the electronic channel. The Privy Council Office oversaw the development of a consultation portal, and departments are now required to post all their consultations on it. While the main focus for consultations has been government departments, there have been some originating at the political level; for example, the House of Commons website supports online petitions, and in 2003, the House of Commons Sub-Committee on the Status of Persons with Disabilities, then chaired by the technologically avant-garde Carolyn Bennett, undertook an online consultation about the pension plan disability program.

The Ontario government went from an aversion to consultation when Mike Harris was premier at the beginning of the millennium, to experiments with consultation under his successor Ernie Eves, to an enthusiastic embrace of consultation under Dalton McGuinty. The Liberals undertook numerous consultation exercises both centrally (for example, the 2004 budget) and departmentally in their first year, and established a high-profile consultation portal. After a year in office, they shifted their focus from consultation to implementation, and as a consequence there have been far fewer consultations, and the portal has become a low-profile archive for the completed consultations. The Legislature has not had any unique role in e-consultation, which has been conducted entirely through the government's websites.

Electronic Clients

Here, too, we can approach the analysis in terms of the supply of content on the electronic channel by the government and the demand by clients to use the electronic channel, as opposed to traditional channels. Both the federal and Ontario governments created their Web portals early in this period. The Canada Site was relaunched in 2001 and its format stayed constant through the Chrétien and Martin governments. Its emphasis was on electronic services, and it was structured around three gateways (Canadians, business, non-Canadians) and thirty-one sub-portals, referred to as Clusters. Interdepartmental Cluster teams have continuously worked at enhancing content.

The Ontario portal has undergone several iterations, the most recent in the fall of 2005. In all of them, the portal has incorporated considerable political content, including a high-profile premier's page and buttons linking to pages on key government priorities as well as a prominent display of government news stories. Services are presented in three ways on the home page: target groups, life events, and popular topics.

Two months after taking office, the Harper government undertook a major restructuring of the Canada Site, boosting its political content by enhancing the prime minister's page, displaying government news stories and its key priorities more prominently, increasing the use of the Conservatives' traditional blue, and relegating the three service gateways to the left sidebar. In essence, the Canada Site now closely resembles the Ontario portal.

The demand side can be broken down into informational and transactional services. By 2005, 90 per cent of the information disseminated for forty-three targeted federal government informational services was being provided over the electronic channel. As more people are accessing the Internet for government information, the government is making more information available online. Also by 2005, for eighty-nine targeted federal government transactional services, approximately 30 per cent of the transactions were being completed online. Other channels, in particular postal service and in-person, continue to account for substantial but slowly declining shares of completed transactions. The federal government has completed development of its Secure Channel, but it remains to be seen what public take-up of online service will be, as well as how many different transactions the government will be willing to authenticate by means of the Secure Channel.

In addition to integrated service over Web portals and the integrated service delivery organizations that the federal and Ontario governments are building, there are a variety of initiatives at other levels of government and across multiple levels. While not nearly as many large Canadian municipalities have put in place integrated telephone service (311) as have large U.S. municipalities, there have been a number of early adopters, both large and small, including Halifax, Calgary, Gatineau, QC, and Tillsonburg and Halton, ON. By 2005, a number of pilot projects provided client groups with electronic services that were integrated across jurisdictions. At the federal-provincial level, these have included the Canada Business Service Centres and Seniors Canada On-Line. Notable initiatives spanning the federal, provincial, and municipal governments are Brockville (Ontario) Seniors Information, and Victoria Connects.

To summarize the evidence from the federal and Ontario governments, it is clear that there has been substantial progress in the last five years in implementing IT within government.[3] Politicians and public servants are choosing an electronic workplace, and IT organizations are building the infrastructure to support it. While voters are not yet choosing the Internet as the main source of political information or locus of political participation, parties increasingly recognize their websites as an integral channel for campaigning. The electronic channel is also playing a greater role in bureaucratically hosted consultation. In client service, the electronic channel has taken over information dissemination almost entirely and is playing an increasing role in transactions. Not only is there a growing number of integrated service delivery initiatives, but the structure of government is starting to reflect the new emphasis on IT-enabled integration. Taking all these developments into account, can we say that IT has transformed government?

The Question of Transformation

The methodological approach of this study has been anthropological, in the sense that we have tried to get inside the black box of public sector IT management through observation, interviews, and questionnaires conducted over several years. It is fundamentally different from studies that have focused on government websites as the output of a transformational process and defined transformation in terms of the capacities of those websites. For us, the evidence of transformation is to be sought in changes in patterns of interaction between government and society, changes in the public sector as a workplace, and changes in the organizational structure and cost of government. This places our perspective on transformation closer to Fountain than to West. We therefore discuss three areas where there is the potential for transformation: first, greater transparency of government, representing new patterns of interaction between government and society; second, workplace transformation in government, emerging from IT-enabled changes in both the pattern of work and structure of organizations; and third, a reduction in the cost of government.

Greater Transparency

The fact that the electronic channel has become by far the most popular for information made available by government for public access is of enormous significance. Traditionally, there has been a distinction between records held internally by government and material published by government for public use. Publication is expensive and time-consuming, and there is no certainty that published materials will be widely accessible. Putting government records on the Internet is inexpensive and quick and makes them universally accessible. The interviews with Ian Wilson and Reg Alcock demonstrate two different but reinforcing perspectives on this phenomenon. For Wilson, the Internet is extending the reach of Library and Archives Canada by making its holdings far more readily accessible than in the past. For Alcock, government is responding to the public's demand for information about both its outputs (performance indicators, grants, contributions) and inputs (contracts, travel and entertainment expenses of politicians and public servants) by posting this material online. For both, there is now a self-reinforcing cycle, in that the demand for government information online is stimulating supply, hence further increasing demand.

There is a cynical view that the best way for a government to bury embarrassing information is to publish it many levels down on a website, but the alternative view is that, with powerful search engines that can be applied to government websites, no piece of online information is too obscure to be uncovered. Similarly, Google, Yahoo, and Microsoft have all recently produced software tools that enable users to match publicly available databases with online maps to create their own geographic information system applications (O'Connell 2005). More generally, we can expect a continuing flow of software tools that people outside government can use to do their own analysis of databases created and made available by government. The Internet is the most efficient channel for dissemination of policy analysis done by civil society, as well as public policy commentary posted on individuals' blogs and organizational websites. Having it available makes it difficult for government to suppress information that civil society wants. A recent example: the Gomery Commission's restriction on Canadian media from disseminating testimony at some of its hearings was easily flouted by observers at the hearings providing accounts to the operator of a website based in Minnesota.

The Internet, and in particular blogging, has increased the transparency of political debate and comment during election campaigns. The most recent manifestation is that, as political parties attempt to move to the ideological centre, they search for embarrassing comments made by activists of opposing parties that then can be used to paint their opponents as extremists. The most notable example in the 2006 election campaign involved the Liberals and NDP seizing on a speech that Conservative Party leader Stephen Harper made in 1997 (when he was director of the National Citizens Coalition, not an MP) referring to Canada as 'a northern European welfare state in the worst sense of the term' and posted on the website of a conservative policy organization to argue that Harper is still to the far right of the political spectrum (Galloway 2005).

Yet another aspect of transparency is increased accessibility of politicians and public servants by e-mail. Politicians' e-mail addresses are posted on the legislative website, and it is clear from our survey in chapter 8 that they receive considerable amounts of e-mail from citizens regarding both service and policy. E-mail has the potential to make public servants more readily accessible than did the telephone directories of the past. In some countries, such as the United Kingdom, a decision has been made not to post contact details for most public servants on the Internet. In Canada, however, the practice has been to post such information. While an individual public servant may choose not to list his or her e-mail address, there are enough names and addresses listed that it is easy to infer the unlisted address. Very rarely do departments or individual public servants block outside e-mail. Many public servants, even at the most senior levels, access their own e-mail. Sitting for long hours in meetings, but connected to their e-mail via BlackBerrys, they may well see outside e-mails and have the time to answer them.[4]

In the introduction, we noted that one of the essential differences between public and private management is that actions of public managers are much more intensely scrutinized by oversight institutions and the media, giving rise to the term *management in a fishbowl*. The electronic channel has made the public management fishbowl even more transparent by enhancing civil society's capacity for oversight through policy commentary and analysis, and ready e-mail contact with politicians and public servants.

Workplace Revolution

It appears that, due to the influence of IT, there are major changes happening in the public sector workplace at both the micro level of the characteristics of individuals' jobs and the macro level of organizational structure. At the individual level, there has been considerable reduction in the ranks of clerical and data-entry workers, the former because office software makes it easy for professionals to do their own clerical work and the latter because users of services are doing their own data entry. The number of IT workers has grown considerably; for example, Ontario's IT organization encompasses 3500 workers, approximately 6 per cent of a public service of 60,000. If a broader definition such as *knowledge-intensive workers* is used, the ranks of this community expand considerably.

Particularly at the senior levels, technology has increased immediacy. BlackBerrys, cell phones, and text messaging allow senior public servants, political staff, politicians, and ministers all to be in faster and more frequent contact with one another than before. As discussed in chapter 7, immediate communication is essential to responding to the media during political campaigns. It also facilitates crisis management. Information technology both encourages and facilitates collaboration, as discussed in chapters 2 and 4. The Government On-Line project gave rise to thirty-one sub-portals, each a collaborative virtual organization. The interdepartmental and inter-jurisdictional service-delivery partnerships discussed in chapter 4 require public servants to work cooperatively across organizational boundaries. There are now more partnerships with organizations outside government, such as non-profits delivering social services, or the corporate sector building IT infrastructure. To manage these partnerships successfully, public servants need to understand private and voluntary sector organizational cultures as well as be able to shape a consensus of partner institutions. While not a substitute for these soft skills, there are capabilities built into widely used office technologies that support collaboration. These include the easy distribution of e-mail and documents, the 'track changes' document format, automatic conference calling, and video-conferencing. More powerful software that facilitates collaboration is also becoming available (Fallows 2006).

Not only are public servants required to spend more of their time working across organizational boundaries, but technology is facilitating the reshaping of organizations. By the end of our research period, we have seen the birth of two integrated service delivery organizations – Service Canada and Service Ontario – as well as integrated support initiatives in Public Works and Government Services Canada and the Ontario Ministry of Government Services. The Ontario Ministry of Government Services is taking integration even farther, by incorporating service delivery, shared services, the IT organization, and human resource management.

While analysing the evolution of these organizations is the work of another research project, we can at least speculate about their future. Two key issues concern their relationship with existing line ministries and their accountability structure. The service-delivery and support functions of line ministries have traditionally been important as the locus of political patronage. It has always been of great concern to politicians where front-line offices or backroom support functions are located, or whether procurement processes favour suppliers in one region over another, or small Canadian businesses over large multinationals. Integrated service delivery and support organizations are likely to attempt to reduce patronage to lower cost and increase efficiency. We can thus expect line ministers and ministries to resist ceding these functions to integrated service delivery or support organizations.

In establishing the accountability structure for these organizations there are several choices: regular ministries, operating agencies, or even more arms-length structures, such as Crown corporations. Currently, Service Canada is part of Human Resources and Social Development Canada, and Service Ontario is part of the Ministry of Government Services. If Service Canada or Service Ontario becomes larger, there may be a rationale for giving them each its own minister. Making them more arms-length, for example, service agencies or Crown corporations, would facilitate introducing efficiency-driven regimes, such as user fees or other incentives to shift users to the Internet channel.

Greater Efficiency

One of the arguments for transformation, often made by IT consulting firms soliciting government business, is that the application of technology will produce large savings. We now have several data points from which to make educated guesses about the magnitude of those savings. To begin, it is helpful to separate government spending into two components: operating expenses (personnel, transportation and communications, supplies and equipment, land, buildings, machinery) and program expenses. In 2002–3, operating expenses made up 14 per cent of total spending by the Ontario government and 27 per cent of total spending by the federal government (Borins 2004). Averaging the two, we will assume that, in general, governments spend 20 per cent on overhead and 80 per cent on programs. With respect to operating expenses, it is argued that IT projects substitute machinery (capital) for labour, thereby driving down operating expenses. An example would be online tax filing, which eliminates the need for legions of government clerks doing data entry.

Program spending includes interest payments on public debt; entitlement-based transfers to individuals, such as pensions or income support; and overhead and service-delivery costs for institutions receiving government grants, for example, provincial support of the health care and educational systems.[5] Much of government program spending is on entitlements, and it is assumed that IT projects aid in determining more accurately who is entitled to program benefits, and preventing benefits from going to those who are not. It is also assumed that, on balance, increased accuracy would reduce total spending for a given program. This reduction was clearly one of the key objectives of the Ontario Ministry of Community and Family Services Business Transformation Project designed by the Harris government. Similarly, one of the potential benefits of IT-based integration of health records is to identify individuals who are using the health system to excess.

A third area in which the implementation of IT could affect government finances is taxation. By more extensive matching of databases, government could more effectively uncover tax evasion, with the result that the tax yield for a given tax rate increases.

Taking capital-labour substitution, more accurate targeting of entitlements, and reduced tax evasion together, how much could IT improve public finances? Improvements will come from the implementation of IT projects, many large in scale. If there are cost overruns or delays, the benefits of the projects will be reduced. The eighty-twenty split between the program and overhead costs of government means that projects involving capital-labour substitution affect only 20 per cent of government spending, so that to make major inroads, projects would have to reduce improper targeting of entitlements. It is an open question whether entitlements are currently so ineffectively targeted that there is room for substantial improvement.

There are now a number of estimates of cost-savings that would come about through IT projects. The Treasury Board Secretariat's 2003 estimates of service delivery costs by channel, mentioned in chapter 4, put the average of an in-person visit at $38.00, a letter at $19.00, and an Internet transaction at $0.84.[6] These estimates imply that shifting users from other channels to the Internet would provide enormous cost-savings in service delivery. Service delivery, however, is only a thin slice of the overhead component of the cost of government. That said, these estimates were based on both information dissemination as well as transactions. By far the largest proportion of information dissemination uses the Internet channel, while the other channels increasingly are being used mainly for transactions. A more appropriate comparison would involve transactions on all channels. It is likely that, in such a comparison, given the complexity of establishing secure authenticated services, the Internet would not have quite as compelling an advantage as in the Treasury Board Secretariat estimate.

A second way of approaching the question of savings is to look at government plans to achieve them. As part of its expenditure review in the 2005 budget, the federal government presented a package of net savings of $11 billion over the five years from 2005–6 to 2009–10 (Department of Finance Canada 2005a). The two areas where IT plays the largest role in achieving savings are Service Canada and procurement reform. Service Canada is expected to deliver ongoing (base budget) savings of approximately $800 million, based on an upfront investment of $500 million, and procurement reform ongoing (base budget) savings of $900 million, based on an upfront investment of $90 million. Taken together, expected annual base budget savings from Service Canada and procurement reform are $1.7 billion, or approximately 1 per cent of total federal government spending of $180 billion. Some of the other areas of savings in the package, such as program efficiencies (which are expected to deliver base budget savings of approximately $300 million) and administrative efficiencies (which are expected to deliver base budget savings of approximately $350 million), could possibly be traced to the application of IT. Even so, adding another $650 million in savings would still leave IT-based annual savings at $2.3 billion, less than 2 per cent of federal government spending. Peter Gershon's report to the U.K. government on efficiency savings, discussed in chapter 12, identifies base budget savings of £20 billion by 2008, approximately 2.5 per cent of total government spending.

It would appear from the Department of Finance and Gershon studies that IT-based reductions in total government spending are not huge. It could be argued that neither took into account increased tax yields and that neither looked closely at improved targeting of entitlements. It could also be argued that there is a learning curve, and after initial savings are made, government will increase its capacity to make savings or to handle increased volumes of work with current levels of resources. Nonetheless, it does not appear that the implementation of IT-based projects in the next five years will deliver savings of more than 5 per cent of the government's base budget. While the sums of money may be impressive, their visibility is more likely a function of the proportion of total government spending they represent. Political parties of the left, such as the Liberals or U.K. Labour Party would use these savings to fund new programs, while parties of the right, such as the Canadian or U.K. Conservatives would use them to fund tax cuts.[7]

To return to the question with which this section and chapter began: has IT transformed government? To find an answer, we must look at all aspects of a potential transformation together, rather than each separately. We believe that, taken together, there is evidence of a transformation. Reduction in spending is, however, a relatively minor component of such a transformation. More important components are the increase in the transparency of government; the restructuring of its workforce; the heightened immediacy and faster pace of political and bureaucratic work; the increased requirement for, and means of, collaboration; and the advent of organizational restructuring due to integrated service delivery and support organizations.

Reason for Optimism or Cause for Concern?

Are the transformations discussed above reason for optimism or cause for concern? This is a challenging question because IT has many components, because there are many groups that can be expected to gain or lose, because the time frame chosen for the analysis may affect the answer, and because the status quo alternative is not itself clear. All these considerations come into play in making an assessment. Despite this complexity, techno-optimists would likely answer that society will be better off because government is providing more information about itself, thus increasing democratic accountability; the quality of public services is improving because of the increased convenience of the e-channel; and greater efficiency is driving down the cost of government. Even so, each of these assumed improvements has distributional implications in that some people would be made worse off.

Consider cost reduction by means of more precisely targeting entitlements. It involves a transfer from those who use the welfare and health care systems more frequently to those who have no involvement with welfare and those who use the health care system less often. No matter how much IT helps target entitlements, there will still be incidents where entitlements were erroneously given or denied. Critics of IT-enabled entitlement reform, such as the Harris government's welfare reforms, contend that they have tilted the balance between the two types of errors to the side of erroneously denying entitlements.

Capital-labour substitution, another area of cost reduction, clearly has distributional implications in that the beneficiaries are consulting firms, often large multinationals, which build the new systems, and the highly skilled workers who operate them, while the losers are the relatively low-skilled and low-paid workers who are laid off.

Improving service by increasing the use of the e-channel benefits those who have access, particularly broadband. The poor seldom can afford to buy a computer and connect it to the Internet, some elderly people have difficulty mastering the technology, and remote areas may not have broadband. As was argued in chapter 4, government is encouraging users to migrate to the e-channel. If at some point government reduces the quality of service on alternative channels, or abandons them altogether, then the groups on the wrong side of the digital divide may experience deterioration in the quality of service they receive. A recent example: after making topographical maps available online, the federal government has seen demand for printed topographical maps drop from 330,000 per year in 2003 to fewer than 10,000 per year in 2005. It is now proposing to stop printing maps entirely, and leave it to individuals and the private sector to determine what to download and how to reproduce it (Walton 2005). The techno-optimists hope, however, that the significance of the digital divide will diminish over time as computing prices keep falling and broadband service expands.

Another concern about shifting to service delivery on the e-channel is that the institutional identity of government is increasingly its website, rather than bricks-and-mortar buildings flying the Canadian or provincial flag. The federal government has traditionally considered its facilities to be a way of asserting its identity in the face of regional challenges, and an approach to service delivery that emphasizes the electronic channel and call centres necessarily reduces the number and visibility of federal facilities. This change in emphasis puts government on a par with other large institutions, such as banks, telephone companies, and cable television companies, which increasingly are handling their customer transactions over the e-channel. The federal government has tried to mitigate this concern by branding its place in cyberspace with strong Canadian images and requiring all its websites to have a common look and feel.[8]

It is the utilization of information that often delivers the benefits of IT-enabled transformations. Politicians and public servants increasingly see the value of automatic data integration to improve service. Critics argue that this creates potential invasions of privacy. People may accept data integration if government can convince them that the information is being used only for a specific purpose proposed in advance. For example, most taxpayers annually check the box on their returns agreeing to release their addresses to Elections Canada to maintain the permanent voters list. There has, however, been much less public support for more broadly defined uses proposed by government, such as the creation of a national identity card or the creation of a longitudinal database for social scientific research. Thus, there is a tension between the desire of government to move forward on data integration and public concern that it would enhance the possibility of tracking and surveillance of individuals, if not immediately, then in the future and under different circumstances (Perri 6, Bellamy, and Raab 2005).

A second privacy issue concerns data posted on government websites. While many people's general reaction is that more information equals more transparency, they may question this in specific areas – or as it concerns information about themselves. For example, while court proceedings are a matter of public record, should all documents associated with court cases be made available online? In the past, documents were available at courthouses where the cases were filed – a much more restricted form of access. An advisory committee to the Canadian Judicial Council recently recommended a more restrictive policy, making available judgments and docket information in certain areas, such as family law, with personal identifiers removed. Online access would be restricted to individuals and lawyers involved with the case, and journalists would be required to file special requests for access (Blackwell 2005).

This section does not have an unassailable conclusion. We think that the transformation brought about in the public sector by the use of IT provides net benefits for society, but we can understand how others, particularly those who bear the costs, may reach a different conclusion. We recognize that scholars like Barney (2005) who desire more responsive, inclusive, and participatory government conclude that the use of IT has not yet led to a realization of their ideal state. Furthermore, we also understand how some issues, such as the trade-off between the benefits of integrated databases and the fear of invasion of privacy, are complicated and uncertain, and will necessitate careful observation as they evolve (Bennett and Raab 2003).

The Next Five Years

Regardless of one's evaluation of the merits of IT-based transformation of government to this point, it is useful to speculate about what is likely to be on the horizon. Given the pace of change, these speculations are limited to a short span of five years. They concern the areas of impact discussed throughout this book: politics and campaigning, and information, transactions, and organization in government.

Our research has shown that politicians have become increasingly proficient in their use of technology. We expect this trend will continue as an ever-increasing majority of legislators are members of the 'post' generation. How will this affect politics? It is normally assumed that IT, by democratizing the flow of information, tends to undercut hierarchy and central control. In Canada, however, political parties have traditionally exerted tight control over their backbenchers, and this still seems to be the case in the Internet age. For example, legislators are not permitted to link their biographies on legislative websites to personal sites, and political parties, by developing website templates and providing them to their candidates and legislators, are ensuring that they all adhere to the party line in cyberspace. The minority governments headed by Paul Martin and Stephen Harper have been characterized by cohesive party discipline, as opposed to the freewheeling American legislative model. Legislators could use their websites to launch consultations, but most appear content to leave e-consultation to the bureaucracy. We expect that legislators will continue to become technologically more sophisticated, but most will not use technology to break the bonds of party discipline. (The exceptions will be technologically advanced and independent-minded backbenchers like Conservative Garth Turner who have little ambition to become ministers.) Another way in which we are likely to see increased party discipline is that during election campaigns, parties wanting to move to the political centre will exert pressure on both their candidates and activists to ensure that all materials posted in their blogs are 'on message.' Paradoxically, this focus would reverse blogging's original objective of facilitating individual expression.

In the United States, political campaigns are long and expensive, electoral finance laws prohibit large contributions, the audience for network television is diminishing in total and fracturing internally, and a significant proportion of the population is not registered to vote. These conditions have made the Internet an essential campaign channel for fund-raising, voter registration, candidate blogging, and increasingly for online advertising (Nagourney 2006). Only one of these conditions holds true in Canada, which has short election campaigns, a continuing large market for network television, substantial public funding for political parties, limits on total spending by parties during campaigns, and a reasonably effective government-operated voter registration system. The Harper government's proposals to ban contributions by corporations, unions, or organizations and limit to $1000 annually individual donations to parties, their local entities, or leadership candidates, if enacted, would put pressure on parties to focus on smaller donations. If parties do focus on smaller donations, they might begin to emulate American practice in open-source politics, using participation through meetups or blogs as a prelude to financial donations. Whether or not this happens warrants close attention.

One political context in which the Web could play a significant role is a possible Quebec referendum. The last referendum occurred just before widespread Internet use, so we cannot simply extrapolate. As soon as the Parti Québécois is elected, the de facto referendum campaign will begin, and citizens' groups and bloggers in Quebec and elsewhere on both sides and in both official languages, as well as a variety of ethnic languages, will quickly begin to mobilize online. Legislation on spending limits by the official yes and no campaigns will be unable to cover Web-based activities by groups and individuals, especially if hosted outside Quebec. The fact that the referendum is winner-take-all and each vote counts equally is an incentive to widespread mobilization. Rumours, ad hominem attacks, and speculation will be rife during a referendum campaign, and these are the stock-in-trade of the political Internet. We therefore look to a possible Quebec referendum for the most active and creative political use of the Internet.

In government, a few trends are likely. The Internet is now dominant for the dissemination of information by government, but, as shown in chapters 2 and 6 as well as in the interview with Ian Wilson, information or knowledge management is less advanced than other aspects of e-government. This situation is likely to stimulate initiatives in information management that are oriented towards the public and are internal to the government. The former would include improving the structuring of online information for users outside the government and determining the extent of commercialization of the government's information holdings, as opposed to free provision. The latter would include enhancing government's organizational memory and extending the sharing of information within government.

The next area to consider is the use of the electronic channel for transactions with government. While the infrastructure is in place, the question is whether users will shift from other channels. Our expectation is that the shift to the electronic channel will be more pronounced on the part of business for two reasons. First, businesses are more frequent users of public services than are individuals, for example, a commercial tax-preparer compared to an individual who completes an income tax return once a year. A second reason is that government, especially if service delivery agencies operate on a cost-recovery basis, can charge businesses user fees that represent differential channel costs – an approach that might be politically difficult for services to individuals. Therefore, the take-up by individuals of electronic transactions with the government remains uncertain.

Government at the municipal level will also face questions of service integration. Municipal governments, which are generally the most resource-constrained in Canada, will have to choose between investing in website development and instituting 311 integrated call centres. This will move them towards relying on the provinces to provide support for Web development or to integrate their websites with those of their parent provinces.

The federal and Ontario governments' new integrated service delivery and support organizations, as discussed earlier in this chapter, will deserve close attention. Will they be effective? How far will their reach extend? What will be their accountability structure? Will other provinces move forward with similar initiatives? The success of integrated service delivery also depends on the attitudes of individuals and businesses. Will they support the sharing of information that makes integrated service initiatives possible? We expect that, if government provides a clear justification for each instance of information sharing, public support for will be forthcoming.

Another aspect of e-government is organization. Will the radical merger of integrated service delivery, support, the IT organization, and human resources embodied in Ontario's Ministry of Government Services work? We expect that, by the end of the decade, it will either be an effective organization or it will be deconstructed, with its components located elsewhere. Will governments, particularly Ontario, become more effective at managing major IT-based projects? Our expectation is that this is an area where progress can be made. It has received high-level attention and there is now a well-developed and reasonably well-tested set of smart practices that can be applied. What of senior IT leadership – will it continue to be imported from the private sector, or will governments be able to groom their own for such positions? If senior IT leaders come primarily from the private sector and are paid far more than other senior public servants, they will continue to operate in a gilded ghetto. Our expectation, however, is that IT skills have become sufficiently widespread that the next generation of IT leaders within government will be developed internally.

A final area of speculation is new technologies or new applications. Some technologies, such as mobile communications and GIS, will see many more public sector applications. In the last five years, there have been many surprises, such as the interaction of technology (meetup, blogging) and demographics that made Howard Dean's campaign for president more effective than electoral observers had expected. The generation that has grown up with the Internet is at the leading edge in adopting new technologies, and it is difficult to predict how they may apply that to their interactions with politics and government. Given the unpredictability of new technologies, it is a certainty that there will be surprises in store in the next half-decade.

Lessons from Canada: Management Practices for Export

This section provides lessons based primarily on the Canadian experience analysed in this book. It is aimed at practitioners in Canada and elsewhere. In each section we indicate the source of the lessons. To some extent, the lessons are recommendations, but we recognize that resource constraints or the distribution of power within organizations may prevent all from being acted upon. We start with lessons at the political interface, then move to the consultation interface, the service interface, and finally the internal operations of government.

Campaigning Online

While a very small percentage of Canadian voters use the Internet as their primary source of election information, a larger percentage uses it as one source in combination with others, and journalists for other media give it considerable attention. On the basis of our observation of federal and provincial election campaigns from 2003 to 2006 (see chapter 7), we believe online campaigning must be comprehensive, responsive, and time-sensitive, giving rise to the following lessons:

- Use cross-media integration, for example, posting downloadable television and radio ads on the website, video-streaming campaign events on the website, and prominently displaying the URLs for party and candidate websites in other media, such as television ads, signs, literature, and speaker's podiums.
- If an essential element of a campaign is negative, such as attacks on other parties and their leaders, the negative messages should be displayed prominently on your own website, rather than just relegated to sponsored attack sites, which are less credible.
- The party's researchers should pay careful attention to all online discussion of the campaign (news, blogs, attack sites, etc.) to respond quickly to attacks on the party or rumours about its leader, and to find material damaging to the other parties that can be exploited. Conversely, parties, responding to the inevitable pressure of an election campaign to move to the ideological centre, should minimize

damage to their own cause by encouraging their candidates and activists to stay 'on message.'

- The party website should contain the platform in a modular version, so that voters can download the components of greatest interest. The campaign can easily measure the relative importance of different issues by the frequency with which each component of the platform is downloaded.
- The party's webmaster should be in direct contact with the senior strategist or campaign manager to implement changes immediately.
- If a party leader performs well in a leaders' debate, supportive external reviews should immediately be posted on the website.

Connecting the Legislature

Our survey in chapter 8 found legislators increasingly comfortable with technology, leading to these lessons:

- Connectivity should be provided on the floor of the Legislature, as the House of Commons has now done.
- All the debates of the legislature as well as its committee meetings should be webcast.
- Legislatures should facilitate online petitions.
- Legislators' personal websites should be linked to their official résumés on the Legislature's website.
- Legislators should enhance their personal websites' capacity for policy consultation, blogging, and assistance to constituents for the delivery of public services.

Consulting Electronically

On the basis of chapter 9, which discusses recent federal government and Ontario experience with consultation, we propose the following lessons:

- The central agency (Privy Council Office for the federal government, Cabinet Office in Ontario) should be responsible for managing consultation strategically, by setting priorities among consultations when many are planned simultaneously; providing expertise to departments; and establishing a community of practice. Departments should be responsible for undertaking consultations within

central guidelines, and sharing best practices within the community
of practice.

- A consultation portal should be established on the government portal, listing all ongoing consultations, with links to the sponsoring
  department.
- Departments should be responsible for outreach to those who are
  likely to be interested in a given consultation, using the most appropriate channel(s).
- Public meetings that are part of a consultation should be webcast.
- Detailed graphical material should be made available online, as it is
  faster and less expensive than in print.
- Governments should move to the next level in consultation, by
  experimenting with interactivity, for example, by posting individual
  responses and summary information about responses online, or
  establishing moderated discussion forums.

Going from an Effective Portal to Integrated Service Delivery

The federal government's efforts starting with Government On-Line
and now moving to integrated service delivery have led to its first-
place ranking by Accenture for the last five years. In chapters 2 and 4,
we identified a number of strengths in Ottawa's approach, and these
give rise to a number of lessons. The first group deals specifically with
the government's portal:

- In developing the government's portal, begin by testing user preferences for how information should be displayed, and on that basis
  choose a structure that can remain in place for a considerable period
  of time.
- Ensure that all connected sites have a common look and feel and
  governmental identity.
- Establish a stable set of sub-portals, assign staff to developing them
  over several years, and provide some central funding to support
  sub-portal development.
- Set targets over time for increasing the capacity of the electronic
  channel.
- Establish a central oversight committee of deputy ministers, coordinating committees for the sub-portals, and an external advisory
  committee.

Moving more generally to integrated service delivery, we derive the following lessons:

- A full program of research should be conducted into patterns in utilization of services by channel, user preferences regarding channels, and costs of service by channel.
- A nation-wide council of public sector experts in service delivery is an effective structure to drive the research program as well as facilitate projects that integrate service across levels of government.
- Integrated channel delivery requires that managers evaluate demand, user satisfaction, and cost across channels and then be able to shift resources among channels. Migrating users to channels such as the Internet that involve self-service will require communication and incentives.
- Integrated service delivery initiatives require clear assurances to the public that their privacy will be protected and data will be shared only for purposes to which they have given consent.
- Service delivery partnerships require clear, transparent, and comprehensive agreements at the outset. Governance, accountability, funding, and branding should all be part of the agreement.
- Integrated service delivery initiatives must be explained and marketed to both the public and to politicians.

Establishing the Local Call Centre (311)

Local call centres are also a form of integrated service. On the basis of the considerable experience of large American cities that have established them, we identified the following lessons in chapter 5:

- If a local government establishes 311 service, it should have support from key decision makers, a private sector contractor capable of developing a system and training staff, and one department assigned to lead an interdepartmental development team.
- Calls should be tracked so that users can follow the status of the service being provided and so that managers can analyse service trends.
- The service should be effectively marketed, particularly to distinguish between emergency (911) and non-emergency service (311).

Getting Project Management Right

In chapter 3, we dealt with the difficulties the Ontario government has experienced in managing major IT projects, and chapter 12 continued that discussion on major projects in the United Kingdom. The two chapters provide a number of lessons for governments seeking to do better in this area:

- Projects should not be too large and of too great duration. Size increases complexity and duration increases the probability of changes in scope and leadership of the project. Instability in both these areas increases the probability of failure.
- Contractors should have some equity stake in major projects and there should be performance-based penalties and rewards. The equity stake, however, should not be too large, for example, a contract that prevented contractors from receiving any return on their investment until the project is completed. Too large an equity stake gives contractors incentives to shift risk back to government, reduce exposure, or inflate cost, as was the case with Ontario's common purpose procurement system.
- Government should provide internal leadership for major projects. To do this requires the development of in-house expertise.
- Transparency should be increased for major projects, both within the public service and outside.

Getting Started on Knowledge Management

Canadian governments are still at an early stage in their application of knowledge management, but in chapter 6 several lessons emerged from initiatives that have been undertaken:

- Strengthen policy and institutional arrangements for managing information as a strategic public administration resource, for example, by seeking the commitment of top organizational leaders to the importance of knowledge management and locating initiatives in the deputy minister's office, rather than IT or human resources units.
- Undertake knowledge audits based on surveys with individuals throughout the organization to determine existing knowledge management practices and to understand needs.

- Establish communities of practice at all levels, within departments, across departments, and across governments.
- Interview the large wave of public servants who are, or soon will be, retiring, to capture their knowledge of the organization's environment and their experience within the organization.
- Establish Web-based applications that enable members of organizations to contribute and share lessons learned (as, for example, the Canadian Forces are doing for peacekeeping missions).

When All Is Said and Done, There Is Still More to Be Said and Done

In writing this book, we set out to take a longitudinal and holistic approach to the study of public sector IT. We chose to look at many aspects of public sector IT in both politics and public administration for five years (2000–5) for two jurisdictions that are considered to be at the leading edge. This project, we believe, will occupy a distinctive place in the literature. The study of public administration reform has, to a great extent, not known what to make of IT, and has tended to say little about it (Dunleavy and Margetts 2000; Kernaghan and Gunraj 2004). There has been considerable study of the emerging role of the Internet in politics, but that research has not been linked to research in public administration. We believe our research has integrated IT into public administration and has demonstrated the linkages between the study of IT in politics and in administration. In the normative debates about IT, we have assumed a techno-realist stance, rather than those of the optimists, who see only benefits, and the pessimists, who see unmitigated problems.

We end our study with a sense of ongoing curiosity about what will happen next in both jurisdictions in the role of IT in political campaigning, public consultation, and service delivery. The creation of IT-facilitated integrated service delivery and support organizations represents the potential for a major reshaping of government, and they warrant ongoing observation. Initiatives coming from government, for example, in knowledge management, and practices originating in civil society such as blogging, also warrant ongoing observation. The public sector IT sagas in the two jurisdictions we have observed most closely, the governments of Canada and Ontario, are intrinsically interesting, and also contain lessons for other jurisdictions. We are certain that this unfolding story will continue to fascinate both scholars and practitioners.

Notes

1 Five of the six co-authors of this book are career academics and have wit-
nessed an IT-based transformation in our own work in the last fifteen years.
While our core work remains teaching and research, how we teach and do
research has changed dramatically. Teaching has been affected by online
distance education, the smart classroom (equipped with computers for
both faculty and students), the use of the Internet as a research tool by
students, and e-mail and online discussion among faculty and students.
Research has been affected by basic office automation, the use of the Internet as a research tool, the dramatic increase in computational power, and
the use of the Internet and e-mail to globalize academic communities and
facilitate collaboration at a distance. These changes in our own work environment should increase our sensitivity to similar changes in the work
environments of politicians and public servants.
2 In the Martin government, Service Canada reported to Parliament through
the minister of human resources and skills development. The Harper government, which prefers larger ministries, reintegrated Human Resources
and Skills Development Canada and Social Development Canada into
Human Resources and Social Development Canada, and made Service
Canada part of that ministry.
3 Our intention in this section, as in the entire book, has been to use the
Ontario and federal governments to benchmark the progress of leading-
edge jurisdictions in applying IT to government. A secondary purpose
was to contrast and compare the two jurisdictions. Doing so highlighted
the following contrasts: Ontario's more powerful corporate CIO, Ontario's
earlier commitment to shared support services, the federal government's
greater success with large IT projects, and the federal government's more
structured and better-funded approach to portal development through
the GOL initiative. On the other hand, there are many similarities, such as
their virtually simultaneous launch of integrated front-line service delivery
organizations, and, following the Harper government's revisions to the
Canada site, the look and feel of their portals. The two jurisdictions are
well aware of each other's IT practices, and constantly learning from each
other.
4 I exchange a considerable amount of e-mail with public servants and have
found that senior public servants often return external e-mail quickly using
a BlackBerry while in meetings. An instance of BlackBerry technology facilitating an indiscretion concerns former Liberal cabinet minister Scott Brison, who sent e-mails to an investment banker friend anticipating changes

in the tax treatment of income trusts announced by the minister of finance (Stewart and Taber 2006).

5 Some program spending includes overhead to institutions such as hospitals, schools, colleges, and universities. As discussed in chapter 3, while government would like to see them reduce cost through IT-based capital-labour substitution, their institutional autonomy prevents government from ordering them to undertake such projects.

6 These estimates are based on operating costs and make no allowance for capital. It could be argued that the estimate of Internet costs is downwardly biased because it ignores the costs recently incurred in establishing networks. Those who did the studies argue that this omission is appropriate, however, because capital costs incurred long ago for the other modes (for example, government buildings) are also ignored.

7 Neither parties of the left nor the right would be likely to use such savings to pay down the public debt, because, at current interest rates – which are the rates that would prevail if government attempts to retire public debt regardless of maturity – every dollar of debt service eliminated from the annual budget would require a payment of approximately twenty dollars.

8 The Harper government's revision of the Canada site has led critics to claim they are rebranding it to closely approximate the Conservative Party brand, and to argue that such a rebranding is inappropriate (Tossell 2006).

References

6, Perri. 2003. *Entitlement cards: Benefits, privacy and data protection risks, costs and wider social implications.* Wilmslow, UK: Office of the Information Commissioner.

– 2004a. *E-governance: Styles of political judgment in the information age polity.* Basingstoke, UK: Palgrave Macmillan.

– 2004b. Joined-up government in the Western world in comparative perspective: A preliminary literature review and exploration. *Journal of Public Administration Research and Theory* 14 (1): 103–38.

6, Perri, C. Bellamy, and C. Raab. 2005. Joined-up government and privacy in the United Kingdom: Managing tensions between data protection and social policy, part 1. *Public Administration* 83 (1): 111–33.

6, Perri, K. Seltzer, D. Leat, and G. Stoker. 2002. *Towards holistic governance: The new agenda in government reform.* Basingstoke, UK: Palgrave.

6, Perri, A. Warren, C. Bellamy, C. Raab, and C. Heeney. 2005a. The governance of information sharing in networked public management. Paper presented at the Public Management Conference, Los Angeles.

– 2005b. Social policy as judgment: Risks of injustice and the injustice of risk in the use of personal information. Paper presented at the annual conference of the Social Policy Association, Bath.

Accenture. 2002. eGovernment leadership – Realizing the vision. http://www.accenture.com/xd/xd.asp?it=enWeb&xd=industries/government/gove_welcome.xml.

– 2004. eGovernment leadership: High performance, maximum value. http://www.accenture.com/Countries/Canada/Research_And_Insights/eGovernmentValue.htm.

– 2005. Leadership in customer service: New expectations, new experiences.

http://www.accenture.com/xdoc/ca/locations/canada/insights/studies/leadership-cust.pdf.

– 2006. Leadership in customer service: Building the trust. http://www.accenture.com/Global/Services/By_Industry/Government/R_and_I/BuildingtheTrust ES.htm.

Accenture Digital Forum. 2005a. Accenture develops, launches New York's 311 citizen contact centre. http://www.accenture.com/Global/Services/By_Industry/Government/AccentureInNewYork.htm.

– 2005b. City of New York: NYC 311: Accenture report. http://www.accenture.com/Global/Services/By_Industry/Government/AccentureInNewYork.htm.

Alberts, David, and Richard Hayes. 2003. *Power to the edge: Command ... control ... in the information age*. Command and Control Research Program Publication Series. Washington, DC: Department of Defense.

Alcock, Reg. 2005. Speech to the Ottawa Centre for Research and Innovation. http://www.tbs-sct.gc.ca/media/ps-dp/2005/0124_e.asp.

Alexander, Cynthia. 2000. Cents and sensibility: The emergence of e-government in Canada. In *How Ottawa spends: 2000–01*, ed. Leslie Pal, 185–209. Toronto: Oxford University Press.

– 2001. Digital leviathan: The emergence of e-politics in Canada. In *Party politics in Canada*. 8th ed. Ed. Hugh G. Thorburn and Alan Whitehorn, 460–83. Toronto: Prentice-Hall.

Allison, Graham, and Phillip Zelikow. 1999. *Essence of decision: Explaining the Cuban missile crisis*. 2nd ed. New York: Addison Wesley Longman.

American Productivity & Quality Center. 2001. *Building and sustaining communities of practice*. Houston: American Productivity & Quality Center.

– 2003. *Expertise locator systems: Finding the answers*. Houston: American Productivity & Quality Center.

Anderson, E.W., and C. Fornell. 2000. Foundations of the American customer satisfaction index. *Total Quality Management and Business Excellence* 11 (7): 869–82.

Attallah, Paul, and Angela Burton. 2001. *The Canadian general election of 2000*. Ed. J.H. Pammett and C. Dornan. Toronto: Dundurn.

Austin City Council. 2004. *311 Citywide customer information centre (CIC) implementation: Audit report No. AU04103*. Austin, TX: Austin City Council.

Automated Business Systems and Services. 2003. *REACT: Citizen relationship management solution*. Upper Marlboro, MD: Automated Business Systems and Services.

Babble. 2005. Which party has the best campaign edition website? http://www.rabble.ca/babble/ultimatebb.php?ubb=get_topic&f=35&t=001099.

Bai, Matt. 2004. Who lost Ohio? *New York Times Magazine*, 21 November. http://www.nytimes.com/2004/11/21/magazine/210HIO.html?ex=1258779600&en=2a9da5f1ef2 7580c&ei=5090&partner=rssuserland.

Bailey, Sue. 2005. New website tracks MPs; Voting records, absences, words spoken documented. *St John's Telegram*, 5 July, A9.

Bard, Louis. 2003. XML on Parliament Hill: Changing 100 years of tradition; Is XML alone enough? Paper presented at the XML Europe Conference, London. http://www.idealliance.org/papers/dx_xmle03/papers/03-05-02/03-05-02.html.

Barney, Darin. 2005. *Communications technology.* Vancouver: UBC Press for the Canadian Democratic Audit.

Barzelay, Michael, and C. Campbell. 2003. *Preparing for the future: Strategic planning in the U.S. Air Force.* Washington, DC: Brookings Institution Press.

Bedi, N. 2004. Keeping KM relevant to the needs of the public sector. Paper presented at McMaster World Congress, Hamilton, ON.

Bellamy, C. 2002. From automation to knowledge management: Modernising British government with ICTs. *International Review of Administrative Sciences* 68:213–30.

– 2003. *In-depth case study of the UK's Universities and Colleges Admissions Service (UCAS).* Brussels: European Back Office Project, European Commission.

Bellamy, C., Perri 6, and C. Raab. 2005. Joined-up government and privacy in the United Kingdom: Managing tensions between data protection and social policy, part 2. *Public Administration* 83 (2): 393–415.

Bellamy, C., and John Taylor. 1998. *Governing in the information age.* Buckingham, UK: Open University Press.

Bennett, Colin, and Charles Raab. 2003. *The governance of privacy: Policy instruments in global perspective.* Hampshire, UK: Aldgate.

Bent, Steven, Kenneth Kernaghan, and Brian Marson. 1999. *Innovations and good practices in single window service.* Ottawa: Canadian Centre for Management Development.

Beveren, J.V. 2003. Does health care for knowledge management? *Journal of Knowledge Management* 7 (1): 90–5.

Bichard, M. 2004. *The Bichard Inquiry Report*, HC 653. London: House of Commons.

Bimber, Bruce. 2003. Quoted by Alaina Sue Potrikus. Website engaging lots of people in politics, *Miami Herald*, 14 October. http://www.miami.com.

Bimber, Bruce, and Richard Davis. 2003. *Campaigning online: The Internet in U.S. elections.* New York: Oxford University Press.

Blackwell, Richard. 2005. Panel wants most court files kept off Web. *Globe and Mail*, 6 October 2005, A8.

Blakeney, Allan, and Sandford Borins. 1998. *Political management in Canada.* 2nd ed. Toronto: University of Toronto Press.

Blythe, Marie, and Brian Marson. 1999. *Good practices in citizen centred service.* Ottawa: Canadian Centre for Management Development.

Bontis, N. 1998. Intellectual capital: An exploratory study that develops measures and models. *Management Decision* 36 (2): 63–76.

– 1999. Managing organizational knowledge by diagnosing intellectual capital: Framing and advancing the state of the field. *International Journal of Technology Management* 18 (5–8): 433–62.

– 2001. Assessing knowledge assets: A review of the models used to measure intellectual capital. *International Journal of Management Reviews* 3 (1): 41–60.

– 2004. National Intellectual Capital Index: A United Nations initiative for the Arab region. *Journal of Intellectual Capital* 5 (1): 13–39.

Borins, Sandford. 1998. *Innovating with integrity: How local heroes are transforming American government.* Washington: Georgetown University Press.

– 2001. Encouraging innovation in the public sector. *Journal of Intellectual Capital* 2 (3): 310–19.

– 2002. Transformation of the public sector: Canada in comparative perspective. In *The handbook of Canadian public administration,* ed. Christopher Dunn, 3–17. Toronto: Oxford University Press.

– 2003a. *Contracting and partnerships in IT services to government.* A report to the Panel on the Role of Government in Ontario. http://www.law-lib.utoronto.ca/investing/reports/rp38.pdf.

– 2003b. *New information technology and the public sector in Ontario.* A report to the Panel on the Role of Government in Ontario. http://www.lawlib.utoronto.ca/investing/reports/rp12.pdf.

– 2004. A holistic view of public sector information technology. *Journal of Electronic Government* 1 (2): 3–29.

Bouey, Kathryn. 2004. Memorandum to all MBS staff on supply chain management. 12 August. Borins Collection, Toronto.

Boutin, Paul. 2004. Net-savvy campaign boosts Bush. *Wired News,* 23 June 2004. http://www.wired.com/news/politics/0,1283,63942,00.html?tw=wn_tophead_1.

Boyne, Walter J. 2003. *Operation Iraqi Freedom: What went right, what went wrong, and why.* New York: Forge.

Brautigam, Tara. 2005. Liberal exec quits over slurs on Web. cnews, 26 December. http://cnews.canoe.ca/CNEWS/Politics/CanadaVotes/2005/12/26/1369003-cp.html.

Brennan, Richard, and Robert Benzie. 2004. $20M to fix pay delay: Glitch in welfare computer program has Liberals, Tories playing blame game. *Toronto Star*, 7 July, A1.

Broadbent, Ed. 2004. Quoted by Sherry Morley. Jumping on the blog bandwagon. capitalnewsonline, 19 March. http://temagami.carleton.ca/jmc/cnews/10932004/n1.shtml.

Brown, David. 2005. Electronic government and public administration. *International Review of Administrative Sciences* 71 (2): 241–54.

Brown, David, Milaine Alarie, Alana Cattapan, and Jonathan Dignan. 2006. *Report on PPF survey of government citizen-centred, Web-based service delivery: June 27th—July 23rd, 2005*. http://www.digitalstate.ca/supp/ch2/html.

Brown, David, Gabe Eidelman, and Milena Isakovic. 2004. *Gateways and Clusters: The Government of Canada's experience with client-centred single-window electronic service delivery; Report on year 1*. Ottawa: Public Policy Forum. http://www.digitalstate.ca/supp/ch2.html.

Brown, J. 2000. Ontario town answers citizens' calls. *Computer Dealer News* 16 (21): 12.

Brynjolfsson, E., and L.M. Hitt. 2000. Beyond computation: Information technology, organizational transformation and business performance. *Journal of Economic Perspectives* 14 (4): 23–48.

Butters, George. 2004. Canadian candidates woo voters on Web. *theglobeandmail.com*, 10 June.

Cabinet Office. 2000. *Successful IT: Modernising government in action* ('The McCartney report'). London: Cabinet Office. http://www.ogc.gov.uk/embedded_object.asp?docid=2633.

Canada, Government On-Line Advisory Panel. 2002a. First Report of the Government On-Line Advisory Panel. 12 April 2002. http://www.gol-ged.gc.ca/pnl-grp-reports/first/first_e.asp.

– 2002b. Transforming government to serve Canadians better: Report of the Government On-Line Advisory Panel. http://www.gol-ged.gc.ca/pnl-grp-reports/transform/transform_e.pdf.

– 2003. Connecting with Canadians: Pursuing service transformation; Final report of the Government On-Line Advisory Panel. http://www.gol-ged.gc.ca/pnl-grp/reports/final/final00_e.asp.

Canada, Governor General. 1997. *Speech from the Throne to open the first session, thirty-sixth Parliament of Canada*. 23 September. http://www.parl.gc.ca/information/about/process/info/throne/index.asp? Language=E&param=sp &parl=36&sess=1.

– 1999. *Speech from the Throne to open the second session, thirty-sixth Parliament of Canada*. 12 October. http://www.pco-bcp.gc.ca/default.asp?Language=E&Page=sftddt&doc=sftddt1999_e.htm.

Canada, House of Commons. 1999. *Building the future: House of Commons requirements for the Parliamentary Precinct.* Ottawa: House of Commons.

– 2004. Standing Committee on Procedure and House Affairs. Overview and status of technological projects. Report tabled by Clerk of the House. March 23.

– 2005. Evidence, Standing Committee on Procedure and House Affairs. February 3. http://www.parl.gc.ca/infocomdoc/38/1/PROC/Meetings/Evidence/PROCEV18-E.pdf.

Canada, House of Commons Administration. 1999. Report on plans and priorities, 1999–2000. http://www.parl.gc.ca/information/about/process/house/plans99/cover-e.htm.

– 2004a. Performance report, 2003–2004. Fall. http://www.parl.gc.ca/information/about/process/house/performance04/01-toc-e.htm.

– 2004b. Report on plans and priorities, 2004–2005. Spring. http://www.parl.gc.ca/information/about/process/house/plans04/cov-e.htm.

– 2004c. Strategic outlook for the 38th Parliament. December. http://www.parl.gc.ca/information/about/process/house/StrategicOutlook/08-rap-e.htm.

Canada, Office of the Auditor General. 2003. Information technology: Government on-line. In *Report of the Auditor General of Canada to the House of Commons,* chap. 1. Ottawa: Office of the Auditor General.

– 2006. Canadian Firearms Program. In *Status Report of the Auditor General to the House of Commons,* 95–139. Ottawa: Office of the Auditor General.

Canada, Public Works and Government Services. 2006. *Government On-Line 2006.* Ottawa: Public Works and Government Services Canada.

Canada–Ontario. 2004. Memorandum of agreement on collaboration in the delivery of public services. http://www.hrsdc.gc.ca/en/cs/comm/hrsd/news/2004/040513.shtml#101.

Canadian Radio-television and Telecommunications Commission. 2004. Telecom decision CRTC 2004-71: Assignment of 311 for non-emergency municipal government services. Ottawa: Canadian Radio-television and Telecommunications Commission. http://www.crtc.gc.ca/archive/ENG/Decisions/2004/dt2004-71.htm (accessed 28 February 2005).

– 2005. Broadcasting public notice CRTC 2005-9. Distribution of Spike TV by broadcasting distribution undertakings. http://www.crtc.gc.ca/archive/ENG/Notices/2005/pb2005-9.htm.

Canadian Wireless Telecommunications Association. 2002. Assignment of '311' to non-emergency municipal services: Canadian Wireless Telecommunications Association. Letter to Diane Rhéaume, secretary general, Canadian Radio-television and Telecommunications Commission. http://

www.crtc.gc.ca/PartVII/eng/2003/8665/cwta/040112.doc (accessed 25 January 2004).

Carr, Nicholas. 2004. *Does IT matter? Information technology and the corrosion of competitive advantage*. Boston: Harvard Business School Press.

Cavoukian, Ann. 2005. About the Office of the Information and Privacy Commissioner/Ontario. http://www.ipc.on.ca/scripts/index_.asp?action=31&N_ID=1&P_ID=17&U_ID=0.

Cellucci, Paul. 2005. *Unquiet diplomacy*. Toronto: Key Porter.

Chadwick, A., and C. May. 2003. Interaction between states and citizens in the age of the Internet: 'e-government' in the United States, Britain and the European Union. *Governance* 16 (2): 271–300.

Chancellor of the Duchy of Lancaster. 1996. *government.direct: A prospectus for the electronic delivery of government services*. London: Her Majesty's Stationery Office.

Chandler, Alfred. 1977. *The visible hand: The managerial revolution in American business*. Boston: Belknap.

Chase, Steven, Gloria Galloway, and Campbell Clark. 2006. Harper's lead takes a hit. *Globe and Mail*, 20 January.

Chatzkel, J. 2002. Conversation with Alex Bennet, former deputy CIO for enterprise integration at the US Department of Navy. *Journal of Knowledge Management* 6 (5): 434–44.

Chen, Peter. 2002. Australian elected representatives use of new media: Research report. http://www.anu.edu.au/mail-archives/link/link0207/0009.html.

Chenier, John, and Joseph Peters. 2003. Is e-consultation everything it's cracked up to be? *Ottawa Hilltimes*, 2 June.

Chief Information Officer Branch, Treasury Board of Canada Secretariat. 2004. *Serving Canadians better: Moving forward with service transformation at the enterprise level*. http://www.tbs-sct.gc.ca/cio-dpi/2004/canada/canada00_e.asp.

Cinca, C.S., C.M. Molinero, and A.B. Queiroz. 2003. The measurement of intangible assets in public sector using scaling techniques. *Journal of Intellectual Capital* 4 (2): 249–75.

Clients Speak. 2001. *A report on single-window government services in Canada*. R.A. Malatest and Associates for the Public Sector Service Delivery Council and the Institute of Public Administration of Canada. http://www.iccs.org/eng/pubs/clientsreport.pdf.

Clinton, Bill. 1996. Remarks to the community in Sacramento, California, 23 July. http://www.highbeam.com/library/doc-Free.asp?DOCID=1G1:18659748.

Coase, R. 1937. The nature of the firm. *Economica* 4:386–405.

Coleman, S. 2001. *What do we want from MPs Web sites?* London: Hansard Society for Parliamentary Government.

– 2004. Connecting Parliament to the public via the Internet: Two case studies of on-line consultations. *Information, Communication and Society* 17 (1): 1–22.

– 2005. Blogs and the new politics of listening. *Political Quarterly* 76 (2): 273–80.

Cong, X., and K.V. Pandya. 2003. Issues of knowledge management in the public sector. *Electronic Journal of Knowledge Management* 1 (2).

Congressional Management Foundation. 2005. *Communicating with Congress: How Capitol Hill is coping with the surge in citizen advocacy.* http://www.cmf-web.org/cwreport1.asp.

Coram, Robert. 2002. *Boyd: The fighter pilot who changed the art of war.* Boston: Little, Brown.

Cordesman, Anthony H. 2003. *The Iraq war: Strategy, tactics, and military lessons.* Washington, DC: Center for Strategic & International Studies.

Cornfield, Michael. 2004. *Politics moves online: Campaigning and the Internet.* New York: Century Foundation.

– 2005. The Internet and campaign 2004: A look back at the campaigners. PEW Internet & American Life Project. http://www.pewinternet.org/pdfs/Cornfield_commentary.pdf.

Cornfield, Michael, and Lee Rainie. 2003. *Untuned keyboards: Online campaigners, citizens and portals in the 2003 elections.* N.p.: Institute for Politics, Democracy and the Internet.

Corporate Architecture and Standards Branch. 2005. Open source software: Product evaluation criteria and TCO framework. Management Board Secretariat, Government of Ontario. Borins Collection, Toronto.

Corporate Security Branch. 2003. Management Board Secretariat, Government of Ontario. Borins Collection, Toronto.

– 2004a. OPS patch management strategy. Management Board Secretariat, Government of Ontario. Borins Collection, Toronto.

– 2004b. Safeguarding the OPS network. Management Board Secretariat, Government of Ontario. Borins Collection, Toronto.

– 2005. Proposed security requirements: BlackBerry devices, wireless LANs, remote access services. Management Board Secretariat, Government of Ontario. Borins Collection, Toronto.

Coughlin, Shannon. 2003. Building the infrastructure you require to maintain an integrated approach to service delivery. Paper presented to Conference of the Institute for Citizen-Centred Service, Ottawa.

Cross, M. 2005. Public sector IT failures: Special report. *Prospect* (October): 48–52.

Crossing Boundaries III Political Advisory Committee. 2002. *E-Government: The message to politicians*. Ottawa: KTA Centre for Collaborative Government.

Crossing Boundaries National Council. 2002. MP website study results. Ottawa: KTA Centre for Collaborative Government. http://www.crossing-boundaries.ca/index.php?page=MPdata2&lang_id=1&page_id=94.

– 2005a. About the council. http://www.crossingboundaries.ca/abouten.html?page=about&lang_id=1&page_id=2.

– 2005b. Privacy in the information age: Government services and you. http://www.crossingboundaries.ca/files/kta_final_report_050805.pdf.

Culver, Keith, and Paul Howe. 2004. Calling all citizens: The challenges of public consultation. *Canadian Public Administration* 47 (1): 52–75.

Darr, Carol. 2004. Quoted by Richard Robbins. Internet cuts campaign corners nationally and locally. *Pittsburgh Tribune-Review*, 7 November.

d'Auray, Michelle. 2002. Government on-line: Serving Canadians in a digital age. Presentation to CIPS Breakfast, annual federal CIO update, Ottawa, 18 April.

David, Paul A. 1985. Clio and the economics of QWERTY. *American Economic Review* (papers and proceedings) 75 (2): 332–7.

Davis, Joshua. 2003. If we run out of batteries, this war is screwed. *Wired Magazine* June. http://www.wired.com/wired/archive/11.06/battlefield_pr.html.

Davis, Richard. 1999. *The Web of politics*. New York: Oxford University Press.

Defence Research and Development Canada. 2004. OCTAS 'E-training and knowledge management.' http://www.valcartier.drdc-rddc.gc.ca/e/actualitesdisplay_e.asp?lang=e&page=33&news=83.

Democratic Renewal Secretariat. 2005. Citizen engagement: Definition and scope. Presentation to Deputy Minister's Committee on Transformation, February, Borins Collection, Toronto.

Denis, Pierre. 2004. Federal website study. 9 September.

Department for Constitutional Affairs. 2003. *Public sector data sharing: Guidance on the law*. London: Department for Constitutional Affairs.

Department of Finance Canada. 2005a. *Budget 2005: Expenditure review for sound fiscal management*. http://www.fin.gc.ca/budget05/pdf/bkexpe.pdf.

– 2005b. *Strengthening and modernizing public sector management*. http://www.fin.gc.ca/budget05/pdf/bkmgte.pdf.

DeWitt, J. 2003. Performance management: The impact of measurement and accountability. *American City and County Special Reports* 1 (3). http://enews.primediabusiness.com/enews/americancitycounty/v/37.

Diamond, E., and R. Cooper. 2003. Citizen relationship management. *Optimum Online* 33 (4). http://www.optimumonline.ca/article.phtml?id=190.

Dinsdale, Geoff, and Brian Marson. 1999. *Citizen/client surveys: Dispelling myths and redrawing maps.* Ottawa: Canadian Centre for Management Development.

Directorate-General for Information and Media (European Commission). 2005. *On-line availability of public services: How is Europe progressing? Web based survey on electronic public services. Report of the Fifth Measurement October 2004.* Brussels: Directorate-General for Information and Media (European Commission). http://ec.europa.eu/information_society/soccul/egov/egov_benchmarking_2005.pdf.

Directorate of Land Strategic Concepts. 2003. *Future force: Concepts for future army capabilities.* Kingston: Department of National Defence.

Dispatch. 2005. Cities with 311 non-emergency telephone service. *Dispatch Monthly Magazine.* http://www.911dispatch.com/info/311map.html.

Docherty, David. 1997. *Mr Smith Goes to Ottawa.* Vancouver: University of British Columbia Press.

Dunleavy, Patrick, and Helen Margetts. 2000. The advent of digital government: Public bureaucracies and the state in the Internet age. Paper presented to the annual conference of the American Political Science Association, Washington, DC.

Dunleavy, Patrick, Helen Margetts, Simon Bastow, and Jane Tinkler. 2004. Government IT performance and the power of the IT industry: A cross-national analysis. Paper presented at the American Political Science Association annual conference, Chicago.

e-Citizen Engagement Support Office. 2005. Electronic citizen engagement by the Ontario public service. Presentation to Deputy Ministers' Committee on Transformation. Borins Collection, Toronto.

Earl, M. 2001. Knowledge management strategies: Toward a taxonomy. *Journal of Management Information Systems* 18 (1): 215–33.

Eaton, B. 2005. Gatineau forges ahead with 311 service. *it World Canada,* 24 June 2005. http://www.itworldcanada.com.

Erin Research Inc. for the Citizen-Centred Network and the Canadian Centre for Management Development. 1998. *Citizens First.* Ottawa: Canadian Centre for Management Development.

Erin Research Inc. for the Institute for Citizen-Centred Service and the Institute of Public Administration of Canada. 2003. *Citizens First 3.* Toronto: Institute of Public Administration of Canada.

Erin Research Inc. for the Public Sector Service Delivery Council and the Institute of Public Administration of Canada. 2001. *Citizens First 2.* Toronto: Institute of Public Administration of Canada.

Fallows, James. 2005. Bush didn't invent the Internet, but is he good for tech? *New York Times,* 23 January.

– 2006. Working at the PC isn't so lonely anymore. *New York Times*, 1 January, B3.

Ferguson, Rob. 2004. Personal data sent to strangers: Privacy chief demands audit, Government promises reforms. *Toronto Star*, 17 December.

Ferguson, R., and M. Howell. 2004. *Political blogs: Craze or convention?* London: Hansard Society for Parliamentary Government.

Ferris, N. 2004. Gaining taxpayer respect. *Computerworld* 38 (38): 40.

Ford, D. 2003. Trust and knowledge management: The seeds of success. In *Handbook on knowledge management*, ed. C.W. Holsapple, 553–76. Berlin: Springer.

Foreign Affairs and International Trade Canada (DFAIT). 2004. A dialogue on foreign policy. http://www.foreign-policy-dialogue.ca/en/welcome/index.html

Fountain, Jane. 2001. *Building the virtual state*. Washington, DC: Brookings.

Fountain, Jane, with Carlos Osorio-Urzua. 2001. Public sector: Early stages of a deep transformation. In *The economic payoff from the Internet revolution*, ed. R.A. Litan and A. Rivlin, 235–68. Washington, DC: Brookings.

Gale, Robert J.P. 1997. 'Canada's Green Plan.' In *Nationale Umweltpläne in ausgewählten Industrieländern.* (A study of the Development of a National Environmental Plan, with expert submissions to the Enquete Commission, 'Protection of People and the Environment,' for the Bundestag). Berlin: Springer-Verlag Berlin, 97–120.

Galloway, Gloria. 2005. Eight-year-old speech haunts Harper. *Globe and Mail*, 15 December, A9.

Gershon, P. 2004. *Releasing resources to the front line: Independent review of public sector efficiency.* London: HM Treasury.

Gibbins, Roger. 2000. Federalism in a digital world. *Canadian Journal of Political Science* 33 (4): 667–89.

Gibbons, Robert. 2003. Team theory, garbage cans and real organizations: Some history and prospects of economic research on decision-making in organizations. *Industrial and Corporate Change* 12 (4): 753–87.

Gibson, Rachel, and Ian McAllister. 2003. Cyber campaigning and the vote: Online communication in the 2001 Australian election. Paper presented to the annual conference of the American Political Science Association, Philadelphia.

Gibson, Rachael, Paul Nixon, and Stephen Ward. 2003. *Political parties and the Internet: Net gain?* London: Routledge.

Gibson, R.K., W. Lusoli, and S. Ward. 2005. On-line participation in the UK: Testing a 'contextualised' model of Internet effects. *British Journal of Politics and International Relations* 7(4): 561–83. http://www.esri.salford.ac.uk/ESR-CResearchproject/papers/gibson_et_al_2005_bjpir_preprint.pdf

Girard, J. 2004. Defence knowledge management: A passing fad? *Canadian Military Journal* 5 (2): 17–27.

– 2005a. Combating information anxiety. *Management of Organizations: Systematic Research Journal* 35 (1): 65–80.

– 2005b. The Inukshuk: A Canadian knowledge management model. *Journal of Knowledge Management Professionals Society* 2 (1): 9–16.

– 2005c. Taming enterprise dementia in public sector organizations. *International Journal of Public Sector Management* 18 (6): 534–45.

Globerman, Steven, and Aidan Vining. 1996. A framework for evaluating the government contracting-out decision with an application to information technology. *Public Administration Review* 56 (6): 577–87.

Gonzales, A.R., T.A. Henke, and S.V. Hart. 2005. *Calling 311: Guidelines for policymakers.* Report #NCJ 206257. Washington, DC: National Institute of Justice, U.S. Department of Justice.

Good, David. 2003. *The politics of public management: The HRDC audit of grants and contributions.* Toronto: University of Toronto Press.

Government of Ontario. 2005. *Report of Ontario's special task force on the management of large-scale information and information technology projects.* Toronto: Queen's Printer.

Government On-Line. 2003. *Government On-Line 2003.* http://www.gol-ged.gc.ca/rpt2003/rpt00_e.asp.

– 2005. *Government On-Line 2005: From vision to reality – and beyond.* Ottawa: Queen's Printer.

– 2006. *Government On-Line 2006: Serving Canadians better.* Ottawa: Public Works and Government Services Canada.

Graham, William. 2003. *A dialogue on foreign policy: Report to Canadians.* Ottawa: Department of Foreign Affairs and International Trade. http://www.foreign-policy-dialogue.ca/en/final_report/index.html.

Hammer, M. 1990. Reengineering work: Don't automate, obliterate. *Harvard Business Review* (July–August): 104–12.

Hansen. 2004. *Halifax regional municipality, Nova Scotia call centre processes one million citizen service requests.* Press release. http://www.hansen.com/news/press-release/09-21-2004.asp.

Hillwatch. 2004. Political Web sites: Strategic assets or virtual lawn signs? http://www.hillwatch.com/Publications/Research/Virtuallawnsigns.aspx.

– 2006. Still virtually lawn signs: Benchmarking Canadian political Web sites during the 2006 campaign. http://www.hillwatch.com/VirtuallyLawnSigns1.aspx.

Hines, Matt. 2004. US election 2004: The year the Web came of age. *CNET News,* 28 October. http://insight.zdnet.co.uk/internet/0,39020451,39171897,00.htm.

Howell, David. 2004. Web helps Green party gain political ground. *Canada.com News*, 7 June.

Huber, Nick. 2003. Hitting targets? The state of UK IT project management. *Computer Weekly*, 5 November. http://www.computerweekly.com/Articles/2003/11/05/198320/HittingtargetsThestateofUKITpro jectmanagement.htm.

Hughes, Thomas P. 1998. *Rescuing Prometheus: Four monumental projects that changed the modern world.* Boston: Pantheon.

Human Resources Development Canada. 1999. *Service delivery in the new millennium: HRDC's service delivery policy.* Ottawa: HRDC.

Human Resources and Stakeholder Education Branch. 2004. *Government of Ontario I&IT organization: Recognizing our effort and successes.* Management Board Secretariat, Government of Ontario. Borins Collection, Toronto.

Ichniowski, C., and K. Shaw. 2003. Beyond incentive pay: Insiders' estimates of the value of complementary human resource management. *Journal of Economic Perspectives* 17 (1): 155–80.

Industry Canada. 1996. *Building the information society: Moving Canada into the 21st century.* Ottawa: Supply and Services Canada.

– 2005. *Stopping spam: Creating a stronger, safer Internet.* http://e-com.ic.gc.ca/epic/Internet/inecic-ceac.nsf/en/h_gv00317e.html.

Information and Information Technology Controllership Branch. 2003. *An executive 'Project Health' dashboard.* Corporate Chief Strategist, Office of the Corporate Chief Information Officer, Management Board Secretariat, Government of Ontario. Borins Collection, Toronto.

– 2004a. *Final 2003–04 OPS I&IT corporate performance report.* Internal report, 2 December. Corporate Chief Strategist, Office of the Corporate Chief Information Officer, Management Board Secretariat, Government of Ontario. Borins Collection, Toronto.

– 2004b. *Major I & IT projects report for period ending September 2004.* Corporate Chief Strategist, Office of the Corporate Chief Information Officer, Management Board Secretariat, Government of Ontario. Borins Collection, Toronto.

– 2004c. *A proposed process to update ITELC on status of major I & IT projects.* Corporate Chief Strategist, Office of the Corporate Chief Information Officer, Management Board Secretariat, Government of Ontario. Borins Collection, Toronto.

Information Technology Executive Leadership Council Retreat. 2003. Author's minutes. 3 November. Borins Collection, Toronto.

Information Week. 2003. Dean's not the only one who's learned online lessons. *Information Week*, 12 August. http://www.informationweek.com/story/showArticle.jhtml?articleID=13100030.

Ingram, Matthew. 2005. Parties not using Web to fullest in this campaign, *theglobeandmail.com*, 5 December.

Institute for Citizen-Centred Service. 2003. *Citizens first 3*. Toronto: Institute of Public Administration of Canada.

– 2004. *Taking care of business*. Toronto: Institute of Public Administration of Canada.

Jansen, Harold. 2004. Is the Internet politics as usual or democracy's future? Candidate campaign Web sites in the 2001 Alberta and British Columbia provincial elections. *Innovation Journal* 9 (2): 1–20.

Johnson, Dennis W. 2004. *Congress online: Bridging the gap between citizens and their representatives*. New York: Routledge.

Jones, D.G. 2003. Case study: Managing knowledge management from audit to strategy; The RCMP experience. *Proceedings of the Conference on Knowledge Management in Government*. Ottawa: Federated Press.

Kalakota, R., and M. Robinson. 2000. *e-Business 2.0: Roadmap for success*. 2nd ed. Reading, MA: Addison-Wesley Professional.

Kamarck, Elaine Ciulla. 2002. Political campaigning on the Internet: Business as usual? In *Governance.Com. Democracy in the information age*, ed. Elaine Ciulla Kamarck and Joseph S. Nye Jr, 81–103. Washington, DC: Brookings Institution Press.

Kernaghan, Kenneth. 2005. Moving toward the virtual state: Integrating services and service channels for citizen-centred service. *International Review of Administrative Sciences* 71: 119–31.

Kernaghan, Kenneth, and Jennifer Berardi. 2001. Bricks, clicks and calls: Clustering services for citizen-centred service. *Canadian Public Administration* 44: 417–40.

Kernaghan, Kenneth, and Justin Gunraj. 2004. Integrating information technology into public administration: Conceptual and practical considerations. *Canadian Public Administration* 47 (4): 525–46.

Kernaghan, Kenneth, Nancy Riehle, and James Lo. 2003. *Politicians' use of ICTs: A survey of federal parliamentarians*. Ottawa: KIA Centre for Collaborative Government. http://crossingboundaries.ca/reports/CBStudy_Politicians_Use_of_ICTS.pdf.

Kernaghan, Kenneth, and David Siegel. 1999. *Public administration in Canada: A text*. Toronto: Nelson.

Kerner, Sean Michael. 2004. Americans click their way toward elections. 27 October. http://www.clickz.com/stats/big_picture/traffic_patterns/article.php/3427901.

Kippen, Grant. 2000. *The use of new information technologies by a political party: A case study of the Liberal party in the 1993 and 1997 federal elections*. Vancouver: SFU-UBC Centre for the Study of Government and Business.

Kirby, Patrick, and David Brown. 2005. *Report on PPF survey of government citizen-centred, Web-based service delivery: December 3rd, 2004–January 3rd, 2005*. http://www.digitalstate.ca/supp/ch2.html.

KM Review. 2003. Profile – Nilam Bedi: Aligning with strategy and convincing skeptics in the Canadian government. *KM Review* 6 (5): 5.

KM World. 2005. New approaches to KM in government. *KM World Magazine* (June): 7–8.

Laming, Lord. 2003. *The Victoria Climbié inquiry: Report of an enquiry by Lord Laming, Cm 5730*. London: Stationery Office.

Lausin, A., K.C. Desouza, and G.D. Kraft. 2003. Knowledge management in the U.S. army. *Knowledge and Process Management* 10 (4): 218–30.

Lavigne, Brad. 2004a. Quoted in Mary Nersessian. Sites may not click with voters. *theglobeandmail.com*, 9 June.

– 2004b. Federal website survey. 6 October.

Layton, Jack. 2004. A letter from Jack Layton. *ENDP*, 27 June.

Leblanc, Daniel. 2005. Rules broken in federal executive-exchange program, officials say. *Globe and Mail*, 15 August.

Legris, P., J. Ingham, and P. Collerette. 2003. Why do people use information technology? A critical review of the technology acceptance model. *Information and Management* 40 (3): 191–204.

Lewis, D., and D. Bridger. 2000. *The soul of the new consumer: Authenticity; What we buy and why in the new economy*. London: Nicholas Brealey.

Liebowitz, J. 2003. A knowledge management implementation plan at a leading U.S. technical government organization: A case study. *Knowledge and Process Management* 10 (4): 254–59.

– 2004. *Addressing the human capital crisis in the Federal Government: A KM perspective*. Burlington, MA: Butterworth-Heinemann.

Liebowitz, J., and Y. Chen. 2003. Knowledge sharing proficiencies: The key to knowledge management. In *Handbook on knowledge management*, ed. C.W. Holsapple, 409–24. Berlin: Springer.

Liebowitz, J., B. Rubenstein-Montano, D. McCaw, J. Buchwalter, C. Browning, B. Newman, and K. Rebeck. 2000. The knowledge audit. *Knowledge and Process Management* 7 (1): 3–10.

Lin, William. 2004. Greens cotton on to Web's populist power. *Toronto Star*, 10 June.

Linden, Russel M. 1994. *Seamless government: A practical guide to reengineering in the public sector*. San Francisco: Jossey-Bass.

Lonti, Zsuzsanna. 2000. The impact of work characteristics and technological change on the adoption of workplace practices in government workplaces. PhD diss., University of Toronto.

Lonti, Zsuzsanna, and Anil Verma. 2003. The determinants of flexibility and innovation in the government workplace: Recent evidence from Canada. *Journal of Public Administration Research and Theory* 13 (3): 283–310.

Lusoli, W., and S. Ward. 2004. Digital rank and file: Party activists' perceptions and use of the Internet. *British Journal of Politics and International Relations* 6 (4): 453–70.

Lyon, David. 2001. *Surveillance society: Monitoring everyday life.* Buckingham: Open University Press.

– 2003. *Surveillance after September 11.* Cambridge, UK: Polity.

Makin, Kirk. 2005. Computer lawsuit costs Ontario $63 million. *Globe and Mail*, 1 June, A1.

Malbin, Michael J. 2005. Will the Bipartisan Campaign Reform Act of 2002 strengthen the political system? *Journal of Policy Analysis and Management* 24 (3): 599–610.

Malloy, Jonathan. 2003. *To better serve Canadians: How technology is changing the relationship between members of Parliament and public servants.* Toronto: Institute of Public Administration of Canada.

Mantagaris, Elena. 2003. The Canada Site: Bringing it together the Canadian way. Public Works and Government Services Canada. Presentation, Ottawa, 10 February.

Marland, Alex. 2003. Political marketing in modern Canadian elections. Paper presented at the Canadian Political Science Association Conference, Halifax.

Marson, Brian, and Peter Ross. 2004. *Survey of DMs and CAOs: Deputy ministers identify the top management issues.* Toronto: Institute of Public Administration of Canada.

– 2005. Targeting managers. *Public Sector Management* 16:4–11.

Martin, Paul. 2003. Finding our digital voice: Governing in the information age. Remarks at the Crossing Boundaries National Conference, Ottawa. http://www.crossingboundaries.ca/files/paul_martin_david_zussman_transcript.pdf.

Mazerolle, L., D. Rogan, J. Frank, C. Famega, and J.E. Eck. 2003. *Managing citizen calls to the police: An assessment of non-emergency call systems.* Cincinnati: University of Cincinnati Press.

McAdam, R., and R. Reid. 2000. A comparison of public and private sector perceptions and use of knowledge management. *Journal of European Industrial Training* 24 (6): 317–29.

McDonald, Helen. 2003. *Developing the GoC service strategy.* Presentation to the Government Exchange Conference on Multi-Channel Service Delivery for Government, Ottawa.

McGuinty, Dalton. 2003. Memo to all Ontario Public Servants. 23 October. Borins Collection, Toronto.

McMahon, Tom. 2000. The impact of the Internet on Canadian elections. *Electoral Insight*, June. http://www.elections.ca/eca/eim/pdf/insight_2000_06_e.pdf.

Mechling, Jerry. 1999. Information age governance: Just the start of something big? In *Democracy.com? Governance in a Networked World*, ed. Elaine Kamarck and Joseph Nye, 161–91. Hollis, NH: Hollis.

Meckbach, G. 2001. Crown agencies use CRM to integrate data. *Technology in Government* 8 (8): 8.

Ministry of Government Services. 2005. Ontario to improve management of large-scale I & IT Projects. News release, 17 November. http://www.mgs.gov.on.ca/english/ministry/releases/nr111705.html.

Motorola. 2002. Guide to understanding 311 systems. White paper RO-20-2005. Schaumburg, IL: Motorola.

Motsenigos, A. 2002. IDC reports on KM activity. *KM World Magazine* 11 (9): 3.

Murphy, E.C., and M.A. Murphy. 2002. *Leading on the edge of chaos: The 10 critical elements for success in volatile times*. Upper Saddle River, NJ: Prentice Hall.

Myron, D. 2004. CRM.GOV. *Customer Relationship Management* 8 (7): 26–29.

Nagourney, Adam. 2006. Politics faces sweeping changes via the Web. *New York Times*, 2 April.

National Aeronautics and Space Administration. 2002. *Strategic plan for knowledge management*. Washington, DC: National Aeronautics and Space Administration.

National Audit Office. 2003a. *Difficult forms: How government agencies interact with citizens*. London: Stationery Office.

– 2003b. *New IT systems for the magistrates courts: The Libra project*. London: Stationery Office.

– 2004. *Improving IT procurement: The impact of the Office of Government Commerce's initiatives on departments and suppliers in the delivery of major IT-enabled projects*. London: Stationery Office.

Nersessian, Mary. 2004. Sites may not click with voters. *theglobeandmail.com*, 8 June.

Newcombe, Tod. 2001. Customer satisfaction. *Government Technology*, March. http://www.govtech.net/magazine/story.php?id=3882&issue=3:2001

New York City. 2000. *The newest New Yorkers 2000: Immigrant New York in the new millennium*. New York: Department of City Planning, Population Division.

Nonaka, I., and N. Konno. 1998. The concept of 'ba': Building a foundation for knowledge creation. *California Management Review* 40 (3): 40–54.

Nonaka, I., and H. Takeuchi. 1995. *The knowledge-creating company: How Japanese companies create the dynamics of innovation*. Oxford: Oxford University Press.

Norris, Pippa. 2002. Revolution, what revolution? The Internet and U.S. elections, 1992–2000. In *Governance.com: Democracy in the information age*, ed. Elaine Ciulla Kamarck and Joseph S. Nye Jr, 59–80. Washington, DC: Brookings Institution Press.

O'Connell, Pamela. 2005. Do-it-yourself cartography. *New York Times Magazine*, 11 December.

Ofcom (Office of Communications). 2005. Ofcom consumer panel report: Consumers and the communications market – where we are now. London: Ofcom. http://www.ofcomconsumerpanel.org.uk/publications/ consumer_panel_report.pdf.

Office of the Corporate Chief Strategist. 2004a. *Strategic asset management: IT equipment acquisition*. Corporate Chief Strategist, Office of the Corporate Chief Information Officer, Management Board Secretariat, Government of Ontario. Borins Collection, Toronto.

– 2004b. *Strategic IT asset management: Equipment life-cycle management and financing*. Corporate Chief Strategist, Office of the Corporate Chief Information Officer, Management Board Secretariat, Government of Ontario. Borins Collection, Toronto.

– 2005. *I & IT horizontal review: Implementation and immediate priorities*. Corporate Chief Strategist, Office of the Corporate Chief Information Officer, Management Board Secretariat, Government of Ontario. Borins Collection, Toronto.

Office of the Corporate Chief Technology Officer. 2004a. *Mobile devices report back: Trends and recommendations*. 14 May. Borins Collection, Toronto.

– 2004b. *New connections: Technology outlook and directions*. Corporate Chief Strategist, Office of the Corporate Chief Information Officer, Management Board Secretariat, Government of Ontario. Borins Collection, Toronto.

Office of the Corporate CIO. 2002. *Sustaining the momentum toward e-government: I & IT medium term priorities*. Management Board Secretariat, Government of Ontario. Borins Collection, Toronto.

– 2004. Presentation to Information Technology Executive Leadership Council. 9 March. Borins Collection, Toronto.

Ohler, Shawn. 2005. Liberals, Tories: New kids on the blog. *canada.com*, 11 December. http://www.canada.com (accessed 12 December 2005).

Oldenburg, B. 2003. Call 311: Simplifying customer service. *Summit Magazine* 6 (October): 16–17.

Ontario Liberal Party. 2003. Government that works for you: The Ontario Liberal plan for a more democratic Ontario. http://www.ontarioliberal.com (accessed 25 September 2003).

Ontario, Ministry of Consumer and Business Services. 2005. Service integration: Identifying issues at ServiceOntario. Presentation to Managing Government Information 3rd Annual Forum, 8 March. http://www.governmentevents.ca/mgi2005/Stream%204b(i).ppt.

Ontario, Office of the Auditor General. 2002. *Annual report 2002.* http://www.auditor.on.ca:81/isysquery/irl11fb/12/doc.

Ontario, Public Accounts Committee. 1998. *Hearings on the 1998 annual report of the provincial auditor: Ministry of community and social services.* 17 December. http://www.ontla.on.ca/hansard/committee_debates/36_parl/session2/accounts/p008.htm#TopOf Page.

– 1999a. *Hearings on the report of the provincial auditor on the Accenture agreement.* 9 December. http://www.ontla.on.ca/hansard/37_parl/session1/Committees/Accounts/pdfP006.pdf

– 1999b. *Hearings on the report of the provincial auditor on the Accenture agreement.* 16 December. http://www.ontla.on.ca/hansard/37_parl/session1/Committees/Accounts/pdfP006.pdf

Organisation for Economic Co-operation and Development (OECD). 2001. *The hidden threat to e-government.* Paris: OECD. http://www.oecd.org/dataoecd/19/12/1901677.pdf.

– 2003. Conclusions from the results of the survey of knowledge management practices for ministries/departments/agencies of central government in OECD member countries. In *Unclassified Report JT00138295.* Paris: Human Resources Management Working Party, Public Governance and Territorial Development Directorate, Public Management Committee, Organization for Economic Co-operation and Development, 1–50.

Orlov, L. 2004. When you say 'KM,' what do you mean? *CIO Magazine* 9 (21): 21.

Pal, Leslie. 1998. A thousand points of darkness: Electronic mobilization and the case of the Communications Decency Act. In *Digital democracy: Politics and policy in the wired world,* ed. Cynthia Alexander and Leslie Pal, 105–31. Toronto: Oxford University Press.

Pammett, Jon H., and Lawrence LeDuc. 2003. *Explaining the turnout decline in Canadian federal elections: A new survey of non-voters.* Ottawa: Elections Canada. http://www.elections.ca/content.asp?section=loi&document=internet&dir=tur/tud&lang=e&text only=false.

Pan, S.L., C.W. Tan, and E.T K. Lim. 2006. Customer relationship management (CRM) in e-government: A relational perspective. *Decision Support Systems* 42(1): 237–50.

Parliamentary Office of Science and Technology. 2003. *Government IT projects.*

London: Parliamentary Office of Science and Technology. http://www.parliament.uk/post/pr200.pdf.

Parycek, P., and H. Risku. 2004. Intercultural e-government. *Proceedings of the 5th International Working Conference on Knowledge Management in Electronic Government of the International Federation for Information Processing*, 47–53. Krems, Austria: Springer.

Peppard, J. 2000. Customer relationship management (CRM) in financial services. *European Management Journal* 18 (3): 312–27.

Performance and Innovation Unit. 2002. *Privacy and data-sharing*. London: Performance and Innovation Unit, Cabinet Office.

Pfeffer, J. 1998. *The human equation: Building profits by putting people first*. Boston: Harvard Business School Press.

Phase 5 Consulting Group Inc. for the Institute for Citizen-Centred Service and the Institute of Public Administration of Canada. 2004. *Taking Care of Business*. Toronto: Institute of Public Administration of Canada.

– 2005. *Citizens First 4*. Toronto: Institute of Public Administration of Canada.

PoliticsOnline. 2005. Kerry smashes every online fundraising record. *Netpulse* 9 (1). 5 January. http://netpulse.politicsonline.com/netpulse.asp?issue_id=09.01.

Potier, Beth. 2004. How did Internet affect election? *Harvard University Gazette*. 16 December. http://www.news.harvard.edu/gazette/2004/12.16/13-netvote.html#Zack%20Exley.

Procurement Policy and IT Procurement Branch, Management Board Secretariat, Government of Ontario. 2003a. Government of Ontario: Procurement policies and procedures. PowerPoint presentation by Neil Sentence, Toronto. Borins Collection, Toronto.

– 2003b. *MBS lessor of record update*. Borins collection, Toronto.

– 2004a. *Microsoft software licensing and software support services agreement*. Borins collection, Toronto.

– 2004b. *New corporate IT vendor of record*. Borins collection, Toronto.

– 2004c. *Reducing OPS reliance on consultants for enduring roles*. Borins collection, Toronto.

Public Sector Council of Chief Information Officers of Canada / Public Sector Service Delivery Council (PSCIOC/PSSDC). 2004. *Cross-jurisdictional identification, authentication and authorization working group: Identification, authentication and authorization framework policy and guidelines—Consultation draft*. http://www.iccs-isac.org/eng/pubs/IAA_guidelines.pdf.

Public Records Office. 2001. *e-Government policy framework for electronic records management*. Kew, UK: Public Records Office. http://www.nationalarchives.gov.uk/electronicrecords/pdf/egov_framework.pdf.

Public Sector Service Delivery Council. 2003a. Integrated service delivery: A critical analysis. Project sponsors: Ellen Waxman (ON) and Bette-Jo Hughes (BC). http://www.iccs-isac.org/eng/pubs/ISD%20Critical%20Analysis_report_11%20Aug%2003.pdf.

– 2003b. *Interjurisdictional service delivery: HR issues and challenges*. Project sponsors: Wynne Young (SK) and Ed Fine (federal Treasury Board Secretariat). Available from Wynne Young, Government of Saskatchewan, Regina, SK.

PublicTechnology.Net. 2005. 84 million savings so far from government-Microsoft software deal. http://www.publictechnology.net (accessed 30 June 2005).

Public Works and Government Services Canada (PWGSC). 2004. *Government On-Line*. Ottawa: Public Works and Government Services Canada.

– 2005. Consulting with Canadians website: http://www.consultingcanadians.gc.ca.

Reschenthaler, Gil, and F. Thompson. 1996. The information revolution and the new public management. *Journal of Public Administration Research and Theory* 6 (1): 125–44.

Richardson, Tim. 2004. Quoted in Mary Nersessian, Sites may not click with voters. *theglobeandmail.com*, 8 June.

Richter, Andrew. 1999. The revolution in military affairs and its impact on Canada: The challenge and the consequences. University of British Columbia Institute of International Relations. Working paper no. 28, March 1999. http://www.iir.ubc.ca/pdffiles/webwp28.pdf.

Riley, T.B. 2004a. e-Democracy seminar report. Brussels: eGovernment Unit, Information Society Directorate General, European Commission.

– 2004b. *E-Government: The digital divide and information sharing; Examining the issues*. Ottawa: Report by the Commonwealth Centre for E-Governance and Riley Information Services.

Roberts, Alasdair. 2006. *Blacked out: Government secrecy in the information age.* Cambridge: Cambridge University Press.

Roberts, A., and S. Bretschneider. 2005. Patterns of work within government agencies: Analysis using EDRMS data. Paper presented at the 8th annual Public Management Research Association conference, Los Angeles.

Robillard, Lucienne. 2003. When e-government becomes simply government: Making the case for radical incrementalism in public sector governance. Paper presented at Crossing Boundaries Conference, Ottawa.

Rounce, Andrea D., and Norman Beaudry. 2002. *Using horizontal tools to work across boundaries: Lessons learned and signposts for success.* Ottawa: Canadian Centre for Management Development.

Rumsfeld, Donald. 2002. Transforming the military. *Foreign Affairs* 81 (3): 20–32.

Samuel, Alexandra. 2004. Web plays wild card in US election. *Toronto Star*, 19 October.

Sasser, D.P., and S.E. Bartczak. 2004. Identifying the benefits of knowledge management in the Department of Defense: A Delphi study. *Proceedings of the 10th Americas Conference on Information Systems*, New York.

Schmidt, Faye, and Teresa Strickland. 1999. *Client satisfaction surveying: A common measurements tool (CMT)*. Ottawa: Canadian Centre for Management Development.

Schultz, R. 2003. *C stands for citizen: Direct marketing business intelligence*. Direct Job Zone. http://www.directmag.com/mag/marketing_stands_citizen.

Service Canada. 2005. *Service Canada: We're open for business*. http://www.servicecanada.gc.ca/en/about/launch.html.

Sibley, K. 2003. Quiet revolution in the North. *Government Technology's Public CIO*, November. http://www.public-cio.com/story.php?id=2003.11.18-77916

– 2004. Canadian cities call out for 311 non-emergency number. *IT business.ca*, 4 May 2004. http://www.itbusiness.ca/it/client/en/Home/News.asp?id=2549&bSearch=True.

Simos, Louise. 2004. *Greenbelt consultation: Increasing citizen engagement*. Toronto: Ministry of Municipal Affairs and Housing. Borins Collection, Toronto.

Simpson, R. 2004. Why projects succeed. Sungard Sherwood Systems. http://www.sungard.com/products_and_services/psnps/ukpublicsectorsolutions/information/why projectssucceedwhitepaperv1.002dec04.pdf.

Skyrme, D.J. 2003. *Public sector—public knowledge: The KM contribution to better government*. Highclere, Newbury, UK: Ark Group/David Skyrme Associates.

Smith, Graeme. 2003. PCs solicit votes with mass e-mail campaign. *Globe and Mail*, 27 September, A-16.

Smith, K.D., and W.G.K. Taylor. 2000. The learning organisation ideal in civil service organisations: Deriving a measure. *Learning Organization* 7 (4): 194–206.

Snellen, I. 2003. E-knowledge management in public administration: An agenda for the future. *Proceedings of the 4th International Working Conference on Knowledge Management in Electronic Government of the International Federation for Information Processing*, Springer, Rhodes, Greece, 70–5.

Sobers, Tracey. 2004. Memorandum to all executive assistants, Office of the Premier staff, Cabinet Office staff. 29 August. Borins Collection, Toronto.

Stewart, Cheryl. 2004. The Internet and e-democracy: An opportunity to create a space for engagement between Parliament and citizens. Paper presented to symposium on A New Agenda for e-Democracy, Oxford.

Stewart, Sinclair, and Jane Taber. 2006. Brison sent e-mail to Bay Street's star 'income-trust guy.' *Globe and Mail*, 9 March.

Stewart, T.A. 2001. Intellectual capital: Ten years later, how far we've come. *Fortune*, 28 May, 192–4.

Suellentrop, Chris. 2003. We'll see if it happens: Will Howard Dean do what he just said he would? Slate.com, 7 November. http://slate.msn.com/id/2090927.

Sullivan, H., and C. Skelcher. 2002. *Working across boundaries: Collaboration in public services.* Basingstoke, UK: Palgrave.

Tatle. 2005. Norwegian minister: Proprietary formats no longer acceptable in communication with government. http://www.andwest.com:16080/weblog/tatle/agenda/2005/06/27/Norwegian_Minister_Proprietary_Standards_No_Longer_Acceptable_in_Communication_with_Government.html.

Technology in Government. 2005. Ontario saving money by consolidating services. 1 May. http://www.itbusiness.ca/it/client/en/TechGovernment/Home.asp (accessed 2 May 2005).

Telus. 2004. Joint Part VII Application by the City of Calgary, the City of Toronto, the Halifax Regional Municipality, La Ville de Gatineau, and the Regional Municipality of Halton seeking CRTC Designation of 3-1-1 for Non-Emergency Municipal Government Services in Canada: Telus Corporation. http://www.crtc.gc.ca/PartVII/eng/2003/8665/telus/040112.doc (accessed 25 December 2004).

Ticoll, David. 2004. Why a $180 million computer can't deliver a welfare hike. *Globe and Mail*, 15 July, B12.

Tierney, Tim, Liberal Party Webmaster, 2004. Federal website survey. 9 September.

Toronto Star. 2004. Sour grapes over MPPs BlackBerries. http://www.thestar.com, 3 May.

– 2005. Don't lose that number (Toronto 311). Editorial.

Tossell, Ivor. 2006. We stand on-line for the Tories. *Globe and Mail*, 5 May.

Transformational Government Strategy Project Team. 2005. *Transformational government: Enabled by technology.* Report to the CIO Council and the Service Transformation Board. London: E-Government Unit, Cabinet Office. http://www.cio.gov.uk/documents/pdf/transgov/strategy-workfile.pdf.

Treasury Board of Canada. 2005. *Management in the government of Canada: A commitment to continuous improvement.* www.tbs-sct.gc.ca. October.

Treasury Board Secretariat. 1994. *Blueprint for renewing government services using Information Technology.* Ottawa: Supply and Services Canada.

– 2004. *Service delivery network profile summary report*. March. Borins Collection, Toronto.

United Nations. 2004. *UN global e-government readiness report 2004: Towards access for opportunity*. New York: United Nations. Produced by Department of Economic and Social Affairs, Division for Public Administration and Development Management. http://unpan1.un.org/intradoc/groups/public/documents/un/unpan019207.pdf.

Van Riper, Paul, and F.G. Hoffman. 1998. Pursuing the real revolution in military affairs: Exploiting knowledge-based warfare. *National Security Studies Quarterly* 14 (3): 1–19.

Velenosi, Jill. 2002. The GOC service strategy. Presentation to TBS Academic Advisory Council, Ottawa.

Vincent, Charles, and Nicholas Prychodko. 2002. Working horizontally across the Canadian public sector. *Canadian Government Executive* 6: 18–20.

Walker, D. 2002. Homeland security: Critical design and implementation issues. Statement of David Walker, comptroller general of the United States, GAO-02-957T. Washington, DC: United States General Accounting Office.

Walton, Dawn. 2005. Ottawa plots making maps without paper. *Globe and Mail*, 4 October, A3.

Walton, G., and A. Booth, eds. 2004. *Exploiting knowledge in health services*. London, UK: Facet Publishing.

Ward, S., and W. Lusoli. 2005. 'From weird to wired': MPs, the Internet and representative politics in the UK. *Journal of Legislative Studies* 11 (1): 57–81.

Ward, S., W. Lusoli, and R. Gibson. 2005. Old politics, new media: Parliament, the public and the Internet. Paper presented at the Political Studies Association annual conference, Leeds.

Watkins, Mike. 2005. Election 2006: Party Web sites. *mikewatkins dot net*, 28 November.

Weick, K.E., and K.M. Sutcliffe. 2001. *Managing the unexpected: Assuring high performance in an age of complexity*. San Francisco: Jossey-Wiley.

Weinstock, M. 2001. Human capital: People persons. *Govexec.com*, 1 May. http://www.govexec.com/features/0501/0501s2.htm.

West, Darrell. 2003. *Global e-government survey*. Providence: Center for Public Policy, Brown University.

– 2005. *Digital government: Technology and public sector performance*. Princeton, NJ: Princeton University Press.

Wiig, K.M. 2002. Knowledge management in public administration. *Journal of Knowledge Management* 6 (3): 224–39.

Winsor, Hugh. 2004. Attack ads attacked. *Globe and Mail*, 19 June.

Woods, G., C. Lantsheer, and R.E. Clark. 1998. Focusing learning on customer service: An example from the public sector. *Learning Organization* 5 (2): 74–82.

Xenakis, A., and A. Macintosh. 2003. Using knowledge management to improve transparency in e-voting. *Proceedings of the 4th International Working Conference on KM in Electronic Government of the International Federation for Information Processing*, Springer, Rhodes, Greece, 2003, 274–84.

Zaharova, S., and K. Zelmene. Knowledge management in delivering customer oriented services in public sector. *Proceedings of the 5th International Working Conference on Knowledge Management in Electronic Government of the International Federation for Information Processing, Springer*, Krems, Austria, 2004, 37–46.

Index

The Institute of Public Administration of Canada
Series in Public Management and Governance

Networks of Knowledge: Collaborative Innovation in International Learning, Janice
   Stein, Richard Stren, Joy Fitzgibbon, and Melissa Maclean
*The National Research Council in the Innovative Policy Era: Changing Hierarchies,
   Networks, and Markets*, G. Bruce Doern and Richard Levesque
*Beyond Service: State Workers, Public Policy, and the Prospects for Democratic
   Administration*, Greg McElligott
*A Law unto Itself: How the Ontario Municipal Board Has Developed and Applied
   Land Use Planning Policy*, John G. Chipman
Health Care, Entitlement, and Citizenship, Candace Redden
*Between Colliding Worlds: The Ambiguous Existence of Government Agencies for
   Aboriginal and Women's Policy*, Jonathan Malloy
The Politics of Public Management: The HRDC Audit of Grants and Contributions,
   David A. Good
*Dream No Little Dreams: A Biography of the Douglas Government of Saskatchewan,
   1944–1961*, Albert W. Johnson
Governing Education, Ben Levin
*Executive Styles in Canada: Cabinet Structures and Leadership Practices in Canadian
   Government*, edited by Luc Bernier, Keith Brownsey, and Michael Howlett
The Roles of Public Opinion Research in Canadian Government, Christopher Page
The Politics of CANDU Exports, Duane Bratt
Policy Analysis in Canada: The State of the Art, edited by Larent Dobuzinskis,
   Michael Howlett, and David Laycock
Digital State at the Leading Edge, Sandford Borins, Kenneth Kernaghan, David
   Brown, Nick Bontis, Perri 6, and Fred Thompson